Becoming a Teacher
in Texas

A Course of Study for the
Professional Development ExCET

Edited by

CYNTHIA GIFT HENRY

University of Houston

JANICE L. NATH

University of Houston

WADSWORTH

TM

THOMSON LEARNING

Australia • Canada • Mexico • Singapore • Spain
United Kingdom • United States

WADSWORTH
THOMSON LEARNING

Education Editor: Dan Alpert
Associate Development Editor: Tangelique Williams
Editorial Assistant: Alex Orr
Marketing Manager: Becky Tollerson
Marketing Assistant: Ingrid Hernandez
Project Editor: Trudy Brown
Print Buyer: April Reynolds

Permissions Editor: Joohee Lee
Production Service: Buuji, Inc.
Copy Editor: Linda Ireland
Cover Designer: Qin-Zhong Yu
Compositor: Buuji, Inc.
Text and Cover Printer: VonHoffmann Graphics

Library of Congress Cataloging-in-Publication Data

Becoming a teacher in Texas: a course of study for the Professional Development ExCET / edited by Cynthia Gift Henry and Janice L. Nath.—1st ed.
    p. cm.
    Includes bibliographical references and index.
    ISBN 0-534-55714-7
    1. Teaching—Texas—Examinations—Study guides. 2. Teachers—Certification—Texas. I. Henry, Cynthia Gift. II. Nath, Janice L.
LB1763.T4 B43 2000
371.12'09764—dc21   00-043977

Wadsworth/Thomson Learning
10 Davis Drive
Belmont, CA 94002-3098
USA

For more information about our products, contact us:
Thomson Learning Academic Resource Center
1-800-423-0563
http://www.wadsworth.com

International Headquarters
Thomson Learning
International Division
290 Harbor Drive, 2nd Floor
Stamford, CT 06902-7477
USA

UK/Europe/Middle East/South Africa
Thomson Learning
Berkshire House
168-173 High Holborn
London WC1V 7AA
United Kingdom

Asia
Thomson Learning
60 Albert Street, #15-01
Albert Complex
Singapore 189969

Canada
Nelson Thomson Learning
1120 Birchmount Road
Scarborough, Ontario M1K 5G4
Canada

This book is dedicated to the future teachers of Texas.
May you give the schoolchildren that you teach your very best each and every day.

Contents

＊

Foreword

KIP TELLEZ
UNIVERSITY OF HOUSTON

Becoming a teacher in Texas should not be an easy task. As our state continues to move toward an economy based on advanced technology, and as the options for our leisure time grow more diverse, teachers will be called upon to help children and youth develop the knowledge and skills needed for a new world we can now only imagine. In order for today's children to lead satisfying lives as citizens of 21st century Texas, the schools must remain a powerful tool for developing cognitive growth, encouraging social justice, and sustaining the democracy. I believe that this book, in its own way, will help to ensure that future teachers in Texas can meet the challenge.

When future educators look back on our era, they will no doubt describe it as the "age of accountability." In particular, Texas has embarked on a strategy of school improvement marked by both freedom and responsibility. Schools now have more liberty than ever to design innovative programs, alter existing curricula, and develop new instructional strategies. However, with additional freedom has come school achievement measures, such as the Texas Assessment of Academic Skills, that hold educators accountable for student performance. Educators in our state are no longer told *how* to help children achieve high standards, but they are held accountable if their students do not meet those standards.

As an emerging teacher, you are no doubt aware that the age of accountability has affected your education as well. In order to be awarded a Texas teaching certificate, you will need to pass at least two Examination for the Certification of Educators in Texas (ExCET) tests. Your professors or instructors, like their K–12 counterparts, have not been given mandates regarding how to teach you, but they know that you will not be awarded a teaching certificate without successful completion of these examinations. I believe that this book will help them to prepare you for the Professional Development ExCET, one of the mandatory examinations you will take.

As you leaf through the pages, you will notice that the book is organized according to the competencies developed for the ExCET Professional Development (PD) test. Each chapter is devoted to one of the 15 ExCET PD competencies. I think that you will agree that each of these competencies is important for all beginning teachers to know. And although the book's structure is aligned with the ExCET, it is much more than a study guide. On the contrary, this book provides a full treatment of the knowledge and skills required for the beginning teacher in Texas. Naturally, no book can explore the specific teaching skills needed for each and every discipline or grade level, but this book does provide a strong foundation in those issues that span all content areas. In short, it is designed to prepare you for both the ExCET PD and the classroom.

At the turn of the millennium, Texas public schools are responsible for educating nearly 4 million students, representing a fascinatingly diverse number of cultures and languages. And if current projections are accurate, we will reach 5 million students by 2015. As a teacher, you will be responsible for leading some of these students into the future, and it is indeed daunting to think about the important role teachers must play in the lives of future Texans. But with a well-developed knowledge of the teaching/learning process and a commitment to care for children and youth, you will be ready. I hope this book will contribute to your success.

Preface

HISTORY AND PURPOSE

In the past several years, numerous changes have been implemented in teacher education at the state level. Many of these changes have greatly impacted educator preparation entities (colleges and schools of education and regional service centers). For example, many universities and colleges have moved their teacher education programs into professional development sites (PDSs) located in school districts. The changes that have come about as a result of this field-based move have been exciting and profitable for preservice and inservice teachers. No longer do preservice teachers only talk about theories regarding students and classrooms, but they are actually immersed in the real work of schools.

Parallel to the Professional Development Site movement, Texas has instituted greater accountability for teachers-to-be through the Examination for the Certification of Educators in Texas (ExCET) criteria. Currently, all individuals seeking state teacher certification must pass the Professional Development ExCET. This rigorous examination is based on 15 competencies that measure a teacher's ability to deal with the challenging roles and expectations that must be faced in the classroom. In addition, many teachers moving to Texas from other states and other adults making a change in careers are finding it challenging to understand the theories upon which the Professional Development ExCET competencies are based. After having so many calls that ask, "Please, is there a book that will help me pass the Professional Development ExCET?" we began to investigate the possibility of combining theory and practice to answer this need. It was through this expressed concern by Texas teachers-to-be that this book was developed.

It is our hope that by using this course of study you will gain an excellent background in the knowledge and skills needed to understand and pass the Professional Development ExCET as well as enter your classroom fully prepared to lead the schoolchildren of Texas into the 21st century.

GOALS FOR YOU

The Professional Development ExCET has been designed to include 15 competencies that Texas believes teachers must demonstrate in the classroom. Growing with the examination itself at times has been problematic and frustrating for many of us. However, the competencies upon which the Professional Development ExCET is based have been investigated thoroughly and represent best practice for students, parents, teachers, and schools. Without question, the knowledge and skills in these competencies can be highly supported by all. We also know that teachers-to-be can pass this test and never look back, becoming negative stereotypes of teachers no parent wants their child to have. Therefore, it is our goal to not only help you pass the Professional Development ExCET but to also help you internalize this body of knowledge of best practice so you will enter your classroom every day being able to do what is best for the schoolchildren of Texas.

HOW THE TEXTBOOK IS ORGANIZED
AND SPECIAL FEATURES

The book is organized into 15 chapters corresponding to the 15 Professional Development ExCET competencies. Each chapter includes research, theory, and practical classroom examples. These chapters have been authored by teacher education professors from a number of universities throughout Texas. These authors bring to this book a wide range of knowledge and experiences in teacher education. They come from inner-city urban universities, from both small and large rural universities, and from the school districts with whom they partner. Each chapter provides: (1) definitions of terms to know for the Professional Development ExCET, (2) a body of content knowledge, (3) websites, and (4) a variety of other resources to access further information.

The Professional Development ExCET items are designed to test application of theories rather than the simple recall of information. Therefore, practice test items with explanations are given in this same application scenario format for each competency.

ACKNOWLEDGMENTS

We greatly appreciate the helpful comments of all those who helped to review chapters and offer suggestions:

Laura Allen
Trinity University

Angela Breidenstein
Trinity University

Norma G. Hernandez
University of Texas, El Paso

Priscilla A. Hoke
Southwest Texas State University

John Huber
Sam Houston State University

Sandra R. Hurley
University of Texas, El Paso

Shana Pate-Moulton
Southwest Texas State University

Cynthia Peterson
Southwest Texas State University

Milagros Seda
University of Texas, El Paso

Steve Tipps
University of North Texas

We particularly appreciate those students at the University of Houston and our colleagues throughout the state who added their comments to make this book answer the needs of those seeking teacher certification. Helen Farran, a jewel of an assistant, contributed in so many ways and in all areas of this project. We cannot thank her enough for all her hard work. Thanks also goes to Eileen Westerman and Denise McDonald for their last-minute assistance. We are grateful to the guidance of Dianne Lindsay at Wadsworth/Thomson Learning and Linda Ireland at Buuji, Inc. Finally, we would like to applaud the authors of the chapters. Their hard work and dedication to this project will ensure that many teachers will, indeed, complete certification and share their gifts with Texas schoolchildren.

About the Editors

Dr. Cynthia Gift Henry is a professor in the Department of Curriculum and Instruction at the University of Houston and serves as the Coordinator for the Teacher Internship Program. She has been actively involved in field-based teacher education. Dr. Henry has been an elementary classroom teacher and has worked extensively with gifted and talented students and ESL students. She is also co-editing a textbook on the Elementary Comprehensive ExCET. Her research interests include teacher education, gifted and talented education, and parent involvement.

Dr. Janice L. Nath is a professor in the Department of Curriculum and Instruction at the University of Houston and serves as the Coordinator for Elementary Education, Director of the PUMA TRACS Program (for post baccalaureate certification), Assistant Coordinator of the Teacher Internship Program, and heads one of the university's Professional Development School (PDS) sites. Teacher education is her main area of interest and research, along with technology in teacher education, action research, and others. She has been actively involved in field-based teacher education for many years and is currently chair of the AERA (American Educational Research Association) Professional Development School Research Special Interest Group (PDRS SIG).

✳ Contributors

Virginia R. Beidelman
University of Texas—Tyler

Terry Brandt
University of St. Thomas

JoAnn Canales
Texas A&M University—Corpus Christi

Lillian Chenoweth
Texas Woman's University

Diane Clay
University of St. Thomas—Houston

Gary R. Clay
Houston Baptist University

Myrna D. Cohen
University of Houston—Downtown

Donna Cunningham
Texas Woman's University
College of Professional Education

JoAnn Engelbrecht
Texas Woman's University

Veronica Lopez Estrada
University of Texas—Pan American

Emiliano Gonzalez
University of St. Thomas

Cynthia G. Henry
University of Houston

Gena Jerkins
University of Houston

Stephanie L. Knight
Texas A&M University

Pam Lindsey
Tarleton State University

Jennifer L. Martin
Texas Woman's University

Janice L. Nath
University of Houston

Mary E. Parker
West Texas A&M University

Judith Ponticell
University of New Mexico

Angela Spaulding
West Texas A&M University

Understanding Learners

1

✳

Understanding
Human Development

TEXAS A&M UNIVERSITY

This chapter focuses on Competency 1 of the areas tested in the Examination for the Certification of Educators in Texas (ExCET). The first competency, Understanding Human Development, is included within the broader category of Domain I, Understanding Learners, of the five domains of knowledge considered important for the professional development of aspiring teachers in Texas. Although the proficiencies are linked to a specific state test, they represent knowledge and skills that teachers in any state might need in order to be effective in a variety of classrooms.

Competency 1: The teacher uses an understanding of human developmental processes to nurture student growth through developmentally appropriate instruction.

The teacher recognizes that students' developmental characteristics affect what and how they learn and that effective decision making about instructional content and methods takes into account individual students' levels of development in the various domains (e.g., cognitive, social, emotional, aesthetic). The teacher is aware of expected developmental progressions and ranges of individual variation in each domain, knows how to foster growth in each domain, and understands how development in any one domain may affect performance in other domains. The teacher applies knowledge of human development to design instruction that helps students at various developmental levels make connections between their current skills and understandings and those that are new to them.

TERMS TO KNOW

Development
Physical
Cognitive
Personal
Social

Developmentally appropriate

Readiness

Maturation

Piaget's stages of development
Sensorimotor
Preoperational
Concrete operational
Formal operational

Organization

Disequilibrium

Equilibration

Adaptation

Accommodation

Assimilation

Schema

Information processing capacity

Vygotsky's sociocultural theory
Guided participation
Zone of proximal development
Scaffolding
Private speech

Stages of psychosocial development
Initiative
Industry
Identity

Kohlberg's stage theory of moral reasoning

Can you think of teachers you have had in the past who appeared to know their content areas very well, but had difficulty getting information across to students because they failed to give concrete examples or applications? Or, perhaps you know teachers who experience classroom management problems because they require relatively young students to remain seated and inactive for long periods at a time. These teachers may know their content very well. They may have a repertoire of instructional strategies at their command. Nevertheless, effective teaching requires more than just knowledge of content and instructional strategies. Teachers also need knowledge about developmental levels and the variation in developmental levels that might be expected from students in their classes in order to design appropriate learning experiences. While many teachers acquire the knowledge and skills to provide developmentally appropriate instruction in their classrooms by observing and interacting with students, beginning teachers typically have not had the time or experience with students needed to acquire this knowledge. The study of child and adolescent development theory in advance or concurrent with field experiences provides a more efficient means of enabling teachers to integrate their knowledge of students, strategies, and tasks needed for effective instructional decision making.

This chapter will examine several areas related to Competency 1 that inform prospective teachers about child and adolescent developmental progression and the implications for teaching these students in Texas classrooms. Areas of emphasis include cognitive, social, and emotional development and the range of characteristics that students in certain grade levels exhibit in these areas. Although the competencies are the same for both elementary and secondary levels, prospective teachers will choose either the elementary or the secondary professional development test depending on their certification level. While reading this chapter, pay particular attention to characteristics of students in the level you have chosen.

THEORIES OF GROWTH AND DEVELOPMENT

How many times have you heard, in formal education courses as well as in informal discussions with teachers, that you have to "know" your students in order to match your teaching to their learning needs and interests? One way to know them involves recognizing the physical, intellectual, social, and personal characteristics that occur as humans develop capacities in these areas.

Development refers to systematic, lasting changes that take place over the course of the human life span. While there has been a great deal of controversy over the source of this change, most educators recognize that development takes place as a result of both internally determined change, referred to as **maturation**, and the interaction of the individual with the environment, an external influence. The relative importance of the internal and external, or "nature and nurture", varies depending on the area of development we are discussing. For example, variations in **physical development**, changes in the human body, depend to a large extent on genes. Nevertheless, environmental influences such as nutrition or exposure to certain chemicals can impact growth. On the other hand, **social development** occurs as humans interact with others, although inherent personality traits may influence the nature of these interactions. In all developmental areas, the environment appears to be an important factor.

The definition of development includes recognition of certain principles that all types of development exhibit, despite the differing influence of nature and nurture. In general, developmental changes are continuous and gradual rather than sudden, although periods of rapid physical growth can often make teachers and parents remark that a certain student "sprouted overnight." Some changes are highly visible, as in physical development, while others, such as changes in **cognitive development** (i.e., mental processes), are less readily observed. Since students in a typical classroom exhibit biological as well as experiential differences, we would not expect all students to develop at the same rate. Even a classroom with students of exactly the same age would contain a rather broad range of developmental levels, since people develop at different rates. This potential diversity may seem initially overwhelming to the novice teacher, but developmental theory helps us organize the changes and make predictions about behavior that can guide our teaching. Although theorists often argue about the nature and order of stages, humans appear to develop in similar, orderly stages. This orderly progression enables us to make predictions about "typical" characteristics and behaviors at certain grade levels that help us plan appropriate instruction. Therefore, the role of the teacher is to be aware of the range of possible developmental levels and the characteristics that students exhibit in these levels and provide **developmentally appropriate** instruction in a way that learning experiences lead to optimal development for each child. Theories of students' cognitive, social, emotional, and moral reasoning development provide tools for teachers to become proficient in this role. Using the knowledge of characteristics of different levels in combination with knowledge about the cognitive, social, or physical demands placed on a student in specific tasks or activities enables teachers also to assess student **readiness** for various learning experiences, that is, the student is now capable.

Piaget's Stage Theory of Cognitive Development

Anyone who has worked with children recognizes that they do not think like adults. The difference is not solely a matter of capacity. For example, sunflowers grow from seeds, but not by becoming very large seeds. Likewise, the cooing and babbling of infants changes to adult language, but only after progressing through various stages that are qualitatively different.

A Swiss biologist, Jean Piaget, noted the qualitative differences between adults and children in their cognitive development—in the ways that their knowledge, thinking, and problem solving change over time (see, e.g., Piaget, 1963, 1970, 1985). He devised a theory that explains the way that people make sense of their environments and how their cognitive processes change as they grow older. According to Piaget, maturation, social experiences, actions on the environment (activity), and the process of equilibration interact to impact our cognitive development. Humans innately engage in the constant combination and arrangement or **organization** of actions and thoughts into systems or structures that he called **schemata** (the plural of **schema**). Schemata enable us to understand our world and help guide our interactions with objects and events. As we mature and encounter new information through interaction with objects and people, the way thought is organized in these schemata changes. The change occurs through the process of **adaptation**, the adjustment of existing knowledge structures through the two processes of assimilation and accommodation. When we perceive that our current experience and prior mental structures or schemata that represent understanding of the environment are consistent, we merely incorporate the new knowledge into our existing knowledge through the process of **assimilation**. In other words, in order to make sense of the new information, we use an existing schema. For example, if you have a schema for birds based on characteristics such as "has feathers and flies" and you see a robin for the first time, you are able to assimilate easily the fact that a robin is a bird. In some cases, the new knowledge may have to be somewhat distorted in order to do this. This distortion may result in a misconception. An example is the misconception held by some children that a whale is a fish because it swims.

On the other hand, when we perceive that the information we receive from interaction with the environment is not consistent with our prior representation of events or objects, we experience dissonance or **disequilibrium**. To alleviate the incongruity between what we know and conflicting new information, we must change our existing structure to accommodate the new information through a process called **accommodation**. The constant search for a balance between what we know and what we are learning through activity or social experiences is known as **equilibration**. Equilibration helps us understand why students enjoy "brain teasers" and why they persist at challenging tasks even without the promise of some external reward. Motivation stems from the child's desire to balance what she already knows with novel events or information.

From this perspective, teachers would want to design experiences that result in some disequilibrium to motivate students to pursue puzzling situations. They might provide information or experiences that challenge students' existing beliefs. For example, a science teacher might conduct an experiment using two glasses of clear liquid—one water and the other alcohol. When she places an ice cube in one glass, it floats as students expect. When she places an ice cube in the other glass, which is actually alcohol, it sinks to the bottom. Students become curious about a situation that challenges their previous understanding of the way objects in the natural world act. They become motivated to learn about scientific principles. However, if new information is too far in advance of a student's current knowledge, the student may choose to ignore it.

With these processes in mind, Piaget suggested specific differences in the way children's thinking evolves as they develop. He proposed four stages of cognitive development: **sensorimotor, preoperational, concrete operational,** and **formal operational.** Although children may enter these stages at different ages, according to Piaget, each child goes through the same sequence of developmental stages. Furthermore, these stages can be represented by a typical range of ages that help teachers predict and verify the range that might exist in a particular grade level. Piaget developed a series of tasks to determine the developmental stage of a child, and these tasks can be used by preservice teachers to become familiar with characteristics of students representative of the grade levels they will teach. Although current research has modified our thinking about stages in relation to information processing capacity, knowledge and expertise, and cultural influences (see, e.g., Case, 1985; Rogoff, 1990; Siegler, 1991), these stages still serve as a useful guide for thinking about the kinds of experiences that will benefit students at different grade levels.

Sensorimotor During infancy, from birth to approximately 2 years of age, humans rapidly develop the ability to act on their environment. As a result, they form initial schema from physical interactions with the objects and people around them. Their primary accomplishments during this period include the following: understanding that objects exist even when not in sight or sound range (object permanence), imitation of the actions of others, combination of simple actions into more complex routines, the ability to reverse an action (reversibility), and evidence of goal-directed or intentional behaviors tied to physical actions. Infants can dump objects from a container and then reverse the action by refilling the container. They also engage in enthusiastic repetition of actions that produce a pleasing effect or reaction. In fact, caretakers of infants and toddlers quickly recognize that many of their young charges have developed a schema for dropping a spoon from their high chair and expecting it to be retrieved for them—only to be dropped and retrieved again and again.

Preoperational During early childhood, which includes the early elementary school years (2 to 7 years), students move from the development of schemata that are tied to physical actions to actions that are carried out mentally by thinking them through (operations). In other words, this stage marks the transition to symbolic thought. Despite the ability to use symbols, children at this stage cannot yet perform the mental experiments or operations characteristic of later cognitive development. When confronted with a task or problem, they tend to focus on a single aspect of the situation and ignore other aspects. They may be able to think operations through in one direction but cannot mentally reverse the operations.

Preoperational children also are considered egocentric in that they are unable to view situations from the perspectives of others. For example, try asking a young child if he has a sibling (brother or sister). Then if the answer is yes, ask him if his brother or sister has a brother. His answer to the second question is typically no because preoperational children have difficulty putting themselves in their sibling's place. Preoperational children also tend to play side-by-side in groups, chattering happily about what they are doing, but without direct interaction or dialogue with other children.

Teachers can provide a range of experiences through field trips and invited guests that preoperational children can draw on for development to the next stage. Given the limited use of symbolic language at this stage, concrete items, visuals, and role-play are desirable whenever possible. Experiences that help preoperational children see other viewpoints will benefit those on the verge of moving to the next stage. For example, rather than lecture children about the importance of sharing with others, demonstrate what it would look like if you were sharing the crayons with someone else. Then have students provide demonstrations of sharing other objects in other settings. Providing students with hands-on practice in basic skills also provides the background they will need later for development of more complex skills in language, math, and reading. Teachers also can use large magnetized or velcro letters to build words and have students divide the morning snack into equal portions to share with others. While Piaget found that children in this stage could not perform operations such as categorization, more recent research indicates that preoperational children may exhibit operations in areas of greater knowledge (e.g., Chi & Koeske, 1983; Siegler, 1991). Even young children may be able to classify dinosaurs into different related groups because they have a relatively large knowledge base about them. However, these same children may be unable to use this skill in other areas.

Concrete Operational During a large part of elementary school (7 to 11 years), students exhibit characteristics of a concrete operational stage of cognitive development. They can now perform mental experiments, but their operations are constrained by what they have actually experienced. During this stage, when confronted with a task or problem, they can consider more than one aspect of the task simultaneously and solve hands-on problems logically. They can group objects according to characteristics that the objects have in common (classification) as well as arrange objects in an orderly fashion using a quantitative dimension such as size (seriation). But the major accomplishment of this period is development of conservation—the realization that a change in appearance of an object does not necessarily change the characteristics of the object. Development of conservation requires use of three other reasoning skills acquired during this same period: (1) identity—when nothing is added or subtracted, the material is not changed; (2) compensation—a change in one dimension or direction can be balanced by a change in another dimension or direction; and (3) reversibility—the ability to conjecture what would happen if an action were reversed or "undone." Despite these accomplishments, concrete operational students are unable to deal with abstract concepts.

Teachers of concrete operational children will most likely need to continue to use concrete objects and visuals to help students understand complex concepts and procedures. Although students have more complex mental skills than in the previous stage, long readings and presentations are difficult for concrete operational children to follow, and teachers may need to break these into more manageable segments separated by periods of activity. Graphic organizers (charts, diagrams, webs, time lines, etc.) and models are helpful for presentation and learning of complex information and serve two purposes. They help the teacher organize material for presentation to students so it is clear and logically arranged. In addition, graphic organizers provide students with opportunities to analyze and compare objects and ideas at a more complex level. As in the previous stage, opportunities for activity enable the students to explore the world and to make connections between what they know and the new material. Simple science experiments, opportunities to act out historical or fictional events, and manipulation and crafting of objects representative of time periods provide the experiential base that concrete operational students need. Likewise, use of familiar examples to explain unfamiliar material helps them make connections between the known and the unknown. Teachers would not want to introduce topics that require the higher reasoning skills of later stages until students exhibit some capability in that area. For example, problems that involve fractions or decimals would be difficult to teach until students have some ability to reason proportionally. Even then, the teacher would want to enable students to understand proportions by providing objects or props such as slices of pie or rods that can be broken into smaller pieces.

Formal Operational   The ability to deal with abstract concepts emerges for adolescents and adults during the formal operational stage (11 years to adult). While some students stay at the concrete operational stage during all their school years, others acquire the ability to move beyond concrete operations and solve abstract problems containing a number of variables logically. They develop hypothetico-deductive reasoning—the ability to consider a hypothetical situation and hypothesize implications through use of logical reasoning. Due to the focus on abstract reasoning at this stage, adolescents often become interested in the "ideal" and focus on political or social issues that fall short of abstract perfection.

Characteristic of entry into this stage is adolescents' tendency to focus on their own beliefs and ideas and assume that everyone else is as interested in them as they are (adolescent egocentrism). However, unlike the egocentrism characteristic of preoperational thinkers, adolescents are capable of perceiving situations from different viewpoints. They often are just more interested in their own ideas.

Not everyone reaches the formal operational stage. Some adults may never acquire formal operational thought in any area. Furthermore, individuals may reach formal operational thought in some areas but not others. For these reasons, teachers may need to continue some of the same instructional strategies that were suggested for concrete operational learners, while looking for signs that students are in the process of moving from one stage to another. More sophisticated graphic organizers can be used by the teacher or developed by students at this stage to help learners organize information and make connections with prior knowledge. Opportunities to explore hypothetical situations, design experiments, and solve problems through writing and discussion support the development of formal operations. In addition, relating material to students' lives by using popular music or events of interest to adolescents, captures their interest.

In summary, Piaget's theory provides the basis by which teachers at all levels can design active learning environments that fit with students' active construction of knowledge. Teachers can help students acquire new information by taking care to tie it to something the students already know. Likewise, as students advance, they will encounter information that does not fit with their simpler conception of the world. In this case, teachers need to provide discrepant events that challenge or contradict students' existing conceptions and motivate them to reconcile the two opposing beliefs. Students at all levels can benefit from hands-on manipulation of concrete objects in order to form a bridge between preoperational and concrete operational stages or between concrete and formal operational stages. Finally, the opportunity for students to interact, whether through play at lower levels or through academic discussions at upper levels, contributes to the development of expanded perspectives.

Information Processing Theories of Development

Information processing theorists tend to disagree with the stage theory proposed by Piaget (e.g., Case, 1985). In contrast, they suggest that the development of cognitive processes occurs through more gradual processes involving increasing capability and capacity of attention, learning strategies, knowledge, and metacognition. Younger children are more distractible than older and less purposive in their goals of learning. As students progress, they are better able to direct their attention to learning despite outside interference and can focus on specific aspects of material to learn while ignoring others.

Furthermore, older students have strategies they can apply to help them learn material (see Gagne, Yekovich, & Yekovich, 1993). Children use more complex strategies as they increase in age and knowledge, and they use them more effectively. For example, kindergarten students rarely use a rehearsal strategy to remember information. During elementary years, children use rehearsal more frequently and with better results as they progress through school. The same students also tend to organize information in meaningful categories that aid memory as they continue through elementary school. As they reach puberty, elaboration of information, adding information they already know to new information, develops as a learning strategy. However, high-ability adolescents tend to utilize elaboration to aid learning more than lower-ability students, despite similarities in age.

Concurrent with the development of more effective learning strategies is the expansion and integration of the knowledge base. As students progress through school, they acquire more and more information that becomes interrelated with existing knowledge. Since we learn best by relating new information to existing information, the more knowledge a person has, the more she can acquire. While younger students may have knowledge bases consisting of isolated facts, older students are more likely to have better organized systems of concepts and ideas.

Finally, differences between younger and older learners exist in metacognitive ability—their knowledge about their cognitive processes and their use of these processes to facilitate learning. Older children are better able to predict how well they can learn material and identify what they know and do not know, while younger learners are typically overly optimistic in their predictions and descriptions. In addition, as students progress through school, they become increasingly aware of the advantages of some strategies over others and are more likely to use them effectively.

Although information processing theory represents a somewhat different conception of cognitive development than that proposed by Piaget, many of the implications are similar. Consistent with Piagetian theory, we need to remember that younger students are not as effective or efficient in performance of learning tasks as their older counterparts. In particular, distractions may pose more of a challenge to younger students than older ones. Teachers will have to be explicit in directing student attention and in minimizing distractions caused by materials or activities that compete with completion of the target task. Also consistent with a Piagetian perspective, teachers need to enable students to see connections between new material and information they already possess, since new learning builds on existing knowledge. Information processing theories build on Piagetian approaches by suggesting that teachers may need to teach learning strategies directly to some students, model their use for all students, and point out the advantages of using particular strategies for learning. Furthermore, students should be encouraged to determine how well they know material and to examine discrepancies in their predictions of accuracy and their actual performance.

Vygotsky's Sociocultural Theory of Cognitive Development

Vygotsky, a contemporary of Piaget, provides a somewhat different view of the cognitive development of children (Vygotsky, 1978, 1986). In contrast to Piaget's focus on the individual's construction of meaning through activity, Vygotsky emphasizes the role of social interaction and the development of language in cognitive development. While Piaget viewed self-talk (which he called collective monologue) as an example of the characteristic of self-centeredness (egocentrism) exhibited in the preoperational stage, Vygotsky interpreted this characteristic differently. He described **private speech**, his term for self-talk, as a critical factor in guiding and monitoring the thinking and problem solving of young children. In addition, in contrast to Piaget, he emphasized the role that adults and more capable peers play in children's learning through scaffolding and assisted learning. He suggested that children operate within a **zone of proximal development**. The zone of proximal development refers to the difference between the intellectual tasks that students can perform alone and those that they can perform with the assistance of an adult or a more skilled peer. In his words, this is the difference between the "actual developmental level as determined by independent problem solving and the level of potential development as determined through problem solving under adult guidance and under the direction of a more capable peer" (Vygotsky, 1978, p. 86).

The classroom implications of Vygotsky's theory emphasize the importance of determining the zone of proximal development for students and providing instruction within that zone. In other words, we provide tasks that students would not be able to do without some assistance. That assistance is typically given in the form of questions, hints, or clues or uses some type of structure or procedural facilitator such as a checklist to provide a prompt. **Scaffolding**, appropriate guidance and support from adults or peers that is gradually withdrawn as competence improves, arises from the notion that students develop cognitively when they are involved in tasks that are more difficult than those they could accomplish alone, but which are attainable with varying degrees of help from others. The terms *assisted learning* and *guided participation* describe the process a teacher might use when providing scaffolding within a student's zone of proximal development. For example, a child may not be able to generate the causes of the Civil War on her own after reading a chapter in a book. However, if the teacher provides a concept map with some of the causes provided, the child may be able to fill in the remainder. In math, the teacher could provide examples that are partially completed and have students complete the remainder of the problems. Story maps or other kinds of webs may provide prompts when reading fictional text that result in student understanding of themes or character and plot development. Likewise, the teacher may direct students to keep cue cards for complex processes, such as long division or factoring, that they can use as they work.

Teachers also can plan instructional groupings involving cooperative learning or paired problem solving to take advantage of guidance provided by peers who are more skilled in certain areas. Students can collaborate with adults or peers when doing particularly challenging or novel tasks. In addition, instructional strategies such as reciprocal teaching, in which the teacher first models and then students gradually assume the role of teacher, also enable students to gradually advance beyond their zone of proximal development. In all cases, "thinking out loud" while doing complex tasks, talking about what you are doing and thinking as you solve a problem, provides a model for students to accomplish tasks, particularly when they encounter difficulties. The teacher, as well as other students, can model the use of language as a means of organizing thinking.

Social and Emotional Development

Although we think of school as primarily a place for cognitive development, schools foster other kinds of development, and the reverse is also true—other kinds of development have an impact on how students learn. Students develop **personally** in areas of self-concept and emotions, **socially** in their relationships with others, and **morally** in their sense of what is right and wrong. All these areas of development occur as a result of the combination of certain maturations and experiences. We often refer to the sum of these areas as **psychosocial development.**

Just as Piaget described a stage theory of human cognitive development, Erik Erikson proposed a stage model of psychosocial development based on critical periods for the development of certain personality characteristics (Erikson, 1963, 1968). In this theory, social or societal demands interact with individual needs and bring about a conflict that must be successfully recognized and resolved or the individual will have difficulty in personality development at later stages. Prior to school, children encounter conflicts that determine whether they learn to trust or mistrust people (trust versus mistrust—ages birth to 18 months) and whether they develop personal autonomy or end up doubting their abilities to cope with the world (autonomy vs. shame and doubt—ages 18 months to 3 years). While the results of these stages influence school-age children's later development either negatively or positively and are of great interest from that perspective, the stages that are of most importance to teachers include the three stages that span the years from the ages of 3 to 18 years. Although many of the influences on personality development occur within the family, teachers are in a position to foster healthy social and emotional development within the classroom.

Initiative Versus Guilt During the stage of **initiative versus guilt**, children from about 3 until 6 years of age test their independence and explore their environment as they master language, cognitive, and social skills. If children are provided with opportunities to try out new behaviors and are successful, they develop initiative. On the other hand, if these attempts are limited or punished too frequently, children may develop a sense of guilt and become overly dependent on adults. Teachers of preschool, kindergarten, and first-grade students can support early efforts of children as they plan and implement activities.

Industry Versus Inferiority From the ages of 6 to 12, children engage in attempts to develop the academic and social skills and abilities needed for successful societal and social interaction (**industry versus inferiority**). When they see themselves as incompetent in dealing with social situations and with their peers, a sense of inferiority or worthlessness may emerge. This feeling of incompetence may be "self-fulfilling" in the sense that a child who has a self-view of incompetence may approach new situations in a manner that builds in failure. Students in elementary schools will benefit from success at academic tasks and genuine praise from teachers for this success. Teachers can provide realistic opportunities for successful attainment of skills coupled with the guidance toward mastery needed during this period. Since comparison with peers is a powerful indicator of success, teachers may want to downplay competition with classmates. Instead, teacher emphasis on individual criteria and progress toward individual goals may be more positive.

Identity Versus Role Confusion During secondary school years, from about 12 to 18 years of age, students are searching for self-identity (**identity vs. identity confusion**). This can be a particularly difficult time for students in junior high and high schools as they try out different roles. Students' self esteem, their sense of their own worthiness or value, may drop during the onset of this stage, particularly for females. Students who encounter nonsupportive environments may develop a poor definition of their occupational, sexual, or moral identities.

Typically, four identity statuses can result from this stage (Marcia, 1980). Identity achievement describes those students who have successfully resolved their identity crises and have a secure sense of who they are and what they want to be. On the other hand, identity diffusion is characterized by a lack of direction on the part of adolescents. Identity foreclosure suggests that adolescents have committed to an identity but have not given it much thought. In this case, they may adopt the identities or expectations of parents or peers without questioning whether there is a good match between their needs and skills and the adopted roles. Finally, moratorium describes the status characterized by the active search for identity by students who are currently undergoing identity crises. The student who dons the clothing and hairstyles of popular sports or music idols one year and the preppy clothing of college-bound peers the next may be experiencing identity moratorium. Extremes of behavior may be common for adolescents in this stage. Teachers can facilitate the adolescent search for self by facilitating the exploration of different roles through classroom discussions and choice of reading materials and activities. In particular, discussions about different career options and investigation of belief systems different from their own are of interest to adolescents.

Teachers play an important role in recognizing and helping students and their caregivers seek help for developmental problems that emerge during school years. Although there is a very broad range of differences that teachers and other adults should accept and encourage, unusual or serious problems may require consultation and special attention of counselors or school psychologists. Even when problems are not serious enough for outside intervention, students who have not emerged as successful in previous stages may need further opportunities to develop trust, autonomy, and initiative. Teachers can involve them in opportunities to choose activities, assume classroom responsibilities, and work independently at all levels of schooling.

Stages of Moral Development

In addition to his work on cognitive development, Piaget also studied children's moral reasoning in relation to their ideas of right and wrong and their understanding of the rules of games they played (Piaget, 1965). By posing moral dilemmas and observing the reasoning of children, he proposed a stage theory of moral development that begins with a premoral period in which children are unaware of rules or standards of right and wrong. Children then progress through a stage of moral absolutes at about the time they enter school. At this stage, rules are inviolable despite possible motives or circumstances justifying changes in certain rules. At the end of the elementary years, children enter a stage of autonomous morality, which recognizes motives or circumstances as an important factor. For example, a school-age child in the moral absolute stage would consider that a child who spilled sugar while trying to help his mother should be punished the same as a child who spilled sugar as a result of playing with the sugar bowl. The child in the stage of autonomous morality would consider that the first child intended to do something good and that the spilling of the sugar was an accident. Therefore, the first child would not be as "guilty" as the second.

Kohlberg posed a similar, but more elaborate, stage theory of moral development based on reasoning about moral dilemmas in the form of stories (Kohlberg, 1981). Using the justifications provided by children for what children in the stories should do, he proposed his **stage theory of moral reasoning** with three levels of moral reasoning—preconventional, conventional, and postconventional. Each level consists of two stages. Students at a preconventional stage of moral reasoning choose a course of action because they will receive certain rewards or punishments for doing so. They define right and wrong in terms of the consequences that they would receive. Preschool children, most elementary-age children, and a few junior and senior high school students exhibit this level of moral reasoning.

In contrast, students at a conventional level focus on gaining approval of others as a result of a particular course of action. They often view societal rules and laws as guidelines that should be followed inflexibly. A few older elementary students and some junior high school students may exhibit this level of moral reasoning, but it is seen primarily in high school students.

The last level, postconventional, reflects moral decisions in light of the interests of the majority and the rights of the individual and moves in its last stage to establishment of a personal code of ethics. Laws are seen as flexible and subject to change when they no longer fulfill their purpose in society. This level is rarely seen in students younger than college level, and most people never reach the highest stage of this level.

Although Kohlberg's theory was based on males only and has not proven to be an adequate portrayal of female moral reasoning (Gilligan, 1982), the stage theories of both Piaget and Kohlberg provide some useful implications for teachers. Children develop morally through opportunities to play and interact with others. Social play provides opportunities for children to acquire social skills as well. Children recognize the necessity of making and adhering to rules in interaction with others on the playground and in the classroom and learn to use social skills rather than aggression. For older students, provision of real-life experiences in which moral decisions may be encountered often serves as a catalyst for more mature moral reasoning and behaviors. Interaction with others at higher levels of moral reasoning may provide the catalyst for elevation to a higher level. Opportunities to hear moral reasoning at a higher level challenge the reasoning of students at lower levels. These theories can be combined with other theories that encourage students to think of the perspectives of others as a basis for moral decision making and behavior (Selman, 1980).

Teachers can model appropriate behaviors for students and reinforce appropriate classroom behavior. At lower levels of schooling, teachers may want to describe how students should behave in class and apply the consequences of misbehavior consistently. Students at preconventional stages may be preoccupied with how "fair" the teacher is, requiring the teacher to provide similar opportunities for all students to the extent possible. Students at this level in elementary classrooms might be given opportunities for sharing of materials to enable them to understand why following guidelines for equitable use might be desirable. Opportunities for playing the roles of others and discussing how they feel in particular situations may also encourage development in perspective-taking. With high school students, teachers may have opportunities to discuss more abstract principles such as human rights and to explore through literature and history situations in which rules or laws might not be productive. At all levels, teachers can help students view situations through the perspectives of others, particularly those of different genders, cultures, races, and religions.

SUMMARY

This chapter focused on Competency 1, Understanding Human Development, of the areas tested in the Examination for the Certification of Educatiors in Texas (ExCET). Competency 1 forms a part of the broader category of Domain I, Understanding Learners, of the five domains of knowledge considered important for beginning teachers in Texas. While other areas of the ExCET emphasize knowledge of instructional strategies or assessment of student learning, this competency highlights teachers' need to understand developmental levels and the variation in developmental levels that might be expected from students in their classes in order to create developmentally appropriate lessons.

Developmentally appropriate instruction considers the physical, intellectual, social, and personal characteristics that occur as humans develop capacities in these areas. Piagetian, Vygotskian, and information processing theories sensitize teachers to differences in cognitive processes and capacities of students as they progress through school and suggest instructional practices that enable students to progress intellectually. Psychosocial developmental theories that describe the ways that students develop personally and socially provide a framework for understanding internal and external influences on intellectual development. Students develop personally in areas of self-concept and emotions, socially in their relationships with others, and morally in their sense of what is right and wrong. While schools may emphasize cognitive development, these other kinds of development influence how students learn academic content and are important when we consider development of the disposition for lifelong learning as an important educational outcome. With the knowledge of cognitive, social, and emotional developmental theories and the range of characteristics that students exhibit in these areas, teachers can better design learning experiences that are appropriate for the grade and age levels they teach.

SUGGESTED ACTIVITIES

1. Interview students at the grade levels you will teach using one of Piaget's tasks (available in most college-level educational psychology or child development texts). How do students respond to the questions? What stage do they exhibit? How might this impact the way you teach them?

2. Conduct a similar set of interviews for students at the level you will teach using one of Kohlberg's moral dilemmas. How do students respond to the questions? What stage do they exhibit? How might they respond to different approaches to classroom management or discipline as a result?

3. Observe students on the playground or in the school cafeteria. Describe their interactions with peers or adults. Analyze these interactions in terms of Erikson's psychosocial stage model of personality development.

4. Summarize the major changes brought about by cognitive and psychosocial development at each of the following ages: early childhood, elementary school, adolescence. Construct profiles of students at different levels in school.

5. Make a list of activities you could do to encourage (a) initiative in preschool children, or (b) industry in elementary school-age children,

or (c) identity formation in adolescents. Ask someone familiar with these ages to comment on your list.

6. Shadow a student at the grade level you will teach. What do you notice about this student in relation to cognitive, social, and emotional development?

7. Scan the newspapers for several days for stories about children or adolescents at the age level you will teach. What societal pressures or challenges do they depict that might endanger the childrens' or adolescents' social and emotional development? Are these similar to the challenges you faced at that age?

8. Consult one of the websites listed in the following Web Links section for additional information about students' cognitive, social, or emotional development.

9. Look at the contents section of a text designed for the level you will teach. At what cognitive level will students in your classes need to be in order to be able to learn this material as presented? What can you do to make the concepts more concrete for students?

10. Ask teachers at the level you plan to teach about the range of developmental levels in their classes. How do they deal with the diversity?

PRACTICE DECISION SET

1. John Anderson has just accepted a position as a fourth-grade teacher in a large suburban school district. As a member of a grade-level team, he will be responsible for developing the math activities for the entire fourth-grade team. From a cognitive developmental perspective, when Mr. Anderson is planning these activities, he should incorporate:

   a. Opportunities for students to interact with their peers during math
   b. Hands-on activities using concrete materials/manipulatives
   c. Competitive games to increase interest level
   d. Packets of worksheets for each math skill taught

2. Susie Smith is teaching junior English in a large urban high school. As she plans activities for her classes, she takes into consideration that from a psychosocial developmental perspective, the students will be most interested in:

   a. Whether they will do better than their peers on her tests
   b. How fair she is in giving grades
   c. The relevance of studying literature for future occupations
   d. The requirements for the research paper assigned to all juniors

3. Curriculum coordinators in the Walton ISD have designed a curriculum to be used by teachers in their classes to enhance students' decision-making capabilities. For one of the activities, they include Heinz's Dilemma, a story about a man who could not get the money to pay a druggist's exorbitant prices for a drug that would cure his dying wife and who subsequently steals the drug in order to save her life. They ask students to discuss whether Heinz was right in what he did. Which of the following responses might teachers expect from a typical elementary-school student?

   a. "I think what Heinz did wasn't so bad because his wife is more important to him than the druggist's money. But if he gets caught he could go to prison. I would do it so no one would ever know it was me."
   b. "Although I have a hard time blaming Heinz for wanting to save his wife, he has to think about what others would say about stealing—I mean, think how embarrassed he would be in church and all that."
   c. "Heinz was right in what he did in this particular situation because he had exhausted all other alternatives and she would have died if he hadn't. Sometimes the laws don't fit certain situations."
   d. "Nothing justifies breaking the law. What if everyone did that?"

Answer 1: Students at the upper elementary level are most likely in the concrete operational stage of cognitive development. For this reason, Mr. Anderson would want to provide concrete experiences for students to facilitate understanding of abstract math principles. While teachers may want to incorporate the use of groups or provide practice in basic skills for other reasons, from the standpoint of cognitive development, *b* is the best answer.

Answer 2: Applying Erikson's guidelines for psychosocial development, we know that adolescents are concerned with occupational choices and the future roles they will play in the workplace. Although they might have short-term concerns about course requirements and grading, their overriding concerns from a psychosocial perspective most likely will involve how what they are doing currently will impact their future occupational needs and goals. Therefore, *c* is the best answer.

Answer 3: Most elementary-age students are at a preconventional stage of moral reasoning characterized by concern over the consequences that breaking a law will have for them. Answers *b* and *d* reflect conventional morality based on pleasing authority figures and maintaining a law-and-order stance. Answer *c* is characteristic of postconventional morality. Therefore, *a* is the best answer.

WEB LINKS

Remember that website locations may change. If any of these sites have moved or cannot be located, use the Terms to Know in this chapter to search for further information.

http://ericps.ed.uiuc.edu/ericeece.html
Development in the early childhood and elementary grades

http://idealist.com/children
Erikson's psychosocial theory of development

www.vanderbilt.edu/kennedy/topics/cogdev/html
Preschool curriculum based on developmental theory

http://pixel.cs.vt.edu/melissa/projects.htmls
Learning project that deals with social problems currently confronting students

www.wimsey.com/~chrisl/jps/jps.html
Jean Piaget Society home page

www.piaget.org/biography/biogg.html
Piaget's biography

www.snycorva.cortland.edu/~andersmd/kohl/content.html
Kohlberg's theory of moral development with classroom dilemmas and applications

www.forum.swarthmore.edu/mathed/vygotsky.html
Vygotsky's sociocultural theory

www.vanderbilt.edu/kennedy
Research in human development

http://gwis2.circ.gwu.edu/~kearsley
Theory into practice database for theories of learning and instruction that includes Piaget and Vygotsky

REFERENCES AND SUGGESTED READINGS

Case, R. (1985). *Intellectual development: Birth to adulthood.* New York: Academic Press.

Chi, M., & Koeske, R. (1983). Network representation of a child's dinosaur knowledge. *Developmental Psychology, 19,* 29–39.

Erikson, E. (1963). *Childhood and society.* New York: Norton.

Erikson, E. (1968). *Identity, youth and crisis.* New York: Norton.

Gagne, E., Yekovich, C., & Yekovich, F. (1993). *The cognitive psychology of school learning.* New York: HarperCollins.

Gilligan, C. (1982). *In a different voice: Psychological theory and women's development.* Cambridge, MA: Harvard University Press.

Kohlberg, L. (1981). *The philosophy of moral development.* New York: Harper & Row.

Marcia, J. (1980). Ego identity development. In J. Adelson (Ed.), *The handbook
of adolescent psychology.* New York: Wiley.

Piaget, J. (1963). *Origins of intelligence in children.* New York: Norton.

Piaget, J. (1965). *The moral judgement of the
child.* New York: Free Press.

Piaget, J. (1970). *The science of education and the
psychology of the child.* New York: Orion.

Piaget, J. (1985). *The equilibrium of cognitive
structures: The central problem of educational
development.* Chicago: University of
Chicago Press.

Rogoff, B. (1990). *Apprenticeship in thinking.*
New York: Oxford University Press.

Selman, R. (1980). *The growth of interpersonal
understanding: Developmental and clinical
analysis.* New York: Academic Press.

Siegler, R. (1991). *Children's thinking.*
Englewood Cliffs, NJ: Prentice-Hall.

Vygotsky, L. (1978). *Mind in society: The
development of higher mental processes.*
Cambridge, MA: Harvard University
Press.

Vygotsky, L. (1986). *Thought and language.*
Cambridge, MA: MIT Press.

ABOUT THE AUTHOR

Dr. Stephanie L. Knight is a professor in the Department of Educational Psychology at Texas A&M University. She also directs the Center for the Study and Implementation of Collaborative Learning Communities in the College of Education at Texas A&M. Her research interests include the impact of classroom processes on student outcomes and the use of teacher research as professional development. She has published numerous books, chapters, and journal articles in these areas. Dr. Knight teaches graduate and undergraduate courses in educational psychology and received the university award for outstanding teaching in 1998.

2

✳

Considering Environmental Factors That Affect Learning

ANGELA SPAULDING
WEST TEXAS A&M UNIVERSITY

This chapter will deal with Competency 2 of the Professional Development Examination for the Certification of Educators in Texas (ExCET). Competency 2 is part four of five competencies that make up Domain I, Understanding Learners.

Competency 2: The teacher considers environmental factors that may affect learning in designing a supportive and responsive classroom community that promotes all students' learning and self-esteem.

The teacher understands how various external factors (e.g., conflict within students' families, peer relationships, gang- or drug-related community problems, malnutrition) may affect students' lives and their performance in school and knows how to create a learning environment that takes advantage of positive factors and minimizes the effects of negative factors. The teacher recognizes signs of stress in students (e.g., a sudden drop in grades, an increase in aggressiveness) and knows how to respond appropriately to help students deal with stress. The teacher understands factors inside and outside the classroom that influence students' perceptions of their own worth and potential (e.g., grouping practices, parent and teacher expectations, prior experiences in school), and recognizes the effects of these perceptions on learning, and knows how to plan instruction to enhance all students' self-esteem and to create an environment in which all students feel safe, accepted, competent, and productive.

TERMS TO KNOW

Perception	**Self-esteem**
Life position	**Classroom environment**
Conflict	**Stereotypes**
Maslow's hierarchy	**Individual security**
Bullying	**Conflict resolution**
Culture	**Environmental factors**
Transactional analysis	**Self-actualization**
Needs	

There are so many factors that impact the learning that occurs in classrooms. These factors may come from within the classroom (e.g., teaching methods, equipment and supplies, teacher-student interactions, etc.), or they may be what students bring with them to class (e.g., attitudes, beliefs, experiences, clothing choices, etc.). Effective teachers know this; they constantly scan their classrooms for signs of environmental influences and use this information to better serve their students and to keep them safe. The very best way a teacher can identify these influences is by knowing each of the students. When a teacher knows his or her students well, he or she can then detect changes in student attitudes or behaviors that may be caused by **environmental factors**. By understanding environmental factors that affect students, the teacher can create a classroom environment that helps counter the negative influences that students may have experienced or may be presently experiencing.

A **classroom environment** can be defined as a setting in which classroom members (i.e., teacher and students) reside for the purpose of learning. This environment includes all the factors or influences that impact the classroom members and all the interactions of members of the classroom and how these interactions affect the students. An examination of some of these environmental factors will help the teacher become more knowledgeable on how to create a classroom environment that is supportive, fun, motivating, and full of learning.

ENVIRONMENTAL FACTORS
THAT IMPACT LEARNING

Perception

Perception is often defined as "how the world is seen through each individual's eyes." A student's individual perception certainly impacts the learning experience in numerous ways. This individual perception is often referred to as selective perception. We see selectively as individuals because each of us has had hundreds of different experiences that have brought us to this moment in time, as have our students. Our culture, stereotypes, life positions, and even our own individual security influence this selectivity. Detective shows on television indicate that one of the most difficult tasks at a crime scene is trying to put all the stories of witnesses together, as each may have seen the act from a different angle or perspective. Teachers must remember that a student's perception is reality to that student. Each perception and the interpretation of virtually any event are based on a combination of historical experience, present needs, and the inherent properties of the scene being perceived (Napier & Gershenfeld, 1999, p. 3). Because what is seen is always a combination of what is actually occurring and what is happening within us at that moment, it is unlikely that two people will ever perceive the same thing in exactly the same way (Harrison, 1976, pp. 100–107).

To be an effective teacher, one must understand that each student comes to the classroom with a different set of perceptions and that many of these perceptions can be distorted. According to Napier and Gershenfeld (1999), "even with the most objective task, it is nearly impossible to keep our subjective views from altering our perception of what really exists" (p. 3). So the way students view their teacher, peers, classroom, subject matter, or purpose for learning is impacted greatly by their perceptions. The following discussion examines perception in relation to the four areas of culture, stereotypes, life positions, and individual security.

Perception and Culture Cultural experiences affect the way students behave. They affect how students think, how they treat others, and how they treat themselves. Basically, culture consists of behaviors absorbed or learned from a group. In education, we often refer to **culture** as students' behaviors learned in their lives outside of school. A teacher cannot understand his or her classroom without making reference to the cultural and personal backgrounds of all the students and examining his or her own cultural baggage as well.

Cultural differences are well documented. For example, cultural differences in eye gaze and eye contact affect the perceptions of others. In addition, these cultural differences impact classroom communication. For instance, when one person greets another, the following sequence generally takes place: gaze—smile—eyebrow lift—quick head nod (Eibl-Eibesfeldt, 1972). This behavior may seem ordinary until you realize that all students do not share the same cultural behaviors.

The most distinguishing feature in the cross-cultural use of eye contact is the focus of the listener's eyes (Burgoon, Buller, & Woodall, 1989). According to Spaulding and O'Hair (2000), Anglos are socialized to gaze directly at the speaker's face when they are listening; students from other cultures often refuse to look directly into the eyes of an authority figure, such as a teacher. In their culture, direct eye gaze with an authority figure is considered rude and inappropriate and to not look up is a sign of respect, especially to a teacher. Japanese-Americans, for example, avoid eye contact when listening by focusing on the speaker's neck. An Anglo teacher can easily misread a student because of the student's eye contact if he or she is not aware of cultural differences. The teacher might, for example, perceive that the student is not paying attention or is acting inappropriately. This is just one example of how perception and culture can impact the classroom learning environment.

Body language, mannerisms, and deep-rooted beliefs may be different in various cultures. These differences may be based on ethnicity, religion, gender, or even on being raised in a certain area of a country. They may be profoundly related to a student's socioeconomic background. Because students are in various stages of cultural growth, they may exhibit very strong cultural differences or none at all.

Perception and Stereotypes **Stereotypes** are preconceived notions of how individuals from certain groups think, feel, and act. As classroom members, students rapidly turn for support to other students they believe share their own stereotypes (Kelley, 1951; Napier & Gershenfeld, 1999; Slater, 1955). Stereotypes can have negative consequences for the classroom environment. Students may form stereotypes that result in the acceptance or unacceptance of other class members. Students are then discriminated against because of this acceptance or nonacceptance (Locksley, Ortiz & Hepburn, 1980). Anyone who has ever felt unaccepted in a group knows how miserable it is. This issue has been examined as one of the factors in the Littleton, Colorado, shooting in the spring of 1999. Feeling unaccepted in a classroom may not result in violence, but it often inhibits the learning process. Students who are accepted and valued do better in school. Teachers need to make sure that all students feel accepted in the classroom environment.

Stereotypes can be based on family background, race, ethnic background, religion, parental occupation, grades, athleticism, hobbies, economic status, or any number of other factors. Stereotypes are often the result of generalizing one person's behavior to a whole population of people (Quattrone & Jones, 1980). Teachers must be aware of such stereotypes so as to promote a classroom culture that accepts and celebrates differences. When a teacher values each student for who he or she is, the teacher sets a strong example for other students to follow. Teachers must be conscious of any stereotypes that they may consciously or unconsciously carry as well as the stereotypes that exist within the classroom. These stereotypes often come with set expectations about another group's abilities or behaviors. For example, several stereotypical myths are: athletes are more brawn than brains; students with disabilities cannot learn; and people with blond hair lack common sense. In recent years, some schools have promoted uniforms as a way of removing visual stereotypes, as students often dress according to their group either by choice or economics or try to wear a symbol of their stereotyped "gang." Thinking about stereotypical myths can help the teacher see how these myths could create negative learning conditions in the classroom.

Teachers must keep in mind that students are complex, unique individuals— no two are the same! It is the teacher's job to not only enjoy this uniqueness, but to teach students to do the same.

Perception and Life Position Our present perceptions are the result of past experiences. The theory of **transactional analysis** (TA) (Berne, 1976, pp. 44–45,

123–135); Woollams & Brown, 1978, pp. 118–120) explains this premise. According to TA, all of our experiences in life, starting as infants, contribute to the development of our concept of self-worth and assist us in formulating a sense of worth of others. Napier and Gershenfeld (1999) describe our development of self-worth this way:

> We did this by crystallizing our experiences and making decisions about the kind of life we would have (sad, happy); what parts we would play (strong hero, loner); and how we would act out the parts of our life scripts (adventurously, in fear, slowly, with permission). (p. 6)

For example, a person who is continuously praised as a child begins to see himself or herself as worthy of praise. A person who is ridiculed frequently as a child may see himself or herself as unintelligent, with little to offer. It is through these experiences that we form a life script or a **life position**. As we grow older, we become a self-fulfilling prophecy—continuing to reinforce what we learned about ourselves as children.

The students who enter the classroom will have life positions already established. Some students, based on the way they have been treated in life, will already feel they are going to fail at school. A teacher's job is to help such students find a way to overcome and redefine that life position. Nobody said teaching is simple! It is clear how a life position can impact learning in the classroom and it is also evident that, as a part of the many experiences that students will have in the classroom, the teacher can make a difference—positively or negatively.

Perception and Individual Security When students enter a new classroom group, they often experience a lack of **individual security** that results in anxiety (Bennis & Shepard, 1987). Feelings of anxiety may be mild to extreme depending on the student. Holtgraves (1991) defines anxiety as a feeling of uneasiness that is brought about by a conscious or unconscious feeling of danger (not necessarily real) and a readiness to meet that danger. When experiencing anxiety, students feel insecure about themselves. They feel as if other class members may harm them in some way. Harm may come in physical, emotional, or mental ways. In this state of anxiety, students experience self-doubt about the way others perceive them. As a result, their behavior is based on these feelings. Students may act out in various ways because of this self-doubt. Some students may withdraw while others may become loud and rambunctious. Other students may lash out (as if cornered). At this point, teachers may see students caught in self-conflict between their wish to interact with others and their need to protect themselves, and between their desire to succeed within the group and their doubts about their ability to contribute (Turquet, 1978).

Napier and Gershenfeld (1999) remind us that when individuals join a group, they change. Thus, a student's in-group behavior may differ from his or her out-of-group behavior; peer pressure and group membership can impact students. Students can have membership in many different groups, both large and small—everything from the key club to rival gangs. A student's group behavior differs drastically from group to group. A teacher should consider the classroom to be a group that students join and, as the leader of that group, create an environment that makes students want to have membership.

Conflict

A natural by-product of human interactions is **conflict**. Effective teachers must understand conflict and its role in the classroom and school. Most people see conflict as purely negative, which is not always the case. What is always true, however, is that conflict does not manage itself. Students will bring conflict into the classroom that originated outside the classroom. On the other hand, some conflict will originate within the classroom. Wherever it originates, conflict has the potential to negatively or positively impact classroom learning, depending on how it is dealt with. In order for a teacher to effectively deal with conflict and to teach students to do the same, the teacher must have skills in managing conflict. Teachers develop these skills by (1) understanding conflict contaminants, (2) identifying types of conflict, and (3) implementing appropriate conflict resolution strategies.

Conflict Contaminants Conflict contaminants are conditions in which negative conflict grows and thrives. These are conditions that have a negative effect on classroom learning. Several authors (Harvey & Drolet, 1994; Roberts, 1982, Spaulding & O'Hair, 2000) refer to these contaminants as pollutants that clog and choke a classroom climate. The following are examples of conflict contaminants that could occur in the classroom with a detrimental impact on learning.

Negativism Students get into more conflict when negativity is predominant in the classroom (Harvey & Drolet, 1994). Teachers must promote a positive classroom environment with students. They achieve this by being accepting, welcoming, and encouraging to students. A positive classroom environment is one in which the teacher has made allowances for different personalities and learning styles and does not play favorites. Furthermore, the actions of the teacher must always represent what is best for students. For example, some teachers see sarcasm as a way of teasing or "fitting in" with kids. Its use is not in the best interest of students, however, because sarcasm is often misunderstood by students, resulting in hurt feelings and anger. It is better left out of the school environment.

Unrealistic Expectations If teachers have unrealistic expectations of students, students are likely to experience failure. With failure comes negative conflict, which is often created by finger pointing, excuses, and feelings of inadequacy. Students need to experience success in order to achieve more success. A teacher's job is to help students find success in academic, social, and mental ways. Teachers need to provide opportunities for each student to succeed at small tasks before moving him or her to more complex tasks. In addition, teachers should build in opportunities for success throughout longer projects to encourage students to continue working and learning. Teachers must also be careful to guard against placing an expectation label on a culturally different child (e.g., not expecting a low socioeconomic student to succeed academically because of his or her lack of experiences and resources). Effective teachers stop and celebrate successes because they know that success breeds success.

Poor Communication Skills When poor communication exists between students, between the teacher and students, or between the teacher and parents or administration, conflict will likely occur. Without effective communication, teachers leave their classrooms open to rumors, incorrect information, and missed information. They also miss opportunities to get to know their students. Teachers who do not get to know their students cannot effectively meet students' individual needs. Use of various types of delivery systems (e.g., written and oral) and frequent feedback (e.g., oral, written, and/or nonverbal) will help to ensure that students interpret the teacher's messages in the way he or she intends for the messages to be interpreted.

Personal Stressors Personal stressors are personal conditions that teachers and students experience, such as health problems, lack of sleep, financial difficulties, improper nutrition, pregnancy, or lack of organizational or social skills. Personal stressors, for many students, can also be issues of a social nature, such as number and quality of friendships, perception of students' own physical attractiveness, athletic abilities, and dating. All these stressors have the potential to affect student learning and the classroom climate as well as promoting conditions for conflict. A teacher may be limited on what he or she can do with many of these stressors; however, seeking the help of school administration, community services, or counselors can assist teachers in getting help for students. The classroom teacher is generally the first person to note and report these stressors because of his or her daily contact with students.

Savior Syndrome Some teachers have a condition known as the savior syndrome. These are teachers who, though well-meaning, try to fix every student problem. This often gets teachers into conflict situations. "When you try to solve someone else's problems, you do two perilous things. First, you rob the other person of the opportunity to grow. . . . Second, you increase the chances that you will become an actor in the conflict yourself" (Harvey & Drolet, 1994, pp. 75–76). All teachers need to be involved in helping students with problems, but when students become dependent on teachers for help with every problem, without thinking or acting for themselves, that can create conflict. Also, teachers who make choices for students—who give them the answers to all their questions and problems— become accountable for the consequences of those choices. A good rule of thumb to bear in mind is that teachers want students to depend on them, not to become dependent upon them.

Jumping to Conclusions Students, parents, and teachers alike are guilty of jumping to conclusions before getting all the necessary information to make a judgment or decision. For example, a teacher may assume that the student who is often in trouble is the cause for all problems that occur in the class. This creates harmful conflict because the true facts are not considered. Jumping to conclusions creates unnecessary conflict. Teachers must try to avoid jumping to conclusions by always getting the facts before saying or doing anything. Taking time to get the story correct saves time in the long run.

Lack of Support and Trust Students need to feel supported in the classroom. Students who feel supported show signs of increased creativity, communication, and personal growth. Without support, students will be less likely to try new academic challenges for fear of failure and the consequences that result. Teachers can show students support in many ways. For instance, they can attend school activities in which their students are involved and, at the first opportunity, praise the involved students and acknowledge their efforts in the activities. In addition, teachers can engage students in conversations about topics that interest them, be available to answer questions when students need it, gear classroom teaching to include all the learning styles of the students, and use a tremendous amount of positive reinforcement and encouragement. These are only a few of the hundreds of supportive actions that teachers can use to build trust and support. Teachers should think about the kinds of actions that others demonstrate to them that make them feel supported, since these are likely to be the same types of actions that will be important to students. The more students feel supported by the teacher, the more their trust will develop and grow.

Preference Protection Some teachers operate under the condition of preference protection. Preference protection is the protection of one's preferred way of doing something. It is often exemplified by the statement, "It is my way or the highway." Teachers must spend more time thinking about where they want their students to go academically, and less time demanding that there is only one way to get there. Tunnel vision occurs when a teacher feels that his or her way is the only way. This will limit student creativity and success. Students operate out of many different learning styles. Many of these styles will be different from the teacher's learning styles. The goal is for students to learn—not for all of them to learn in the same way.

Types of Conflict Teachers must accept the fact that conflict is a necessary and inevitable part of life in the classroom. They must also be able to identify the types of conflict that occur in the classroom so that they can properly manage them. Conflict does not necessarily feel good, but it is necessary for personal and classroom growth. If we think about the times in our lives when we have grown the most, whether personally or professionally, we can see that more times than not, those growing situations were full of conflict. By managing the conflict, we became stronger people. Whether or not we want to acknowledge it, we all need conflict to challenge and enrich our lives.

Harvey and Drolet (1994) provide a five-way classification of conflict that is helpful in defining the types of conflict with which teachers deal. The five types of conflict are the following.

Value Conflict Value conflict is the most difficult type of conflict to resolve because it deals with a person's individual beliefs, values, or convictions. These may be deep-seated religious, moral, or political beliefs that a student has carried over time. For example, recent conflicts over prayer at school events can lead to conflict between students who want to pray and those suing to stop the practice.

Tangible Conflict Tangible conflict is conflict over resources. These are resources that can be measured and may include time, money, supplies, parking spaces, and classroom space and location. For students, these resources can also be the type of car they drive and the clothes they wear (or want to drive or wear). When resources decline, tangible conflict increases.

Interpersonal Conflict This is a very common type of conflict in classrooms and schools. It is often seen in the conflict between student "cliques" based on academics, sports, music, or other common interests. Interpersonal conflict results when an individual or group has feelings of dislike toward another individual or group. It is interesting to note that interpersonal conflict is often a secondary conflict resulting from another unresolved type of conflict.

Territorial Conflict Territorial conflict occurs as the result of territorial invasions, or as the result of someone expecting another to expand his or her present territory or responsibility (Harvey & Drolet, 1994; Spaulding & O'Hair, 2000). Consider the student who is asked to share her supplies or textbooks with another student. She feels her supplies are her private property. In this case, conflict is created through the feeling that another student is invading the first student's territory. Or, consider the student who is doing a group project and learns that his partner did not hold up his end of the bargain. The first student now feels that he must complete not only his part of the project, but his partner's part as well. Conflict is created in this case by territorial expansion because the first student is being forced to expand his territory into someone else's in order to get the project finished.

Perceptual Conflict As we discussed earlier in the chapter, people often have distorted images of each other. This is certainly true in the classroom. Students and teachers often jump to conclusions about the motives and goals of others. Most perceptual conflicts occur because the conflicting parties do not have the facts. For example, perceptual conflicts can arise in classes with immigrants who have come from countries whose culture is dramatically different from our own, and the students are unsure how to relate to one another. According to Meyer (1987), conflicting parties often have mirror-image perceptions of one another—each attributes the same virtues to themselves and vices to their adversaries. In other words, each party to the conflict believes they are taking the most logical and beneficial action possible while they see their adversary as taking an illogical and detrimental action. Perceptual conflicts often grow into other types of conflict if not resolved early on. Ruby Payne (1995) describes students who live in poverty as having very limited vocabulary, used only for casual interactions. These students seem very rough and, at times, impolite. Conflict may occur in their conversations with others because the receiver of their messages may perceive the message to be inappropriate and offensive. As a result, interpersonal conflict may develop.

Conflict Resolution Strategies After identifying one or more of the five types of conflict (value, tangible, interpersonal, territorial, or perceptual), the teacher must next know what strategies to utilize to resolve the conflict. The following **conflict resolution** strategies have been found to be effective in resolving conflict effectively (Ball, 1989; Filley, 1975; Harvey & Drolet, 1994; Huse, 1975; Meyer, 1987).

Using Conciliatory Gestures It is common for communication between two conflicting students or student groups to come to an impasse. When communication ceases, conflict cannot be resolved. At this point in the conflict, a conciliatory gesture can be of tremendous value. A conciliatory gesture can be as simple as a smile or kind word, or it can be as complex as a concession. Conciliation is the process whereby one side of the conflict initiates a gesture of good faith in the hope that the other party will reciprocate with a similar type of gesture (Meyer, 1987; Osgood, 1962, 1980). Choosing an adversary as a partner in the laboratory or as a member of a team in physical education class may be the gesture needed to begin solving the conflict. The initial conciliatory gestures put pressure on the opposing side to act. The intent is to move both conflicting parties toward decreased tension and increased communication and, eventually, cooperation and conflict resolution.

Avoidance Avoidance is a conflict resolution strategy that is overused not only by students but by adults as well. It can be helpful, however, in some situations. For instance, if two students in a classroom are having real difficulties getting along, teaching them the technique of "just don't go there" or helping them maintain a greater distance may help the overall classroom environment and may help them avoid getting into areas where they lose their tempers. At other times, avoidance may make conflict worse. Ignored conflict often mushrooms into deeper conflict or other types of conflict. For example, if the same two students continued to show signs of increasing conflict in the classroom, the teacher would not want to ignore those warning signs. A visit with the school counselor would be a good first step for the teacher in getting help on a potentially volatile situation.

Altering the Group Structure In a classroom, altering the group structure may mean changing the physical space in order to separate two conflicting students, changing a student's schedule, or even changing a teacher's job responsibilities. Like the strategy of avoidance, this strategy may sometimes just push the conflict out of sight temporarily, only to have it return with increased intensity.

Appealing to a Higher Belief or Value When conflict seems unresolvable, sometimes focusing on an overarching value, belief, or goal will help resolve conflict. For example, two teachers involved in an interpersonal conflict may decide to put their differences aside in order to do what is best for students. Developmental levels have a great deal to do with how effective this strategy may be with students. A very young student may not be able to use this strategy, whereas a teacher may appeal to older students to work for the greater good of all. Younger students may not see the value of sharing, for example, for the good of all. Remember, however, that developmental level is very much an individual thing. Teachers often expect too much from older children when they do not consider individual developmental levels.

"I Need You and You Need Me" Strategy   This strategy helps individuals to understand how two conflicting students or student groups may have resources that, when shared, will help each side to achieve its own goals and interests. Sometimes this strategy is stated as the "I'll scratch your back if you scratch mine" resolution. In the classroom, this strategy helps students to realize the value of others. For instance, a student who is strong in math can tutor a fellow classmate in return for help with making jump shots.

Role Clarification   When a student or other individual is uncertain about the role he or she is to have in a group or is confused about the role of the other individuals in the group, conflict occurs. Different perceptions or expectations about roles also can create conflict. A teacher can use role clarification as a resolution strategy by having each student define his or her responsibilities in the group, then having the students define the responsibilities of others in the group, comparing all the responses. From this comparative analysis, the teacher will be able to see where role confusion is occurring. These roles can then be clarified to resolve the present conflict and to prevent future conflict. If a teacher can use this strategy up front, it often avoids conflict.

Direct Order   A direct order is a conflict resolution strategy that is used frequently by teachers. Actually, it is overused. With a direct order, there is no input sought from the conflicting students. And we know that without input, most conflicts will not be completely resolved and will reappear. Harvey and Drolet (1994) suggest using the strategy of direct order when resolution is needed immediately (as with a physical fight) and when the person making the order is accepted as an authority figure by the conflicting students.

Communication   It may sound rather obvious to say that communication is needed to prevent and resolve conflict. Yet, many conflicts occur because of poor communication. To be effective, a communicated message must be sent in a clear and concise manner. Teachers must determine the best way to communicate their intended messages. They may find that the best way to send a message is not just one way but multiple ways. For example, a teacher may first send a message verbally and then send the same message in a written or technological form in order to reinforce the original message. The more reinforcement a message has, the more likely it will be remembered. To determine if a message has been received and interpreted in the manner intended, one must have feedback from the receiver or receivers of one's message. One method of obtaining feedback is having the receiver restate the message in either verbal or written form. Many teachers ask students for feedback with the question, "Does everyone understand?" This is an ineffective way of getting feedback because many students feel insecure about acknowledging that they do not understand something. Plus, a question such as this does not tell the teacher what the students understand. They could understand the wrong thing. Multiple types and levels of communication are always operating at one time, so it is easy to misunderstand a message. To help prevent conflict, teachers should continuously check to see that students understand what they are communicating and that they understand what their students are communicating. Furthermore, this flow of communication extends to parents. Many teachers communicate with parents through newsletters, conferences, telephone calls, or e-mail.

Seeking Additional Information Seeking additional information is a good way to keep from overreacting to misinformation. Misinformation and rumors are everywhere. Many students have become angry or upset over something that they *thought* was said or done, but when the truth was known, the perceived event never occurred or occurred under conditions that were acceptable. Many student conflicts can be resolved through this strategy. When teachers encounter the "He said–She said" conflict, for example, they should immediately seek the facts.

Ruby Payne (1995), in her research on poverty, tells us that the telling of events is different and difficult for children in poverty. Teachers must seek additional information from these students in a more structured way. For example, asking a broad question such as, "Tell me about the fight on the playground today," will stop the flow of communication for these students because often they do not have the skills to express everything they see. Payne suggests that teachers instead help structure conversation by asking more sequential questions, such as, "Who did you see on the playground during the fight?" "What was Romero doing?" "What was the first action you saw that told you a fight was about to occur?" These types of questions allow the teacher to seek additional information in a manner that students can respond to effectively.

Outside Intervention Sometimes conflict becomes so intense that an outside perspective is needed. Outside intervention means involving a third party who can help negotiate, arbitrate, or just offer wise council with regard to the conflict. When teachers are involved in conflict or conflict is occurring in their classroom, their school administrators or counselors may be good resources to contact. Teachers whom students trust may find themselves providing a third-party perspective. Outside intervention can be especially helpful in dealing with conflicts that result from sibling rivalry or blended families.

Group Dynamics Interventions A group dynamics intervention is a strategy that includes a wide variety of programs and events, for example, multicultural awareness projects, personality inventories, challenge courses, retreats, trust-building exercises, team-building exercises, and cooperative learning experiences. These interventions are designed to help conflicting students get to know each other better so as to resolve misconceptions and build unity and cooperation.

Compromise Compromise is a strategy that allows the conflicting students or groups of students to meet halfway. In other words, each side gives up part of what he or she wants in order to resolve the issue. In a compromise, it is important that both parties give equally or resentment and further conflict will result. Teachers may be asked to help discover and mediate what compromises will work. Conflicts requiring compromise can also occur among staff members. For instance, suppose a school receives special funding to expand its reading program, but not enough money for all the teachers to have the materials they want in their classrooms. A compromise might be to set up a literacy closet that would house a variety of reading materials that could be used by all teachers rather than having separate sets in each classroom.

Expanding or Developing New Resources Conflict often occurs when resources are scarce. Resources can be defined as materials, time, territory, personnel, information, or influence (Ball, 1989). When scarcity occurs, individuals begin to scramble to get their fair share. When they come up empty-handed, conflict occurs. This issue can be resolved by expanding the current resources or by developing new resources. Teachers need to be creative in developing new resources. Education systems are always short of resources. One teacher who found her class constantly involved in conflict over computer time in the classroom resolved the issue by writing a grant for more computers in her room and allotting more time for students to use the computers. Assignments may have to be modified, time delegated, or other decisions made to equalize the resources.

Democratic Vote A school is planning a fall festival, and each class is asked to host an activity in their classroom. In order to choose an activity, the teachers ask for suggestions and then allow the class to vote on its favorite. This is an example of resolving conflict through democratic vote. Using a democratic vote to resolve conflict is a majority-rules strategy. With this strategy, a vote is taken of all the students or members of the conflict. The vote can be a written vote, a raised-hand vote, or verbal vote. The group with the most votes wins. Although the democratic vote is certainly an option to conflict resolution, it is much better if the conflict can be resolved utilizing a more cooperative type of resolution strategy first so as not to create winners and losers. In certain conditions, a student may perceive that the teacher already knows that he or she is in the minority and may believe the vote is a "setup" to use peer pressure to vote against him or her.

Other Conflict Resolution Strategies Our discussion has certainly not covered every type of conflict resolution strategy available. An effective teacher develops additional strategies to deal with each individual in the class. For example, humor, when used appropriately, can be used to calm a stressful or highly emotional situation. Teachers should think back to situations of conflict in their own lives.

What types of conflict resolution were used? Were they appropriate for the context or environment? Were they effective? The next section will prompt further reflection on these types of questions and answers.

Matching Conflict Types with Resolution Strategies We have discussed some conflict resolution strategies to use in the classroom, but how does the teacher know what strategy to use when? Actually, this is one of the most difficult tasks in dealing with conflict. The following questions can be used to choose the appropriate resolution strategy (Spaulding & O'Hair, 2000).

- What is the source of the conflict? What additional conflicts are likely to arise as a result of this conflict?
- Do the conflicting groups or individuals have the necessary communication or problem-solving skills to work through their differences?
- Do the potential losses outweigh possible gains?
- Who stands to gain—one party or all parties?
- How much time is available for resolving the conflict?
- Is the issue major or minor?
- Is additional research or information needed?
- Are tempers too hot for a productive resolution?
- Will a temporary solution suffice for the present?
- What communication failures are at the base of the conflict?

When resolving conflict, teachers must keep in mind that all conflict resolution strategies are situational and that conflict rarely ever involves just one conflict type. Teachers must carefully reflect upon the strategies used and their potential outcomes. To help in selecting the appropriate strategy, Table 2.1 matches resolution strategies with conflict types.

Needs

As we continue to study environmental factors that affect student learning, we must understand that students' ability to learn is greatly influenced by the degree to which their needs are being meet. A **need** is a requirement for the well-being of an individual. We can best understand these needs by looking at **Maslow's hierarchy** of needs (1954). According to Maslow (1954), individuals pass through certain developmental stages. These stages are represented in Figure 2.1.

As you can see from Figure 2.1, Maslow discusses five different needs of all individuals. How a student or other person acts in a given situation depends upon the developmental level at which he or she is operating. Theoretically, students move upward through the hierarchy, meeting each need before moving to the next one. The most basic needs are at the bottom of the hierarchy. Each of the needs in the hierarchy can be defined as follows:

Table 2.1 Matching Resolution Strategies with Conflict Types

Conflict Resolution Strategies	Value Conflict	Tangible Conflict	Interpersonal Conflict	Territorial Conflict	Perceptual Conflict
Expanding and developing new resources		♥♥♥♥♥		♥♥♥♥♥	
Compromise	↔	↔		↔	
Group dynamics intervention		↔	♥♥♥♥♥	↔	↔
Outside intervention			↔	♥♥♥♥♥	↔
"I need you and you need me" strategy	♥♥♥♥♥		↔	↔	↔
Altering the group structure		♥♥♥♥♥	↔	↔	
Seeking additional information			↔		♥♥♥♥♥
Communication			↔		♥♥♥♥♥
Direct order	↔	↔	♥♥♥♥♥	↔	
Role clarification			↔	♥♥♥♥♥	↔
Appealing to a higher belief or value	♥♥♥♥♥	↔	↔	↔	
Avoidance	↔		↔		
Democratic vote	♥♥♥♥♥	↔			
Using conciliatory gestures	↔	↔	♥♥♥♥♥	↔	
Using humor[a]		↔	↔	↔	↔

♥♥♥♥♥ Preferred strategy for the conflict type

↔ Possible strategy match for the conflict type

[a]No preferred strategy match is indicated because of the delicate manner in which humor must be used.

SOURCE: *Building Teams, Building People*, by T. Harvey and B. Drolet, 1994, PA: Technomic. Copyright 1994 by Technomic Publishing Company, Inc. Adapted with permission.

■ **Physiological needs** include such basic survival needs as shelter, food, and clothing. Students who come to school hungry, sleepy, or without the appropriate clothing will not be as likely to be successful learners until these needs are met.

■ **Safety needs** are the needs that we all have to feel safe in our environment. Some students may feel threatened by other students in the school environment. This may be a case of bullying or even more extreme types of school violence such as gang-related crime.

■ **Belonging and love needs** are the needs we all have for love and acceptance. Unfortunately, all students will not get the love they need at home. As a result, some students have a hard time adjusting to the social aspects in school. They feel unworthy of acceptance because they have never been accepted in their formative years. As a result, their self-esteem is low. Students

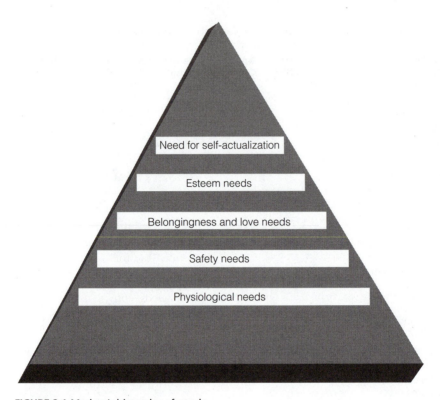

FIGURE 2.1 Maslow's hierarchy of needs.

SOURCE: "A Theory of Human Motivation," 1943, *Psychological Review, 50,* pp. 370–396. Copyright 1943 by the American Psychological Association.

who do not feel a part of the classroom and accepted by the teacher and the school will not be successful learners.

- **Esteem needs** relate closely to love and belonging needs. **Self-esteem** is a condition in which one has confidence and satisfaction with oneself. Research (Biehler, 1978) has shown that slow learners can have low self-esteem. Once students become aware that they are less capable than their classmates at activities (e.g., academics, athletics, music, etc.), they begin to devalue themselves. This devaluation creates self-esteem needs. Teachers must make sure that they show positive feelings toward all students and do not single out the most talented students. Furthermore, teachers may find themselves in the role of helping students discover their own talents. If a teacher believes in each student, the students will have a better chance to believe in themselves. It is a rare person who feels fulfilled in the areas of love, belonging, and self-esteem. Most individuals with self-esteem needs seek personal recognition and strive to win the approval of others— sometimes positively and sometimes negatively.

- **Self-actualization need** is the need to fully realize one's potential. Many people go their entire lives and never realize their potential. This is a higher-order need. Self-actualizing people have worked through their own needs and feel accepted and secure, without the need for approval or recognition of others. Although it is unlikely that students will realize this level during their childhood or adolescence years, the teacher's contribution impacts their ability to meet this future need. With encouragement and challenge, teachers can help students lay a foundation for self-actualizing. Teachers do truly touch the future!

A major implication of Maslow's hierarchy applied to the classroom is that teachers must make sure that the lower-level needs of students are satisfied so that they are more likely to function at higher levels. Students will be better learners if they are physically comfortable, feel safe, feel like they belong and are loved, and, as a result, experience self-esteem. Teachers are very important to the development of students' need gratification because they are responsible for what is happening in the classroom.

Based on Maslow's work, Biehler (1978) provided the following suggestions for meeting student needs:

1. Do everything possible to satisfy the deficiency needs—physiological, safety, belongingness, and esteem.

    - Be aware of the physical condition of students.

    - Make the classroom physically and psychologically safe.

    - Show students that you take an interest in them and that they "belong" in the classroom.

    - Arrange learning experiences so that *all* students can gain at least a degree of esteem.

2. Enhance the attractions and minimize the dangers of growth choices (i.e., if you establish situations in which students feel pressure, tension, or anxiety, students will choose safety and do their best to remain uninvolved; if you minimize the risks and make learning seem exciting, even the less secure student will want to join in).

3. Direct learning experiences toward feelings of success in an effort to encourage a realistic level of aspiration, an orientation toward achievement, and a positive self-concept.

    - Make use of goals and objectives that are challenging but attainable.

    - Provide knowledge of results by emphasizing the positive.

    - Consider the advantages and disadvantages of symbolic and material rewards.

4. Be alert to the damaging impact of excessive competition.

5. For students who need it, encourage the development of a desire to achieve.

6. Take advantage of natural interests, try to create new ones, and encourage learning for its own sake.

7. When appropriate, permit and encourage students to direct their own learning. (p. 525)*

* Reprinted with permission from Houghton Mifflin Company.

OTHER FACTORS THAT IMPACT LEARNING

Teachers spend more time with some students than do their parents. One advantage of spending time with students is that the teacher gets to know them. Knowing students puts the teacher on the front line of defense when it comes to recognizing problem symptoms that may be occurring with a student or group of students. There are many societal ills that affect students. Among them are school violence, suicide, gang activity, eating disorders, and drugs and alcohol—to name only a few. To help students, teachers must learn to identify the symptoms of these ills.

Student Violence

Topping the list of concerns of educators, parents, and students is the increased aggressive behavior of students. It seems that every day we hear of more school-related violence. Unfortunately, this is a situation for which teachers must be prepared. Table 2.2 reveals the contents of the National School Safety Center (1998) report that describes the characteristics found in youth who have caused school-associated violent deaths. As a teacher, knowing and recognizing these student characteristics could save lives. If a teacher feels that a student is exhibiting these symptoms, he or she should discuss the situation with the school counselor and administrator.

Bullying is not often thought of as violent behavior, but in reality, it certainly can consist of or become a precursor to violent behaviors. Bullying can have negative consequences for the general school climate and the right of students to learn in a safe environment without fear (Banks, 1997). It consists of such behaviors as hitting, threatening, teasing, taunting, spreading rumors, enforcing social isolation, and stealing. Research has found that boys tend to engage in aggressive bullying actions such as hitting and threatening while girls tend to utilize more passive strategies, such as spreading rumors and enforcing social isolation (Ahmad & Smith, 1994; Smith & Sharp, 1994). Approximately 15 percent of students are either bullied regularly or are the initiators of bullying behavior (Olweus, 1993).

Bullies tend to be students who desire to feel powerful and in control. They often come from homes where physical punishment is used and where parental involvement and warmth are lacking (Banks, 1997). Students who are victims of bullying are typically anxious, insecure, cautious, and suffer from low self-esteem, rarely defending themselves or retaliating when confronted by students who bully them. They also lack social skills and friends, have overprotective parents, and are socially isolated (Banks, 1997). A bully's actions generally occur when adults are not looking; as such, teachers and parents may not be aware of the situation until it has escalated into a volatile situation. Given this situation, Smith and Sharp (1994) emphasize the need to develop whole-school bullying policies, improve the school-ground environment, and empower students through conflict resolution, peer counseling, and assertiveness training.

Teachers can work with the students in their classes to develop class rules against bullying and can become a listening ear for any students who would like

Table 2.2 Characteristics Found in Youth Who Have Caused School-Associated Violent Deaths

The potentially violent youth . . .

1. Has a history of tantrums and uncontrollable angry outbursts.
2. Characteristically resorts to name calling, cursing, abusive language.
3. Habitually makes violent threats when angry.
4. Has previously brought a weapon to school.
5. Has a background of serious disciplinary problems at school and in the community.
6. Has a background of drug, alcohol, or other substance abuse or dependency.
7. Is on the fringe of his/her peer group with few or no close friends.
8. Is preoccupied with weapons, explosives, or other incendiary devices.
9. Has previously been truant, suspended, or expelled from school.
10. Displays cruelty to animals.
11. Has little or no supervision and support from parents or a caring adult.
12. Has witnessed or been a victim of abuse or neglect in the home.
13. Has been bullied and/or bullies or intimidates peers or younger children.
14. Tends to blame others for difficulties and problems s/he causes.
15. Consistently prefers TV shows, movies, or music expressing violent themes.
16. Prefers reading materials dealing with violent themes, rituals, and abuse.
17. Reflects anger, frustration, and the dark side of life in school essays or writing projects.
18. Is involved with a gang or an antisocial group on the fringe of peer acceptance.
19. Is often depressed and/or has significant mood swings.
20. Has threatened or attempted suicide.

SOURCE: The National School Safety Center. Copyright 1998. Reprinted by permission.

to confide in a teacher with regard to acts of bullying they have witnessed or been victim of. They should watch for symptoms of bullying, such as withdrawal, evidence of physical abuse, a drop in grades, torn clothes, or needing extra money or supplies. And, most importantly, teachers must make sure they do not bully students themselves—physically or verbally. Teachers should use nonphysical, consistently enforced discipline measures as opposed to ridiculing, yelling at, or ignoring children when they misbehave.

Suicide

Students harming other students is just one area of school-related deaths for which teachers must be prepared. Another devastating situation is that of students harming themselves. Teachers may be in the best position to identify students with suicidal tendencies. The warning signs of suicidal behavior are listed in Table 2.3. Taken individually, these signs do not indicate an impending suicide or suicide attempt. If a student displays several of these signs, however, he or she may need professional help. If a teacher is in doubt, it is better to err on the side of intervention than to ignore a potential problem. Before confronting a student, a teacher should seek guidance from the school counselor and administrator. School districts

Table 2.3 Warning Signs of Suicidal Behavior

- Preoccupation with death
- Expressing suicidal thoughts ("death wish" statements, "My family would be happier without me.")
- Changes in sleep patterns
- Change in behavior in school (lower grades, skipping class, loss of interest in school activities)
- Withdrawal from family and friends
- Extreme depression, hopelessness, despair—sees no solution to problems
- Drug or alcohol use
- Recent major life changes (death, end of a relationship, divorce)
- Recent suicide of a family member, friend or other important figure (this can include celebrities)
- Making a will or giving away personal items
- Plan for how to kill himself and the means to carry it out
- Previous suicide attempts
- Sudden sense of peace or relief after a period of great turmoil (may be a sign that the individual has decided to commit suicide to end the problems he is facing)

SOURCE: *The School Crisis and Crime Handbook*. Spaulding & Burleson. Copyright 1999.

have procedures set up for handling crisis situations. These procedures are designed to get the best assistance for students and to protect teachers.

Gang Activity

Another factor that impacts student learning and health is that of gang activity. Students join gangs for numerous reasons. The National School Safety and Security Services (1998) states that students join gangs for power, status, security, friendship, family substitutes, economic profit, and drugs and alcohol use. They also make it clear that gang members cross all socioeconomic backgrounds and boundaries regardless of age, sex, race, economic status, and academic achievement. Gang identifiers* may include:

- Graffiti: unusual signs, symbols, or writing on walls, notebooks, etc.
- "Colors": obvious or subtle colors of clothing, a particular clothing brand, jewelry, or haircuts (even certain types of bandages)
- Tattoos: symbols on arms, chest, or elsewhere on the body
- "Lit" (gang literature): gang signs, symbols, poems, prayers, and procedures, which may be in notebooks or other documents
- Initiations: suspicious bruises, wounds, or injuries resulting from membership requirements
- Hand signs: unusual hand signals or handshakes
- Behavior: sudden changes in behavior or secret meetings

* National School Safety Center, 1998.

Community programs and training available to teachers can be extremely helpful in assisting teachers in identifying and understanding gang activity. Gang identifiers change frequently, so this is an area in which teachers must be constantly updated.

Eating Disorders

Students may also suffer from eating disorders. Eating disorders can take many forms including anorexia nervosa, bulimia nervosa, or compulsive overeating. Adolescence is often the starting place for many eating disorders. At this time, students feel an enormous need to be accepted. Teachers can understand this; after all, they were once adolescents. Students often measure themselves according to the standards they see promoted by the media, which include an often-unattainable body size and shape. Students think that if they can reach this body image, they will be accepted. Some students go to deadly lengths to get their body to look the way they want it to. The characteristics of eating disorders may be more difficult to detect because students may hide their behaviors. Some symptoms, however, cannot be hidden. If a teacher sees or hears about students with any of the symptoms (Thompson, 1996) listed in Table 2.4, he or she would be wise to seek further assistance from the school counselor or administrator.

Taken individually, the signs listed in Table 2.4 do not always indicate an eating disorder. If a student displays several of these signs, however, he or she may need professional help. If eating disorders are caught early, and the person is willing to get help, the chance of recovery is greater (Thompson, 1996). It is very easy for students to get their sense of self-worth from the media-perfect world. One of the wonderful

Table 2.4 Symptoms of Possible Eating Disorders

- Noticeable weight loss
- Excessive exercise
- Fatigue
- Always being cold
- Muscle weakness
- Obsession with food, calories, recipes
- Excuses for not eating
- Complaining of being too fat
- Evidence of vomiting, laxative abuse, diet pills, or diuretics
- Fainting spells and dizziness
- Bathroom visits after eating
- Fasting
- Severe self-criticism
- Tooth decay
- Ipecac abuse
- Depression

SOURCE: Adapted from *www.mirror-mirror.org, Teenagers and Eating Disorders*, by C. Thompson. Copyright 1996. Adapted with permission.

opportunities that teachers have is to know and accept each of their students for who they are. With teachers' acceptance, students can learn to like and accept themselves.

Drugs and Alcohol

Drug and alcohol use can certainly be classified as an environmental factor that impacts learning. Unfortunately, these substances impact a great deal more than student learning. Drug and alcohol abuse continues to rise in the United States. Many factors have contributed to this increase—among them are the increasing availability of drugs and the influence of peers. Many students call themselves "occasional users" of drugs. They have the mistaken belief that they are free from the dangers to which heavy drug users are exposed. There are, however, always serious health hazards associated with any level of drug and alcohol abuse, for example, increased danger of accidents, premature death, increased exposure to more powerful drugs and multiple drug use, and life-controlling addiction. In the United States, students' involvement with drugs follows a clear-cut sequence: (1) beer and wine, (2) tobacco and hard liquor, (3) marijuana, and finally (4) hard illicit drugs such as heroin. Addictions and More (1995), an information source for alcohol and drug abuse, lists warning signs for alcohol and drug abuse in teens (see Table 2.5).

Most, if not all, schools now have alcohol and drug prevention programs. Teachers should find out what is available in their school and eagerly support the program. They should find out what classroom components are available for use with their students. A teacher's influence in the classroom can have a positive impact on the prevention of drug and alcohol abuse. Research by the American Council for Drug Education (1999) shows that success in school academic performance and success in the social environment of the classroom and school can help prevent alcohol and drug use.

It would be easy to feel overwhelmed looking at all the different characteristics of student violence, suicide, gang membership, eating disorders, and drugs and alcohol (and many more areas not even touched on here). Yet, the key to helping students who are struggling in these areas is to be observant and caring. Teachers who are perceived as caring may find that students confide in them and trust their input and help. How does a teacher become known as caring? It really is not that difficult. Teachers can treat their students the way that they would want to be treated, take time to listen to and get to know students, and always go the extra mile to serve their students. Teachers truly have many opportunities to make a positive, even life-changing impact on the lives of their students. What greater reward could they ever receive?

SUMMARY

A teacher must be aware of environmental factors that affect students. Why? Because whatever is affecting students will have consequences for learning in the classroom. The social ills of today are continually increasing in both number and

Table 2.5 Warning Signs for Alcohol and Drug Abuse

- Deterioration in school performance
- Resistance to authority—defiance
- Attitude changes
- Behavior problems
- High-risk behavior such as stealing
- Extreme mood swings (watch for depression)
- Sexual promiscuity
- Physical complaints
- Changes in relationships
- Changes in eating habits
- Changes in sleep patterns
- Difficulty waking
- Odor of gasoline or other household products
- Unexplainable paint around mouth or on hands
- Parents or guardians notice missing money, alcohol, prescriptions, or items (that could be pawned)
- Alcohol on breath
- Slurred speech
- Staggering
- Appearing spaced-out
- Dilated pupils
- Presence of drug paraphernalia (pipes, pill boxes, straws, spoons, cigarette papers, etc.)
- Clothing depicting drug themes

SOURCE: Addictions and More, *www.addictions-net/warning.htm.* Copyright 1997–2000.

intensity. All students today must deal with violence, social acceptance, plus drug, alcohol, and sexual activity choices. Far too many of our students also must deal with the harsh realities of abandonment, broken families, abuse, and poverty. Still other students may be impacted by peer pressure, distorted perceptions, learning disabilities, or low self-esteem. If it impacts students, it will find its way into the classroom and more than likely into the teacher's heart. When it does, the teacher can fulfill the most important role in teaching—that of truly making a positive impact and lifelong difference in the life of a student. The following student plea should constantly ring in every teacher's ears: "Don't tell me how much you know until you show me how much you care."

SUGGESTED ACTIVITIES

Process

1. Observe a school classroom. Identify as many conflict contaminants as are evident. Conflict contaminants are conditions in which negative conflict grows and thrives. Reflect on how these contaminants could create unwanted conflict.

2. Interview several teachers to discover what they feel are the most common environmental factors that impact learning in the classroom.

3. Observe how people around you deal with conflict. What strategies do they use to resolve conflict? What is the most common type of conflict you see?

Application

1. Interview a group of elementary, middle school, and high school students. Generate a list of all the stereotypes that they have encountered in schools. Discuss how the stereotypes affect student behavior. In comparing the different school levels, what differences do you find? What similarities?

2. Practice your conflict management skills. Choose a conflict situation in which you are currently involved. Decide what type of conflict it is and what resolution strategy or strategies you will use. Implement the strategies and reflect on what you have learned.

3. Interview students from four different cultures (racial, religious, economic, or with close ties to another country, for example). Find out how the students differ and how they are the same with regard to the way they view school, engage in communication, and deal with conflict.

Reflection

1. Reflect on a new group you joined in the past. How did you feel when you joined that group? Compare your feelings to those that students may have when joining a new classroom. What can you learn from the comparison that will make you a better teacher?

2. Reflect on the classroom environment that most positively impacted you during your "student" years. List the characteristics of the classroom and the teacher that contributed to that positive impact. What can you learn from this reflection that will help you as a classroom teacher?

3. Reflect on Maslow's hierachy of needs. Think of one classroom example that would apply to each need. Examples may be from your own classroom experience as a student or from observing classrooms as part of your preservice teaching requirements.

PRACTICE DECISION SET

1. Mr. Cogwell has two middle school students he knows are having difficulty getting along. He has witnessed several near alterations during hall change this week. He has also noted that the conflict is impacting other students by the way students are beginning to

discuss the issue in class. What should Mr. Cogwell do?

a. Ignore the conflict because it will go away

b. Determine what course of action the conflicting students should take and tell them to do it or else

c. First, decide on a conflict resolution measure such as one discussed in this chapter

d. First, get the facts by talking to each conflicting student to determine the type and intensity of the conflict before determining the conflict resolution strategy to use

2. Last week, a new student was placed in Mrs. Wellson's fourth-grade classroom. The new student is extremely shy and seems to have difficulty in socializing with the other students. Mrs. Wellson knows that in order for this student to do well academically in her class, he must feel successful and accepted in the classroom group. Which of the following should she do?

a. Realize that the way the student is reacting to his peers and the classroom environment is impacted greatly by his perceptions; and as a result, visit with the student to find out what his perceptions are

b. Find out all she can about his past experiences in school and at home to determine if these experiences are affecting his present behavior

c. Determine the student's cultural background to determine if his behavior is related to cultural differences

d. All the above

3. Which of the following statements are true?

a. If you were continuously ridiculed as a child, you would be likely to see yourself in your school years as a person worthy of praise.

b. The students who enter your classroom will already have life positions established.

c. When students enter a new classroom or group of any kind, they are likely to experience anxiety.

d. Students often act out in disciplinary ways when they feel self-doubt.

Answer 1: The answer is *d*. With regard to answer *a*: This conflict is unlikely to go away, so ignoring it is not helpful. Answer *b*: Determining the course of action that students are going to take without consulting them or getting additional facts is unproductive for several reasons. First, without student input, you will not have their cooperation and the conflict will not end. Second, by resolving the conflict for the students, you rob them of the opportunity to grow and you become responsible for the consequences that result from your solution. Answer *c*: Deciding on a conflict resolution strategy is not a bad idea; it is just not what you would do first. Answer *d*: The first action that needs to be taken is fact finding so that you can identify the type of conflict occurring and match it to the appropriate resolution strategy.

Answer 2: The correct answer is *d*. All of the answers are correct actions that Mrs. Wellson could take to begin to understand why her new student is having difficulties adjusting to her classroom.

Answer 3: The correct answer is *b*, *c*, and *d*. Answer *a*: If you were ridiculed continuously as a child, you would likely experience feelings of lack of self-worth as you got older. Statements *b*, *c*, and *d* are all correct and are discussed in the reading of this chapter.

WEB LINKS

Remember that website locations may change. If any of these sites have moved or cannot be located, use the Terms to Know in this chapter to search for further information.

General Education

www.education-world.com
A large education site with everything from information about lessons plans and curriculum to current issues facing teachers

www.teachers.net
Called the ultimate teacher resource, considering its size, it just may be!

Conflict Resolution

www.stark.k12.oh.us/docs/units/conflict
An example of how to integrate the teaching of conflict resolution in various subject areas

School Psychology

http://mail.bcpl.lib.md.us/~sandyste/ school_psych.html
Research on learning disabilities, ADHD, functional behavioral assessment, autism, adolescence, parenting, psychological assessment, special education, mental retardation, mental health, and more

Student Motivation

www.indiana.edu/~eric_rec/ieo/bibs/ mot-gen.html
A great deal of information on motivation: general theories and classroom strategies and practices

Societal Issues

www.nida.nih.gov/Prevention/Prevopen. html
A great research-based guide by the National Institute on Drug Abuse entitled "Preventing Drug Use Among Children and Adolescents"

http://www.addictions.net/warning.htm
Warning signs for alcohol and drug abuse

http://www.nodrugs.com/peers.htm
Information on how teens influence teens to use drugs

www.schoolsecurity.org
Facts and questions about school safety and gangs

REFERENCES AND SUGGESTED READINGS

Addictions and More. (1995). *http://www.addictions.net/warning.htm*. Copyright 1997–1999.

Ahmad, Y., & Smith, P. K. (1994). Bullying in schools and the issue of sex differences. In J. Archer (Ed.), *Male violence*. London: Routledge.

American Council for Drug Education. (1999). Behavioral signs of substance use and abuse. [On-line]. *www.acde. org/health/Doctors/signsymp.htm*.

Ball, S. (1989). Micro-politics versus management. Towards a sociology of school organization. In S. Walker & L. Barton (Eds.), *Politics and the processes of schooling* (pp. 218–241). Philadelphia: Open UP.

Banks, R. (1997, March). *Bullying in schools*. EDO-PS-97-17. Champaign, IL: University of Illinois at Urbana-Champaign Children's Research Center.

Bennis, W. G., & Shepard, H. A. (1987). A theory of group development. In G. S. Gibbard, J. J. Hartman, & R. D. Mann (Eds.), *Analysis of groups.* (pp. 127–153). San Francisco: Jossey-Bass.

Berne, E. (1976). *Beyond games and scripts*. New York: Grove Press.

Biehler, R. F. (1978). *Psychology applied to teaching.* Boston: Houghton Mifflin.

Burgoon, J. K., Buller, D. B., & Woodall, W. G. (1989). *Nonverbal communication: The unspoken dialogue.* New York: Harper & Row.

Eibl-Eibesfeldt, I. (1972). Similarities and differences between cultures in expressive movements. In R. A. Hinde (Ed.), *Nonverbal communication* (pp. 297–314). Cambridge, England: Cambridge University Press.

Filley, A. (1975). *Interpersonal conflict resolution.* Glenview, IL: Scott Foresman.

Harrison, A. A. (1976). *Individuals and groups.* Monterey, CA: Brooks/Cole.

Harvey, T., & Drolet, B. (1994). *Building teams, building people: Expanding the fifth resource.* Lancaster, PA: Technomic.

Holtgraves, T. (1991). Interpreting questions and replies: Effects of face-threat, question form, and gender. *Social Psychology Quarterly, 54*(1), 15–24.

Huse, E. (1975). *Organizational development and change.* New York: West.

Kelley, H. H. (1951). Communication in experimentally created hierarchies. *Human Relations, 4,* 39–56.

Locksley, A., Ortiz, V., & Hepburn, C. (1980). Social categorization and discriminatory behavior: Extinguishing the minimal intergroup discrimination effect. *Journal of Personality and Social Psychology, 39,* 773–783.

Maslow, A. (1943). A theory of human motivation. *Psychological Review, 50,* 370–396. American Psychological Association.

Maslow, A. (1954). *Motivation and personality.* New York: Harper & Row.

Meyer, D. G. (1987). *Social psychology.* New York: McGraw-Hill.

Napier, R. W., & Gershenfeld, M. K. (1999). *Groups: Theory and experience.* New York: Houghton Mifflin.

National School Safety and Security Center. (1998). Checklist of characteristics of youth who have caused school-associated violent deaths. [On-line]. *www.nssc1.org/reporter/checklist.htm.*

Olweus, D. (1993). *Bullying at school: What we know and what we can do.* Cambridge, MA: Blackwell.

Osgood, C. E. (1962). *An alternative to war or surrender.* Urbana, IL: University of Illinois Press.

Osgood, C. E. (1980). *GRIT: A strategy for survival in mankind's nuclear age?* Paper presented at the Pugwash Conference on New Directions in Disarmament, Racine, Wisconsin.

Payne, R. (1995). *Poverty: A framework for understanding and working with students and adults from poverty.* Baytown, TX: RFT Publishing.

Quattrone, G., & Jones, E. (1980). The perception of variability within in-groups and out-groups: Implications for the law of small numbers. *Journal of Personality and Social Psychology, 38,* 141–152.

Roberts, M. (1982). *Managing conflict from the inside out.* San Diego: Learning Concepts.

Slater, P. (1955). Role differentiation in small groups. *American Sociological Review, 20,* 300–310.

Smith, P. K., & Sharp, S. (1994). *School bullying: Insights and perspectives.* London: Routledge.

Spaulding, A., & O'Hair, M. J. (2000). Public relations in a communication context: Listening, nonverbal, and conflict-resolution skills. In T. J. Kowalski (Ed.), *Public relations in schools* (2d ed., pp. 137–161). Prospect Heights, IL: Longman.

Thompson, C. (1996). Teenagers and eating disorders. *http://www.mirror-mirror. org/teens.htm* (October 4, 1999).

Turquet, P. M. (1978). Leadership: The individual and the group. In G. S. Gibbard, J. J. Hartman, & R. D. Mann (Eds.), *Analysis of groups.* (pp. 86–112). San Francisco: Jossey-Bass.

Woollams, S., & Brown, M. (1978). *Transactional analysis.* Dexter, MI: Huron Valley Institute Press.

ABOUT THE AUTHOR

Dr. Angela Spaulding is an assistant professor in the Department of Educational Leadership at West Texas A&M University. She conducts research in the areas of leadership and group dynamics, classroom and school communications, and school crime and violence issues.

3

✳

Appreciating Human Diversity

EMILIANO GONZALEZ

UNIVERSITY OF ST. THOMAS

GENA JERKINS

UNIVERSITY OF HOUSTON

This chapter addresses Competency 3 of the Examination for the Certification of Educators in Texas (ExCET). Competency 3 is categorized under Domain I, Understanding Learners. Knowledge of this domain is necessary if teachers are to facilitate optimal teaching and learning environments for Texas's diverse populations of student groups.

Competency 3: The teacher appreciates human diversity, recognizing how diversity in the classroom and the community may affect learning and creating a classroom in which both the diversity of groups and the uniqueness of individuals are recognized and celebrated.

The teacher is aware that each student brings to the classroom a constellation of personal and social characteristics related to a variety of factors such as ethnicity, gender, language background, exceptionality, etc. The teacher recognizes the instructional implications of student diversity and knows how to turn the diversity within and beyond the classroom to advantage by creating an environment that nurtures a sense of community, respects differences, fosters learning, and enhances students' understanding of the society in which they live.

TERMS TO KNOW

Acculturation

Assimilation

Bilingual

Biracial/multiracial

Continuum of development

Culture

Cultural capital

Culturally relevant teaching

Stereotyping

Discrimination

Ethnicity

Gender

English as a Second Language (ESL)

Empowerment

Exceptionality

Hidden curriculum

Minority

Monocultural

Physically challenged

Prejudice

Social class/status

Differently-abled

Human/student diversity

> I have learned one great truth. The answer for all our nation's problems—the answer for all the problems of the world—comes to a single word. That word is "education."
>
> LYNDON B. JOHNSON

An examination of public and private educational settings across the United States evidences the changing faces and shades of America's school-age children. If addressed correctly, the dynamics created by this shift in demographics can provide awesome opportunities to cultivate environments where students and teachers can engage in an interchange whereby diverse groups are reciprocally benefited from the enriched knowledge contributed by all involved (Gollnick & Chinn, 1998).

Interestingly enough, the various artifacts that represent distinction and a sense of "special" for various cultures are the same components that form a common thread or "meeting porch" whereby all groups can emphasize that which is common. Art, literature, foods, fads and trends in styles, music, special holidays, traditions, and rituals all provide a wealth of information to explore, and thus provide a greater understanding of those who are different from oneself.

A teacher who is sensitive to areas of **human/student diversity** (areas of distinction for identifying various people groups) can be instrumental in facilitating classrooms where pluralistic student groups can learn from one another. Such a teacher recognizes the strengths that diversity can bring to a classroom and thus emphasizes mutual respect for others regardless of skin color, race, age, gender, religion, social class, national origin, disability, and numerous other distinguishing categories. Such a teacher also portrays sincere appreciation for different cultures and sensitivity to social problems and injustices, and engages in solution-finding instead of blame-shifting. Although the responsibility of being such a teacher may seem overwhelming, the consequences of not being one presents the discriminated student group and society as a whole with a cost that may be detrimental to all involved. **Discrimination** is the usage of negative responses or the absence of positive responses that denies success for certain groups of students.

The question in your mind may be, "So, how do I accomplish all this?" If the question is a sincere one, then this chapter will provide insightful, thought-provoking, and challenging discourse for your consideration. Perhaps many of the presented ideals will stimulate evaluative examination of your present mindset and cause some uncomfortableness. Yet, if you allow this to happen, you will be forced to grow and to challenge those personal beliefs that perhaps hinder you from developing into the best teacher that you can be and also hinder your students from becoming the best people that they can be. And with that, we will begin.

DEMOGRAPHICAL DYNAMICS

In any given classroom, educators across this country must interact with diverse student groups. Pockets of schools consisting of one type of student group are becoming an increasing rarity. Interestingly, in 1988, 3.2 million students attended Texas public schools, with the majority of students falling into the categorization of Anglo. However, within 10 years, the number of students in Texas public schools increased to 3.9 million, with more than half of this number consisting of students from minority groups. **Minority** is typically defined as any ethnicity group (Hispanic, African American, Native American, Asian) other than Anglo.

As recently as November 1999, Texas was ranked as number 12 among states consisting of diverse student groups. The Hispanic population within the state has grown by 45 percent, the African-American population has increased 19 percent, and other minorities such as Asian and Pacific Islanders have expanded by 63 percent. The latter figure must be viewed within the scope of these particular groups having a small initial population within the state, so growth is only relative to the beginning figure (Texas Education Agency, 1996). The Anglo population increased by 5 percent.

The sharp increases in growth within the "minority" student groups and the relatively small growth within the Anglo category presents Texas with a host of cities and counties, and thus school systems, consisting of approximately equal proportions of each student group. This equates to major diversity. The changing demographics of students acquiring public education in Texas is a trend that is predicted to continue for years to come. Educators must conscientiously help all diverse students pursue their own dreams by empowering them to transcend social barriers to become productive and successful citizens.

Becoming a teacher in Texas requires an embracing and an affirmation of human diversity. At times, there is a resistance to the idea of accepting multiculturalism due to the misunderstanding or myth that diversity equates to division.

The fear of this concept is also heightened by the belief that multiculturalism negates those traditions and values that mainstream Americans hold dear. An accurate perception of multiculturalism, however, is based on the understanding that in order to create a bond that extends beyond surface tolerance, the contributions of diverse people groups must be viewed as an enriching and valuable addition to American culture rather than a subtraction.

INTEGRATING MULTICULTURALISM
IN SCHOOL COMMUNITY

Teacher Roles

Empowerment is a student's personal belief that the factors that make up his or her identity (including language, culture, and other factors) are vital contributions to society. To provide students with empowerment, a teacher must examine the role that she or he has in personally shaping the ways that students perceive their worth and the messages conveyed through the student-teacher interactions (Cummins, 1989). A teacher's self-examination of his or her roles and influence provides tremendous insight into the messages that serve to perpetuate failure or encourage images of success in the minds of diverse student groups.

Although simple in description, self-evaluations are often difficult because most teachers are from a certain social class/status background and thus operate with the knowledge of cultural capital. **Social class/status** is the economic bracket within which many teachers fall; usually they are not from extreme poverty. **Cultural capital** is the recognition of those "rules" that generate success in mainstream society including most schools and greater America. For example, cultural capital provides "the ticket" into a good interview with the knowledge that black or navy suits are appropriate for corporate interviews rather than casual sweats or beachwear. In the context of schools, cultural capital allows teachers and students from certain backgrounds to understand the dynamics of appropriate attire, appropriate language or discourse to solve a problem, and so on. Such information is oftentimes so common for the group that it is taken for granted. A teacher may never recognize that some students are unaware of proper school language (e.g., saying "yes ma'am" and "no ma'am," or even "please" and "thank you").

A teacher who is sensitive to cultural capital issues recognizes that this difference is not discriminately race-associated but also includes issues related to diversity in social class or status, gender, religion, and many other areas that may present common knowledge for some which has not been introduced to others. A teacher then must take the time to explain desired or appropriate behaviors for specific situations, procedures for performing those desired behaviors, and consequences and/or benefits for doing so. For example, a teacher may have students practice the correct way to get someone's attention when that person is already speaking with someone else. The teacher might have two students engage in a pretend conversation, then the teacher could walk up to them and politely wait for a moment within eyesight until being noticed and acknowledged, or (if it is an emergency and interrupting is necessary) the teacher could say, "Excuse me Johnny and Scott, we need to line up now! This is an emergency drill!"

Although certain behaviors are definitely more appropriate for certain settings and/or specific times, the teacher must not use this fact as an opportunity to emphasize assimilation, but instead should provide opportunities for acculturation. **Assimilation** is the students' gain of knowledge of dominant culture at the expense of losing native culture and language. In contrast, **acculturation** is the students' successful application of new knowledge from another culture while maintaining their own native culture and language (Nieto, 1996; Ovando & Collier, 1998).

In fact, **culturally relevant teaching** (CRT) theory underscores teacher practices grounded in the understanding of culture and experiences that shape students' ways of knowing the world (Ladson-Billings, 1992a, 1992b, 1992c, 1995; Lipman, 1995). **Culture** is simply a way of life. This concept should not be confused with **ethnicity**, the association of race or skin color with a person's identity. Culture may shift; ethnicity is stable.

Culture can change based on the person's way of life at a specific time or place. A person may also coexist in numerous cultures simultaneously. For example, at this present moment you are a part of student culture, you are also a part of the culture of women or men, and you are a part of a seeing and literate culture. After you pass the ExCET test, however, you will join the culture or profession of certified educators. Yet, your ethnicity in the first cultures will be the same ethnicity that you bring to your later cultures or way of life.

A teacher who grasps a clear understanding of these two concepts, culture and ethnicity, will find it more difficult to make the common mistake of stereotyping. Such a teacher clearly understands that the fact that students share common physical attributes (ethnicity) does not mean they also share common ways of life (culture). **Stereotyping** is the assumption that certain beliefs about people are true based on skin color or other forms of physical identifiers. Teachers must recognize that two African-American students, while sharing a similar skin color, may have two totally different cultural experiences. Yet, a Hispanic student and a White student from the same community or social class/status may have more in common because of their similar culture or way of life. Also, although many Asian people groups have similar physical features, families of Chinese descent have cultures or ways of life that are distinct from Japanese, Vietnamese, Korean, Thai and other Asian descendents. (As a side note, *Oriental* does not refer to a culture of people but is an adjective associated with artifacts like rugs, pottery, and jewelry.)

Through the use of culturally relevant teaching theory, a teacher not only demonstrates an appreciation for the diversity of students' culture within the classroom but also centers teaching and learning around the students and the diversity that they bring into the environment. For example, a teacher who has a large percentage of students who are recent arrivals from another country or even just another city or state may want to include the heritage, customs, beliefs, favorite pastimes, practices, slang or dialectal terminology, and other interesting concepts that may provide opportunity to value the new students while facilitating relationships between them and the rest of the class.

Other practices based on culturally relevant teaching (Ladson-Billings, 1992a, 1992b, 1992c, 1995) that may be beneficial for the classroom include:

- The inclusion of numerous opportunities for all students to experience academic success in areas of literacy, numeracy, technology, social and political arenas, arts and music, and other areas. This is important to develop active and lifelong learners.

- The inclusion of opportunities for students to develop and maintain their cultural heritage through vehicles such as the students' individual culture, music, poetry, community artists, role models, family, traditions, home language, and other areas that depict the diversity within the classroom.

- The inclusion of discussions that foster and develop a critical consciousness through which students challenge the status quo of the current social order with issues such as stereotyping, inequalities, social problems, and prejudices. **Prejudices** are the mindset and resulting action that consistently thrust negative responses on a particular person or group of people.

- The inclusion of multicultural educational experiences into the learning environment even if there is presently only one ethnic group represented within a given classroom. Although a particular classroom may be **monocultural**, or ethnically the same, larger society is not. It is probable that the students, once leaving the classroom, will have the opportunity to work and interact with people of many ethnicities and backgrounds. Teachers should recognize and utilize instructional modes that create and foster an environment in which differences are respected, valued, and enhanced through optimal teaching and learning exchanges.

A teacher who is sensitive to issues of diversity is not responsible for knowing each and every student's language, culture, or traditions. This would be virtually impossible. It merely suggests that in order to be effective, a teacher should be culturally sensitive, aware and respectful of the differences that may exist between his or her own culture and the students' cultures. There is no excuse for a teacher to be unaware of certain cultural issues concerning the students in his or her room. It is the teacher's responsibility to create a conducive learning environment in which all students are respected.

Since the definition of culture, a way of life, incorporates more than racial ethnicity, teachers must also expand their scope of the different categories that make up the diversity within their classroom and the resulting needs and mandated practices. Several factors that may influence a student's culture or way of life include ethnicity, gender, language background, physical challenges, and exceptionalities. Each factor will be discussed in the following text.

Ethnicity is a significant area of diversity within many school environments. As mentioned earlier, ethnicity is described as a person's race or skin color. Many students may be classified as **biracial** or **multiracial**, students whose ancestors are from two or more different racial groups for which the student claims identity.

Teachers must be careful of the dynamics stemming from interactions between persons from different ethnicity groups. In fact, a teacher may bring some issues to the interchange. Teachers must first examine their beliefs and then begin to facilitate an environment whereby students are challenged to forego negative actions associated with racial prejudices. Teachers must have zero tolerance for racial slurs and practices that serve to belittle others based on superficial or surface perceptions. Lawsuits and dismissals have resulted when teachers themselves engage in these practices.

Even with good intentions or positive beliefs associated with a particular race, teachers must still safeguard for the well-being of the student. For example, Asian students are generally perceived as high achievers in areas of math and science. By stereotyping these students with a blanket of positive attributes, teacher often miss the opportunity to help those Asian students who do not excel in these areas and are ridiculed or belittled because they need assistance in these academic areas.

Gender, the distinction between male and female, creates another area of concern as it relates to multiculturalism. Teachers must be careful to avoid actions based on stereotypical assumptions of females and males. For example, it is a common belief that boys are better or more apt to succeed in areas of mathematics and science. Teachers may be more likely to challenge their male students with higher levels and numbers of questions while neglecting to include female students in these areas. Studies emphasize the tendency of male and female teachers to attribute more attention to male students. Without realizing it, teachers often compliment girls for their appearance while praising boys for academic accomplishments. The subliminal message is that the academic success of female students is not valued or emphasized. It is increasingly important for teachers to generate environments whereby all students, regardless of gender, experience success in all areas of academia. With a changing society, both male and female students need the opportunity to actively participate in mathematics, science, technology, and other areas that generate financial success for participants.

Language background presents a distinct area of concern, especially within many of the southern regions of Texas. Students who are ESL (**English as a Second Language**) speakers are unfamiliar with the English language while being fluent in another. ESL speakers sometimes experience discrimination because they are viewed as a nuisance by unprepared classroom teachers. In fact, many times teachers are responsible for the silencing of ESL students.

For example, a teacher may assign a problem-solving task to be completed in a cooperative group. As he or she walks around the room and monitors the students, the teacher may notice that a particular group is working together but speaking in a language other than English. The teacher, because he or she does not understand this language, may command that the students speak only in English. This may cause students to assume that the use of their language is unacceptable. This conclusion may also be transferred to other areas associated with the student's culture. More often than not, these students will begin to withdraw from participating or speaking in the learning environment.

It must be noted that it is totally appropriate for the non–English speaking group to attempt to solve problems in their own language. A university student may experience this phenomenon in a college classroom as a professor explains a lesson in a technical language. However, after leaving the classroom in confusion, the student can experience clarity and understanding by speaking with a peer in a language that is familiar or common among his or her group. The prevention of such peer discussion would hinder the understanding of the information by the student.

Moreover, teachers must remember that students who are classified as ESL or bilingual are not necessarily intellectually inferior to predominantly English-speaking students. **Bilingual** classrooms provide instruction in students' native language *and* in English. Due to a lack of communication, it becomes easy for teachers to fault the students or to react toward them with frustration. Such practices serve only to hinder the positive involvement of these students in the learning environment. An alternative practice for the teacher could be to utilize the unique knowledge and experiences of the ESL or bilingual students within the classroom. This simple action serves as reinforcement of value associated with embracing the diversity of all students within the classroom and school environment.

Physically challenged students provide another cultural (way-of-life) component to multiculturalism. Students who are physically challenged are those who possess some type of bodily condition that prevents them from performing certain actions such as walking, speaking, and seeing. Nevertheless, because of the actions that these students are able to perform, a new terminology is becoming associated with their condition, **differently-abled**. By emphasizing the things that they can accomplish, it is recognized that these students are not handicapped but in fact are able to accomplish tasks in a different way. A culturally sensitive teacher must be willing to put forth the extra effort needed to accommodate the needs of these students. Numerous resources such as specialized materials and supplies, equipment, and trained support teachers are available to assist physically challenged (differently-abled) students. A teacher must be willing to seek out the resources necessary to benefit these students.

Exceptional students exist in a unique culture also. Exceptional children are those who have mental differences that either far exceed or fall short when compared to the typical mental or intellectual capacities of most other children in their general age range. Gifted and talented students, autistic students, and students with mental retardation are all part of this category. Teachers should have specialized training to work with these students.

A teacher who promotes a community of acceptance of diversity by his or her actions encourages students to interact with others who are culturally different. Remember, the teacher serves as the most important model in the classroom because he or she is the authority figure of the group; students will conclude that a teacher's modeled behavior is what is acceptable toward others.

Facilitating Positive Classroom Environments

Teachers are responsible for the creation of a multicultural environment where all learners feel safe and secure. There are practical steps that a teacher can take to ensure that diversity is accepted. These steps include:

- Embracing respect for human diversity by listening, being fair, avoiding harsh words, calling on all students during the day, and selecting all students for privileges, responsibilities, and duties.

- Fostering cultural sensitivity by inviting guest speakers from different ethnic groups represented in the classroom or school community to share their experiences with students.

- Recognizing and evaluating the **hidden curriculum** (rules or expectations that are unvoiced yet known by persons with dominant cultural capital). For example, many students do not recognize that words like "thank you" and "please" are expected words of politeness in schools and social environments. The hidden curriculum may also be seen in the subliminal messages demonstrated by certain actions. For example, one teacher may line up students from the tallest to the shortest boy followed by the tallest to the shortest girl. What value does that show to the short students as well as to the female students?

- Recognizing that parents and children from diverse culture groups are the primary holders of knowledge as it relates to their specific ways of living. A teacher must be encouraged to pursue knowledge of different cultures by interacting and speaking with parents and students from those cultures. A teacher who embraces multiculturalism recognizes that he or she does not know everything about every culture but is willing to learn as much as possible for the betterment of all students.

- Providing democratic classrooms where equity and equality are shown to all students. Teachers must be careful to assign tasks that can be successfully accomplished by all students regardless of privilege or poverty. For example, a teacher who assigns students to turn in typed reports must have adequate assurance that all students have access to typewriters or computers. In special consideration of poverty and privilege issues, it becomes essential to socialize these groups together instead of polarizing and emphasizing the differences between the two. Teachers serve as the leveler of playing fields within the educational environment and must present clear messages of intellectual worth regardless of financial abundance or lack (Banks & Banks, 1993; Nieto, 1996).

- Understanding that all research and information presented on different ethnic groups are based on a **continuum of development**. This continuum of development represents the proportion of a certain group that definitely fits a given research conclusion and the disbursement of others within this same ethnic group who completely defy the summarization. For example, it is commonly accepted that many ethnic groups, especially Hispanics and Asians, view direct eye contact with elders or authority figures as disrespectful. Students from these groups often avoid eye contact and may be punished in school because they are perceived as not telling the truth, acting aloof, or being unconcerned about a given situation. Yet, there are students within the Hispanic and Asian cultures who do not adhere to this practice and will make direct eye contact with a teacher or other authority figure. A child's generation may make a difference in how well he or she is adjusted to practices of mainstream America. A first- or second-generation child may have deep language and cultural ties while a third- or fourth-generation child may have fewer adjustments to make. Thus, many conclusions that are applicable to the first group are inaccurate summarizations for the latter.

As you can see, teachers need to be aware of and sensitive to many ethnic and cultural issues in regard to the students in their classrooms.

Verbal communication practices such as storytelling can vary widely among cultures. For example, many Native-American cultures view persons of few words as wise. Children from these cultures may say very little or be very sketchy or limited in providing information to a teacher. Their dialogue and writings may be extremely brief and to the point. On the other hand, in many African-American cultures, great storytelling and dramatic enactment is heralded as heroic. A child from this culture, when storytelling, will include additional characters and events that did not occur in the original text. Likewise, Jewish and Asian families often teach their children to be inquisitive and question what they do not understand. This may be viewed by some teachers as disrespectful or as an affront to their authority. Yet, for this child, to question the teacher in an effort to understand better is encouraged by the culture. Such cultural misunderstandings explain much of the mislabeling of students that can occur in schools.

As mentioned earlier in this section, teachers are role models, and diversity permeates every aspect of our society. Teachers and school administrators must embrace multicultural education to help students understand and appreciate the diversity and uniqueness of the society in which we live.

Curriculum Restructuring

To provide a well-rounded and inclusive education, teachers of every discipline must integrate multiculturalism into the areas they teach. Subject areas like mathematics and English provide exemplary opportunity to explore diversity in problem solving and literature interpretation. Such areas emphasize the importance of alternative viewpoints, perspectives, and actions, while demonstrating there is not only one correct approach. Multicultural concepts and activities must be included in the curriculum throughout the year. For example, often schools designate October as Hispanic Heritage month, February as Black History month, March as Women's History month, and May as Ecology month. Although these types of activities do give credence to certain groups, they may also prove detrimental in perpetuating images of nonnecessity or "extra" in the minds of students. Thus, when students encounter such practices only once a year, they may conclude that other than at a specific time, the celebrated groups are not very important. Additionally, celebrations of certain groups without the celebration of others may institute a sense of hostility or mockery among students.

A more productive approach would entail the development and organization of activities and instructional materials that are inclusive of all cultural groups throughout the year. Educators should seize every opportunity to teach from multiple perspectives. Although every lesson does not provide the opportunity to discuss a certain person or event, each lesson does provide the opportunity to address a topic from multiple perspectives, brainstorm for various ideas, incorporate the viewpoint of more than one person, and solve or share from different insights and life experiences.

To further restructure curriculum with regard to multicultural considerations, the different voices or multiple perspectives surrounding a given event must be afforded opportunities to enrich and enhance a lesson. For example, there are alternative views to the discovery of America by Christopher Columbus or the Battle of the Alamo in San Antonio, Texas. The diversity of the perspective helps students to develop critical thinking skills while fostering an awareness of self, social issues, and global perspectives of inequalities, injustices, power struggles, oppression, and other societal concerns (Wink, 1997).

In caution, a teacher who is sensitive, proactive, and concerned about addressing multicultural issues must also remember that many topics are extremely emotionally laden for students. Issues like slavery, the Holocaust, welfare, poverty, hate groups and hate crimes, and gender can uncap fears, anxieties, and discomfort for many. Teachers must emphasize with the voices of those who have been hurt while presenting an accurate portrait of the greater hurt that is inflicted upon society as a whole when people are discriminated against because of certain differences. A teacher may have to teach the necessary skills for participating in discussions of such emotional intensity, yet the rewards of allowing students to critically think and analyze while respectfully articulating their viewpoints as well as hearing the viewpoints of others cannot be overstated. It is an invaluable lesson for teachers and students to learn.

Restructuring of Mindsets

Consider the "tossed-salad" analogy as a more accurate depiction of the world's makeup of people. Each piece, whether the tomato, lettuce, or cucumber, has a distinctive taste, aroma, and flavor. Each ingredient is vital and can be clearly identified. Yet, it is only when all come together that the finished product can be called a salad. This analogy is also representative of diverse groups of people. Each individual or group has its own distinction, but when joined together, can serve to enhance society and the world as a whole.

The tossed-salad metaphor is often preferred over the phrases "color blind" or "melting pots." Usually, in a melting pot, one flavor, taste, or aroma is dominant. Such depictions do not give credence to the individuality that gives each person his or her special identity. So, while celebrating or allowing for the differences in each student, a teacher must treat each student fairly.

Fair treatment responds to the specific needs of a child and does not always equate with equal treatment. For example, a child of poverty may come to school in the morning without having eaten since lunch the previous day. A teacher may make the decision to discretely send the child to the cafeteria with a note requesting that he or she be given breakfast. The other students may have already eaten breakfast and do not need this same treatment. Equal says that all of the students must now go to the cafeteria to eat. Fair compensates for the hungry need of one child while recognizing that such action is not necessary for all. A teacher must be concerned that all children be provided with equal opportunity to express themselves, voice their needs/concerns/opinions, and pursue success; and in determining the fair response to each student, the teacher must remember that this response will vary based on the situation.

Another mindset that must remain constant is the assumption that parents from different culture groups do care about the well-being of their children. It is easy to assume that parents do not care when their responses are atypical to what the teacher desires or is accustomed to. For example, it is easy to assume that when parents of children in poverty do not show up for parent conferences or open house events, they do not care for their children. Likewise, it is easy to draw such a conclusion when parents of ESL or bilingual students do not respond to a note sent home or a phone call.

Teachers who are sensitive to issues of diversity, however, will consider that perhaps the parents of the children in poverty did not have transportation to the school site, or perhaps the hours that the teacher suggested for parent conferences or other school events conflicted with parent work schedules. Likewise, for the parents of ESL and bilingual students, the teacher may consider sending notes home or having an interpreter leave a message in the home language. Furthermore, many parents are intimidated by the thought of venturing upon school grounds, the territory of the teacher, in order to address concerns. Alternative sites for conferences and meetings may need to be utilized, like a local restaurant or community center, to provide adequate comfort for all involved.

SUMMARY

Applying multicultural concepts into everyday classroom practices is not difficult. It simply requires treating others like you would desire that someone treat you, your child, or your loved one who has certain traits that define their individuality. It requires giving active and constant respect and consideration for all. It requires a dedication to desire the best education and life for each and every student. It requires a word to be spoken when discrimination and prejudices hurt others, even if you, the teacher, are not directly impacted. Capturing this concept, we remember Martin Niemoller's inaction in Nazi Germany: First they came for the Jews, and I did not speak out because I was not a Jew. Then they came for the communists, and I did not speak out because I was not a communist. They came for the trade unionists, and I did not speak out because I was not a trade unionist. Then they came for me, and there was nobody left to speak out for me.

The issues of diversity are as significant and permanent as the diverse people who create them. Key educators for the millennium recognize, accept, and embrace this fact while pursuing ways of cultivating the diversity within the domains of classrooms and schools for which they are accountable.

SUGGESTED ACTIVITIES

1. Examine the textbooks of different subject areas and analyze the positive integration of persons from diverse culture groups. For example, recognize whether persons from various racial groups and of a specific gender are consistently depicted in subservient or negative roles. Are women consistently depicted as aides or secretaries while men take on roles of doctors, fire fighters, and astronauts? Are persons of color in such roles or totally absent from the pages? What do you think is the significance of inclusion? What is the message that is given by the textbook that you are examining?

2. Examine a school or classroom environment. Analyze the decor (posters, displays, notes, and advertisements) to determine whether it presents messages of inclusion for all students.

3. Create an alternative plan to the traditional open house or parental conferences utilized by many schools. Your plan should promote ways of reaching and including parents from different ways of life. When designing the plan, specify your intended audience and explain how the plan will benefit those in that group.

4. Generate a list of possible resources and activities that would be beneficial for utilizing multicultural concepts within the classroom.

6. Do an *honest* self-evaluation of certain beliefs and stereotypes that you hold regarding different types of people. Explore these beliefs through objective input or interaction with the persons about whom they are held. Reevaluate these beliefs for truths or fallacy. Be open!

6. Analyze the content of personal conversations and other practices that may depict messages of insensitivity to other cultures and begin to eliminate such content from your language usage and other practices. For example, the use of phrases like "Indian giver" or "I worked like a slave" are culturally insensitive remarks to the truth behind the sufferings of persons who were enslaved and the injustices served to Native-American tribes during the early struggles over land rights and ownership.

7. Evaluate a building or service for accessibility for the physically challenged, blind, deaf, and so on. If your school has a wheelchair, an excellent test is to use it to go to all areas of the school your students must visit.

8. Design a layout for your classroom that would accommodate the needs of physically challenged or exceptional students.

9. Identify other characteristics that may distinguish students from a mainstream culture and ways that these differences may be utilized for the benefit of an individual and the greater good. For example, determine ways that the unpopular or nonathletic group of students at school could be shifted so that all students receive opportunity to demonstrate their strengths.

PRACTICE DECISION SET

1. Ms. Sheree notices that during the selection of instructional supplies for the upcoming school year, the majority of resources chosen have little or no representation of other cultures. In order to address this situation, Ms. Sheree should:

   a. Recognize that it is impossible for resources to represent every culture
   b. Accommodate for diversity by utilizing resources from the community including parents and children from her classroom
   c. Find a special day that the diversity of persons can be celebrated in a program
   d. Assume that the absence of diversity is a good thing because diversity helps to illuminate differences and, thus, conflict

2. Ms. Sheree notices that different ethnic groups within her classroom are remaining isolated and are not intermingling with other groups within the class. She wants to promote multicultural education concepts in her ethnically mixed class. Which of the following activities would likely be most effective in promoting cross-cultural interaction?

   a. Have each ethnic group learn about a different culture group and present the information to the rest of the class
   b. Give the class a lecture discussing the dynamics that she is seeing and her disapproval of such developments
   c. Allow the students to form natural bonds where they may and to develop others in their own time
   d. Vicariously regroup students by having everyone with pants, shorts, long socks, tennis shoes, or other distinguishing marks work together, switching the indicator often to make new groups

3. Ms. Sheree notices that the traditional reading list for the English class consists of authors from only one ethnic group. She also recognizes the significant effect that this reading material will have on standardized tests. Ms. Sheree should address the concern by:

   a. Strictly sticking with the curriculum and not concerning herself with the diversity issue
   b. Having a two-week period when writings by diverse groups of authors will be explored
   c. Utilizing additional readings by diverse authors as extra credit or homework assignments
   d. Integrating writings by diverse authors to reiterate and reemphasize concepts from the traditional pieces

4. Ms. Sheree has heard several fellow teachers use phrases like, "They are working us like slaves, "Indian-giver," "trailer trash," or "You're trying to Jew me," in the teachers' lounge. The statements have made her very uncomfortable because she knows the negative connotations that are associated with the meanings of the phrases. Which of the following would be the best response to the situation?

   a. To avoid conflict, Ms. Sheree should remain silent and trust that the teachers will grow to recognize their own insensitivity.
   b. Ms. Sheree should remember that she knows the teachers and that they really are not prejudiced and are probably just blowing off steam.

c. Ms. Sheree should recognize that some stereotypes are accurate and people have a right to use them.

d. Ms. Sheree should voice her concerns in a constructive manner in hopes of helping the teachers recognize the insensitivity associated with their remarks.

Answer 1: It is the teacher's responsibility to seek alternative ways of providing exposure and representation of diverse cultures from other sources. A most practical source would be the parents and children from other cultures within a given community (*b*). Nevertheless, ignoring the lack of diversity by justifying that (*a*) it is impossible or (*d*) it prevents the acknowledgment of differences does not depict an accurate understanding of multicultural ideals and concepts. (*c*) Celebrating through a special program or day *only* gives messages of extra or nonessentialism to the multicultural concept.

Answer 2: The teacher should not draw unnecessary attention to a natural phenomenon in the classroom. She should instead find alternative means of regrouping that will afford students opportunities to learn and work together based on simple concepts (color of socks, those that brought their lunch) and that will not emphasize tensions or differences between groups until a more appropriate or desired time (*d*).

Answer 3: The correct answer is *d*. Remember, integration is the key to utilization of multicultural resources. The other solutions of ignoring diversity and of specialty treatment are a disservice to the scholarship of multi-cultural education.

Answer 4: The correct answer is *d*. The rationale for the answer stems from the latter part of this chapter. For prejudices and discrimination practices to be broken, each person must play a role in speaking out about injustices. Ms. Sheree cannot ignore the situation in hopes that it will get better but must pursue every effort to make the school a discrimination-free environment of learning.

WEB LINKS

Remember that website locations may change. If any of these sites have moved or cannot be located, use the Terms to Know in this chapter to search for further information.

http://gilligan.esu7.k12.ne.us/~esu7web/resources/multi.html
This site includes an outstanding compilation of links to sites that have information related to such topics as culture, diversity, immigration, languages, multicultural education, and multicultural organizations. There are also useful listings of sites with content related to individual ethnic groups.

www.libraries.rutgers.edu/rulib/socsci/hist/afrores.htm
Information at this site organizes resources related to the history of African Americans. There are numerous links to individual documents as well as to entire collections of texts and other key resources.

www.brown.edu/Research/The_Education_Alliance/
The Education Alliance for Equity and Excellence on the Nation's Schools at Brown University examines the theme of culture and diversity.

www.yahoo.com
Information about Native American education is available through this site by choosing the subject Education K–12 and then Indian Education.

www.library.okstate.edu/kappler
This site offers information about

Native Americans, especially laws and treaties.

www.asiasociety.org
This site offers information on Asia and Asian Americans. It provides cultural understanding of some Asian groups.

www.bennington.edu/courses/history
David Phillips, an associate professor of American history at Bennington

College, has developed a collection of on-line resources on American social and cultural history that deal with immigration, women's rights, and other topics dealing with various ethnic groups.

http://www.census.gov
This site provides thorough statistics broken down by race and ethnic groups on the issue of poverty.

SUGGESTED VIDEOS

Prejudice: The Eye of the Storm. VHS, 25 minutes (1981). Insight Media, 2162 Broadway, New York, NY 10024. Phone: 212-721-6316. This Peabody Award winner describes how an elementary school teacher helped students understand the stereotypes that can limit the opportunities available to groups of people.

Learning to Change. VHS, 29 minutes (1990). Southern Regional Council, 134 Peachtree St. NW, Suite 1900, Atlanta, GA 30303-1825. Phone: 404-522-8764. This video describes how

some schools are working to overcome barriers to change in school cultures and practices, particularly to improve the performance of at-risk students.

Visions of Literacy. VHS (1993). Hineman Educational Books, 361 Hanover St., Portsmouth, NH 03801. Phone: 800-541-2086. A series with a number of individual programs relevant to issues raised in this chapter: for example, Children at Risk (30 minutes) and Multicultural Education (28 minutes).

REFERENCES AND SUGGESTED READINGS

Au, K. H. (1993). *Literacy instruction in multicultural settings.* Fort Worth, TX: Harcourt Brace Jovanovich.

Banks, J. A., & Banks, C. A. (1993). *Multicultural education: Issues and perspectives.* Boston: Allyn & Bacon.

Bennett, C. (1995). *Comprehensive multicultural education: Theory and practice.* Boston: Allyn & Bacon.

Carrasquillo, A., & Rodriguez, V. (1996). *Language minority students in the mainstream classroom.* Philadelphia: Multilingual Matters.

Crawford, J. (1995). *Bilingual education: History, politics, theory and practice* (3d ed.). Los Angeles: Bilingual Educational Services.

Cummins, J. (1989). *Empowering minority students.* Sacramento, CA: California Association for Bilingual Education.

Delpit, L. (1995). *Other people's children: Cultural conflict in the classroom.* New York: The New Press.

Dunn, R., & Dunn, K. (1979). Learning styles/Teaching styles: Should they . . . Can they . . . . Be Matched? *Educational Leadership, 36*(4), 238–244.

Dunn, R., & Dunn, K. (1993). *Teaching secondary students through their individual learning styles: Practical approaches for grades 7–12.* Boston: Allyn & Bacon.

Edelsky, C. (1991). *With literacy and justice for all: Rethinking the social in language and education.* New York: The Falmer Press.

Ferguson, R. F. (1991). Paying for public education: New evidence in how and why money matters. *Harvard Journal on Legislation, 28*(2), 465–498.

Gay, G. (1995). Bridging multicultural theory and practice. In A. C. Ornstein & Behar-Horensten, (Eds.), *Contemporary issues in curriculum* (2d ed.). Boston: Allyn & Bacon.

Genesee, F. (1994). *Educating second language children: The whole child, the whole curriculum, the whole community.* Cambridge: Cambridge University Press.

Gollnick, D. M., & Chinn, P. C. (1998). *Multicultural education in a pluralistic society.* Upper Saddle River, NJ: Merrill Prentice Hall.

Gonzalez, N. (1995). Processual approaches to multicultural education. *Journal of Applied Behavorial Science, 31*(2), 234–244.

Grant, C. A., & Gomez, M. L. (1996). *Making school multicultural: Campus and classroom.* Englewood Cliffs, NJ: Prentice-Hall.

Haroutunian-Gordon, S. (1991). *Turning the soul: Teaching through conversation in the high school.* Chicago: University of Chicago Press.

Hollins, E. R., & Oliver, E. I. (1999). *Pathways to success in school: Culturally responsive teaching.* Hillsdale, NJ: Lawrence Erlbaum.

Ladson-Billings, G. (1990). Like lightning in a bottle: Attempting to capture the pedagogical excellence of successful teachers of Black students. *International Journal of Qualitative Studies in Education, 3,* 335–344.

Ladson-Billings, G. (1992a). Culturally relevant teaching: The key to making multicultural education work. In C. A. Grant (Ed.), *Research and multicultural education* (pp. 106–121). London: Farmer Press.

Ladson-Billings, G. (1992b). Liberatory consequences of literacy: A case of culturally relevant instruction for African American students. *Journal of Negro Education, 61,* 378–391.

Ladson-Billings, G. (1992c). Reading between the lines and beyond the pages. A culturally relevant approach to literacy teaching. *Theory into Practice, 31,* 312–320.

Ladson-Billings, G. (1994). *Dreamkeepers: Successful teachers of African American children.* San Francisco: Jossey-Bass.

Ladson-Billings, G. (1995). But that's just good teaching! The case for culturally relevant pedagogy. *Theory into Practice, 34*(3), 159–165.

Lipman, P. (1995). Bringing out the best in them: The contribution of culturally relevant teachers to educational reform. *Theory into Practice, 34*(3), 202–208.

Moll, L., Amenti, C., & Neff, D. (1992). Funds of knowledge for teaching: Using a qualitative approach to connect homes and classrooms. *Theory into Practice, 21*(2), 132–141.

NCSS Task Force on Ethnic Studies Curriculum Guide (1992, September). Curriculum guidelines for multicultural education. *Social Education,* 274–294.

Nieto, S. (1996). *Affirming diversity: The sociopolitical context of multicultural education.* White Plains, NY: Longman.

Noddings, N. (1981). Caring. *Journal of Curriculum Theorizing, 3*(2), 139–148.

Noddings, N. (1984). *Caring.* Berkeley, CA: University of California Press.

Noddings, N. (1992). *The challenge to care in schools: An alternative approach to education.* New York: Teachers College Press.

Ornstein, A. C., & Behar-Horenstein, L. S. (1999). *Contemporary issues in curriculum.* Boston: Allyn & Bacon.

Ovando, C. J., & Collier, V. P. (1998). *Bilingual and ESL classrooms: Teaching in multicultural contexts.* Boston: McGraw Hill.

Powell, R. R., et al. (1996). *Field experience: Strategies for exploring diversity in schools.* Englewood Cliffs, NJ: Merrill Prentice Hall.

Sharp, J. (1994). *Forces of change: Shaping the future of Texas.* Austin, TX: Texas Comptroller of Public Accounts.

Sleeter, C. E., & Grant, C. A. (1989). An analysis of multicultural education in the United States. *Harvard Educational Review, 57*(4), 421–444.

Texas Education Agency. (1996). Snapshot '96. Austin, TX: Division of Performance Reporting Office of Policy, Planning & Research.

Valdez, A. (1999). *Learning in living colors: Using literature to incorporate multicultural education into the primary curriculum.* Boston: Allyn & Bacon.

Wiles, J. (1999). *Curriculum essentials: A resource for educators.* Boston: Allyn & Bacon.

Wink, J. (1997). *Critical pedagogy: Notes from the real world.* New York: Longman.

Yetman, N. R. (1999). *Majority and minority: The dynamics of race and ethnicity in American life.* Boston: Allyn & Bacon.

ABOUT THE AUTHORS

Emiliano Gonzalez graduated from Indiana University in 1998 with a Ph.D. in Curriculum and Instruction. After studying with leading experts in their fields, like Christine Bennett in Multicultural Education and Carlos Ovando in Bilingual Education, he pursued those areas of research. Other areas of interest are issues of poverty, equity, and social justice. While living and working in South Texas, Emiliano gained extensive experience with the instruction of language minority students and students who live in abject poverty.

Gena Jerkins received both her Bachelor of Arts degree with certification and her Masters of Education degree from Texas A&M University. Her doctoral degree is in Educational Administration from the University of Houston. Her interest centers on multicultural issues, and she is the author of *Stand Tall*, a book that delves into diversity concerns. Currently, she is working as an assistant principal in Houston area schools.

4

✳

Understanding How Learning Occurs

VIRGINIA R. BEIDELMAN
JANICE L. NATH
CYNTHIA G. HENRY

THE UNIVERSITY OF TEXAS—TYLER

This chapter will deal with Competency 4 of the Examination for the Certification of Educators in Texas (ExCET). Competency 4 falls under Domain I, Understanding Learners, of those domains Texas considers most important for its teachers to know and use.

Competency 4: The teacher understands how learning occurs and can apply this understanding to design and implement effective instruction.

The teacher understands how students develop knowledge and skills and recognizes instructional strategies that promote student learning (e.g., linking new information to old, fostering a view of learning as purposeful pursuit, promoting a sense of responsibility for one's own learning). The teacher is aware of factors that affect learning (e.g., individual talents, learning styles, teaching styles, prior learning experiences) and can design instruction to facilitate learning in different situations and to help students learn how to learn and to monitor their own performance.

TERMS TO KNOW

Behaviorist theory	Learning styles
Cognitive interactive theory	Teaching styles
Constructivist theory	Multiple intelligences
Social-cognitive theory	Scaffolding
Prior learning experiences	Transactional theory
Schemata	Metacognition
Modality preferences/adeptness	Self-monitoring
Interpsychological	Strategies
Intrapsychological	Zone of proximal development

UNDERSTANDING LEARNING THEORY

How children think and learn has been a focus of study among researchers and educators for centuries (Wood, 1993). Briefly, we will review three of the major categories of learning theories that have emerged that help us to explain the acquisition of learning: (a) behaviorism, (b) cognitivism, and (c) constructivism (Reutzel & Cooter, 2000). We make instructional decisions every day that, consciously or unconsciously, are driven by our theoretical orientation toward the teaching and learning process (De Ford, 1985; Harste & Burke, 1977). Therefore, we need to consciously examine our beliefs in order to choose among various approaches for helping children become successful learners (Reutzel & Cooter, 2000).

A Behaviorist View

Behaviorists view learning as stimulus-response events (Harste & Burke, 1977; Weaver, 1994). This model of learning is based on reinforcement theory whereby the learners' response is either strengthened or weakened through a positive or negative reward. The details of this theory have been covered in Chapter 1. Let us apply how this theory might surface in a subject area. Behaviorism applied to the reading process, for example, represents what is described as a "bottom–up" reading model. In this model, language is processed from "part to whole." This approach reduces the skill of reading to the smallest parts that are then mastered one at a time. Instruction, therefore, begins with the smallest units: letters of the alphabet, and the sounds those letters represent. In a behaviorist view of reading, phonics-first is the basis of learning to read in this subskills model with comprehension as an eventual outcome. When a child is rewarded by being able to "sound out," for instance, the *probability* that he or she will continue to gain more reading skills *is increased*. An underlying belief related to a behaviorist view of reading is that efficiency, or automaticity in decoding letters and words (Gough, 1972; LaBerge & Samuels, 1974), supports comprehension. The next step would be to read a whole word, then a sentence, and so forth. Each is a rewarding step for the learner, so the learner continues. If learners are not able, however, to get through each "part," they "stall out" in overall comprehension due to lack of reward to continue. This is when a learner, for behaviorists, becomes a nonreader. As teachers, it is important for us to remember to provide students with strategies to make each small step in all learning seem possible and to help reward students for taking it. The probability that they will go on to the next step is then greatly increased.

A Cognitive and Cognitive Interactive View

Cognitive theorists in general believe we learn as an outcome of trying to make sense of the world around us, while behaviorists see the learner as passive—the learner acts as a result of a change in the environment. Cognitive theorists, in contrast, see learners as manipulating the environment. In other words, students are seen as active learners, who "initiate experiences, seek out information to solve problems, and reorganize what they already know to achieve new insights" (Woolfolk, 1998, p. 247). Learners acquire knowledge that allows them to change behaviors. Recent cognitive theorists view these active learners as constructivist in nature.

This view of learning has ties to specific areas of learning. In reading, for example, the **cognitive interactive** view of learning emphasizes the construction of meaning through both information gained from print and prior knowledge and **prior learning experiences** of the reader. Within this model of reading, an emphasis is placed on three primary skill areas: decoding, vocabulary, and comprehension. Those who subscribe to this theory believe that during reading and learning to read, language is processed by orchestrating all of these—the features of print, the readers' background knowledge of the world, and various text types. In this view, correctness is expected in reading words; however, various interpretations of the meaning are accepted in relation to the readers' background knowledge.

A Constructivist Transactional View

Constructivists basically believe that a learner builds his or her own learning through interaction with the environment. Therefore, the learner is actively constructing, rather than passively receiving, knowledge. Research into how readers comprehend broadens our thinking in relation to how children think and learn in general. Researchers in the 1970s and 1980s returned to the early work of Dewey (1938) and Rosenblatt (1978) to expand their thinking in relation to literacy learning through constructivist and transactional theories. *Meaningful* learning is at the heart of constructivist theory (Reutzel & Cooter, 2000, p. 30). In reading, for example, from the beginning, the unit of focus for instruction is on *understanding* connected text. Within this model there are three powerful cueing systems: (1) semantics or meaning, (2) syntax or structure of the language at the sentence level, and (3) graphophonics or the sound/symbol relationship of print. These are orchestrated simultaneously in fluent reading. Teachers who adopt a constructivist model of learning view comprehension as central to reading and writing from the beginning. Moreover they consider the learning of "items or parts" as a by-product of the child's search for meaning in print (Clay, 1991). These teachers also know that the acquisition of reading and writing requires the active construction, or orchestration, of a vast network of strategies and that students learn and self-monitor many things in the process of reading and writing to construct meaning.

The more a teacher is able to help students relate these skills to themselves, the more students will be able to self-monitor their own progress in learning. **Self-monitoring** is a great leap into independent learning where learners can, on their own, select those strategies that will help them go forward. However, we have to remember that we first teach a wide variety of strategies in all our subject areas so that learners will have many from which to choose.

Texas supports constructivist theory and learning as an active process. Learners are actively constructing ideas and concepts about language, mathematics, and other subject areas as they engage in purposeful language use in classrooms. This view of learning dramatically shifts the teacher's role as a "dispenser of knowledge" to a "facilitator" who deliberately plans optimum conditions for learning in a classroom. Within this context, learners are engaged in cognitive operations and activities; they are not passively receiving information.

Continuing to look at this theory and how it applies to reading theory, we combine it with **transactional learning theory**, conceptualized by Louise Rosenblatt (1978). This theory describes comprehension as a powerful relationship between the reader and the text whereby the reader constructs a highly personal or idiosyncratic meaning. Conditions such as time, mood, pressures, reason, and intent for reading influence a reader's stance, or purpose, for reading. Following constructivist transactional theory, many of us have made the shift from skills-directed, or "item," teaching toward more balanced, integrated approaches. In reading, for example, students are exposed to texts that are functional *outside* the classroom, including books, menus, signs, packages, and letters to friends. According to exemplary practice, students learn best when the materials they read are authentic and challenging (Zemelman, Daniels, & Hyde, 1993).

Teaching and learning are also directly related to Vygotsky's (1978) **social-cognitive theory** where social interactions are a key part of the learning process. A responsive classroom environment that supports active learning depends upon the strong interactions and transactions among teacher, students, and the materials. In reading, for example, students need many opportunities to actively follow their interests and respond to a wide array of texts in a variety of ways. In this context, students utilize text as *one* kind of knowledge base and collaborate with others to pursue additional resources, pool knowledge, and negotiate meaning.

THOUGHT AND LANGUAGE DEVELOPMENT

Exemplary teachers consistently value, support, and extend the language each student brings to the formal school setting. Valuing linguistic diversity is critical because, according to Clay (1998), before a child enters "formal" schooling, remarkable learning has already occurred. Educational researchers (Au, 1984;

Chomsky, 1957, 1959, 1965, 1980) have documented the impressive language development of young children. Because of this awesome human achievement, Chukovsky (1933), an early force in children's literature, characterized children from 2 to 5 years old as really being geniuses in linguistics because they often spontaneously arrive at word structures that have been developed by people through the ages. Almost miraculously, children at this age master those methods, processes, and peculiarities of word construction that distant ancestors developed in building language.

Knowledge of the development of thought and language has been influenced by two major researchers, Piaget (1977) and Vygotsky (1962). Piaget views language as developing from egocentric (or **interpsychological**) to social. Vygotsky, in contrast, describes the knowledge that children construct as moving from an interpsychological process that occurs between people in a supportive context to an intrapsychological process that is individual and internal (Wertsch, 1979). So while Piaget stresses the individual, developmental nature of cognitive development with little consideration of the social aspects of language development, Vygotsky stresses the social nature of language and learning. In addition, Vygotsky's (1962) research demonstrates the critical role of adult and peer models in a child's learning. The **zone of proximal development** refers to the time in a learner's development when a task can be mastered—if the learner is provided with help and support from adults or more advanced peers. This help, or **scaffolding**, may consist of structure, clues, reminders, help with remembering details or steps, encouragement to keep trying, and so forth (Woolfolk, 1998). As teachers, we must remember to scaffold learning or to ensure that students have cooperative learning situations in which language is used by advanced peers to scaffold into a new task.

Vygotsky's insights influence us to also think about task "readiness," particularly in relation to formal school entry (Bruner, 1966; Vygotsky, 1962). This is an important concept tied to our role of teacher in a classroom. As a result of adult or advanced peer assistance in the ways mentioned earlier, a young child's language develops in powerful ways (Cazden, 1983). Young learners know how to name many things, how to observe conversational and social rules of speaking, how to put their own thoughts into words, and how to construct grammatical rules of oral language (Au, 1993). Therefore, *meaningful* conversations between teachers and students in any classroom setting are *critical* to the enrichment of language development. "It is through these conversations that the teacher gains insight into what the students are understanding" (Cazden, 1983; Clay, 1998) and then makes decisions on exactly what to do to bring them closer to the edge of the zone of proximal development. In this manner, young children create a very powerful language system that generates and extends their control over language (Clay, 1991). Control over language has powerful transfer effects for learning in general for both younger and older students.

School talk is often different from home talk. Outside school children learn to speak in authentic situations, not artificial ones. Therefore, authentic classrooms try to bring the outside world to the student. Purposeful activities involve student-centered inquiry into genuine questions. Students do research—investigate and use literate behaviors in order to provide answers to real audiences other than the teacher. Drilling students over skills that will "eventually" be put to use at some later time is not typical of meaningful learning or a literacy-centered environment. The teaching of skills and **strategies** is integrated into the context of a variety of texts, materials, and authentic literature. Useful problem solving by children is done within the process of reading, writing, listening, and speaking.

Students learn early that talk is empowering because of the useful ways in which it functions; they learn what it can do for them (Halliday, 1975). In this way, students in a purposeful classroom come to understand that reading and writing serve many functions in their lives. Teachers must design learner-centered environments so that students put literacy to use across various content areas and text types to influence others and to enrich their lives. The ultimate goal is that all students become lifelong learners.

SCHEMA THEORY: LINKING AND ORGANIZING INFORMATION

Readers' schema or schemata (background knowledge about *their* world and about how it works) function in the process of understanding or comprehending. A significant part of the learning process is how learners interpret new information and integrate it into their existing schemata—knowledge already stored in memory. Anderson and Pearson (1984) state, "Whether we are aware of it or not, it is this interaction of new information with old knowledge that we mean when we use the term comprehension" (p. 255).

Children are continuously constructing a system of knowledge, or schemata, from birth that allows them to make sense of their world. These schemata consist of background information, life experiences, and expectations for how certain events and people function in the world in particular contexts. Early on, the child directs attention toward the making sense of the events around him or her (Donaldson, 1978). Teachers should be aware of three conditions that affect learning in relation to schemata. First, a student's background knowledge must be accurate and appropriate. Second, the background knowledge must be sufficient for the task at hand. And last, background knowledge must be activated so that known, or partially known, information can be linked, or scaffolded, with new information. Instruction in all content areas should be designed to address prior knowledge that students bring to the task. If students hold inaccurate, alternative, or naive concepts about ideas, simply getting the "correct" information does not alter existing schemata.

Scaffolding is an important part of learning in all subject areas. There are many good strategies that can be used across the content areas to help teachers obtain information about students' prior knowledge and to scaffold it with new information. One good strategy to help identify prior knowledge for all grade levels is a *word association task* (Zakaluk, Samuels, & Taylor, 1986). Using a word or phrase that represents the main idea of a topic, the teacher has students write down as many words or phrases as they can think of in three minutes that are related to the stimulus item. This information can be used to plan more supportive lessons related to the depth of the students' background knowledge. Concept attainment (explained in Chapter 8) is another activity that helps to dispel mistaken ideas about concepts.

A *discussion web* (Alverman, 1991) can be used to help students think through misconceptions and change them. Using responses from the word association task just discussed, the teacher formulates a question(s) that addresses whatever seems to be interfering with student learning—that is, what is confusing students about the concept. Students work in pairs, listing reasons for their "yes" or "no" answers to each stimulus question. Through discussions with partners, students revise their original understandings. Finally, students summarize the shift in their understanding in a brief paragraph.

Macrorie (1988) suggests another strategy, a *freewrite,* that enables a teacher to assess background knowledge. The freewrite asks students to write down everything they know about a topic for a specified length of time. This provides the teacher and the student an opportunity to monitor ongoing understanding of and learning about topics and concepts; by retaining and comparing a number of freewrites, the teacher and student can see how much new learning has been added.

Read-alouds, or shared reading experiences in which teachers share texts with students or students share texts with other students, build from background knowledge and interest. During shared reading, the teacher serves as a model through discussion, scaffolding, and thinking aloud in relation to the author's message. Another good example of adult scaffolding is the interaction that can take place between a parent and child during a bedtime story reading—even at upper levels (Roser & Martinez, 1995; Snow, 1977). Scaffolded instruction in the classroom is often patterned after bedtime story reading through the use of strategies such as reading aloud to students, shared reading of big books or novels, and guided reading in small homogeneous groups.

METACOGNITION: EXTENDING
SELF-IMPROVING SYSTEMS

Metacognition is an important cognitive operation that includes the understanding and monitoring of one's own thinking. In other words, in metacognition we think purposefully about our thinking. This is important because we can begin to self-select strategies that are helpful rather than harmful in accomplishing learning. In order to foster metacognitive activity as teachers, we should be aware of understanding the learner, the learning process, and the strategies used by the student (Brown, 1980). For example, to gain this type of information in reading, many authorities stress the importance of systematic observation by the classroom teacher for insights into the child's thinking in relation to print (Clay, 1993a; Farr, 1991; Goodman, Smith, Meredith, & Goodman, 1987). Running records (Clay, 1993a) taken by the teacher over time and close monitoring of children during classroom interactions provide guidance for prompts, demonstrations, and support for students' acquisition of a network of strategies. In this manner, students gradually exert independent control of "learning to read by reading and learning to write by writing" (Clay, 1991).

In her work with young children, Clay (1982) describes that in early childhood, the student can exhibit self-monitoring behaviors or metacognition. As the learner has opportunities to read and write in connected ways, for example, important behaviors emerge, such as searching the print, checking ongoing understanding, cross-checking one cueing system against another, and self-correcting without prompts from an adult. These are critical behaviors that indicate metacognitive operations that are internalized and, therefore, lead to independent problem solving on the part of the student. Self-monitoring and metacognitive operations are tightly connected.

In reading, when a student begins to exhibit evidence of the formation of inner control (such as searching for and checking prior knowledge in print), much problem solving and decision making during the reading and writing of text is under control. In addition to the development of inner control, a strategic reader shows evidence of generating categories and rules about features in print with or without prompts from the teacher. Transfer of these are enhanced when the student reads new and novel texts (Clay, 1991, pp. 326–327). This means that teachers will "hear" fewer of the readers' problem-solving vocalizations because the mental operations go "underground" or "inside." As a result, better readers are able to read silently and independently.

Self-knowledge and self-monitoring are tandem concepts. To be in command of their own learning, students must know what to do when they run into trouble. Teacher prompts directly related to operations going on in the students' head during learning are critical for support of successful self-monitoring behaviors. For example, classroom use of discussion, questions, and "think-alouds" with students in relation to understanding text is important. A critical part of the challenge for students is "knowing if they know—and knowing if they don't know" (Brown, 1980; Campione, 1987).

Secondary teachers need to have a clear understanding of how older students read and comprehend. According to Manzo and Manzo (1993), a strategic reader is flexible in orchestrating highly skilled and self-directed acts of mature reading in a variety of texts. A learner consciously plans, sets purposes for reading, monitors ongoing understanding, and has a repertoire of "fix-up" strategies if failure to understand occurs. According to several authorities, an older reader who is having reading difficulties is still in the process of internalizing skills that require conscious acts of self-direction. Paris, Wasik, and Turner (1991) refer to these as "skills under consideration" (p. 611). According to Vygotsky (1962), these skills are unrefined and have not yet "gone underground."

Successful teachers deliberately model and teach organizational and thinking strategies that make a significant difference in relation to students' success with text (Adams, 1990). Effective teachers use flexible grouping arrangements such as whole-class, small-group, paired, and other instructional configurations to promote learning. In flexible grouping, teachers regroup the various learners in class often, depending on the needs of students and the task at hand. Holly, a high achiever in reading, may be paired with Karolin, a lower reader; however, she also may be in a foursome with Dwaine, Esther, and Shellie for learning different skills in mathematics. Students should be active learners who construct their own knowledge. Therefore, effective teachers flexibly select from a variety of instructional strategies such as direct instruction, modeling, scaffolding instruction, and small-group and individual activities in order to promote active learning.

Diagnostic Teaching and Direct Instruction

This section discusses strategies that help students gain self-monitoring behaviors and metacognition in reading. Teachers in all subject areas at all grade levels can use these strategies to help students learn materials better. Using this framework, teachers will have the freedom to execute a variety of activities in any classroom within a wide range of student abilities.

Determination of student abilities is directly related to selection of teaching strategies. Diagnostic teaching is discussed in the literature under a variety of names. These include *responsive teaching* and *instructional conversations* (Tharp & Gallimore, 1989a, 1989b); *reciprocal teaching* (Manzo, 1969a, 1969b; Palinscar & Brown, 1985); *dynamic assessment* (Cioffi & Carney, 1983); *clinical diagnosis* (Chall & Curtis, 1987); *intervention assessment* (Paratore & Indrisano, 1987); *trial teaching* (Harris & Sipay, 1990); and *alternative methods* (Lipson & Wixson, 1991).

According to Manzo and Casale (1983), secondary students should be involved in the process of diagnosing and treating their own reading-study needs in an age-appropriate way. They devised the problem-solving approach to study skills (PASS) to guide students in this direction. The steps to PASS are:

1. *Count.* Students are presented with a list of common study skills problems and asked to check those that apply to them.

2. *Characterize.* Students are guided in defining selected problems, and themselves, in specific terms and helped to think about what they are like and what they do well. With older students, this can be done with inventories of learning style, temperament, skills, abilities, and attitudes.

3. *Consider.* Students consider how they typically have dealt with their particular needs and problems and the possible merit in these intuitive self-management and coping strategies.

4. *Collect.* Students discuss and judge standard techniques for dealing with reading-study problems on the basis of their compatibility with their personal styles and values. Where these appear incompatible, the procedures are dismissed as inappropriate, or set aside for reconsideration in the next step.

5. *Create.* Students seek inventive modifications and alternatives that match their personal styles. This step can be handled initially in individual and small-group settings, and then in larger group discussions from which they all may benefit.

In addition to student self-assessment tools, teachers also must have a variety of assessment procedures with which to collect information on how students learn. Paratore and Indrisano (1987) recommend that teachers develop a set of diagnostic methods and materials (passages, tasks, and prompts) to help learners overcome obstacles encountered. Some different types of methods might be unaided retelling, multiple-choice recognition, diverse responses to text, and so on.

Following assessment, secondary students may need direct teaching, especially those who are having learning difficulties. A system developed by Huhn (1982), referred to as RSM2P, can help teachers plan and guide direct instruction. The process is as follows:

Rationale: The teacher tells students what he or she is going to teach them and why.

Steps: The teacher provides the steps of the strategy in writing as well as orally.

Model: The teacher demonstrates the strategy while thinking aloud.

Practice (aided): The student uses the strategy while thinking aloud and with the teacher assisting in the process.

Practice (independent): The student uses the strategy with similar materials, and is permitted to personalize or modify the strategy as long as production remains high.

Direct teaching can be done through the use of KWL charts, the question-answer relationship strategy, and the use of graphic organizers. For example, teachers can use KWL charts (three-column charts with the headings: What do you know? What do you want to know? What did you learn?) to introduce a topic by asking students to reference in one column what they already know about a topic; to pique curiosity by asking students to list in the next column what they would like to know or learn; and to close the reading of a book or presentation of a lesson by asking students to note in the final column what they learned (more on KWLs in Chapter 11). Teachers can make invisible thinking visible by employing metacognitive strategies such as question-answer relationships (Raphael, 1986) with text. In other words, teachers encourage students to employ thinking about where the answer to a question "resides" in the text, whether explicitly or implicitly. In addition, effective teachers demonstrate the use of a variety of graphic organizers such as charts and semantic maps for students to use in understanding and composing their own various text patterns.

Utilizing these models before, during, and after direct instruction makes it more likely that students will become independent learners who know how, why, and when to use strategies for specific assignments. These same teachers encourage students who are reading different types of texts to recognize the importance of analyzing the task that confronts them. They encourage students to reflect upon what they know or do not know about the material to be read. In addition, effective teachers model for students how to devise plans for the successful completion of the task. They provide rubrics and guidelines for students to evaluate and check their own progress in accomplishing tasks (Brown, Bransford, Ferrara, & Campione, 1983). Successful teachers monitor and give specific feedback through modeling and demonstration when task difficulties occur in their class-rooms. Successful teachers employ these strategies in science, social studies, mathematics, and so forth, rather than just in language arts/reading classrooms.

Flexible Grouping Flexible grouping patterns that are reflective of the needs of the learners and the content to be learned (Hiebert, 1991) are used by effective teachers. Opportunities for whole-class, small-group, peer-dyad, and individual configurations to enhance instruction must exist in all classroom settings to provide additional scaffolding opportunities.

Applying this concept to reading, Hiebert (1991) reports that in whole-class settings, very few students are able to share their unique interpretations of books, even though whole-class contexts may be ideal for fostering a sense of community among students. Peer dyads and small groups allow students to read with one another and to share ideas, but peers rarely scaffold learning for one another in ways that encourage students to develop new strategies like predicting. Teacher-led instruction in small or large groups provides the scaffolding that students need, but application of these strategies will depend on the chance to read or write independently.

Guided Reading Guided reading within a literacy program is an essential type of scaffolding that leads to independence for emergent readers and older struggling readers. Through shared reading and guided reading, support is provided for readers to be able to read silently in text that is more and more difficult. According to Fountas and Pinnell (1996), the following components are essential: (1) a teacher works with a small group of students who are similar in their development of a reading process and who are fairly homogeneous; (2) the story is introduced; (3) students are provided with assistance to help them develop independent reading strategies; (4) each student reads the whole text with the goal of reading independently and silently with good comprehension; and (5) students are grouped and regrouped in a dynamic process that involves ongoing observation and assessment by the teacher.

Another way of organizing for effective reading and writing instruction is through cooperative learning. Both older and younger students need time to collaborate, talk, plan, and work with others to complete a task. Cooperative learning groups are small heterogeneous groups of two to five students. Students in a cooperative group work together to accomplish a specific task assigned by the teacher. Each student may have a specific assignment to accomplish independently as a part of the overall group assignment. Wood (1987) suggests grouping by dyads, or pairs, of learners. Students each take a role as they read a couple of pages of text silently or orally. One student recalls the information while the other listens and clarifies. This is an effective strategy that utilizes auditory feedback and encourages good listening skills.

Think-pair-share (Lyman, 1988) is another effective cooperative learning problem-solving strategy. Comprehension, listening, speaking, and thinking are emphasized in this approach. First, students sit in pairs and the teacher presents a mini-lesson. Learners then individually solve the problem. Afterward, they discuss their answers with a partner to reach a consensus. The agreed-upon answer is then shared with the class. This strategy encourages students to be internally motivated, curious, and self-monitoring.

Finally, Heller (1986) offers a method similar to KWL charts that provides a simple way to guide students' initial reading and postreading reflections. On a sheet of paper, a student creates the following three columns: Column A: What I already knew; Column B: What I now know; and Column C: What I do not know. Other teachers use KWL in a different but effective way: What I already know, What I learned, and What I still want to learn about this. Students set up these columns before reading the information and periodically utilize them to assess their on-going understanding of the text. Again, these learning strategies can be used in all content areas and with all levels of students.

LEARNING, THINKING, AND TEACHING STYLES

A great deal of work has been done in the area of *learning styles* and *modalities* during the past few decades. These terms refer to the *how, when, where,* and *with what* a person learns best (Woolfolk, 1990) rather than to intelligence. Some of the most familiar work centers on preferences of sensory input (modalities). Kolb (1985) and Witkin et al. (1977) focused on differences in *how* people perceive and then *process* information—for example, some learners use their senses to probe, while others analyze their thinking. Sternberg (1992) categorized thinking styles, and other researchers have looked at environmental preferences for learning (low light, noise, early morning preferences for learning, etc.). The most recent work has been done by Gardner (1993) in the area of "multiple intelligences."

What creates one's **learning style**? According to Keefe and Ferrell (1990), it is a combination of one's neurobiology, personality, and development. When we perceive, interact with, and respond to the learning environment, these personal elements come into play cognitively, affectively, and physiologically (Hewit & Whittier, 1996; Jacobsen et al., 1993; Keefe, 1982; Schmeck, 1988). All of us know that we have a favorite way to study and learn. Some of us may curl up in a warm, cozy chair all alone with silence and rewrite/reorganize our notes, while others may need a desk with a bright light and the radio playing in the background while we consult our friends on the phone about our work. There are many puzzle pieces to each individual learner's preferred style. It is important to understand these preferences because by matching instruction or environment to students' styles or by never offering certain styles in the classroom, we can enhance or distract from our students' learning. In the real world our students must eventually work in many conditions, so we must also work to strengthen those areas that are not as favored. Finally, we must understand that students who have preferences in some styles are not well served by schools, while students with other styles flourish naturally in traditional settings.

There are many inventories or surveys that are available to determine students' various learning styles. These can help teachers create learning profiles for individuals who are in their classrooms and help teachers in reaching and extending learning in many ways. Intermediate or secondary teachers who have a multitude of students can vary their instruction daily or weekly using many styles so that, at one time or another, they may touch on all of their students' preferences and weaknesses in learning and thinking styles. Remember that finding an individual student's style(s) could be one key to reaching a student who is not doing well with the current teaching style being presented. Vary your approach often.

Modalities

The way in which a student prefers to receive sensory input is termed **modality preference**. **Modality adeptness** refers to the modality in which a student learns best, despite his or her sensory reception preference. In other words, a student may prefer sensory input visually, but actually learn better kinesthetically. We often teach using our own preferred modality. However, a teacher who teaches through a single modality may negatively affect the achievement of children who learn better through other modalities that may not be employed in a classroom often. The modalities listed in Table 4.1 are those that have been identified.

Why should we care about modalities? Sandra Rief (1993), noted educator, researched student retention. She found that students retain:

10 percent of what they read

20 percent of what they hear

30 percent of what they see

50 percent of what they see and hear

70 percent of what they say

90 percent of what they say and do (p. 53)

Teachers who prepare lessons that involve each type of modality will, thus, have students who learn and retain more.

Table 4.1 Modalities

Visual modality	Learns best visually (reading, graphic organizers, seeing it on a video or television, and so forth)
Auditory modality	Learns best through hearing (orally, through lectures, tapes, etc.)
Tactile modality	Learns best through touching (sandpaper letters, writing in shaving cream, manipulatives)
Kinesthetic modality	Learns best by doing and involvement in movement (role-play, laboratory experiments, dressing up, hand movements to concepts, etc.)

Cognitive Learning Styles (Field-Dependent and Field-Independent)

Teachers who would like to understand the concept of field-dependent and field-independent styles for their students should think about how *they* best like to receive and act on information. Table 4.2 presents questions teachers can ask themselves. Teachers who select the (a) statements on the left are field-dependent learners, while those who agree more with the (b) statements on the right are field-independent learners. Neither style has advantages over the other, necessarily, as both are valuable ways of learning for different situations. An effective teacher will offer students opportunities to learn in both styles.

✓Thinking Styles

Perhaps teachers might categorize themselves and their students in other ways as well. Robert Sternberg (1992) chose to focus on thinking styles in terms of "mental self-government." Implementing and doing appeals to the *executive* mind. Solving problems that are structured, following directions or guidelines, and recalling information is a forte for executive thinkers. Students who think in this manner do very well in traditional classrooms. *Legislative* thinkers, however, prefer creating, formulating, imagining, and planning. Creative writing assignments, designing experiments, and imagining different outcomes are all attractive tasks to legislative thinkers. *Judicial* thinkers are those who enjoy tasks that involve judging, evaluating, and comparing. These include critiquing, evaluating solutions and outcomes (rather than creating them), and comparisons of events, books, characters, and so forth.

   Sternberg also identified four other styles in terms of learning based on forms of government. Again, teachers might consider their own preferences. In a monarchic style of government, there is only one central, predominant goal (the king's

Table 4.2 How Do You Learn Best?

Do you see the forest	or	the trees?
(a) like to have the whole picture, general idea, or overall feeling of the materials first, or do you tend to look at the whole to figure out how the parts work? Do you tend to form an overall picture as you read, listen or observe? Do you bog down if faced with a book that begins with many details first? (global orientation)	or	(b) prefer to have a structured view in which each part is categorized and clustered because you tend to look at the parts to see how the whole works? Do you create a structure as you read, listen, or observe? Do you find overviews distracting? Do you prefer step-by-step instruction? (local or analytical orientation)
(a) depend on colleagues and feel more motivated working in a group? Do you like having goals already set for you? (extrinsically motivated)	or	(b) like to work alone much better and have a strong sense of direction? Do you like setting goals by yourself? (intrinsically motivated)
(a) seek the social relevance in materials whenever possible? (socially oriented)	or	(b) seek to focus on the nature of the content or materials? (content oriented)

or queen's). In a *monarchic* form of thinking, a student prefers to do only one thing at a time and is often fixed upon that goal until it is finished. These are not "jugglers" in learning. Monarchic students who are in whole language classes may be confused and frustrated as subjects and assignments merge and blend. Hierarchic forms of government have many goals that are set in order. Students who are *hierarchic* learners can set priorities while juggling several assignments at once. *Oligarchic* governments have equal, multiple goals, all of the same importance. These students are also good jugglers. It is difficult for these learners to set priorities, however, as all seems equally important. They are challenged by juggling many assignments and often do all of them well—or none of them well (due to the inability to set priorities). The *anarchic* thinker, like the anarchic government, has no rules or structure. This type of thinker takes a "potshot" approach to learning that may involve breaking traditional mindsets. Often this student does not do well in traditional classrooms where procedures and guidelines are to be followed.

A teacher may slant instruction toward his or her style. However, a mismatch with students may produce a child who seems uninterested or unwilling to participate in instruction. Sternberg cautions teachers to remember that those students who match the teacher's styles appear to the teacher to be brighter than those who do not. Sternberg also recommends, as do all learning/teaching style researchers, that teachers should provide instruction using a variety of learning and teaching styles in order to meet the needs of all students.

Other Factors Impacting Learning

Dunn and Dunn (1978) investigated many factors that affect learning. In their Learning Styles Inventory, they group these factors into five categories: (1) environmental, (2) emotional, (3) sociological, (4) physical, and (5) psychological. *Environmental factors* include preferences for different light intensities, sound, temperature, and even the arrangement of the room and construction of the furniture (design). *Emotional factors* focus on responsibility, motivation, and persistence, along with the need for (or no need for) structure and supervision in learning. *Sociological factors* center on preferences for learning in groups (large or small), alone, or with an adult, team, or varied group. *Physical factors* are related not only to the senses (all the modalities mentioned earlier) but also to times of the day and need for food intake during learning. *Psychological factors* consider analytic and global thinking as well as reflective and impulsive processing (as described in the next section) and cerebral preferences.

Cognitive Perception and Processing Styles

Another way of looking at the way that learners perceive, interact with, and process an event is related to cognitive perception and processing styles (Kolb, 1984). Table 4.3 describes the cognitive perception and processing styles related to different learning styles.

What do we mean by concrete or abstract perception (how the learner perceives) as shown in the second column of the table? Hewit and Whittier (1996) explained this by asking us to look at people reporting an event or accident. Some

Table 4.3 Cognitive Perception and Processing Styles

	Learning Style	Way Learner Perceives	Way Learner Processes (Conceptual Tempo)	Preferences in Learning	Other
Type 1:	Imaginative (or Relational)	Concretely	Reflectively	Watching, sensing, listening, feeling, personal experience, sharing ideas, loves variety, difficulty with auditory and visual	Asks "Why?"; sees from multiple experiences, so has difficulty with decisions
Type 2:	Analytic	Abstractly	Reflectively	Watching, asking why, thinking, devising theories, sequential thinking, being thorough, seeking "expert opinion"	Prefers traditional classrooms; high achiever, often more interested in ideas than people; fears mistakes
Type 3:	Commonsense (Structured or Solution-Oriented)	Abstractly	Actively	Problem-solving, thinking, doing, practical application, systematic	Asks, "How?"; needs structured classroom
Type 4:	Dynamic (Energetic)	Concretely	Actively	Sensing, feeling, doing, trial-and-error, flexibility, risk-taking, hands-on, spontaneous, plunges into experience	Seeks to influence others, manipulative or pushy; dislikes traditional classrooms

report by relying heavily on their senses (concrete), while others think through and analyze exactly what happened (abstract). For example, "I saw this huge truck coming. I saw the car hit from behind. I heard this large crash. I jumped back," versus, "As the truck approached the car from behind, it was obvious that a crash would occur and that I might be hit." Students who are abstract may be able to problem-solve or work through a problem simply by thinking it through symbolically or by use of numbers, while those who are concrete may need to have manipulatives or other concrete items to "see it or feel it."

What about how students process (or conceptual tempo), which appears in the third column of Table 4.3? Have you also noticed that some learners "jump into" an experience immediately when it is offered (active), while others "step back" and watch for a bit first (reflective)? Reflective learners first tie a new experience to past learning to help make sense of the event, while the active learners go for the experience opportunity first, then reflect. We would tend to believe that reflective thinkers do better, but at the extreme, they can ponder for so long that they bog down in decision making. The extreme active learner can be so quick as to be impulsive and error-prone. Both can be taught to become more efficient in each area.

Multiple Intelligences

Howard Gardner's theory of **multiple intelligences** speaks of capacities that reside inside of a person. He currently identifies eight intelligences: verbal-linguistic, logical-mathematical, intrapersonal, visual-spatial, musical-rhythmic, bodily-kinesthetic, interpersonal, and naturalist. This theory offers us a new look at children as we ask, "How is this child smart?" rather than "How smart is this child?" The chart shown in Table 4.4 (Campbell et al., 1996) offers an overview of these intelligences. All of these intelligences are believed to be a part of each child, but by school age, it is believed that a child will already show strength or favor in certain areas. There is also the capacity to develop all of these intelligences to high levels.

Why is this concept of multiple intelligences important for teachers to understand? This work is particularly exciting because it offers some fundamental principles to students and teachers. First, it supports the philosophy that "all children can learn" because children respond to learning in different ways. Therefore, if teachers provide situations for learning in each of these areas, their students, more likely than not, will respond and learn more easily and retain more of what they learned. Next, intelligence can be learned. This is motivating to students as well, as they understand that over time they can increase their intelligence in all of these areas. Thus, intelligence is not viewed by Gardner as fixed at birth. By offering students an opportunity to work in their dominant learning style or intelligence, they can excel. Certainly, the classroom is more inviting to students when instruction and environment are matched to their preferences or strengths at some point during the day or week. When offered another style or intelligence in which to work, students will have the opportunity to work on building intelligence in that area.

Table 4.4 Gardner's Multiple Intelligences

Intelligence	Attributes	Some Successfully Matched Careers
Verbal-linguistic (Smart with Words)	Ability to think in words and use language to express and appreciate complex meaning; learns through listening, reading, writing, and discussing; creates original writing or oral communication	Journalists, poets, authors, speakers, political debaters, lawyers
Logical-mathematical (Smart with Numbers)	Ability to calculate, quantify, consider propositions and hypotheses, and carry out complex mathematics; perceives patterns, relationships, and abstract symbols, and problem-solves by posing and testing hypotheses	Engineers, mathematicians, computer scientists and designers, scientists, accountants
Visual-Spatial (Smart with Pictures)	Ability to perceive external and internal imagery to recreate, transform, or modify images, to navigate oneself and objects through space, and to produce or decode graphic information; learns by seeing and observing (with graphic representation or through visual media); thinks in pictures of mental imagery	Architects, painters, sculptors pilots, astronauts, designers, sailors, photographers, videographers, art critics, mechanics
Bodily-kinesthetic (Smart with the Body)	Ability to manipulate objects and fine-tune physical skills; learns by touching, handling, or manipulating what is to be learned along with concrete experiences such as field trips or role-play; needs to move; is able to express ideas and feelings through the body	Athletes, surgeons, dancers, workers of crafts, builders
Musical-rhythmic (Smart with Music)	Possesses a sensitivity to pitch, melody, rhythm, and tone; immediately reacts to music; sensitive to environmental sounds	Musicians, composers, conductors, instrument makers, music teachers, music critics
Interpersonal (Smart with People)	Capacity to understand and interact effectively with others; perceives the feelings, thoughts, motivations, behaviors, and lifestyles of others; communicates effectively both verbally and nonverbally; easily	Teachers, social workers actors, politicians, counselors, comics

Intelligence	Attributes	Some Successfully Matched Careers
	adapts to different environ-ments or groups; uncanny ability to "read"people; has "people skills"	
Intrapersonal (Smart with Self)	Ability to construct an accurate perception of oneself and to use such knowledge in planning and directing one's life; works independently; empowers others; uses self-discipline, self-esteem, etc., to function well in situations	Theologians, psych-ologists, and philo-sophers
Naturalist (Smart with Nature)	Ability to classify patterns in nature, and to recognize flora and fauna and weather change patterns	Botanists, forestry careers, zoologists, meteorologists

Emotional Intelligence

Emotional intelligence is an area addressed by Daniel Goleman (1995). Emotional intelligence refers to recognizing, using, understanding, and managing emotions. Testing involves measurement in stress tolerance, motivation, innovation, intuition, empathy, optimism, happiness, self-actualization, flexibility, social skills, and so forth. Children who lack emotional intelligence are often those who are labeled as behavior management problems, inappropriate, or "outcasts" because they lack the ability to read emotions in others. Success in schools and beyond can be affected by the inability of a student to use the emotional intelligence area, although he or she may be intelligent in many other areas.

Investigating Students' Styles

There are numerous inventories that have been constructed for measuring learn-ing styles, intelligences, and modalities. Many teachers will survey all students in order to determine learning style preference and to better meet individual needs in the classroom. However, when one student is having difficulties, teachers need to investigate these options carefully.

One instrument that identifies learning styles was developed by Manzo, Lorton, and Condon (1975) and Manzo and Casale (1983) and is informally administered. The Learning Preference Inventory (LPI) is not limited to early age–grade ranges or to modality issues, as are most other learning styles inventories. Another strong point for using this inventory is that it promotes awareness as to whether a student has a strong dislike for a commonly used mode of presentation.

Teaching Styles

Along with learning styles, much research has examined **teaching styles** (Fischer & Fischer, 1979). A teacher's choice of emphasis, instruction, interactions/ways of communicating, and classroom mannerisms make up a style of teaching. A teaching style is developed through knowledge of education, beliefs, and past experiences—coupled with the teacher's own personality. As in learning styles, we can look at these styles in different ways, often noting overlaps in labels.

One classification system identifies three types of teaching styles: teacher-centered, content-centered, and student-centered. A *teacher-centered style* involves the teacher filtering and processing information for students. All instruction, content, assessment, and so forth are decided by the teacher (autocratic). *Content-* or *subject-centered* teachers are often "respected experts." Methods of instruction are often lecture and text-driven readings with assignments. On the one hand, these experts can impart a great deal of knowledge and can be noted as brilliant and/or entertaining lecturers, but on the other hand, covering the material is more important—at the cost of the learner. Within this classification, the student-centered teacher is basically what Texas would like the teaching style to be. *Student-centered teachers* employ a facilitating manner and constantly focus on the needs of the learner in every respect. Teachers continuously ask if students are able, ready, interested, and so forth. Student decisions about learning are respected and encouraged, and the teacher is a learner in the classroom as well. Some educators make a more distinct category of *purely student-centered*. In this pure style, the curiosity of the child is followed completely, so the curriculum emerges from whatever the child wishes to learn. There is no preset curriculum, because teachers cannot know what the child will be interested in each day. When "student-centered" appears on the test, however, Texas is referring to more of a *learning-/student-centered style* rather than a purely student-centered style (see Table 4.5). Unless a test item specifically indicates a *purely* student-centered style, the assumption is that it refers to a learning-/student-centered style.

Another classification presents a dyad in which two styles are contrasted sharply with one another: the traditional style and the facilitating style. In a *traditional teaching style*, teachers are autocratic (*they* make the decisions), subject-centered, task-centered, formal, and prescriptive. They most often teach in classrooms with desks in rows facing the front. Their lessons are, as a rule, lecture-type or other teacher-centered instruction where *they* do the demonstrations and have students learn in a deductive manner. The

Table 4.5 Teaching Styles

Teacher-Centered	Learning-/Student-Centered	Purely Student-Centered
Traditional	Facilitating	Completely child-centered
Task-oriented	Student-centered	Laissez-faire
Subject-centered	Equal concern for task, material, and students	Child decides what interests him or her and teacher follows (emergent curriculum)
Autocratic	Democratic	
Formal	Cooperative planner (respects and asks for student input)	
Prescriptive		
Top-down instruction		

transference of knowledge is from teacher to student in a *top-down* approach. This, at first glance, may sound like a teacher that you would not enjoy. However, there are times that this can be an appropriate style, and there are students in the room who shine when matched with this style. The difficulty comes when this is the *only* style employed by a teacher.

A *facilitating teacher*, however, is mostly democratic in style (some joint learning decisions with students are made). Instead of desks in rows, such teachers often have students arranged in small groups or in a circular pattern, demonstrating that this is a student-centered classroom. The instruction is often cooperative and inductive in nature with many inquiry and problem-solving activities in evidence. Concrete rather than abstract learning is emphasized. In this type of classroom, teachers are seen as fellow learners. Although some learners respond very well to traditional teaching styles, Texas maintains an overall interest in teachers who employ a more facilitative manner.

Using knowledge of teaching and learning styles, a teacher can plan and instruct more effectively. A teacher cannot justify using only one approach or providing only one type of environment for learning. Neither can a teacher accommodate each learner every moment. However, the more that teachers know about their learners and the various learning styles and the more that teachers know themselves and their own teaching styles, the better they can design instruction that will let students excel in their areas of preference/dominance while challenging students in areas of nonpreference that may need strengthening. It is one more step toward teachers knowing themselves and knowing their students as individuals in order to provide the best in instruction.

SUMMARY

"Our image of children-as-learners is a reflection of our definition of what it means to teach" (Wood, 1993, p. 1). Thus, learning about various theories that offer "different accounts of the way in which children think and learn also leads to alternative views on what is involved in teaching them" (Wood, 1993, p. 14). The diversity of today's classroom demands much from any teacher. Both teacher and students are engaged in a highly complex interaction of materials, tasks, and contexts. We must respond to the needs of *all* students and reflect constructively on *what* we are requiring students to do. As important is the question of why we are requiring a given task of any student. Responsive teaching, therefore, requires attending to the needs, strengths, and abilities of the student rather than following a predetermined program or curriculum (Galda, Cullinan, & Strickland, 1997; Palinscar & Brown, 1985).

Teachers in classrooms that do teach to individual differences often use inquiry-centered thematic units that allow for incorporation of a variety of strategies to meet student needs. These teachers also use flexible grouping and cooperative learning in the classroom to support language and thought as social events. Talking and thinking are encouraged because students learn best by working and interacting with others about what they are doing in purposeful ways. Within this setting, the emotional and cognitive support of peers encourages authentic engagement in learning. There is powerful influence on learning by the ways in which teachers organize and orchestrate responses in their classroom. Learning and teaching styles are an important consideration in classroom organization and presentation as well as in providing authentic, real-world tasks and helping students understand clearly the reasons for their study. Making links between old and new information and/or connecting prior learning experiences are a necessary part of teaching in Texas. Finally, Texas encourages teachers to help students self-monitor and to take responsibility for their own learning. Thus, if teachers understand how learning occurs and can apply this understanding in order to design and implement effective instruction, they will have success in Texas classrooms.

SUGGESTED ACTIVITIES

1. Design or find a survey that will help you determine "what" students in your grade level or subject area would like to learn and "how" they would like to learn it.

2. Determine your own learning and teaching styles using the information given in the chapter or a survey. Using a lesson that you have constructed, analyze it in terms of students who do *not* match your styles. What does this mean for students?

3. Prepare a short integrated unit outline in which all of the multiple intelligences are used.

4. Develop one of the lessons from your integrated unit outline to include strong scaffolding (linking old information to new) and a strong rationale (fostering a view of learning as a purposeful pursuit).

5. Go back into the lesson you developed in activity 4 to make sure that all modalities are used.

6. Observe a lesson being taught. Note whether the teacher uses scaffolding and presents a rationale. Observe students' reaction during the lesson.

7. Examine the state teacher observation instrument. If a principal were to observe your lesson, where would you gain or lose points for using or leaving out a rationale and scaffolding?

8. Think about how you have self-monitored your learning in this chapter and in preparing for your lesson observation. What are some strategies that you have used to determine if you can go ahead or must go back? Use your own metacognition to "think about your thinking" in this respect. In the lesson that you have designed, find a place where students can "think about their thinking," or use metacognition to select strategies that will help them move forward (self-monitor their learning).

PRACTICE DECISION SET

Vignette 1

Ms. Mayo's first-grade class initiated a thematic unit on community helpers when one of the students shared that his family called the fire department to put out a minor grass fire that weekend. The students had many questions they wanted answered about the fire fighters who helped in the emergency. The class discussion expanded to other types of helpers in the community, how to get help in case of emergencies, who to contact, and what each group of helpers did in the community.

Ms. Mayo capitalized on the students' interest as an authentic opportunity to teach the essential elements required in first-grade social studies curriculum. She worked with the school librarian to have both narrative and informational text, magazines, and newspaper articles about community helpers available in her classroom. She scheduled many opportunities for reading aloud to the children—shared and guided reading, independent reading and writing.

The class wrote letters inviting guest speakers from the fire department, the police department, and the local hospital to discuss their particular community-related responsibilities. The children used learning logs and worked in pairs to formulate questions they wanted to ask the guest speakers. They used the learning logs to record the answers they received during the guest visits.

Ms. Mayo had students brainstorm what they learned, and she demonstrated for the class how to organize information on several semantic maps. Using the semantic maps, the students wrote and published a big book titled "Our Community Helpers."

The first-grade students made maps of their community to locate the fire department, the police department, and the hospital. They used mathematics skills to draw the map and incorporate appropriate map symbols. They worked in cooperative groups to write and perform a play about community helpers. Students decorated the sets, created the costumes, and ended the unit by performing the play for parents and friends.

1. Ms. Mayo is increasing the probability that her students will actively engage in learning in her class by setting supportive conditions. Which of the following strategies *best* supports student engagement?
   a. Allowing student discussions
   b. Including essential elements in the curriculum design
   c. Allowing students' interests and questions to support authentic inquiry and research
   d. Using community helpers as a resource to interest the students

2. Ms. Mayo provided a variety of texts and print materials related to the thematic unit. Which of the following best describes her objectives in this approach?
   a. Daily reading grades can be given using various text types.
   b. The texts provide opportunities to demonstrate how various texts are constructed and used.
   c. A variety of texts provides materials to support the multilevel reading abilities in her class.
   d. Both b and c

3. Which of the following strategies best demonstrates the connection between reading and writing for Ms. Mayo's students?

a. Working in cooperative groups to create a play
b. Using semantic maps to organize information for the purpose of writing a book
c. Recording interview questions and responses to those questions in a learning log
d. Both b and c

4. Ms. Mayo is aware that she needs to provide opportunities for her students to excel in a non-threatening atmosphere using their different learning styles. Which of the following activities offers the best opportunities to accomplish this goal?
   a. Designing a rubric to grade their learning logs
   b. Allowing students to retell their big books to check comprehension
   c. Giving students many opportunities to excel such as creating the play, creating costumes, independent and cooperative groups, and so forth
   d. Using cooperative learning strategies instead of whole group lessons

Vignette 2

Mr. Marshall teaches sixth grade in a school that is characterized as "at-risk." Many of the students are impacted by poverty and have limited experiences with the world and with text. His sixth-grade social studies class is beginning a unit of study on World War II. As an introduction to the study, Mr. Marshall read the first chapter of *The Diary of Anne Frank* to the class. He used "think-alouds" throughout the shared reading, asking students to predict at appropriate times and making his thinking explicit to students. He engaged the class in a discussion of the chapter and encouraged them to make links to their personal lives. Each student had a paperback copy of the book.

Mr. Marshall also planned to have various grouping arrangements for the students to read and respond to a variety of information sources linked to the unit: the social studies textbook, newspaper articles, magazine articles, encyclopedias, and computer-generated searches. Using readers' and writers' workshops, Mr. Marshall deliberately planned opportunities for students to read a variety of genres to search for information. He used mini-lessons to model specific strategies for reading and responding to informational text. Using the workshop format, Mr. Marshall deliberately scheduled independent reading, paired reading, literature discussion circles, journal responses, and dramatic readings.

5. "Think-alouds" support students to think about their ongoing understanding in powerful ways because:
   a. This particular class cannot do the higher-order thinking necessary for this unit of study.
   b. Students need auditory feedback as they follow along in their own novels.
   c. The "think-alouds" explicitly demonstrate metacognitive operations that support strategic reading and writing.
   d. This strategy gives concrete examples to the students to increase their vocabulary.

6. The use of various grouping arrangements enhance the learning of these sixth-grade students because:
   a. All students, regardless of reading level, can learn from one another and make positive contributions in cooperative learning groups.
   b. Individual students are allowed to use different learning styles to

respond to a text and share meaning in diverse ways.

c. Students have opportunities to use their background knowledge and oral language in purposeful ways.

d. All of the above

Answer 1: Answer *b* is a state requirement rather than a method of setting up a supporting condition for student engagement. Allowing student discussion is certainly a positive move for motivation and engagement (answer *a*), as is bringing in community resources (*d*). However, the *most* motivating factor in this exciting lesson is that it was the spark lit by student interest that generated the original question, further inquiry, and research. Answer *c* is, therefore, correct. Plus, it is doubly engaging because it is real-life or authentic inquiry.

Answer 2: Answer *a* should be of least consideration, as it does not address any of the *students'* needs. However, both *b* and *c* are correct, so the correct answer is *d*. Answer *b* is an excellent way to demonstrate the way in which different types of books are written and will offer a "fit" to this particular research need. By offering a variety of books (*c*), there is surely one that will match the interest and the reading level of most children.

Answer 3: Again, the answer is *d*. Answer *a* is not correct because creating a play is a creative writing activity rather than a reading activity *and* everyone in a group might not be assigned a writer's role. There also may be no written work at all depending on the length requirements and so forth. Answers *b* and *c*, however, both offer excellent reading/writing connections. Semantic maps help students generate and organize ideas for writing, and gathering data from interviews for a learning log helps students prepare written answers

to their questions prior to writing their book as well.

Answer 4: Answer *a*, (designing a rubric that tells students *exactly* what is expected for an exact grade) helps students meet a teacher's expectations, but it may or may not allow for different learning styles. Answer *b* is a good way to check for comprehension, but there is no variety of learning style offered here. Answer *d* offers students one alternative style of learning, but does not talk about a *choice* situation. Answer *c*, however, offers students a variety of activities in which they could "shine."

Answer 5: Answer *a* is certainly not correct because intelligence is not related to economic level. Answer *b*, auditory feedback, is a good idea for other learning styles, but not the best answer. Answer *d* is not correct; "think-alouds" may make all kinds of connections, but these are not *all* concrete, perhaps. Answer *c* is the correct answer because this technique supports students in monitoring their own ongoing understanding. As the teacher shares his or her thoughts throughout the reading, students check their thoughts and understanding against the teacher's. Metacognitive thinking is literally "thinking about thinking"—a very active part of "think-alouds."

Answer 6: The correct answer is d, all the above. In *a,* more minds contribute ideas, and more minds are better than only one. Also, contributing positive ideas is not necessarily related to reading level. Answer b reminds us that students do use a variety of styles to gain information from the text, and those perspectives may add to the whole picture. Answer c is also correct. In group activities, it is the students who are orally connecting their knowledge and background with the new task rather than the teacher.

WEB LINKS

Remember that website locations may change. If any of these sites have moved or cannot be located, use Terms to Know in this chapter to search for further information.

Constructivist Theory

www.funderstanding.com/
<http://www.funderstanding.com/>
Practical and enjoyable variety of instructional techniques related to constructivist theory

Learning and Instruction Theory

www.lincoln.ac.nz/educ/tip/1.htm
A comprehensive database that covers both instructional practice, theory, and research. Includes 50 theories related to human learning and instruction. Reviews scope, application, examples, principles, and references

Metacognition

www.ncrel.org/sdrs/areas/issues/students/
learning/lr1metn.htm
Metacognition Pathways home page; provides an outline/overview of a plan of action for studying

Hirsch and Schema Theory

www.ils.nwu.edu/~e_for_e/nodes/NODE-
112-pg.html
An extensive review of Hirsch's schema theory including illustrative stories

related to the instantiation of schemata. Authorities cited include Spiro.

Learning Styles

Search Tip: A number of sources discuss how to determine learning styles and modalities, how to identify ways to work with particular styles, and theory. Do a search using "learning+styles".

http://familyeducation.com
This is a *very* full site for multiple intelligences, learning styles, and emotional intelligences. Once you are into the site itself, you will locate the area that says "site search." Then type in the key words for the subject that you want. A few of the links may not work, but keep going—many do.
http://members.aol.com/susans29/lsa.html
http://www.scican.net/~harnish/mstyles.
html

Multiple Intelligences

http://www.members.tripod.com/
~RheaultK/index.html
http://web.ott.igs.net/~cmorris/faq.html
These sites give further information about multiple intelligences, testing for intelligences, and how to work with students using all intelligences.

Emotional Intelligence

www.eiconsortium.org
http://www.eq.org

REFERENCES AND SUGGESTED READINGS

Adams, M. J. (1990). *Beginning to read: Thinking and learning about print.* Cambridge, MA: MIT Press.

Alverman, D. E. (1991). The discussion web: A graphic aid for learning across the curriculum. *The Reading Teacher, 45,* 92–99.

Anderson, R. C., & Pearson, P. D. (1984). A schema-theoretic view of basic processes in reading. In P. D. Pearson (Ed.), *Handbook of reading research* (pp. 255–291). New York: Longman.

Au, K. H. (1984). Vygotskian perspectives on discussion processes in small group reading lessons. In P. Peterson, L. Wilkinson, & M. Halliman (Eds.), *The social context of instruction: Group organization and group processes.* New York: Academic Press.

Au, K. H. (1993). *Literacy instruction in multicultural settings.* Fort Worth, TX: Harcourt Brace.

Brown, A. L. (1980). Metacognitive development and reading. In R. J. Spiro, B. C. Bruce, & W. F. Brewer (Eds.), *Theoretical issues in reading comprehension* (pp. 453–481). Hillsdale, NJ: Lawrence Erlbaum.

Brown, A., Bransford, J., Ferrara, R., & Campione, J. (1983). Learning, remembering, and understanding. In J. Flavell & E. Markman (Eds.), *Handbook of child psychology* (Vol. 3, p. 716). New York: Wiley.

Bruner, J. (1966). *Toward a theory of instruction.* Oxford: Harvard University Press.

Campbell, L., Campbell, B., & Dickinson, D. (1996). *Teaching and learning through multiple intelligences.* Needham Heights, MA: Allyn & Bacon.

Campione, J. C. (1987). Metacognitive components of instructional research with problem learners. In F. E. Weinert & R. H. Kluwe (Eds.), *Metacognition, motivation, and understanding* (pp. 117–140). Hillsdale, NJ: Lawrence Erlbaum.

Cazden, C. (1983). Adult assistance to language development: Scaffolds, models, and direct instruction. In R. P. Parker & F. R. Davis (Eds.), *Developing literacy: Young children's use of language* (pp. 3–18). Newark, DE: International Reading Association.

Chall, J. S., & Curtis, M. E. (1987). What clinical diagnosis tells us about children's reading. *The Reading Teacher, 40,* 784–789.

Chomsky, C. (1993). *The acquisition of syntax in children from 5 to 10* (Research Monograph No. 57). Cambridge, MA: MIT Press

Chomsky, N. (1957). *Syntactic structures.* The Hague: Mouton.

Chomsky, N. (1959). Review of B. F. Skinner, Verbal behavior. In *Language 35,* 26–58.

Chomsky, N. (1965). *Aspects of the theory of syntax.* Cambridge, MA: MIT Press.

Chomsky, N. (1980). *Rules and representations.* Oxford: Basal Blackwell.

Chukovsky, K. (1933). *From two and five.* Berkeley, CA: University of California Press. (Original work published in 1925)

Cioffi, G., & Carney, J. J. (1983). Dynamic assessment of reading disabilities. *The Reading Teacher, 36,* 764–768.

Clay, M. M. (1982). *Observing young readers: Selected papers.* Portsmouth, NH: Heinemann.

Clay, M. M. (1991). *Becoming literate: The construction of inner control.* Auckland, NZ: Heinemann.

Clay, M. M. (1993a). *Reading recovery: A guidebook for teachers in training.* Portsmouth, NH: Heinemann.

Clay, M. M. (1993b). *An observation survey for early literacy achievement.* Portsmouth, NH: Heinemann.

Clay, M. M. (1998). *By different paths to common outcomes.* York, MA: Stenhouse Publishers.

De Ford, D. E. (1985). Validating the construct of theoretical orientation in reading instruction. *Reading Research Quarterly, 20*(3), 351–367.

Dewey, J. (1938). *Experience in education.* New York: Collier.

Donaldson, M. (1978). *Children's minds.* Glasgow: Fontana.

Dunn, K., & Dunn, R. (1978). *Teaching students through their individual learning styles: A practical approach.* Reston, VA: Reston Publishing.

Farr, R. (1991). *Portfolios: Assessment in the language arts.* ED334603.

Fischer, B., & Fischer, L. (1979). Styles in teaching and learning. *Educational Leadership, 36,* 251.

Fountas, I., & Pinnell, G. S. (1996). *Guided reading: Good first teaching for all children.* Portsmouth, NH: Heinemann.

Galda, L., Cullinan, B., & Strickland, D. S. (1997). *Language, literacy, and the child.* Austin, TX: Harcourt Brace.

Gardner, H. (1993). *Frames of mind: The theory of multiple intelligences.* New York: Basic Books.

Goleman, D. (1995). *Emotional intelligence: Why it can matter more than IQ.* New York: Bantan.

Goodman, K., Smith, E. B., Meredith, R., & Goodman, Y. M. (1987). *Language and thinking in school: A whole-language curriculum.* Katona, NY: Owen.

Gough, P. B. (1972). One second of reading. In J. F. Kavanagh & I. G. Mattingly (Eds.), *Language by ear and by eye.* Cambridge, MA: MIT Press.

Halliday, M. A. K. (1975). *Learning how to mean: Explorations in the development of language.* London: Edward Arnold.

Harris, A. J., & Sipay, E. R. (1990). *How to increase reading ability* (9th ed.). New York: Longman.

Harste, J. C., & Burke, C. L. (1977). A new hypothesis for reading teacher research: Both the teaching and learning of reading are theoretically based. In D. P. Pearson (Ed.), *Reading: Theory, research, and practice* (pp. 32–40). Clemson, SC: National Reading Conference.

Heller, M. F. (1986). How do you know what you know? Metacognitive modeling in the content areas. *Journal of Reading, 29*(5), 415–422.

Hewit, J. S., & Whittier, K. S. (1996). *Teaching methods for today's schools: Collaboration and inclusion.* Boston: Allyn & Bacon.

Hiebert, E. H. (1991). Research directions: Literacy contexts and literacy processes. *Language Arts, 68,* 134–139.

Huhn, R. H., Jr. (1982). RSM2P: A metacognitive approach for teaching cognitive strategies to facilitate learning. In G. H. McNich (Ed.), *Reading in the discipline* (pp. 67–68). Second yearbook of the American Reading Forum.

Jacobsen, D., Eggen, P., & Kauchak, D. (1993). *Methods for teaching: A skills approach* (4th ed.) New York: Merrill.

Keefe, J. W. (1982). Assessing student learning styles: An overview. In National Association of Secondary School Principals (Ed.), *Student learning styles and brain behavior.* Reston, VA: Author.

Keefe, J. W., & Ferrell, B. G. (1990). Developing a defensible learning style paradigm. *Educational Leadership, 48*(2), 57–61.

Kolb, D. (1984). *Experiential learning: Experience as the source of learning and development.* Englewood Cliffs, NJ: Prentice-Hall.

Kolb, D. (1985). *The learning style inventory.* Boston: McBer & Co.

LaBerge, D., & Samuels, S. J. (1974). Toward a theory of automatic information processing in reading. *Cognitive Psychology, 6,* 293–323.

Lipson, M. Y., & Wixson, K. K. (1991). *Assessment and instruction of reading disability.* New York: HarperCollins.

Lyman, F. (1988). Think-pair-share, Wait time two, and on. . . . *Mid-Atlantic Association for the Cooperation in Education Cooperative News, 2,* 1.

Macrorie, K. (1988). *The I-search paper.* Portsmouth, NH: Heinemann.

Manzo, A. V. (1969a). Improving reading comprehension through reciprocal questioning. (Doctoral dissertation, Syracuse University, Syracuse, NY, 1968.) *Dissertation Abstracts International, 30,* 5344A.

Manzo, A. V. (1969b). The ReQuest procedure. *Journal of Reading, 13,* 123–126.

Manzo, A. V., Lorton, M., & Condon, M. (1975). *Personality characteristics and learning style preferences of adult basic education students.* Research monograph of Center for Resource Development in Adult Education, University of Missouri—Kansas City.

Manzo, A. V., & Casale, U. P. (1981). A multivariate analysis of principle and trace elements in mature reading comprehension. In G. H. McNinch (Ed.), *Comprehension: Process and Product* (pp. 76–81). First Yearbook of the American Reading Forum.

Manzo, A. V., & Manzo, U. C. (1993). *Holistic diagnosis and remediation.* New York: Harcourt Brace Jovanovich.

Palinscar, A. S., & Brown, A. (1985). Reciprocal teaching: Activities to promote "reading with your mind." In E. J. Cooper (Ed.), *Reading, thinking, and* concept development: Interactive strategies for the class. New York: The College Board.

Paratore, J. R., & Indrisano, R. (1987). Intervention assessment of reading comprehension. *Reading Teacher, 40,* 778–783.

Paris, S. G., Wasik, B. A., & Turner, J. C. (1991). The development of strategic readers. In R. Barr, M. L. Kamil, P. Mosenthal, & P. D. Pearson (Eds.), *Handbook of reading research* (Vol. 2, pp. 609–640). New York: Longman.

Pearson, P. D., Barr, R., Kamil, M., & Mosenthal, P. (Eds.) (1984). *Handbook of reading research.* New York: Longman.

Piaget, J. (1977). Piaget's theory. In P. Mussen (Ed.), *Carmichael's manual of child psychology* (Vol.1, 703–732). New York: Wiley.

Raphael, T. E. (1986). Teaching question/ answer relationships, revisited. *The Reading Teacher, 39,* 516–522.

Reutzel, F. R., & Cooter, R. B., Jr. (2000). *Teaching children to read: Putting the pieces together.* Upper Saddle River, NJ: Prentice-Hall.

Rief, S. F. (1993). How to reach and teach ADD/ADHD children: Practical techniques, strategies, and interventions for helping children with attention problems and hyperactivity. The Center for Applied Research in Education.

Rosenblatt, L. M. (1978). *The reader, the text, the poem: The transactional theory of the literary work.* Carbondale, IL: Southern Illinois University Press.

Roser, N. L., & Martinez, M. G. (Eds.). (1995). *Book talk and beyond: Children and teachers respond to literature.* Newark, DE: International Reading Association.

Schmeck, R. (Ed.). (1988). *Learning strategies and learning styles.* New York: Plenum.

Snow, C. (1977). The development of conversation before mothers and babies. *Journal of Child Language, 4,* 1–22.

Sternberg, R. (1992). In K. Ryan & J. Cooper (Eds.), *Kaleidoscope* (pp. 109–116). Boston: Houghton Mifflin.

Tharp, R. G., & Gallimore, R. (1989a). *Rousing minds to life: Teaching, learning, and schooling in social context.* New York: Cambridge University Press.

Tharp, R. G., & Gallimore, R. (1989b). Rousing schools to life. *American Educator, 13* (92), 20–25, 46–52.

Vygotsky, L. (1962). *Thought and language.* Cambridge, MA: MIT Press.

Weaver, C. (1994). *Reading process and practice* (2d ed.). Portsmouth, NH: Heinemann.

Wertsch, J. (1979). From social interaction to higher psychological processes: A clarification and application of Vygotsky's theory. *Human Development, 22,* 1–22.

Witkin, H. A., Moore, C. A., Goodenough, D. R., & Cox, P. W. (1977). Field-dependent and field-independent cognitive styles and their educational implication. *Review of Educational Research, 47* (1), 1–64.

Wood, D. (1993). *How children think and learn: The social contexts of cognitive development.* Cambridge, MA: Blackwell.

Wood, K. (1987). Fostering cooperative learning in middle and secondary level classrooms. *Journal of Reading, 31,* 10–18.

Woolfolk, A. (1998). *Educational psychology* (4th ed.). Englewood Cliffs, NJ: Prentice-Hall.

Zakaluk, B. L., Samuels, S. J., & Taylor, B. M. (1986). A simple technique for estimating prior knowledge: Word association. *Journal of Reading, 30,* 56–60.

Zemelman, D., Daniels, & Hyde, A. (1993). *Best practice: New standards for teaching and learning in America's schools.* Portsmouth, NH: Heinemann.

ABOUT THE AUTHORS

Virginia R. Beidelman is an associate professor in the College of Education and Psychology, Department of Special Services at The University of Texas at Tyler. She received her Ph.D. in Reading from Texas Woman's University (TWU) with major areas of study in supervision and special education including language/learning disabilities and gifted and talented education. As a doctoral student at TWU, she taught College and Adult Reading and Study Skills and Content Area Reading. In addition to extensive classroom teaching experience in K–adult in the Dallas metroplex, she has served as Director of Language Arts K–12 for the Richardson Independent School District. As a certified Reading Recovery Teacher Leader, she has trained teachers in major districts in East Texas in early intervention for children at-risk. Her current areas of interest are the promotion of outreach literacy programs through the university and interdisciplinary research related to family literacy.

Dr. Janice Nath teaches at the University of Houston in the Curriculum and Instruction Department. She is the Coordinator for Elementary Education, Director of PUMA TRACS for post baccalaureate certification students, Assistant Director of the Internship Program, and heads one of the university's Professional Development School (PDS) sites. Teacher education is her main area of interest and research along with technology in teacher education, action research, and others. She has been actively involved in field-based teacher education for many years and is currently the chair of the AERA (American Education Research Association) Professional Development School Research Special Interest Group (PDSR SIG).

Dr. Cynthia Gift Henry is a professor in the Department of Curriculum and Instruction at the University of Houston and serves as the Coordinator for the Teacher Internship Program. She has been actively involved in field-based teacher education. Dr. Henry has been an elementary classroom teacher and has worked extensively with gifted and talented students and ESL students. She is the coeditor and author of a textbook on the Professional Development ExCET. Her research interests include teacher education, gifted and talented education, and parent involvement.

5

✳

Motivating Students

THE UNIVERSITY OF TEXAS—

PAN AMERICAN

This chapter will deal with Competency 5 of the Examination for the Certification of Educators in Texas (ExCET). Competency 5 is the last of five competencies that fall under Domain I, Understanding Learners.

Competency 5: The teacher understands how motivation affects group and individual behavior and learning and can apply this understanding to promote student learning.

The teacher understands the importance of motivation to learning, knows how to help students become self-motivated, and is able to recognize factors and situations that are likely to promote or diminish motivation. The teacher is aware of the characteristics and effects of intrinsic or extrinsic motivation and knows how to use a variety of techniques (e.g., relating lessons to students' personal interests, allowing students to have choices in their learning, giving students control over their learning experiences, leading individuals or groups of students to ask questions and pursue problems that are meaningful to them) to engage students in learning activities and to help them develop the motivation to achieve.

TERMS TO KNOW

Active learning	Metacognitive, metacognition
Age appropriate	Modeling
Agent (agency)	Motivation (intrinsic, extrinsic)
At-risk	Negative reinforcer
Autonomy, autonomous	Positive reinforcer
Cognitive motivation theory	Reinforcement theory
Conceptual understanding	Resilient, resiliency
Extracurricular activities	Rote learning
Facilitate, facilitator, facilitation	Self-motivated, self-motivation
High interest	Self-efficacy
Higher-order thinking	Social-cognitive theory
Learner-centered	Student empowerment
Lifelong learning	Teacher-centered
Locus of control (internal, external)	Vicarious learning

One of the most challenging things for new teachers to master is the art of motivating students to learn. Let's face it. Not every child (or adult for that matter) is always **self-motivated** for academic learning. Having a classroom filled with eager young minds is a rarity indeed! It is not enough to merely hope our own enthusiasm for learning will rub off on our students; nor is it acceptable to ignore, or be complacent about, having unmotivated students in our classes. Moreover, given that our role as teachers has shifted from a traditionally **teacher-centered** model of teaching to a **learner-centered** one, it is now more imperative than ever that we become **facilitators** of learning rather than "dispensers" of knowledge. As facilitators, we must get to know who our students are. We need to inquire about their past experiences, their current interests, and their hopes and dreams for the future.

Technological advances have changed the way children and adolescents prefer to obtain information. Computer games, "surfing the web," and MTV and other television programming are often preferred over reading books and other print media largely because electronic media can provide large quantities of information quickly and relatively effortlessly. These media are attractive and entertaining to young people and thus valuable resources; however, they are flawed in the educational sense in that they do not require **higher-order thinking** of their viewers. Watching television, for example, is a passive act. Images and messages project onto the monitor, requiring the audience to do nothing more than watch and listen. Computers are, comparatively, more interactive but often do not require users to engage in complex thinking. Both forms of media deliver information expediently and efficiently—so much so that the challenge for teachers is to motivate students to spend sustained periods of time learning in ways that are interactive, meaningful, challenging, relevant, fun—*and* that require them to read, write, compute, evaluate, make judgements, infer, synthesize, and so on. In light of this, the questions most teachers, both new and seasoned, continue to grapple with are: *How do I get my students motivated to learn in my class? And how do I keep them motivated?*

In attempting to answer these questions, we must initially address the importance of **motivation** to academic learning by reviewing how motivation has been theorized in the field of education. Secondly, we must recognize factors and situations that are likely to promote or diminish motivation in our efforts to help students become self-motivated. Third, we must understand the characteristics and effects of **intrinsic** and **extrinsic** motivation and know how to use a variety of techniques to engage students in learning activities to help them develop the motivation to achieve. Finally, we must be able to motivate hard-to-reach students by creating motivational learning environments. These are the many things we cover in the remainder of this chapter so that we may be well-prepared to tackle the questions related to Competency 5 on the Professional Development ExCET examination.

IMPORTANCE OF MOTIVATION TO ACADEMIC LEARNING: THEORETICAL BACKGROUND

Many teachers believe that while some students are naturally motivated to learn in school, others simply are not. Of course, understanding motivation is not as easy as that. In fact, motivation is such a complex concept, it is quite difficult to pin down. We can say with certainty, however, that different teachers have different notions of what motivation is and how to apply it to academic learning. Some conceive of it as the act of gaining students' interest so that they are inspired to perform in desired ways. Others attribute motivation to the act of choosing materials that are of high interest to particular age groups so they appeal to the students and compel them to complete their work enthusiastically. Still others think of motivation as the act of offering rewards so that students are likely to work harder to succeed academically. Most teachers agree, however, that motivation is necessary for active learning and that it is the teacher's responsibility to promote motivational techniques and strategies that will enable students to learn in the classroom.

> Motivation is relevant to learning because learning is an active process requiring conscious and deliberate activity. Even the most able students will not learn if they do not pay attention and exert some effort. If students are to derive the maximum benefits from school, educators must provide a learning context in which students are motivated to engage actively and productively in learning activities. (Stipek, 1998, p. xi)

In Motivation to Learn: From Theory to Practice (1998), Deborah Stipek reviews psychological theories that have been used to explain behavior in achievement contexts. Over the past three decades, she explains, there has been a shift from a focus on observable behavior (behaviorist theory) to a focus on psychological variables (cognitive theories) such as beliefs, values, and goals that can be inferred from behavior, but cannot be observed directly. **Reinforcement theory**, based on Skinner's work, was first developed to explain all human behavior, rather than only achievement-related motivation, and dominated educational psychology literature for many years. It conceptualized motivation entirely in terms of observable behavior:

> [I]ndividuals exhibit a particular behavior in achievement or other settings because they have been reinforced (rewarded) for that behavior in the past. Accordingly, students who are rewarded (e.g., with good grades) for working hard on school tasks and persisting when they face difficulty will continue to work hard and persist in the future. . . . Motivation is not considered a quality of a person, but a set of behaviors and their contingencies (i.e., whether they are rewarded or punished). (Stipek, 1998, p. 11)

Reinforcement theory is used in academic settings substantially today. We recognize it when we give students *praise* **(positive reinforcer)** for behaving appropriately in class by smiling and verbalizing our approval (e.g., "I liked the way you raised your hand, Suzy."). In contrast, the broken record technique (teacher continuously repeats a request, but stops immediately when the student complies) is an example of a **negative reinforcer**. As soon as the desired action happens (student complies), the negative annoyance (teacher's repetitive voice) is taken away or negated. Compliance will come more quickly next time, as the student wants to avoid the teacher's repeating voice focus on his or her behavior again. While reinforcers (both positive and negative) involve strengthening or making an action quicker, **punishment** should stop or decrease a behavior by the addition of something that is disliked (or subtraction of something that is liked). In other words, a behavior occurs, followed by a punishment, followed by a decrease of the behavior. One might see the difference in the "Grandma Rule." As soon as you eat your peas, you may have dessert (reinforcer), *but* if you whine about it, you have to go to your room without television, which you hate (punishment). The next time there will probably be less whining.

Positive Reinforcers (behavior encouraged by reward)	Negative Reinforcers (behavior encouraged by avoidance)	Punishment (behavior suppressed by + a dislike or − a desire)
■ Praise	■ Broken record technique	■ Public humiliation
■ Public recognition	■ Finish work before being able to go to recess	■ Corporal punishment
■ Giving tangibles (stickers, etc.)	■ Wait quietly in line before starting to lunch	■ Demerits, running laps
■ Positive body language		■ Assigning extra work
■ Extra privileges		■ Removal of privileges

In the 1960s, **cognitive motivation theorists** were critical of behaviorist theories because they seemed too limiting and mechanistic, so they began to explore unobservable psychological variables.

> They claim[ed], however, that cognitions (beliefs), such as expectations, "mediate" the effect of rewards. Thus, for example, they claim[ed] that students work hard because their past experiences lead them to expect hard work to be rewarded in the future, not because they have been rewarded for working hard in the past. (McCombs & Pope, 1994 p. 11)

Cognitive motivation theorists viewed motivation as "based on an individual's learned beliefs about his or her self-worth, abilities, or competencies (e.g., academic self-concepts); goals and expectations for success or failure; and the positive or negative feelings (e.g., curiosity, anxiety) that result from self-evaluative processes" (McCombs & Pope, 1994, p. 12). Cognitive theorists helped us understand that learned self-beliefs, goals, expectations, and feelings are factors that influence motivation and performance.

In the 1970s, **social-cognitive theory** entered educational literature regarding motivation. Largely through the works of Bandura (1977, 1986, cited in Stipek, 1998), teachers learned that children and adolescents do not need to personally experience reinforcement and punishment to have behaviors manifested. In a classic study by Bandura and Walters (1963, cited in Stipek, 1998), these researchers found that individuals sometimes exhibit behaviors because they observe other individuals being reinforced for these behaviors. Thus, they learn *vicariously* through the experiences of others (**vicarious learning**), or by seeing others rewarded or punished for certain behaviors. Teachers frequently use this principle of reinforcement in comments such as the following: "I like the way Yi-Ling followed my directions exactly" or "Row 2 may now line up for lunch first because they have finished their work and are quietly waiting." Students usually react with the teacher's desired behavior when they hear these types of comments. Other aspects of social-cognitive theory include the following:

- *Personal evaluation serves as a means of positive reinforcement* (e.g., if Miguel scores lower than he expected on his mathematics test, this may give him the incentive to study harder next time).

- *The feeling of satisfaction for achieving a goal serves as a reward, which in turn increases future effort* (e.g., Jason does better than expected on his mathematics test, and this gives him the incentive to keep up his strong study habits).

- *Individuals are active agents in their behaviors*; hence, individuals are able to deal with environments as a means of controlling behaviors (e.g., DeMarcos realizes that by studying an hour every day after school, he is better prepared for pop quizzes or chapter exams; or, Kathy rewards herself with an hour of TV viewing after her homework is completed).

Intrinsic motivation theorists have helped us understand that individuals have a natural tendency to be motivated from "within themselves" when they focus on personal learning goals. Research indicates that individuals are naturally motivated to "self-start" their learning and continuously maintain their work without outside help or pushing when they do not fear failure, when they perceive what they are learning as being personally meaningful and relevant, and when they are in supportive and respectful relationships with teachers. Moreover, students are more motivated to learn when teachers involve them in decision making, for example, by giving them some control over their own learning processes (McCombs & Pope, 1994).

Intrinsic motivation theory is based on the assumption that people are "naturally motivated to develop their intellectual and other competencies and that they take pleasure in their accomplishments" (Stipek, 1998, p. 12). Striving to achieve something is the "intrinsic pleasure one experiences from developing an understanding and mastery of it" (p. 12).

Stipek (1998) discusses three perspectives on intrinsic motivation that are all based on the premise that "humans have a natural inclination that render some tasks intrinsically motivating" (p. 117). She explains that humans are innately disposed, or born with the drive, to do the following:

1. *Seek opportunities to develop competencies* (e.g., an infant who has learned to grasp objects with his hands attempts to grasp almost any object within sight, a child reads a story repeatedly until she learns to read every word, an adolescent plays a song over and over until he memorizes every word and note)

2. *Seek novelty—events and activities that are somewhat discrepant from their expectations* (which may explain why so many children like cartoons, science fiction, and video games—these types of activities "provide some level of surprise, incongruity, complexity, or discrepancy from their expectations or beliefs")

3. *Be autonomous and engage in activities of their own volition (or choice)* (i.e., "individuals are motivated intrinsically to develop their competencies, and . . . feelings of competence enhance intrinsic interest in activities;" humans are also "naturally disposed to wanting to believe that they are engaging in activities by their own volition—because they want to rather than because they have to") (p. 123)

Stipek (1998) lists the following as characteristics and advantages that students have when they are intrinsically motivated to learn, or when they are provided conditions that foster intrinsic motivation:

- Learning activities outside of school
- Preference for challenge
- Conceptual understanding
- Creativity
- Pleasure and involvement (pp. 14–15)

Most recently, academic motivation has been described as a **metacognitive** approach to the extent that it focuses on our abilities to "think about our own thinking" and "on how we can engage higher levels of self-awareness, or consciousness, in order to control our thinking" (McCombs & Pope, 1994).

The focus in this research is on an understanding of the self as **agent**. . . . When individuals can be taught to understand and control their thinking, they can step outside the influence of negative beliefs about their abilities or fear of failure. As a result they can access higher level processes such as insight, creativity, wisdom, and common sense. They can operate outside the cognitive system and see beyond a conditioned belief system or personal frame of reference.

In a nutshell, what is emerging as a new perspective related to motivation is that students are capable of understanding the relationships between their beliefs, their feelings, and their motivation. At higher levels of understanding or consciousness, students can see that they have personal control (or **agency**) over thought content and thinking processes, they can understand the role of thought, and they can know that they have the ability to be self-motivated. . . . Because motivation is inherent, it needs to be elicited, rather than established. (McCombs & Pope, 1994, pp. 13–15)

Educational psychologists Barbara McCombs and James Pope (1994) contend that students are able to draw on their inherent motivation to learn if they understand the ways their thinking influences their moods and behavior. This means understanding the concept of *self as agent* and recognizing that if they perceive that certain background or ability factors can interfere with their success, then they can "redirect their thoughts, gain a different perspective, and work to overcome these barriers with effort and training in skill enhancing strategies that can offset these negative influences" (p. 15). For example, a student who has negative beliefs about himself or herself in a given subject, may override these beliefs by understanding that he or she "can control the thoughts (and emotions) that feed those beliefs" (p. 15).

IDENTIFYING FACTORS AND SITUATIONS
LIKELY TO PROMOTE
OR DIMINISH MOTIVATION

Jack Frymier, a leading researcher on the topic of academic motivation and risk, directed a major research study that culminated in a national report entitled *Growing Up Is Risky Business, and Schools Are Not to Blame* (1992). In this report, he clearly states that schools are not to blame for most of the problems young people in America face today—in fact, our *culture* is, and our *society* is responsible. Frymier's work is significant because it sheds light on students who are **at-risk** of failing school. His powerful message is clear and positive. Risk is prevalent everywhere; no one goes through life "risk-free." Not all children who are at-risk at school will fail at life, however. In fact, "many youngsters will make it, and make it big, but every youngster needs assistance, instruction, care, and love" (p. 3). All children and adolescents are "at risk" to fail academically, just as they are "at promise" to succeed.

Frymier's research included 21,706 students. The prevalent pattern emerging in the data was that if a student is at-risk in one area, that student is very likely to be at-risk in many other areas; thus, efforts to help the student may be confounded because other problems are involved. In addition, the research identified five factors contributing to risk. *These are factors and situations likely to diminish motivation to academic learning*, and they are listed in the following. Review them closely.

1. *Personal pain.* The personal pain factor consisted of ten items that correlated highly with each other:

   ■ Student had been suspended from school
   ■ Student had attempted suicide
   ■ Student had been involved in a pregnancy
   ■ Student sold drugs
   ■ Student used drugs
   ■ Other family members used drugs
   ■ Student used alcohol
   ■ Parents drank excessively or one was an alcoholic
   ■ Student had been arrested
   ■ Student had been physically or sexually abused

2. *Academic failure.* The academic failure factor consisted of eight items that correlated highly with each other:

   ■ Student got low grades at school
   ■ Student failed courses in school
   ■ Student was overage in grade
   ■ Student had been retained in grade
   ■ Student had excessive absences
   ■ Student had low sense of self-esteem
   ■ Student had been referred to special education
   ■ Student had low scores on standardized test in reading

3. *Family tragedy.* The family tragedy factor consisted of six items that correlated highly with each other:
   ■ A parent was sick last year
   ■ A parent died last year
   ■ A parent lost his or her job last year
   ■ A friend died last year
   ■ The student was seriously ill or in an accident last year
   ■ A sibling died last year

4. *Family socioeconomic situation.* The family socioeconomic situation factor consisted of six items that correlated highly with each other:

- Student's father was unemployed or held an unskilled laborer's job
- Student's father had not graduated from high school
- Student's mother was unemployed or held an unskilled laborer's job
- Student's mother had not graduated from high school
- Parents had a negative attitude toward education
- English was not the language spoken at home

5. *Family instability.* The family instability factor consisted of four items that correlated highly with each other:

- Student did not live with real mother and real father
- Student moved frequently
- Student changed schools frequently
- Student's parents divorced last year

What can teachers in Texas do to promote students to be academically motivated in spite of factors and conditions in their lives that are often barriers to their success? One answer appears obvious. Teachers can start by getting to know their students. *Knowing* what kind of home lives our students have provides clues about their belief systems and about how their belief systems affect their motivation to learn. Teachers must be sensitive to the fact that not all children grow up in the best of circumstances. Preservice teachers must go into the teaching profession understanding that many students may not do their homework because they are distracted by conditions and/or events in their lives that make the things we teach them in school seem irrelevant, stupid, or even a waste of time. For instance, poor students may not have a place that is quiet and conducive for study, or school supplies to use. In the "big scheme of things" and needs in their lives, homework may come far behind other stressors. For example, a field-based student shared a story with her class not long ago:

> A little boy came to tell her he didn't have his work because his "mom" had a baby the night before. I wanted to ask him which "mom" because his real mom is in prison. He lived with an aunt for a time, but she couldn't keep him in a one bedroom apartment. Now, the woman he lived with was a friend of the family he also called "Mom" for the brief time he had been with them during the first two months of school when I had met him in my assigned classroom.

By contrast, students of higher socioeconomic status may have parents who overstimulate them with so many after-school activities that they do not have time to complete their homework.

In short, students need *understanding* and *caring* teachers who are willing to be there for them—to listen and to offer good advice, not to ignore them or distance themselves from them. Frymier (1992) adds that teachers need to provide positive and unconditional regard, or acceptance of one person by another without conditions. That is not to say, however, that teachers will not make judgments about behaviors or that they will accept behaviors that are harmful to themselves or others.

> In teaching, acceptance means acknowledgement and recognition of the worth of a student, just because the student exists. Acceptance does not imply approval of what the student does or agreement with that person's beliefs or values. It means a positive and helping relationship is rooted in the belief in the inherent worth and value of the student as a person. (p. 75)

In other words, students should not be valued more because they are "good students" who never give their teachers any problems, or always follow the teacher's instructions, or constantly abide by their academic expectations, or have influential or well-to-do parents in the community. They should be valued because they are students in one's classroom—period. As Frymier states, "They need someone who cares about them, who accepts them, who honors their uniqueness and their individuality, just because they exist" (p. 76).

It is critical for teachers to understand that for many students with at-risk factors and life conditions, having an understanding and caring teacher is often the only reason they remain in school and is often the only constant source of love, support, and hope for the future. Many teachers notice that negative behaviors escalate near times that students will be at home for longer periods—holidays or summer vacations. This is often because the student is acting out against leaving a stable, loving environment provided by a caring teacher for one that may be scary in some way for that student.

Another way teachers can promote motivation is to *cultivate a sense of responsibility* for who the students are and what they do. Frymier (1992) correctly maintains that students must "learn to take charge of their own lives, to get on top of things. Students at risk must develop and exhibit an **internalized locus of control**." (p. 76). An internalized locus of control is a psychological term meaning that one has a sense of self-worth and feels responsible for one's own actions. People with internalized loci of control feel that they are individuals who are important, and they are able to respond to situations in their lives so they can make a difference. The opposite is true of an **external locus of control**. People with external loci of control do not believe they are in control of their lives at all. In fact, they feel that other people in their lives are in control of their actions and fate, and so they adopt a fatalistic attitude—"whatever will be will be, and there's nothing I'm responsible for in my life because I'm not in control." Either luck or other people are responsible and, thus, can be blamed. This may sound familiar, since many of us know people who have these beliefs about themselves and their roles as human beings in this world. Frymier (1992) suggests six things that teachers need to instill in their students so the students will develop a sense of responsibility and an internalized locus of control:

1. Understanding and acceptance of one's own abilities and strengths

2. Acceptance of one's uniqueness

3. Belief in the importance of doing more than is expected

4. Belief in the importance and fun of behaving responsibly

5. Understanding of the power and possibilities inherent in exercising choice

6. Ability to make intelligent decisions

How can teachers foster these positive attitudes and beliefs to promote **self-motivation** in their students? They can begin by making their classes as *learner-centered* as possible. As the term suggests, a learner-centered classroom reflects the interests, viewpoints, goals, and achievements of the learners. Students have a voice in their educational process when teachers adopt a learner-centered teaching philosophy because they are involved in the decision making. A learner-centered classroom does not require teachers to abandon their curricula; it only allows students to have more choices in the way they want to interact with the content that teachers provide for them. Figure 5.1 lists the Learner-Centered Proficiencies adopted by the Texas State Board of Education in 1995. Review these thoroughly before taking the ExCET examination, and consider these proficiencies as you take it.

One additional thing teachers can do to motivate their students to learn is to *nurture their students' academic achievement and skills* (Frymier, 1992). Notice that nurturing students' academic achievement and skills comes *after* teachers have established an understanding and caring relationship with their students, *and* have helped their students assume responsibility for their own learning and lives. Without these conditions in place, it is often difficult for students to concentrate on succeeding academically—particularly for those students who have at-risk characteristics.

I. Learner-Centered Knowledge
The teacher possesses and draws on a rich knowledge base of content, pedagogy, and technology to provide relevant and meaningful learning experiences for all students.

II. Learner-Centered Instruction
To create a learner-centered community, the teacher collaboratively identifies needs; and plans, implements, and assesses instruction using technology and other resources.

III. Equity in Excellence for All Learners
The teacher responds appropriately to diverse groups of learners.

IV. Learner-Centered Communication
While acting as an advocate for all students and the school, the teacher demonstrates effective professional and interpersonal communication skills.

V. Learner-Centered Professional Development
The teacher as a reflective practitioner dedicated to all student's success, demonstrates a commitment to learn, to improve the profession, and to maintain professional ethics and personal integrity.

FIGURE 5.1 Proficiencies for teachers in learner-centered schools.

SOURCE: From *Learner-Centered Schools in Texas: A Vision of Texas* Educatiors (pp. 3–7), State Board of Education, 1995, Austin: Texas Education Agency.

What does it mean to nurture students' academic achievement and skills? Put simply, it means providing students with activities that are accessible to them, thereby giving them opportunities to experience success. This is a key component to promoting a sense of **self-efficacy** with one's students. Students with a high degree of self-efficacy tend to exert greater effort to meet their academic challenges because these students believe they are capable; they are able to visualize themselves as being able to do whatever they set their minds to do. In essence, they have a perception of themselves as having control over their learning (an internal locus of control), and they are less likely to give up when they confront unfamiliar or challenging material. In fact, they are more likely to choose learning strategies and approaches that require them to use deep thinking processes or elaborative approaches (Pintrich & Garcia, 1994, cited in Brozo & Simpson, 1999). Moreover, because they are active learners who are metacognitively aware of their learning processes, they are more successful students, and ultimately, better-prepared young adults.

Metacognition is "the knowledge and control we have over thinking and learning activities" (Baker & Brown, 1984, cited in Brozo & Simpson, 1999, p. 39). When students are able to self-monitor their reading or listening, for example, they can detect errors, or contradictions in a text. They are able to identify topics or ideas they do not understand, and use a variety of task-appropriate reading and learning strategies to "fix up" or alleviate their difficulties in understanding. Finally, in all subject areas, active learners use a variety of self-monitoring strategies such as self-questioning, paraphrasing, comparing key ideas, and using their prior knowledge, which only enhances their self-motivation to learn (Brozo & Simpson, p. 39). Some students are able to do this almost automatically, but others need to be taught both the learning strategies and to think about how well each works for that individual, so that those strategies that work can become part of a learning repertoire.

My own research (Estrada, 1997) on academic motivation yielded several factors and conditions that facilitated **resiliency** in three teenage girls who had multiple at-risk characteristics and succeeded academically despite the odds. Although we cannot draw generalizations from three single-case studies, these deeply developed case studies can reveal much that is general. The following themes are useful *indicators of factors and conditions likely to promote self-motivation in children and adolescents:*

Themes Emerging from Three Single-Case Studies of Resilient Mexican American Adolescents: Factors and Conditions that Facilitate Resiliency

1. Live with at least one caring and responsible parent
2. Are goal-oriented
3. Cope with stressful life events in a variety of ways
4. Have positive self-concepts
5. Have good decision-making skills
6. Expect a positive personal future
7. Form close positive friendships

8. Maintain a close relationship with at least one parent
9. Seek opportunities to learn and grow
10. Accept and adapt to situations that are beyond their control
11. Take time to think before making important decisions
12. Believe a close family is important

EFFECTS OF INTRINSIC
AND EXTRINSIC MOTIVATION

Before discussing the effects of intrinsic and extrinsic motivation for learners, we ought to review what these terms mean. *Intrinsic motivation* refers to the motivation to engage in an activity in the absence of any extrinsic reward or purpose (Stipek, 1998, p. 135). *Extrinsic motivation*, however, refers to the motivation to engage in an activity only in the presence of an extrinsic reward or purpose. As stated in a previous section, there are clear advantages to having intrinsic motivation and to fostering intrinsic learning in one's classroom. Teachers who have intrinsically motivated children or adolescents in their classes often notice that they are more apt to be involved in learning activities outside of school, or to be involved in **extracurricular activities**, where they are not rewarded extrinsically with grades, with tangible objects such as pencils, stickers, money, and candy, or with privileges like "free time," extra credit, or test exemption. Intrinsically motivated students often prefer to engage in more challenging tasks than extrinsically motivated students. They learn at the conceptual level and are not satisfied with surface understandings of material or rote memorization. This is why it is so important to incorporate **high-interest** and **age-appropriate** reading materials and activities into one's curriculum. Success breeds success, so students who experience being able to successfully complete tasks will feel motivated to try the next time. Research has shown that the conditions that produce interest and enjoyment, or foster intrinsic motivation, especially facilitate understanding and conceptual learning, but not **rote learning** (Stipek, 1998). That is why teacher educators encourage teachers to design lessons that have "a spark," along with a meaningful rationale for learning the skills of the day.

Another advantage intrinsically motivated students have is their tendency to be more creative than extrinsically motivated learners. Researchers are unsure about why extrinsic motivation does not foster conceptual and creative thinking to the extent that intrinsic motivation does; however, they note it is possible that extrinsic rewards and contingencies may create "an instrumental focus that narrows attention and orients individuals to take the quickest and easiest solutions" (Stipek, 1998, p. 125). In other words, students focus on finishing a task as quickly as possible with little or no concern for the quality of their product or understanding of what their work means. This is seen in elementary classrooms quite often. The teacher offers candy or another extrinsic reward upon completion of her students' work, causing the children to rush to finish as quickly as possible.

The end results are usually sloppy, thoughtless, and careless products. It is also possible that extrinsically motivated students may be used to being evaluated on rote learning and are not used to being tested on **conceptual understanding**. If this is the case, then it is highly likely that students who are motivated with extrinsic rewards memorize course material for the short term and do not really engage in conceptual understanding for **lifelong learning**. We have probably all experienced the feeling that accompanies intrinsic motivation with a hobby or in anticipation of travelling somewhere on vacation. For example, suppose one learns in school that San Antonio is the place where the battle of the Alamo was fought and an old Spanish city, but in planning a weekend trip, one wants to know much more. Such a person may delve into resources to find there is a great Jazz Festival, review history to establish sequence of events, and discover that there are many missions (including one that is "intact" and still offers a mariachi service at the mission church). All of these things the person learns are sought out because that person is now interested. That is the same type of intrinsic interest we hope to spark in our students.

Lastly, intrinsic motivation is associated with *pleasure* and *involvement*. Students are more likely to enjoy learning when they discover learning can be fun, interesting, relevant, and worthwhile. In fact, studies have shown that under certain circumstances, "offering extrinsic rewards for engaging in tasks actually undermines intrinsic motivation" (Stipek, 1998, p. 126). Moreover, external rewards can undermine interest in a learning task, thus contradicting reinforcement theory (that which assumes that a reward contingent on a behavior increases the frequency of that behavior).

CREATING MOTIVATIONAL LEARNING ENVIRONMENTS FOR ALL STUDENTS

Thus far, we have discussed several things that directly relate to creating motivational learning environments that have to do with the *teacher*. This is a key idea, for creating a motivational learning environment begins with the teacher. Initially, it was mentioned that teachers ought to take the role of facilitator in their learner-centered classroom. Two educational buzzwords appear in this statement: *facilitator* and *learner-centered*. Carl Rogers, a noted counselor, psychologist, and therapist, maintains that significant learning depends on certain attitudinal qualities that exist in the personal relationships between facilitators and learners. He believes that the term *facilitator* emphasizes what happens to learners rather than to teachers, and he contends that an effective facilitator has three *attitudinal* qualities that all serve to promote motivation among students (Ryan & Cooper, 1998). They include the following:

1. *Realness or genuineness.* The facilitator must be a real person who is "being himself or herself" and who is free to be enthusiastic, bored, interested, or angry, instead of presenting a front or playing a role.

2. *Valuing the learners.* The facilitator must respect his or her learners—their feelings, opinions, persons as worthy in their own right, accepting both their imperfections and potentialities. He or she must recognize learners as individuals who are motivated to learn in different ways (i.e., what motivates one student does not necessarily motivate another, and it is the teacher's job to find out what motivates each individual student).

3. *Empathetic understanding.* The facilitator must be able to understand his or her learners without judging or evaluating. For instance, if a student says, "This is a stupid assignment. Why do we have to write a research paper anyway?" a nonevaluative statement might be, "You don't like writing much. What do you find difficult with this assignment?" This is an empathetic statement that is helpful in assisting the student with his or her reluctance to engage in a task that is unfamiliar or that he or she has failed to achieve before. (Ryan & Cooper, 1998)

One can see how the teacher is the major motivating force in the classroom. With the concept of teacher as facilitator, the view of the teacher as the sole source of knowledge in the classroom and the students as passive receptors has changed dramatically. The old view is sometimes referred to as the "empty vessel" theory, where the teacher pours all the knowledge into the students, whether or not the student wants it, and whether or not that knowledge is valuable or relevant.

Teachers as facilitators are more like guides or resources for helping students access knowledge and for helping students learn to be self-directed and self-motivated. Students are encouraged to take on more responsibility for their learning as they become more involved in personally relevant learning activities. As facilitators, teachers support their students by encouraging them in their quests to learn, and by getting out of their students' way when the situation deems it necessary.

Nonfacilitating teachers do not allow for this kind of learning in their classroom. A nonfacilitating teacher is more concerned with his or her teaching agenda. Most of us can remember a time when we were quite intrigued about a given subject that we were learning about, but we were not allowed to continue our quest for meaningful knowledge because a teacher said, "We don't have time for that," or "We need to move on to something else now." This is not an attitude that promotes self-motivation. That is why educators should value such a "*teachable moment*"—even though the teacher may give up time on information or skills that he or she feels pressured to teach, what the teacher receives in return is positive student intrinsic motivation.

The current underlying philosophy of the Professional Development ExCET examination promotes a motivational environment where teachers are facilitators as described by Rogers, for his approach intends to create a classroom environment conducive to self-initiated (or self-motivational) learning. As Ryan and Cooper (1998) sum up:

> [Rogers] maintained that the teacher's skills, knowledge of the field, curricular planning, lectures, and selection of books and other learning aids are all peripheral; the crux of the learning situation is the relationship between the facilitator and the learner, which should be characterized by

realness, valuing, and empathy. In the absence of these three attitudinal predispositions, Rogers contended, the learning environment is sterile and cannot produce significant learning. . . . The atmosphere in your class-room will make possible for you and your students a joy, excitement, and closeness absent from many classrooms. (p. 161)

It is important to stress that all teachers must be enthusiastic about the subject matter they teach because bored teachers convey boredom to their students. A teacher who is not excited about teaching a subject he or she has been assigned to teach must try to develop a positive attitude about it anyway. Think of a sales-person who, when trying to make a sale, acts as if the product is not particularly exciting to him or her. Most people would not feel very excited about buying the product if even the salesperson was bored by it. Teachers must "sell" their product(s) too, as students read attitudes quite easily. Effective teachers are enthu-siastic teachers! Enthusiastic teachers make it possible for students to reach their full learning potential.

Another aspect of creating a motivational learning environment that was pre-viously mentioned and described is that of making the classroom as *learner-centered* as possible. If one accepts Rogers's idea regarding attitudinal qualities of teachers as facilitators, then adopting a learner-centered philosophy makes sense. This means that teachers should have learner-centered knowledge that provides rele-vant and meaningful learning experiences for all students. Offering a variety of reading and writing assignments that apply to the "real world," is, of course, fun-damental. In the case of our students, relevant and meaningful knowledge may be fostered in activities that incorporate "real-life" or authentic forms of literature such as the following: comic books or comic strips, newspapers, magazines, print ads, trade books, maps, recipes, graphics, directions, shopping lists, environmental print, business letters, propaganda, medical pamphlets, utility and credit card bills, and so forth.

Explaining a rationale for each lesson or skill can also show students its rele-vance to the real world. For instance, basic math skills could be taught by instruct-ing children to shop for their families on a specific budget using print ads from a local Sunday newspaper. A science lesson in middle school, or junior high, could involve tracking tropical storms and hurricanes using maps provided by local news stations. Students in a high school business class could learn about finance by read-ing interest rate information on monthly mortgage statements, automobile state-ments, or credit card bills. All students can be motivated to learn to write well if they are given relevant reasons to do so, such as publishing in class or school liter-ary magazines, yearbooks, newsletters, bulletin boards, student-made books, poster-boards, websites, and so on. Other authentic activities include taking students on field trips, inviting guest speakers, integrating learning across content areas so that subjects are not taught in isolation, and having scavenger hunts where objects that relate to specific themes are brought into class so students can experience them by sight, sound, touch, smell, and taste (Cunningham & Allington, 1999).

Learner-centered instruction involves **facilitation** of learning, rather than dis-semination of knowledge—a key component to creating a motivational learning environment. The teacher has a vision of his or her goals for the students, and works with the students to establish how to accomplish those goals. Because learner-centered instruction has the learners' interests and needs in mind, students feel **empowered** in their learning processes and are more likely to take a vested interest in their work. Teachers are like coaches who guide students through the material they need to cover, offering assistance to their students as the students discover how to do things for themselves.

There are several simple ways that teachers make their instruction learner-centered. For instance, they can offer their students opportunities for *self-selected reading* time. In many classrooms, this time is called USSR or Uninterrupted Sustained Silent Reading. Other people call it DEAR time (Drop Everything and Read) or SQUIRT time (Sustained Quiet Reading Time). The goal of this learner-centered instructional activity is to allow students daily uninterrupted time to read a trade book or magazine of their choice for pleasure. While the students read, the teacher reads a book as well. By joining students in this activity, the teacher is **modeling** the purposeful and pleasurable aspects of reading, and not just paying lip service to it. When children and adolescents see that their teachers are readers and learners, they are motivated to be readers and learners themselves.

Self-selected writing activities are also motivational. Many elementary and secondary teachers have incorporated a time for journal writing on a daily basis on self-selected topics. Students are encouraged to write about whatever they have on their minds on that day, or to *freewrite*. This means, they do not need to be concerned about punctuation, spelling, or grammar because the journal entries will not be graded. Only their content is emphasized, which frees the students to take risks while improving their writing fluency skills. Self-selected reading and writing activities are not the only motivational forms of instruction, of course. There are too many to mention in the scope of this chapter. However, one may remember the following important *characteristics of learner-centered instruction*:

- *Teachers model and demonstrate active learning in learner-centered classrooms.* When students write, teachers write. When students read, teachers read. When students do math problems, teachers do math problems. When students experiment, so do teachers.

- *Teachers make an effort to bring in "real-world" reading materials, and assign learning tasks designed for "real-world" purposes.* Authentic tasks are seen as relevant by students. Teachers can engage students by providing them with a rationale for when students will be able to use the skill or information in the "real world" rather than "just on a test."

- *Teachers set aside time for students to engage in thinking aloud, writing, and reading with one another on a regular basis.*

- *Teachers tap students' prior knowledge when introducing new topics or lessons.* This is motivating because students can bridge their prior experiences with a given topic to something new or different.

- *Teachers keep their students' ages and interests in mind when they plan lessons.* High-interest and age-appropriate materials motivate children and teens because they typically address common themes and interests of children and teens.

- *Teachers allow students to take part in decision making.* They do this by offering students choices in the way they prefer to respond to subject matter. (Note: For very young children, it may be better to give them only two choices in responding to texts, writing, drama, or art activities. More than two is sometimes hard for children to deal with. For older children, offering choices is quite different. For example, they may be allowed to budget their own time for completing a major project, although the deadline is set by the teacher; given the option of writing three different types of poems in whatever order they want; or allowed to choose who they want to work with for particular thematic unit activities or projects.)

- *Teachers assess students formally and informally using a variety of assessment tools including norm and criterion-referenced standardized tests, inventories, portfolios, checklists, and other forms of authentic assessment.*

In essence, learner-centered instruction is motivational because students feel empowered in their learning process. Teachers guide them through the content the teachers want to cover, giving their students choices in ways that are appropriate. *Reader and writer workshops* are good examples of learner-centered motivational environments where teachers are facilitators of instruction. In fact, many aspects and strategies found in these workshop environments can be incorporated into most content area classrooms. (For more information on Reader/Writer workshops, see Atwell, 1987; Cunningham & Allington, 1999.)

Equity in excellence for all learners, another proficiency, means that teachers respond appropriately to all their students, particularly in our increasingly diverse communities of learners. Teachers must be sensitive and respectful to all learners, modeling "appreciation for all students' cultural heritages, unique endowments, learning styles, interests, and needs. [Teachers must] also design learning experiences that show consideration for these students' characteristics" (State Board of Education, 1995, p. 5).

Two important things come to mind when discussing equity in excellence for all learners. First, by respecting all learners' cultural heritages, unique endowments, learning styles, interests, and needs, it is clear that teachers must be, or become, knowledgeable about their students as individuals with particular and diverse histories (i.e., how their family lives, how their particular ethnic backgrounds affect their interpretations of everything they learn, what their talents and interests are, how they learn best, and in what areas they need the most assistance). This is a tall order indeed! However, it is not impossible to manage this if one takes the time to get to know one's students. "Equity in excellence for all learners" suggests that all learners must be given ample opportunities to be successful in school. It assumes that teachers have high expectations of all learners despite ethnic or gender differences, learning styles, and ability levels; it paints a powerful portrait of teachers as positive, respectful, effective, democratic, and caring individuals. Treating each child exactly the same may not always equal equity.

Learner-centered communication is another feature of learner-centered classrooms. It means that teachers are expected to communicate professionally and appropriately with their students, colleagues, families, and community members.

It also means teachers must model their ability to communicate in verbal, non-verbal, and technological ways so that students may learn how to express their ideas to others in appropriate ways. Learner-centered communication also requires that teachers demonstrate how to think at deeper levels, thus promoting higher-level thinking skills. Texas teachers must then be able to communicate in many ways, for many purposes, and always appropriate to the given situation. Our state proficiencies also indicate that teachers must be advocates for each learner, be sensitive to the concerns that affect learners, and take advantage of community strengths and resources for our students' welfare.

Finally, learner-centered classrooms have learner-centered teachers who are reflective and dedicated to all students' success, demonstrate a commitment to learn, improve the profession, and maintain professional ethics and personal integrity. This commitment to *professional development* is a motivating aspect for students for obvious reasons. Most students appreciate having teachers who are committed to their profession. They appreciate having teachers who "practice what they preach," or demonstrate their love of teaching by engaging in continuous professional development activities.

Experience teaches us that not all teachers are who they perceive themselves to be. For instance, there are teachers out there who never pick up a book, magazine, or newspaper, but somehow view themselves as highly literate individuals. This is also the case with others who view themselves as specialists in their field or content areas, but who have not kept up with current theories, trends, and research in their content areas or areas of expertise. Students are very intuitive about these factors and find it motivating when they see that their teachers are learners who consistently model ways to learn and keep up with current theory and practice in their professional fields of study. Most importantly, teachers should foster understanding of the importance of lifelong learning to their students.

SUMMARY

There are many factors and situations that create barriers to academic success for students. Therefore, it is imperative that teachers in Texas, and everywhere, make strong efforts to get to know students. Teachers must take the time to discover who their students are, where they come from, what their home lives are like, and how belief systems affect their motivation to learn. At the same time, students need to see their teachers as understanding and caring adults in their lives—adults who work hard to promote motivation in their students by cultivating a sense of responsibility, helping students to develop an internal locus of control, and nurturing students' academic achievement and skills.

Thus, it is important that teachers create learner-centered classroom environments because they provide positive, motivational sites for students of all ages. Teaching from a learner-centered perspective requires that one teaches his or her content curriculum in a manner that considers the learners' interests, viewpoints, goals, and achievement. A learner-centered classroom, then, revolves around *the learners* in that classroom. By creating motivational learning environments, teachers are better able to facilitate intrinsic motivation in their students, so that students engage in activities for the sake of their own learning as opposed to learning for extrinsic rewards or purposes.

SUGGESTED ACTIVITIES

Process—Field-Based Journal Writing Assignments

1. Observe several teachers' classrooms in your content area. Pay attention to the type of motivation theory that underlies their practice. In a journal entry, identify the theory or theories and reflect on the effectiveness of the strategies. Then, think about how you would handle any or all of these classroom scenarios if you were the teacher.

2. Observe a particular classroom in your content area and concentrate on the interactions between the teacher and the students. Who are the more active learners in the class? Describe them, then reflect on the recognizable factors and conditions that promote their motivation to learn. Next, identify the passive students in the class. Describe them and reflect on the recognizable factors and conditions that diminish their motivation to learn. Finally, reflect on learner-centered strategies that would enable you to motivate these students to learn.

3. List the five learner-centered proficiencies and describe ways you have seen them manifested in some of the classrooms you have visited. If they have been absent in the classrooms you have visited, describe how the teacher-centered approaches you have seen could be redesigned for more effective, learner-centered instruction.

Application—Field-Based Instructional Assignments

1. Design a lesson that is motivating to students of a particular age group and of a particular region in Texas. Remember to include "real-world" purposes or objectives for teaching the lesson, pre-reading/thinking/writing activities that activate prior knowledge of your students, age-appropriate and high-interest student activities, and questions that promote higher-order thinking skills.

2. Obtain permission to teach this lesson, teach it, and reflect on your effectiveness. What would you do differently if given another opportunity to teach it? Why? What did you learn about your students and about motivating them to learn?

Reflection—Field-Based Research Assignments

1. Interview a mentor teacher that you found particularly motivating during your field experience or student teaching. Ask questions regarding ways he or she elicits students' intrinsic motivation, creates a motivational learning environment, and develops teacher qualities that are conducive for effective learner-centered teaching. Reflect on what you learned in this interview in a write-up of your findings.

2. Generate a working list of strategies and techniques in the classrooms

you have observed throughout your fieldwork and student teaching. Describe each of them in a field journal for your own reference.

Underneath each description, write a few sentences where you reflect on the effectiveness of each strategy and its motivational value.

PRACTICE DECISION SET

A week before school starts, the teachers at Greenbriar Junior High are informed by their principal, Mrs. Diaz, that all content areas will be required to adopt a learner-centered approach to teaching. After five days of inservice, the teachers seem to have a better idea of how to teach within this perspective and are generally positive about the whole idea. Mrs. Diaz encourages her faculty to address any questions or concerns directly to her once classes begin.

1. Mr. Robles, a seventh-grade math teacher, is the first faculty member to take up Mrs. Diaz's offer. During his conference hour, an exasperated Mr. Robles comes into her office and says, "A learner-centered approach doesn't work for me because math is a subject that has to be drilled. I put the students in small groups so they could work out a few math problems together, but I definitely disagree on letting them talk through their math problems as we were told. Furthermore, I heard them talking and applying it to things outside of school, and it seems to me they are just wasting time. I don't see why they can't be working silently on their math problems on their own after my lecture. The students are so noisy and they appear to be having too much fun." What did Mr. Robles fail to understand about learner-centered instruction as a means of fostering motivation for his students?

I. Socializing is a great promoter of motivation and will always contribute to high math scores.

II. Students are more likely to want to learn when their lessons are meaningful and relevant to the "real world."

III. As a facilitator of learning, the teacher should model and encourage appreciation for students' cultural heritage, unique endowments, learning styles, interests, and needs.

IV. Allowing students to think aloud about their thinking processes, or giving them opportunities to develop meta-cognitive awareness, promotes the development of an intrinsic locus of control in students. Once students feel they are in control of their own learning, they tend to become self-motivated.

  a. I and II
  b. II and III
  c. II, III, and IV
  d. II and IV

2. Miss Wells, a science teacher, decides to visit Mrs. Diaz for a few minutes during her lunch hour because she is having a few problems of her own. She tells Mrs. Diaz that she gave her sixth-graders a packet of materials that included a research report assignment requiring them to "specialize" in learning everything they could about a particular North American bird. In an attempt to help her

students get started, Miss Wells included a list of references from the library so students could obtain their information from encyclopedias, websites, computer software programs, and other library reference materials. She told them they had two weeks to complete their paper and they should use class time to conduct the research and write. Two weeks later, Miss Well laments, "Despite the fact I gave them so much time in class and allowed them to budget their own time to do the work, they produced very shabby, incomplete products, Mrs. Diaz!" What did Miss Wells not understand about being a motivational teacher in a learner-centered classroom?

I. As the leader in a learner-centered community, the teacher takes on a variety of roles when teaching. For example, the teacher must be a facilitator who helps students link ideas in the content area to familiar ideas, to prior experiences, and to relevant problems.

II. The teacher must give explicit directions and always give students as much time as they request to finish their assignments.

III. The teacher must be a manager who effectively acquires, allocates, and conserves resources. By encouraging self-directed learning and by modeling respectful behavior, the teacher effectively manages the learning environment so that optimal learning occurs.

IV. The teacher must select materials, technology, activities, and space that are developmentally appropriate and designed to engage interest in learning.

a. I and II
b. II and III
c. I, III, and IV
d. I, II, III, and IV

3. John is a student in Miss Wells's class who produced one of the "shabby" research papers on the North American bald eagle. In fact, he did not turn in much of a paper; at best, he turned in notes copied from an encyclopedia entry. When John's parents came in for a parent-teacher conference, they asked Miss Wells to help explain John's sudden loss of interest in her class. Miss Wells said she had noticed John was not spending much time on-task in her class for those two weeks, but she never did anything about it because she assumed that John probably did not care enough about the assignment and would simply have to take responsibility for his actions. After all, a learner-centered philosophy of teaching does stress that students develop a sense of responsibility for self-directed learning. What is the best way of explaining what is wrong with Miss Wells's attitude in this situation?

I. She is not taking any responsibility for creating a motivational teaching environment for her students, particularly John.

II. Nothing. John's parents simply do not understand her role as a facilitator in a learner-centered community.

III. She is not communicating effectively as an advocate for her student, nor is she exhibiting a caring, understanding, or empathetic attitude toward him.

IV. She is not communicating effectively to the parents because she is not expressing her views clearly.

a. I and IV
b. II
c. III and IV
d. I and III

Answer 1: This teacher has not yet understood the underlying philosophy of learner-centered teaching and how learner-centered teaching is motivational if implemented correctly. By putting his students in small groups to work together to solve math problems, he has given them the opportunity to talk through problems with their peers, hence providing them time for "meta-talk," or talking about their thoughts aloud. Often when students are trying to make sense of something new, they make links to their prior knowledge as a means of bridging old knowledge with new conceptual knowledge. Making connections to the "real world," of course, is motivating because the subject becomes less abstract or unfamiliar, and more relevant and real. The best answer is *d*.

Answer 2: Answer *c* is the best answer, for it shows that the teacher has many roles in the instructional process that motivate students to learn (instructor, facilitator, coach, leader, manager). This teacher has the wrong idea of learner-centered teaching and does not understand what a facilitator is at all.

Answer 3: This teacher has a negative attitude about students who do not produce in her classroom. She immediately blames the student for his "laziness" and defends herself with a false understanding of a learner-centered philosophy. She does not understand the importance of learner-centered communication, which requires that teachers act *as advocates* for all their students and demonstrate effective professional and interpersonal communication skills. Moreover, she does nothing to create a motivational learning environment that may help students like John to get interested in learning. The answer is *d*.

WEB LINKS

Remember that website locations may change. If any of these sites have moved or cannot be located, use the Terms to Know in this chapter to search for further information.

http://www.aol.com/webcenters/research/education.adp
This web link is a great resource for educators. It includes everything from

lesson-planning tips to book reviews. For resources on student motivation, click on Education, then Education World, Quick Browse, and finally Student Motivation.

http://www.ole.net/ole/LINKARCHIVE
This web link provides weekly websites on education and motivational tools or teachers. A great resource!

REFERENCES AND SUGGESTED READINGS

Atwell, N. (1987). *In the middle: Writing, reading, and learning with adolescents.* Portsmouth, NH: Boynton/Cook.

Brozo, W. G., & Simpson, M. L. (1999). *Readers, teachers, learners: Expanding literacy*

across the content areas (3d ed.). Upper Saddle River, NJ: Prentice-Hall.

Cunningham, P. M., & Allington, R.L. (1999). *Classrooms that work: They can all read and write* (2d ed.). New York: Addison-Wesley.

Estrada, V. L. (1997). *Expecting the best: Case studies of resilient Mexican American girls in a South Texas high school.* Unpublished doctoral dissertation, The Ohio State University, Columbus.

Frymier, J. (1992). *Growing up is risky business, and schools are not to blame.* Bloomington, IN: Phi Delta Kappa.

McCombs, B. L., & Pope, J. E. (1994). *Motivating hard to reach students.* Washington, DC: American Psychological Association.

Ryan, K., & Cooper, J. M. (1998). *Those who can, teach* (8th ed.). Boston: Houghton Mifflin.

State Board of Education. (1995). *Learner-centered schools for Texas: A vision of Texas educators.* Austin, TX: Texas Education Agency.

Stipek, D. (1998). *Motivation to learn: From theory to practice.* Needham Heights, MA: Allyn & Bacon.

ABOUT THE AUTHOR

Veronica Lopez Estrada is an assistant professor at The University of Texas—Pan American (UTPA) at Edinburg, Texas, where she specializes in Language, Literacy and Culture. She received her doctorate from the Ohio State University in 1997. Her research has focused on resiliency theory, beginning teacher induction, and diversity issues in education. Currently, she serves as the Program Coordinator of Secondary Reading at the College of Education at UTPA. Dr. Estrada teaches undergraduate and graduate courses in reading, and research methods courses for doctoral students. Her current research is a study that explores biliteracy development of preservice teachers in a two-way bilingual education teacher preparation program. She resides in Edinburg, Texas, with her husband, Edward, and her daughter, Megan.

Enhancing Student Achievement

6

✴

Planning and Designing Instruction

JOANN CANALES
TEXAS A&M UNIVERSITY—CORPUS CHRISTI

This chapter will address Competency 6 of the Examination for the Certification of Educators in Texas (ExCET). Competency 6 is the first of six competencies that fall under Domain II, Enhancing Student Achievement.

Competency 6: The teacher uses planning processes to design outcome-oriented learning experiences that foster understanding and encourage self-directed thinking and learning in both individual and collaborative settings.

The teacher understands the relationship between careful planning and student success in the classroom. In designing instruction, the teacher takes account of factors relevant to instructional planning (e.g., learners' backgrounds, desired learner outcomes, content of instruction, integrated curriculum, input from students, available materials and resources, time and space constraints). The teacher chooses lessons and activities that reflect the principles of effective instruction and that help students achieve an in-depth understanding and acquire the will to set and accomplish their own long-term and short-term goals. The teacher makes use of collaborative processes (e.g., working with other teachers) in planning instruction and in designing individual and group activities.

TERMS TO KNOW

...nic learning time (ALT)

Anticipatory set

Bloom's taxonomy

Knowledge
Comprehension
Application
Analysis
Synthesis
Evaluation

Checking for understanding

Closure

Curriculum

Hidden
Interdisciplinary
Integrated
Intradisciplinary
Spiral

Goals

Guided practice

Independent activity

Instructional input

Modifications for special populations

Modeling

Plans

Long-range
Unit
Daily

Objectives

Broad (goals)
Behavioral
Instructional
Learner outcomes
Performance

Objective domains

Cognitive
Affective
Psychomotor
Linguistic
Social

Reflection (cognitive monitoring)

Texas Essential Knowledge and Skills (TEKS)

Thematic

The ExCET is an examination focused on *decision making*. The premise for the examination is that professional educators, irrespective of grade level or subject matter taught, ought to be astute, focused, and competent decision makers. This particular skill is especially critical for the sixth competency that addresses *planning and designing instruction*.

Effective planning is planning that promotes student achievement. Too frequently, lack of experience, lack of time, and lack of resources result in a day-to-day approach to planning focused on *activities rather than objectives*. An activity is a diversion that students engage in to pass the time such as completing a generic English grammar worksheet, tracing/coloring a map, working math problems in isolation, or watching a movie. In contrast, an objective is a purposeful mission that is contextually based. Examples include completing a worksheet or writing a narrative that emphasizes specific grammar skills studied; tracking or marking on a map to indicate the path of a hurricane or the journey followed by a main character in a novel; working math problems to determine specific measurements studied in a thematic unit; or watching a movie to examine the literary license taken when producing a movie based on a novel the students have read. Focusing instruction on activities versus objectives tends to result in a fragmented, unscaffolded presentation of material and requires that students be responsible for determining the relevancy of their own learning as well as be responsible for making sense of their own learning without the explicit support of the classroom teacher. In other words, they are left to "read into it" whatever they can. For example, a teacher may present three math activities, each based on a male-dominated sport. The teacher does not talk about the general use of the concept or skill, so students may "gather or infer" that "this skill/concept" is one that applies only to males.

Another term for the **curriculum** resulting from this ineffective approach to planning is the **hidden curriculum**. It is called the hidden curriculum because it is never explicitly taught, yet students are held accountable for the content. This phrase is also applied to any set of expectations that is not made explicitly clear to students and may include expectations for linguistic and social performance.

Among practitioners, there is a wide range of practices when it comes to planning for instruction. At one end of the continuum are practitioners who invest considerable time and effort in developing elaborate **spiraled** units and daily plans that build on each other and help to scaffold student learning as well as keep the students actively engaged. This type of instruction demands that a teacher touch on past learning as he or she begins new skills or content in a daily lesson. In looking at long-term planning, the mathematics curriculum is often an excellent example of this. Each year in elementary mathematics, a student "comes back" to addition. At first, the student only adds two single-digit numbers but gradually, as he or she advances through the grades, adds columns of single- and double-digit numbers and uses the skill for other mathematical operations such as multiplication and division.

At the opposite end of the continuum are teachers who invest considerably less time and rely on activities, worksheets, or straight text from a book to fill the instructional time. This broad range of practices creates a tension for preservice or beginning teachers who are being taught, or have been taught, to produce thoughtful, elaborate, detailed, lengthy plans.

As a beginning teacher, it is important to keep in mind that the primary goal of effective planning should be to maximize students' **academic learning time (ALT)**. Academic learning time is defined as the amount of time students spend *successfully* engaged in acquiring new knowledge and skills. (Kindsvatter et al., 1996, p. 31). The key word is *successfully* because it is possible for students to spend time practicing poor reading habits, poor writing skills, or poor problem-solving, which does not benefit the student, the teacher, or society in general.

As a beginning teacher in Texas, it is particularly important to address the **Texas Essential Knowledge and Skills (TEKS)**. The TEKS are a core body of learnings identified as essential for all students graduating from an accredited public school system. The TEKS are the basis for the Texas Assessment of Academic Skills (TAAS), the statewide educational accountability measure of a student's academic performance. Students, schools, and school districts are held highly accountable for successful performance on the TAAS. As such, all teachers must ensure that the TEKS are appropriately, effectively, and explicitly addressed on a regular basis.

There are several assumptions that a beginning teacher should also keep in mind relative to planning. These include:

- Successful teachers recognize the importance of the major elements of an effective lesson plan and know the theories that buttress the plan and each of its components.

- Although experienced successful teachers may not always prepare extensively written plans, they always have clear goals/objectives/rationales for their lessons.

- Student and beginning teachers require more detailed, formal written lesson plans than do veteran teachers, who generally are more familiar with the school, students' abilities and prior learning experiences, and the content of the subject.

- Teachers are more apt to teach "to the lesson," and more apt to teach the same lesson again in the same way, when it is written formally. This fourth assumption is particularly critical if there are to be equitable opportunities and access to information for all students during the course of a day or over a span of time, or if the same lesson is to be taught to multiple sections or at particular grade levels or disciplines.

There are also several common sense reasons for generating explicit detailed plans. Developing detailed plans:

- Provides an important sense of security that helps the teacher stay on course.

- Helps the teacher organize material and search for loopholes, loose ends, or incomplete content. The process enables reflective teachers to ask, "What questions will students ask here about this topic (or skill)?"

- Provides a context that is required to help the teacher assess his or her own teaching, the students' learning, and the curriculum.

- Helps other members, especially substitutes and members of a teaching team, understand what the teacher is doing and how he or she is doing it.

- Provides a blueprint. By quickly noting any reflective changes immediately after teaching the lesson, the teacher creates an updated, improved version of the plan for the next time it is taught—whether that be next class period or next year.

- Enables the teacher to become a reflective decision maker.

- Reflects a high degree of professionalism and shows that the teacher has been thoughtful about the process to be undertaken.

In addition to building a teacher's sense of worth and self-confidence regarding his or her profession, for the reasons given here, such planning also serves to contribute to a climate of collegiality and student success. Accomplishing these noteworthy goals entails using a nested approach to planning. This chapter will focus on the use of this nested approach and will highlight the important considerations for developing long-range plans, unit plans, and daily plans.

THE PROCESS OF PLANNING

The nested approach to effective planning takes into consideration the amount of time allocated to meeting with students, the state standards for which students and teachers will be held accountable, and the topics/content/skills that are the medium for meeting the state standards and students' academic, linguistic, and social proficiencies.

In planning, the first step is to develop **long-range plans** identifying goals (or **broad objectives**) and their corresponding topics. **Goals** are written utilizing such verbs as: *will realize, understand, appreciate, and become familiar with/aware of.* Goals are not observable (we cannot look at a student or even inside a student to see what is happening in this regard) and, thus, are not measurable. Goals do voice our overall learning aims. For example:

- Students will appreciate art produced during the Renaissance period. (Topics: Perspective, Religion, Anthropocentrism)
- Students will understand the influence of the environment on our daily lives. (Topics: Plants, Animals, Health)
- Students will become familiar with the concept of fair play. (Topics: Competition, Cooperation, Sportsmanship)

The second step is to organize the topics into **integrated thematic unit plans** using **instructional objectives.** Instructional objectives address both *audience* and *behavior* and answer the following questions:

Who does the task? (Audience)

What is the task to be completed? (Behavior) (Kindsvatter et al., 1996, p. 159)

Instructional **objectives** have traditionally been organized into three **domains—cognitive, affective,** and **psychomotor.** Given the demands on teachers to address the needs of the *whole* child, I have added two additional domains—**linguistic** and **social** (see Table 6.1). Historically, teachers have addressed the cognitive domain using **Bloom's taxonomy of higher-order thinking skills** (see Tables 6.2 and 6.3). Including the linguistic and social domains will ensure that the teacher attends to developing students' communication skills, namely, listening, speaking, reading, and writing, which will result in true integrated learning. Including the social domain will ensure students will acquire collaborative skills that enable them to be successful participants in a democratic society. Such skills as turn taking, seeking help when needed, sharing materials/resources, contributing to each other's learning, and building on others' responses are all interpersonal dynamic skills that must be explicitly taught using content as a medium.

Table 6.1 Linguistic and Social Domains

Examples of Social Objectives

- Accept individual responsibility
- Acknowledge peers' contributions
- Analyze own work reflectively
- Brainstorm possible answers to a question
- Bring necessary materials to the group
- Build on peers' contributions
- Call partner by name
- Check partner's understanding of directions for the assigned task
- Coach each other through the steps on a task
- Compare or combine each other's answers/homework
- Conduct face-to-face interactions
- Contribute ideas
- Encourage participation
- Generate hypotheses/outcomes
- Get into groups quietly and quickly
- Give help when asked
- Keep the group focused on task
- Listen attentively/actively
- Listen to partner(s)
- Make inferences and predict
- Offer constructive criticism
- Perform/complete assigned tasks
- Praise each other
- Reach consensus
- Read each other's notes
- Request help only when needed
- Review/drill on assignments
- Share materials
- Stay with the group until the task is finished
- Support points with evidence
- Take risks
- Take turns talking
- Trade initial responses to a film or story
- Use indoor voices
- Utilize humor appropriately

Examples of Linguistic Objectives

Listening

1. Follows directions
2. Listens actively
3. Demonstrates appropriate nonverbal behaviors
4. Diagrams/maps lecture accurately

Speaking

1. Cohesively constructs appropriate responses
2. Uses appropriate vocabulary
3. Addresses audience with confidence
4. Supports response logically

Reading

1. Employs decoding strategies
2. Determines the meaning of unfamiliar/technical/specialized words using context clues
3. Skims for information
4. Predicts possible consequences

Writing

1. Uses appropriate vocabulary
2. Formulates correct grammatical structures
3. Demonstrates correct punctuation usage
4. Justifies problem-solving strategy

Table 6.2 Listing of Process Words and Possible Products Correlating to the Six Different Levels of Bloom's Taxonomy

LEVEL OF PROCESS	PROCESS VERBS	POSSIBLE PRODUCTS
Recall (Knowledge) (Lowest Level)	define, fill in the blank, identify, know, label, list, locate, match, memorize, name, recall, record, relate, repeat, spell, state, tell, underline	books, diagrams, events, films, filmstrips, magazines, models, newspapers, people, radio, records, tapes, TV commercials/programs
Comprehension	describe, discuss, explain, express, interpret, paraphrase, put in order, recognize, report, restate, retell in own words, summarize, trace	books, diagrams, events, films, filmstrips, magazines, models, newspapers, people, radio, records, tapes, TV commercials/programs
Application	apply, compute, conclude, construct, demonstrate, determine, dramatize, draw, employ, experiment, find out, give an example, illustrate, interview, make, manipulate, operate, paint, practice, schedule, shop, show, sketch, solve, state a rule or principle, teach, translate, use	collection, diagram, diary, diorama, illustration, map, mobile, model, photographs, puzzle, scrapbook, sculpture, stitchery
Analysis	advertise, analyze, appraise, calculate, categorize, classify, compare, contrast, critique, debate, determine the factors, diagnose, diagram, differentiate, dissect, distinguish, examine, inspect, inventory, question, relate, separate, solve, sort, specify, survey, test	chart, commercial, diagram, graph, questionnaire, report, survey
Synthesis	change, collect, combine, compose, construct, create, design, find an unusual way, formulate, generate, hypothesize, imagine, infer, invent, manage, organize, originate, plan, predict, prepare, pretend, produce, propose, reconstruct, reorganize, revise, role-play, set-up, suggest, suppose, visualize, write	advertisement, cartoon, invention, magazine, new color/game/machine/smell/ taste, news article, pantomime, play, poem, product, puppet show, radio/TV show, recipe, song, story, structure
Evaluation (Highest Level)	appraise, assess, choose, debate, decide, defend, discuss, editorialize, estimate, evaluate, interpret, in your opinion, judge, justify, measure, prioritize, rank, rate, recommend, revise, score, select, support, value	conclusion, court trial, group discussion, letter, news item, panel, recommendation, self-evaluation, survey

SOURCE: Compiled by Dr. JoAnn Canales, Associate Professor, Texas A&M University—Corpus Christi, July 1999.

Table 6.3 Examples of Instructional Objectives Using Bloom's Taxonomy

The student will:

Knowledge	List the organelles found in animal cell cytoplasm.
Comprehension	Describe each of the organelles found in animal cell cytoplasm.
Application	Sketch the organelles found in animal cell cytoplasm.
Analysis	Discriminate under the microscope the organelle found in the cytoplasm of animal cells.
Synthesis	Design a classification scheme of the organelles found in animal cell cytoplasm according to their functions.
Evaluation	Justify the interpretation that certain structures are specific organelles while observing living animal cell cytoplasm under the microscope.

The student will:

Knowledge	Identify the major parts of speech in the sentence.
Comprehension	Discuss the major parts of speech in the sentence.
Application	Diagram complete sentences.
Analysis	Analyze a paragraph for misuse of major parts of speech.
Synthesis	Write a paragraph that correctly uses each of the major parts of speech.
Evaluation	Evaluate a paragraph written by another student for proper use of major parts of speech.

The student will:

Knowledge	Name the positions of players on a soccer team.
Comprehension	Describe the positions of players on a soccer team.
Application	Demonstrate how the positions of players on a soccer team depend upon one another.
Analysis	Contrast the different positions of players on a soccer team.
Synthesis	Generate an offensive plan that uses the different positions of players on a soccer team.
Evaluation	Interpret the reasons for an opposing team's offensive use of the different positions of players on a soccer team.

The thematic units, driven by these instructional objectives, usually span grade reporting periods or large segments of reporting periods. Preferably these units are **interdisciplinary,** which means that various disciplines (e.g., language arts, history, math, science, art, music, and physical education) are addressed under a single theme (see Figure 6.1). Incorporating both core and elective type subjects under a unifying, universal theme—such as Interdependence, Rhythm, Friendship, or Unity—enables students to see and make explicit connections and provides them multiple opportunities to enrich their vocabulary and language skills in a variety of contexts. If a teacher teaches in a classroom devoted to one subject area, having an interdisciplinary philosophy can also help students to see that *all* subjects are related to each other in the real world—for example, a scientist uses oral and written language to clearly communicate his or her findings, a civil engineer uses physics and mathematics to build bridges, and a doctor

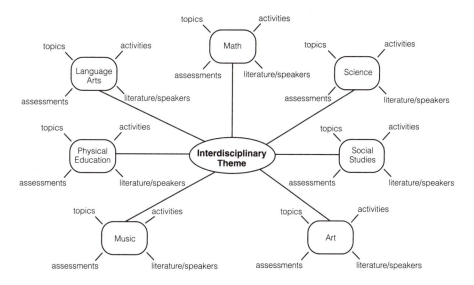

FIGURE 6.1 Model web for an interdisciplinary thematic unit.

uses biology, chemistry, and psychology to examine and treat a patient. **Intradisciplinary,** or single-subject, thematic units can also be developed using a unifying theme that spans topics covered over multiple weeks (see Figure 6.2).

The third step in the planning process involves developing the **daily detailed lesson plans** using **performance** objectives. Also known as **behavioral** objectives or **learner outcomes,** these objectives are more specific than instructional objectives. In addition to *audience* and *behavior,* performance objectives also address *condition* and *degree.* Such objectives answer the questions:

Audience—Who is to accomplish the task?

Behavior—What is the task to be accomplished?

Condition—What are the circumstances for performing the task?

Degree—At what level of proficiency is the task to be accomplished? (Kindsvatter et al., 1996, p. 160)

Examples of performance objectives are:

- Students will identify the various stages of photosynthesis while observing a variety of plants with 80 percent accuracy.

- Students will accurately compare and contrast jazz music written between the 1930s and 1960s using a matrix listing the various elements.

The circular graphic shown in Figure 6.3 clearly illustrates the steps involved in the nested approach to planning, and the following sections elaborate on each type of planning.

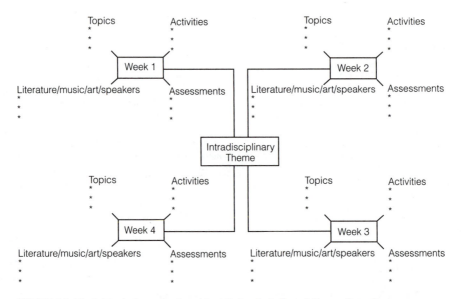

FIGURE 6.2 Model web for a single-subject (intradisciplinary) thematic unit.

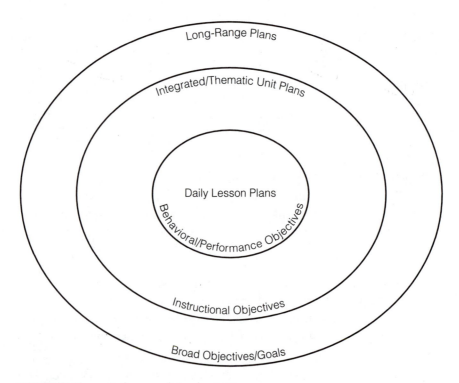

FIGURE 6.3 The nested approach to planning.

LONG-RANGE PLANS

In developing long-range plans, teachers should first obtain the school district calendar, the state-adopted materials for their subject(s), and a copy of the Texas Essential Knowledge and Skills (TEKS) for their particular grade level or discipline. Second, teachers should determine the number of student contact days they will need to consider, which can be easily determined by using blank grids for each calendar month and:

- Note the beginning and end of the academic year.
- Subtract all staff development days, testing days, holidays, weekends, and so on.
- Note the beginning and end of the grade reporting periods.

Third, teachers should examine the topics addressed in the state-adopted textbook(s). Elementary teachers will need to examine all the subject-area textbooks. Then teachers can determine which topics can best be organized along a unifying theme. Examining the TEKS will ensure that all the state competencies for students will indeed be covered, although textbook publishers should have addressed these competencies in the development of   their materials. Also, teachers may want to make decisions on the order of TEKS introduced related to the Texas Assessment of Academic Standards (TAAS) objectives based on:

1. Information obtained in students' records about difficulties in skills.
2. Generally accepted scope and sequence knowledge, that is, introducing skills/content with which students have more difficulty (square root, expository writing) early, the premise being that students will do better if that skill is taught first and reviewed frequently and prior to the administration of the TAAS so that it is familiar and fresh in their minds.

It is also a good idea to consider matching content, when possible, to seasonal changes and any special programs offered by the school or community during the school year, such as Earth Day in April, to take advantage of things happening around students.

This long-range planning task is most efficiently accomplished in collaboration with subject and/or grade-level colleagues. Working in collaboration with colleagues helps to ensure consistency and continuity for student learning.

UNIT PLANS

Like long-range planning, unit planning is most efficiently accomplished when done in collaboration with colleagues. If the members of the planning team have not worked together on previous occasions, it is always a good idea to first "come to terms with terms." Every individual has his or her own working definitions of "educationese." Often, colleagues engage in similar practices while having different operational terms for the practices. For example, *interdisciplinary, transdisciplinary, thematic,* and *integrated units* may represent units that incorporate a variety of disciplines and all communication skills (listening, speaking, reading, and writing) under a single theme. They may also signify units that solely reflect a variety of disciplines. Further, identifying a theme to some teachers may be as simplistic as selecting an animal (e.g., pigs, bears, etc.), or it may mean identifying some socially relevant cause/event.

Coming to a consensus on terminology is always easier when there are philosophical underpinnings that can serve as guidelines, or criteria, in identifying a theme. (See Figure 6.4.) The guidelines that follow are presented in what appears to be a sequential format; however, there is no hierarchy for these guidelines. Each one should be considered on its own merit. Some suggested guidelines for identifying a theme are:

- *Must be interesting to students.* Students are more likely to be motivated to learn something when the topic is appealing.

- *Must be something students consider important.* Students are also more likely to be motivated to learn if they find the subject matter relevant to their daily lives.

- *Should have implications for a broad audience including the community, the nation, the world, and possibly the universe.* Students need to understand that their learning is part of a larger context that will enable them to be successful participants in a variety of contexts.

- *Should have multicultural awareness.* Students need to appreciate as well as tolerate diversity as we move toward a more globalized society. While we

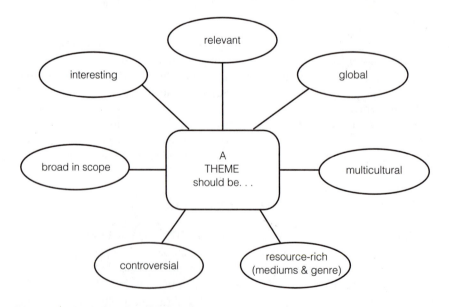

FIGURE 6.4 Criteria for identifying a theme.

have made strides toward honoring and valuing diverse populations of individuals, we must go beyond the narrow approach to celebrating diversity that classifies ethnic/racial groups by day, week, or month. Our society is not a fragmented colored-by-number masterpiece. It is a rich colorful fabric *interwoven* with diversity of religion, race, ethnicity, language, culture, ability, and preference; this should be reflected in our everyday curriculum so that students can began to see the unifying elements rather than the fragmenting elements.

- *Must have multiple resources available in a variety of mediums and genre.* Students need to be exposed to multiple ways of learning that enhance the auditory, visual, oral, and tactile senses.

- *Should be controversial,* that is, focus on political issues, historical debates, or environmental dilemmas. Such a focus will help stimulate inquiry and contribute to self-directed learning.

- *Should be broad enough to cover subtopics and multiple disciplines.* (Wolfinger & Stockard, 1997)

One excellent example of a theme that capitalizes on all of these guidelines is borrowed from a unit developed by a group of secondary education students working together at the University of North Texas. Their unit was entitled "Man's Inhumanity to Man." The team incorporated contemporary music by Billy Joel, classical art capturing the cruelty of royalty toward dwarfs, a variety of literature focused on the plight of humanity because of poverty that transcends racial/ethnic groups, and the historical practice of resolving differences through world wars. The theme and the approach taken by the group provide students of today with a means for appreciating historically significant events while relating them to current events using a variety of mediums. If this theme title was going to be used, the teacher would want to explicitly state to the students that *man* is a traditional way of denoting *human;* thus, the term represents *woman,* as well as *man.*

Another possible theme could be Walls. Mathematics teachers can teach about the angles and slopes of walls found in a variety of housing; science teachers can teach about the composition and subsequent strength of materials; social studies teachers can teach about castles, moats, ghettos, and famous walls in places such as China and Berlin; and language arts teachers can introduce poetry and have students write about "the walls" human beings put up and take down between themselves in relationships.

For elementary students, application of similar guidelines could result in a socially relevant unit using Interdependence, Friendship, or Unity as the central theme (see Figure 6.5). The perspective of how "parts work together to become a whole" could also be the basis for a unit incorporating:

- Math (concept of addition or fractions)

- Language arts (concept of grammar, literacy, or writing)

- Science (concept of body parts, plants, or animals)

- Social studies (concept of communities or community helpers)

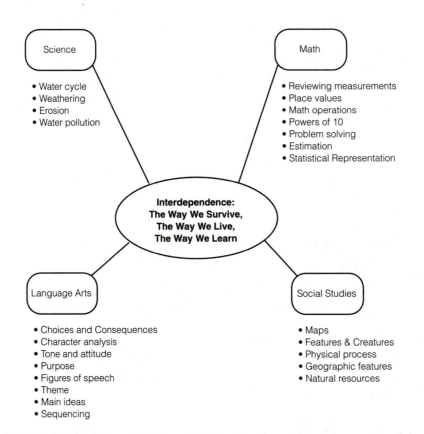

FIGURE 6.5 Interdisciplinary thematic unit—Interdependence: The way we survive, the way we live, the way we learn.

SOURCE: Developed by Anna Lisa Torres, Fernando Valenzuela, Dave Birt, and Leoneissa Lopez, Texas A & M University—Corpus Christi, Fall 1999.

- Art (concept of shapes, forms, or colors)
- Music (concept of instruments, notes, lyrics, or stanzas)
- Dance (concept of steps and movement)
- Physical education (concept of skills)

Developing the thematic unit is an *iterative* process, that is, it requires a continuous reexamination of the steps to ensure continuity, consistency, and relevancy. The steps involved in this iterative process are:

1. *Select a universal theme* after examining the curriculum using state standards, state-adopted materials, and local school district requirements (e.g., conflict, interdependence, exploration).

2. *Create a clever title* for the theme to pique the students' curiosity.

3. *Identify objectives from the various domains,* particularly the cognitive, linguistic, and social domains.

4. *Choose literature and resources* that include a variety of genres (e.g., poetry, short stories, novels) and mediums (e.g., videos, technology, music).

5. *Create a clever "hook"* to introduce the unit and spark student interest.

6. *Brainstorm possible activities,* taking into account that students are highly motivated when they have some choice in learning (e.g., teachers may want to consult their classes or offer choices of some activities).

7. *Organize activities on a planning web* either by discipline or by week as the key "off-shoots" with the following four "sub off-shoots": topics, activities, literature/music/art/speakers, and assessments (see Figures 6.1 and 6.2).

8. *Examine activities to ensure variation* in meeting diverse learning styles and learning proficiency levels.

9. *Sequence the activities* in a logical, meaningful manner.

10. *Detail the activities,* particularly if colleagues will be involved in their implementation.

11. *Centrally locate the materials and equipment* that will be needed.

12. *Decide how to assess* students on the goals.

13. *Notify the students and the parents* so that they can have meaningful discussions about school/classroom events beyond the school walls.

The steps in this sequence are critical to generating a comprehensive unit that will scaffold and anchor students' learning. Steps 2 and 5 are particularly important, as stimulating curiosity should be at the forefront of planning. This trait is a central characteristic of successful leaders, scientists, and space pioneers such as John F. Kennedy (35th president of the United States), Albert Einstein (creator of the theory of relativity), and Eileen Collins (the first female space shuttle commander). It is a quality that we should explicitly help our students to develop if we are to produce generations of lifelong learners.

DAILY LESSON PLANS

Lesson plans constructed from an interdisciplinary thematic unit need even more detail than do lessons from standard units because colleagues and substitutes may need to understand the plans and teach from them. A principal often requires plans to be turned in on a weekly basis so he or she can understand what is happening in the school. Writing good plans is an excellent way to gain respect as an educator from the first moment you enter employment. The majority of school districts in Texas follow a lesson plan design originally conceived by Madeline Hunter (Hunter & Russell, 1981). Her model requires more detail than most veteran teachers usually provide, but the novice teacher will find it useful during the initial teaching years. The level of specificity enables the beginning teacher to focus on teaching the student as well as teaching the content. This focus—teaching *both* the student and the content—should always be a critical premise of planning.

Requirements for lesson plan formats will vary from individual to individual and institution to institution; however, they all contain the following salient major components.

Objectives

All teachers should plan lessons that develop *content knowledge,* develop *linguistic skills*, and develop students' *social skills*. Without specifically detailing objectives that address these three key areas for development, the focus of the lesson will always be content at the expense of developing an articulate, socially adept individual who can function productively in a democratic society. A reflective teacher will always create a plan that focuses on each of these key areas. Bloom's process verbs can be used to frame content and linguistic objectives. Social objectives are drawn from the literature on cooperative learning but should focus on skills needed to accomplish the task and those deemed necessary for members of the classroom to function collaboratively, productively, and efficiently. Examples of such skills are turn taking, constructively elaborating on others' ideas, praising/validating each other's work/thinking, and so forth.

Modifications

Using multiple modalities for teaching and learning, providing advance organizers, and helping students contextualize their learning are all examples of **modifications**. Teachers should provide alternative strategies for second language learners (peer tutoring, advance vocabulary development); for students who need extra help processing a concept (heterogeneous grouping, homogeneous grouping); and for students with exceptional needs (review Individualized Educational Plans and adapt as recommended). (See other related competencies for additional suggestions.)

Anticipatory Set

Other terms used for the component **anticipatory set** are *focus, stage setting,* and *hook*. Young people, much like adults, need a few minutes to "get their heads into" the topic to be taught/learned. Ways in which students' attention may be focused on the lesson include:

1. Engaging students in a motivational activity to pique their curiosity
2. Using personal background experiences, brainstorming, estimating, guessing
3. Conducting a diagnostic assessment activity
4. Showing a related visual or technological production

Instructional Input

Making a lesson comprehensible to students should be the teacher's primary goal. Students should be shown through **instructional input** how the concepts to be learned could fit into their existing schema by relating learning to prior lessons or current events. This can be accomplished by sifting key information, or text material, and presenting it through the use of such strategies as concept attainment and advance organizers (i.e., descriptive, explanatory, and contrastive). (See Competency 8 for a more detailed explanation of these strategies.)

Modeling

Students learn best by being *shown* a process or product and then having an opportunity to explore/modify the means to accomplish an "end." Going over a "freebie," having a finished product or example (or several if there are different ways to do a project), or "walking through" the process are all good ways to provide **modeling**. Teachers should avoid using a series of questions that requires the students to "figure out" what is to be learned, especially if the information will be new to the students. The use of probing questions here can often resemble more of a testing approach than a teaching approach and can prove frustrating for students.

Checking for Understanding

The process of *checking for understanding* should be a formative and summative one. The danger of a linear lesson plan format is that it implies that the elements must happen in a particular sequence and that they can occur only once. In fact, this particular component should be iterative, reoccurring, and focused at the various levels of Bloom's taxonomy. There are many strategies for accomplishing this component including observing behavior, asking random students or the whole class questions and getting responses verbally or with gestures, giving a quiz that does not count toward a grade, using response cards, and using the think-pair-share or heads-together approach (see Competency 8). Thus, checking for understanding should be a strand throughout the lesson cycle.

Guided Practice

This is the opportunity for students to practice what was learned as the teacher or peers monitor to ensure that accurate learning is occurring. *Guided practice* can occur as a whole class, in small groups, or independently. The key word is *guided*. The student is assessed formatively with a "helping hand," and no grade will be taken to count against him or her during this time.

Closure

Revisiting the way in which the instructional input was provided is a good way to "wrap up" a lesson or a portion of a lesson. **Closure** can occur at various points in a lesson as transition statements made between topics and/or activities. For example, a "mini-closure" might be, "Now that we have measured various objects in the room and compared them to the measurements we took last week using our standard rulers, let's review the formula together one more time." This component of the lesson cycle should also be a strand throughout the lesson to ensure "connectedness" for the students. The lesson should always be closed as a whole because it is your last chance that day (or for a unit) to make sure students

(1) understood the main concepts/skills, and (2) leave knowing why that skill is important to them. This is also helpful when a parent asks, "What did you learn today?"

Independent Activity

Students should always be provided opportunities for independent practice to ensure that overreliance on the teacher or peers is minimized. **Independent activity** is an activity where the student does the skill or relates the content by himself or herself and is assessed later by the teacher. This may take *many* forms, but it can be seen as the assignment at the end of class. This component is particularly important to prepare students for standardized achievement test taking and to maximize their attention span to a given task for an extended period of time.

Reflection

This is an oft-neglected but very necessary step in developing lessons. Although teachers engage in continuous reflective practice as they teach and modify instruction on a daily basis, it is also important to include a written **reflection** that addresses the positive elements of the lesson as well as the potential opportunities for modification and the reasons why these might be needed. Reflection can also address the planning process or ways to focus students on the process of learning. Thus, reflection can have a three-pronged benefit by helping the teacher to thoughtfully analyze the planning, as well as the implementation, and helping the students to thoughtfully analyze their own learning processes.

Another term used to describe the reflection process is **cognitive monitoring** (Manning, 1984). Manning suggests that cognitive monitoring should occur during planning, instructing/interacting with students, listening to students, and evaluating instruction. Building on the concept of cognitive monitoring, Neely (1986) identified 16 questions teachers should consider during the preteaching or planning phase. These are:

1. How should I plan for the seating arrangement to use during this lesson?
2. Which students have special needs that should be attended to during the lesson?
3. What discipline and management techniques will I incorporate?
4. What role will I take on during this lesson?
5. Where will I place the materials I have listed?
6. How well do I understand the content of the lesson?
7. What changes will I feel most comfortable with during the lesson?
8. Why should I teach this lesson?
9. Is this going to be too easy/difficult for this group?
10. What attention do I need to give the other students while I am working with this small group?

11. How will I handle interruptions to limit interference in this lesson?

12. How will I check on student understanding?

13. What are my alternative plans if problems arise in this first plan?

14. How will I conclude the lesson?

15. What will students do as this lesson ends?

16. How will I make transitions to the next lesson? (Neely, 1986, p. 31)

Table 6.4 shows a format that teachers may find useful for developing daily plans that address Neely's questions, and Table 6.5 depicts a sample lesson plan.

Table 6.4 Lesson Plan Format

This suggested lesson plan design is a teacher/observer-friendly format. A more linear approach may also be followed. Regardless of the format used, the following are *nonnegotiable* elements: three different types of objectives, use of Bloom's taxonomy, assessment, and getting the students ready for the lesson.

LESSON PLAN FORMAT
(Based on Madeline Hunter)

Preservice Teacher:_____ Grade/Subject:_____

Lesson Focus:_____

Materials/Equipment Needed:

Texas Essential Knowledge and Skills (TEKS) Addressed:

Objectives: (all objectives must be assessed)

      Cognitive:[a]

      Linguistic Development (Listening, Speaking, Reading, Writing):

      Social:

Modifications:

Time Allotment	Process (Teacher)	Activities (Student)	Assessment[a]	Transition
	1. Anticipatory Set			
	2. Instructional Input			
	3. Modeling		Checking for Understanding	Closure
	4. Checking for Understanding			
	5. Guided Practice			
	6. Closure			
	7. Independent Activity			
	8. Reflection			

[a] Objectives should span the six levels of Bloom's taxonomy. A chart listing the various levels, corresponding action/process verbs, and suggested products that require students to perform at the various levels is provided in Table 6.2.

Note: Merely listing a process verb does not mean that the students will actually be engaged at that particular level. Appropriate and specific student expectations that correspond to the process verb must be determined. For example, if students are being asked to "discuss" the pros and cons of a particular issue, but are then asked to merely "List" the pros and cons, the taxonomy level is no longer a comprehension level but is, rather, a recall level.

Table 6.5 Lesson Plan Format

Preservice Teacher: Mr. Math Superstar   **Grade/Subject:** 6/Math

Lesson Focus: 1. Introduction of the thematic unit—Interdependence: The Way We Survive, The Way We Live, The Way We Learn
2. Estimation and measurement of length

Materials/Equipment Needed: Meter sticks, tape of running river

Texas Essential Knowledge and Skills (TEKS) Addressed: 8A, 8B, 8D, 11A, 11D

Objectives: (all objectives must be assessed)

Cognitive: The students will:

Record the measurement of various objects in the room with 100% accuracy using the metric system. (Knowledge)
Discuss the difference between the English and metric units of length using complete sentences. (Comprehension)
Estimate and measure the lengths of various objects in metric units correctly 90% of the time. (Application)
Categorize various objects in the room using the metric system with 100% accuracy. (Analysis)
Write in their journals (2–3 sentences) regarding the concept of interdependency and its relationship to math. (Synthesis)
Write in their journals (2–3 sentences) regarding the concept of math and its relevance to the world around them. (Evaluation)

Linguistic Development (Listening, Speaking, Reading, Writing): The students will:

Follow directions. (Listening)
Clearly articulate responses using complete sentences. (Speaking)
Share their journal entries with peers. (Reading)
Use appropriate and correctly spelled vocabulary in their journal entries. (Writing)

Social: The students will:

Acknowledge peers' contributions in a group activity.

Vocabulary: Metric units, English units, interdependency, meter stick

Modifications:

Pair students with special/linguistic needs with other students.
Require fewer sentences in their journal entries.
Allow LEP (limited English proficient) students to respond in their native language and have a peer translate.
Follow other IEP instructions for special needs students.

Time Allotment	Process (Teacher)	Activities (Students)	Assessment	Transition
5 min	**Anticipatory Set:** Welcome students to the start of a new week. Play tape of running rivers. Use personal backgrounds to introduce "interdependencies."	Close their eyes and imagine running rivers for a few moments.	Observe interest level of students.	"Now that we are relaxed and thinking about rivers, let's see how this relates to this unit."
20 min	**Instructional Input:** A. Using Guided Discussion, introduce students to the concept of "interdependence." Start with a grand scale, i.e., the universe, and work down to examples that students can relate to in their daily lives. Introduce the subtopic of rivers to help in tangible understanding. Explain how interdependencies also exist in math and between subject areas.	Listen actively.	Using adhesive labels, note student responses. Ask questions. Check for comprehension: Give examples of interdependencies and explain your answers. What would happen if there were no interdependencies (in the universe) (in math)?	"These are great responses/questions. It seems like everyone understands the concept of interdependence and how it relates to math and other subjects."
	B. Using Interactive Lecture/Demonstration, review how to take measurements and the difference between metric and English units.	Listen actively. Ask questions.	Ask high-low order questions.	"Now that we've seen the differences between the metric and English units and everyone seems to understand them, I'm

Table 6.5 continued

Time Allotment	Process (Teacher)	Activities (Students)	Assessment	Transition
				going to accurately measure an object."
2 min	**Modeling:** Demonstrate how to estimate and measure with a ruler.	Observe.	Observation of students. Comprehension.	"Since we all seem to understand how to measure with a ruler, let's practice a little."
8 min	**Independent Activity:** Students practice estimating and measuring several objects.	Estimate and measure objects.	Note observation on adhesive labels.	"I'd like everyone to form into your groups. Our next activity will give you practice with measuring concepts as well as let you experience working together in groups."
10 min	**Guided Practice:** Divide students into groups to complete worksheet 1.1. Guide students through the first example.	Work through example. Work in groups.	Completed worksheet— 90% accuracy. Note acceptance of peer responses on adhesive labels.	"Now, you will have an opportunity to show what you have learned individually. For homework, you will complete a similar worksheet."
	Independent Activity: Distribute worksheet 1.2.	Complete worksheet 1.2.	Completed worksheet— 90% accuracy.	
5 min	**Reflection:** Reflect aloud on lesson planning; implementation;	Listen actively.	Analyze whether the lesson and questions	Review concept; review group process work.

144

Time Allotment	Process (Teacher)	Activities (Students)	Assessment	Transition
	teacher/student-generated questions.		stimulated interactions and thinking.	
	Ask students to reflect on what they learned.	Make journal entries.	Review journal entries for appropriateness of mechanics and understanding.	Thank students for participating.

SOURCE: Developed by Dave Birt, a postbaccalaureate student at Texas A&M University—Corpus Christi, Fall 1999.

Historically, school districts have provided their teachers with a "lesson plan" book that is a blank grid of small squares with vertical columns for each day of the week and horizontal rows for either subject areas (for elementary teachers) or multiple periods for secondary teachers. These traditional lesson plan books, typically used by experienced teachers, do not lend themselves to the specificity needed by preservice or beginning teachers. Beginning practitioners are highly encouraged to invest the time in detailed planning. Not only will it help them to successfully "get through the day," but it will also provide a very useful pool of resources for future years.

SUMMARY

Effective planning is a dynamic *decision-making* process. In addition to knowledge of content and pedagogy, it requires effort, thoughtfulness, and time. For the beginning teacher in Texas, it also requires a focus on the Texas Essential Knowledge and Skills (TEKS), a set of explicit subject-specific objectives required for all children attending an accredited public school. Attention to these elements is critical in order to maximize students' academic learning time and to make them successful on the Texas Assessment of Academic Skills (TAAS), the statewide educational accountability measure based on the TEKS.

The process of planning can be viewed as a nested approach. It involves developing long-range plans by identifying broad objectives or goals and the related topics to be covered by subject area; organizing the topics into integrated thematic unit plans using instructional objectives that address content, linguistic development, and social development; and developing daily detailed lesson plans using performance objectives. This approach is essential for developing plans that scaffold and anchor students' learning as well as stimulate curiosity and the desire for lifelong learning.

Central to effective planning are the collaborative and reflective processes. Planning accomplished in collaboration with colleagues can be more efficient and comprehensive, and it facilitates articulation of curriculum across grades and between grades. Reflecting accomplished as an iterative process before, during, and after teaching—on an individual basis, with colleagues, and with students—will greatly enhance a teacher's performance and student achievement.

SUGGESTED ACTIVITIES

There are numerous approaches to developing plans. Therefore, as someone in the process of becoming a teacher, you should explore a variety of resources to maximize your data bank of possible lessons. When examining the many options available, be sure to keep the following questions in mind to ensure that your lessons are quality-based:

■   Do they address state standards?

■   Are they student-centered?

- Do they make learning relevant and meaningful for students?
- Do they help students make connections across disciplines, and within their own discipline, with real-world events/situations?

Process

1. Network with professional colleagues to determine how they develop plans, including long-range, unit, and daily plans. You do not have to reinvent the wheel each day. Colleagues, whether next door or on the Internet, may have the exact lesson you need!
2. Examine state-adopted materials.
3. Browse the Internet sites (see the Web Links section of this chapter).
4. Review commercially produced thematic units.
5. Attend planning workshops.
6. Participate in district/campus/grade-level/departmental curriculum planning meetings.

Application

1. Develop long-range plans for a particular grade level/discipline.
2. Sit in on a meeting at the beginning of school where teachers are discussing long-range plans.
3. If possible, work with colleagues/peers to incorporate a variety of disciplines.

4. Develop daily plans following the format presented in this chapter—incorporating the various types of objectives.
5. Observe a master teacher and note how the lesson plan components are addressed.
6. Videotape yourself teaching a lesson and note how the lesson plan components are addressed.

Reflection

1. In visiting with professional colleagues, consider the correlation between the years of experience in teaching versus the need for planning.
2. In examining state-adopted and commercially prepared materials, compare the depth and breadth of material covered.
3. In browsing the Internet sites, consider using the "substitute lens" before adding the site or lessons from the site to your data bank of lessons. Ask yourself, "Can I take this plan and use it as is or with some modifications? Is it so shallow that even I would be bored teaching it?"
4. While participating in workshops or planning discussions, note the process followed, that is: What were the first considerations addressed? What steps were followed? What criteria drove the final decision making?

PRACTICE DECISION SET

1. Ms. Gonzalez is a first-year fifth-grade teacher. Her principal has just asked her to work with her team of fifth-grade teachers to develop a six-week interdisciplinary thematic unit plan to be taught during the spring semester.

Ms. Gonzalez decides to use a plan she developed during her preservice program. At a grade-level meeting, she presents her ideas to her colleagues who suggest the theme be presented to the whole school before being adopted by the team. Ms. Gonzalez's team members' suggestion reflects:

I. The belief that unit plans need to be a whole-school articulated decision
II. Lack of confidence in a beginning teacher's ideas
III. An understanding of the importance of collegial buy-in
IV. An unwillingness to build on existing work

a. I and III
b. I, II, and III
c. II and IV
d. II, III, and IV

2. Ms. Gonzalez chose the theme of *Interdependence* rather than the traditional focus on dinosaurs for this age group. She proposed that a universal theme allowed each teacher to be more creative with the topics and objectives to be covered. She also proposed that such a theme would enable students to be more creative and to participate more actively in group work. Her choice of a universal theme over a traditional theme suggests that Ms. Gonzalez is:

I. Interested in stimulating student critical thinking
II. Curious to see if students will produce better work
III. Committed to having students make connections across disciplines
IV. Concerned with making learning relevant and meaningful for students

a. I and II
b. I and III
c. I, II, and IV
d. I, III, and IV

3. Central to Ms. Gonzalez's thematic unit was a focus on developing students' linguistic and social skills as well as their cognitive skills.

Consequently, there are numerous activities requiring the students to utilize their communication skills and work collaboratively in groups. The additional activities extend the length of the unit by two weeks. Her rationale for these additional activities reflects her:

a. Understanding that more time spent on a theme will increase student achievement
b. Belief that multiple activities keep students busy and minimize classroom disruptions
c. Philosophy that students internalize information better by manipulating it in various ways
d. Training that exposed her to a variety of ideas and strategies

Answer 1: Although a beginning teacher with new ideas may feel that his or her ideas are being rejected by experienced teachers (II) or that experienced teachers reject university teachings (IV), there are two critical lessons for new teachers to learn. The first is the importance of working collaboratively with colleagues (III), and the second is the importance of having an articulated curriculum that spirals and scaffolds students' learning (I). The correct answer is *a.*

Answer 2: Any departure from tradition will generate resistance from experienced teachers in varying degrees. Ms. Gonzalez's choice of themes will certainly engender some disagreement, in part because many teachers will have invested time, effort, and resources in creating their existing lessons. It is critical that Ms. Gonzalez not convey that students have not been learning or successfully achieving using the traditional themes (II). Thus, gathering support for her unit should focus on helping her colleagues understand how the unit will enhance higher-order thinking (I), make connections among various

subjects taught (III), and increase interest and motivation due to the relevancy
of the subject matter (IV). The correct
answer is *d*.

Answer 3: Although *a* may have some
merit, the issue is not more time
(quantity) but rather what is accomplished during the allocated time
(depth). Answer *b* also has merit but
only if the students are interested and

actively engaged in the activities.
Answer *c* has the most merit because
the linguistic activities will ensure that
students manipulate the information in
multiple ways and that social activities
provide multiple opportunities for multiple perspectives. Answer *d* has potential merit but should not be the
primary consideration for developing a
unit. The correct answer is *c*.

WEB LINKS

Remember that website locations may
change. If any of these sites have
moved or cannot be located, use the
Terms to Know in this chapter to
search for further information.

http://web.lexis-nexis.com
Provides credible, in-depth information
on a variety of subjects ranging from
legal and government to business and
high-tech.

http://www.tea.state.tx.us
Provides the Texas Essential Knowledge
and Skills (TEKS) and a link to lesson
plans based on TEKS.

http://www.tnrcc.com
Useful website for making a model of
the water cycle and getting ideas for
laboratory experiments.

http://www.yahoo.lessonplans.com

http://www.ericsp.org

REFERENCES AND SUGGESTED READINGS

*Examination for the Certification of Educators in
    Texas (ExCET) Professional Development
    Preparation Manual for Elementary and
    Secondary.* (1993). Amherst, MA:
    National Evaluation Systems.

Freiberg, H. J., & Driscoll, A. (1996).
    Universal teaching strategies. Boston: Allyn
    & Bacon.

Hunter, M., & Russell, D. (1981). Planning
    for effective instruction: Lesson design.
    In *Increasing your teaching effectiveness.*
    Palo Alto, CA: The Learning Institute.

Kindsvatter, R., Wilen, W., & Ishler, M.
    (1996). *Dynamics of effective teaching.*
    New York: Longman.

Manning, B. H. (1984). Self-communication
    structure for learning mathematics. *School
    Science and Mathematics, 84*(1), 43–51.

Neely, A. (1986). Planning and problem
    solving in teacher education. *Journal of
    Teacher Education, 37*(3), 29–33.

Wolfinger, D. M., & Stockard, J. W. (1997).
    *Elementary methods: An integrated curricu-
    lum.* New York: Longman.

ABOUT THE AUTHOR

JoAnn Canales is an associate professor at Texas A&M University—Corpus Christi. She began her career as a speech pathologist in Laredo, Texas, in January 1974. Her professional journey has also included working as an elementary language arts teacher, an adult ESL teacher, a student teacher supervisor, a Title I Technical Assistance Center senior evaluation specialist, a director of the Center for Collaborative Research at the University of North Texas, an independent consultant focused on at-risk youth, an interim associate dean for teacher education, and a university professor in education.

Canales currently serves as the Coordinator of Teacher Education at Texas A&M University—Corpus Christi. She is primarily responsible for the implementation of the undergraduate field-based program housed in partner schools and the graduate-level certification program. Other key related activities include serving as a Graduate Associate in John Goodlad's Institute of Educational Inquiry responsible for developing Leadership Associates focused on the Well-Educated Teacher Initiative and the grounding of the Agenda for Education in a Democracy. She also serves as one of nine members on the new National AACTE/ERIC Clearinghouse Committee on Teaching and Teacher Education.

Her publications reflect her many years of experience with the issues of assessment and, in particular, assessment of language minority students. Other publications have focused on issues of faculty involved in teacher preparation, e.g., *Capitalizing on Diverse Faculty Expertise in Universities: Weaving Content Specialization into Generalist Preparation* (1997) and an internationally focused monograph entitled *The Educational Systems of Mexico and the United States: Prospects for Reform and Collaboration, in the Western Interstate Commission on Higher Education's (WICHE) Understanding the Differences* series (1977). She has also been actively involved in one of the initially funded trilateral grants supporting the exchange of faculty and students between the North American countries.

Her numerous presentations at the local, state, national, and international levels include such topics as: partnership development—Texas Partner School Conference (1999); expectations for deans—American Association for Colleges of Teacher Education (1999); and assessing second language learners—International Conference on Education in Puebla, Mexico (1998)/American Educational Research Association (1998).

Canales received her Ph.D. in Curriculum and Instruction from the University of Texas at Austin in 1985. She also holds a master's degree in bilingual education and Spanish from Laredo State University (1978) and a bachelor's degree in speech pathology and audiology from the University of Houston (1973).

7

Verbal, Nonverbal, and Media Communication Techniques

MYRNA D. COHEN
UNIVERSITY OF HOUSTON—DOWNTOWN

This chapter will deal with Competency 7 of the professional development Examination for the Certification of Educators in Texas (ExCET). Competency 7 is the second of six competencies that fall under Domain II, Enhancing Student Achievement.

Competency 7: The teacher uses effective verbal, nonverbal, and media communication techniques to shape the classroom into a community of learners engaged in active inquiry, collaborative exploration, and supportive interactions.

The teacher understands that communication takes place verbally, nonverbally, and through the use of media. Using a variety of modes and tools of communication, the teacher imparts expectations and ideas to create a climate of trust, respect, support, and inquiry. The teacher models effective communication strategies (e.g., monitoring the effects of messages, being a reflective listener, simplifying and restating, being sensitive to nonverbal cues given and received) and encourages students to communicate effectively in a variety of contexts. The teacher is a thoughtful questioner who asks questions that elicit different levels of thinking and recognizes that different ways of questioning achieve different purposes (e.g., promoting risk taking and problem solving, facilitating factual recall, encouraging divergent thinking, stimulating curiosity). The teacher appreciates the cultural dimensions of communication and knows how to foster effective, constructive, and purposeful communication by and among all students in the class.

TERMS TO KNOW

Active inquiry	**Group processing**
Active listening	**Modeling**
Classroom climate	**Nonverbal message**
Community of learners	**Probing question**
Convergent question	**Self-assessment**
Cooperative learning	**Verbal message**
Divergent question	**Wait time**

> I am the decisive element in the classroom. It is my
> personal approach that creates the climate. It is my daily
> mood that makes the weather. As a teacher I possess
> tremendous power to make a child's life miserable or
> joyous. I can be a tool of torture or an instrument of
> inspiration. I can humiliate or humor, hurt or heal. In
> all situations it is my response that decides whether a
> crisis will be escalated or de-escalated, and a child
> humanized or de-humanized.
>
> GINOTT,
> (1971, P. 13.)

Competency 7 supports the notion that one of the pillars of good teaching is good communication. In order to be a master teacher, a teacher needs to be a master communicator. It also implies that it is the teacher who determines the **classroom climate**. Notice the use of the words *shape* and *create* in the competency. The climate does not simply develop, but rather, the teacher creates it and shapes it. The most effective classroom climate is one in which the students feel psychologically safe and free to take risks, because **active inquiry** cannot take place without risk taking. Students need to make mistakes in order to learn through inquiry, and they need to feel comfortable about making them. The competency also stresses that it is the teacher's responsibility to teach students to be master communicators themselves, since learning occurs just as much through interactions among students as it does between teacher and students. Students can learn about communication by observing their teacher's expert skills and by then emulating them. The teacher should also directly teach communication skills as part of the curriculum. In our discussion in this chapter, we will first examine what the teacher can do to excel in communication. Then we will explore the type of learning that is advocated in this competency and for which good communication is a prerequisite.

COMMUNICATION

Teachers are always communicating with their students. They do this by every-thing that they say and do and by everything that they do not say and do not do. The teacher is a powerful figure in the classroom, and even though students may not always show it, they are looking to the teacher as a model. The best teachers are those who understand their influence, are aware of the messages that their stu-dents are receiving, and make sure that those messages are positive ones that facil-itate learning. Good communication is a prerequisite for the type of learning advocated in this competency. It is necessary for building a community of learn-ers, for implementing active inquiry, and for utilizing collaborative exploration. Let us look at some principles of effective communication without which these elements could not be established successfully in a classroom.

Communication Pertaining to Instruction

Teachers need to employ expert communication skills as they teach. This is not such a daunting task, because the skills of effective communication can be learned. Future teachers should be aware of what teachers who excel in this area do. Communicating for instructional purposes is a huge concept and includes topics like developing analogies in the presentation of material, employing reasonable sequencing of concepts, using personal examples and metaphors in explanations, and so forth. However, in Competency 7, the skill of questioning takes promi-nence, and so we will also concentrate on this skill in our discussion. Questioning certainly is the heart of teaching and learning. Whether we ask questions of our-selves or whether others ask them of us, questions direct our thinking.

The content of the questions that are used in the classroom is covered in Competency 8. Competency 7 addresses the ways in which the teacher commu-nicates his or her questions to the students. Different ways of communicating questions determine different results. Teachers are expected to understand the intricacies of this process and to use questions wisely. Even the best question can fall flat on its face if it is not communicated effectively. There are many subtle and some not-so-subtle techniques to take into account as teachers consider how they will use questions in their classroom and how they will give explanations.

Look over the following ways that teachers describe their classrooms:

1. Every one of my students participates when we ask and answer questions in our class discussions.

2. My students think deeply about our questions in class. They give them serious thought.

3. My students are animated and involved in our discussions. They are so motivated and excited!

4. My students listen intently to one another during class discussions.

5. My students follow directions easily and I do not have to waste time repeating instructions.

Are these descriptions too good to be true? Most teachers would love to be able to say these things about their students, and some honestly can. The good news is that these descriptions are not to be found only in utopia. They are not far-fetched and do not depend on a magical potion. In fact, research has found that there are specific ways to bring about these kinds of results with students so that any teacher can one day honestly make remarks like these about his or her classroom. Let us look at each claim in detail and examine how each might be accomplished.

1. *Every one of my students participates when we ask and answer questions in our class discussions.* We have all been in classrooms where a few dynamic students monopolize the discussions while the others inconspicuously fade into the background. One wonders whether the quiet students have ideas of their own or if they are even paying attention to the lesson. Do they have interesting thoughts but are too shy to express them? Or are they thinking about what they will eat for lunch that day? Most teachers and students would rate classes with more student involvement as the more successful ones. But whose responsibility is it if only a fraction of the students are active? Most educators would agree that it is the teacher who determines the level of student participation. For those who value complete student participation, there are a number of points upon which to ponder.

First of all, teachers need to consider whether they are really giving all of their students equal opportunity to participate in class. Teachers often scoff at this question, but in truth, sometimes teachers are not aware that they are being partial. Favoritism can be operationalized by the teacher's use of nonverbal language to encourage selected students to participate by using more eye contact, closer proximity, or encouraging facial expressions with these students. Or, more obviously, teachers may simply call on some students more than others. One type of bias is logistic orientation, where teachers may pay more attention to the students sitting in the front of the room, or on the left or right side. Gender and culture are important to consider as well, and teachers unwittingly may give hidden messages through the patterns of interaction that they direct. Imagine the hidden message of a teacher who calls on boys for higher-level thinking questions and on girls and minority students for lower-level ones. Implicitly, these teachers are saying that they have higher intellectual expectations of boys than of girls or of mainstream than of minority students. Indeed, research has found that teachers often allow more time for boys to answer (**wait time**) than they do for girls, implying that they believe less in girls' abilities (Sadker & Sadker, 1994a). These tacit messages deter the students in question from participating because they are meeting the teacher's expectations as they internalize the implicit prejudice.

What can a teacher do to overcome these behaviors that result in unequal class participation? Fortunately, it is easy to investigate whether one has any biased tendencies by doing audiotape or videotape analyses of lessons or by asking a colleague to observe the class. Being aware of a bias is the first step in overcoming it. In addition, there are a number of techniques that the teacher can employ in order to get all students to respond and to overcome unintended inequities. One way is to call on students in a pattern that is hidden from the students. For example, the teacher may decide to call on students in every other row from front to back.

Teachers should change their patterns frequently so that students will not anticipate their turn. Using the class roll or seating plan can be helpful too. Some elementary school teachers put the names of their students on popsicle sticks and randomly pull out a stick to call on students. The important point is that teachers should be aware of what they want. If only choosing volunteers is in order, that is fine. However, if teachers wish that all students participate, they need to be aware of possible personal biases and should employ methods whereby equity of participation is assured. Teachers can train themselves to be equitable questioners.

Another way of getting all students involved is to have them each individually commit to an answer by demanding a total-class response. A popular technique is the "thumbs up, thumbs down" method. For example, a teacher may say, "Do you think that these two bottles hold the same amount of liquid? All those who think yes, thumbs up, all those who think no, thumbs down." Here everyone in the class has responded within a few seconds, and the teacher can instantly get an idea about the thoughts of the students. Another way to accomplish total participation is to ask students to write down a response. For example, the teacher may say, "What do you think was the primary cause of the Civil War? Write down your choice on a piece of paper and be ready to defend it." The teacher then can walk around the room, glance at the responses, and make comments about the ideas. The important point here is that each student has committed to an answer and hopefully has thought about it. This technique can also easily flow into a think-pair-share activity that is discussed in detail in Chapter 8.

Asking clear questions is an important skill that also impacts participation. Students need to feel safe about expressing ideas, and if they are unsure of what the teacher is asking, they may be reluctant to step forward. Questions that are vague and ambiguous like, "What about the space race in the 1950s?" lead the students to wonder what the teacher is getting at rather than to think about the topic. Run-on questions have the same effect. When students hear questions like, "Could conditions on Mars support life and would you want to live there?" they are left wondering which part of the question is the real one (Kindsvatter, Wilen, & Ishler, 1996). Leading questions are ineffective in that they inhibit students' thoughts. Asking, "Why was Truman a great president?" is more confining than "Would you consider Truman a great president?" In the former leading question, the teacher infers that he or she believes Truman to be great and assumes that the students agree. In this situation, students may avoid considering other opinions or may be reluctant to disagree with the teacher. Furthermore, negative questions are less favorable than positive ones. A negative question like, "Who does not think that Truman was a great president?" would be intimidating, as would a question like, "Who does not know about Truman's accomplishments?" Students may not respond out of embarrassment, in which case the question serves no purpose (Thompson & Kushner, in press).

As these examples indicate, constructing well-phrased questions impacts the level of student participation. Since it is difficult to compose quality questions on the spot in the midst of a lesson, it is advisable to write well-thought-out questions into the lesson plans. The teacher may get to ask them as planned, or may not. However, even if the teacher does not implement them exactly as anticipated, the mental act of writing them out beforehand will increase the likelihood of coming up with well-phrased questions during instruction. It is also important to be sensitive to students' feedback when engaged in discussions. Confused looks or unrelated student responses are cues to the teacher that his or her questions were not clear. In these instances, rephrasing or simplifying questions is in order.

2. My students think deeply about our questions in class. They give them serious thought. The teacher also determines the quality of answers offered by students. Different questions are asked for different purposes. If a teacher asks a lower-level, **convergent question**, where all answers should converge, or be the same, the teacher should anticipate a simple, recall response. An example is, "Which is the most densely populated country in the southern hemisphere?" There is a right or a wrong answer that the students either know or do not know. These recall type questions are beneficial and should be used appropriately. However, they should be taken for what they are—questions that do not require creative or higher-level thinking. There is no problem with using recall or convergent questions. The only problem comes with using them too often and at the expense of **divergent questions**, questions with many possible answers. Bloom's taxonomy (see Chapter 8) offers a stepladder for teachers to follow not only for creating objectives, but also for constructing questions on various levels.

Teachers who ask a good, thought-provoking, divergent question should anticipate a thoughtful response, assuming they have asked the question skillfully. For example, a teacher should not undermine his or her own question by expecting students to answer quickly. Students need time to think about the question. A teacher who calls on a student a split second after asking a question is essentially telling the class that the question does not require much reflection—that it can be answered on the spot. However, by waiting after posing the question before entertaining student ideas, the teacher communicates the opposite—that the question is complex and cannot be answered quickly. The time between the asking of a question and the calling on a student to answer it is termed *wait time*. Research shows that if a teacher extends wait time, more students will have answers and more students will attain a deeper level of thought. Sometimes teachers find it difficult to refrain from calling on students who eagerly wave their hands and beg to be called on immediately. But the teacher is in control, and if the students see that the teacher insists on reflection time, they will change their behavior to meet the teacher's expectations. Some teachers have devised gimmicks to condition themselves to allow for wait time. Counting silently to 10 or walking across the room before calling on a student may be helpful. It is difficult to fight the impulse that most of us have to "fill the silence" and shorten wait time. However, it is worth the effort as it encourages more and deeper thinking.

Another way to encourage reflection is by using **probing questions**. Rather than just accepting students' initial responses as the best that they can do, teachers can probe students so that they will refine and sharpen their thinking. For example, if a student responds that Heathcliff is his favorite character in *Wuthering Heights*, the teacher can ask what differences the student sees between Heathcliff and Catherine and why the student chose one over the other. These questions will stretch students to deeper levels of thinking as they ponder aspects that they might not have considered on their own. A teacher who uses no probes conveys to the students that they are not capable of more than the initial response. Lev Vygotsky, a Russian psychologist born in 1896, has gained popularity among educators for his theory of the zone of proximal development that supports the importance of probing questions. Vygotsky (1987) believed that "with assistance, every child can do more than he can by himself—though only within the limits set by the state of his development" (p. 187). Teachers expand students' mental capacities by helping them think on deeper levels, as with the use of probing questions. While initially the students only reach these deeper levels with assistance, eventually they will be able to reach those same levels independently. Once this occurs, their level of independent thinking moves up a notch and their teacher's assistance brings them to an even higher point (see Figure 7.1). The space where the students can expand their thinking with the assistance of the teacher is called the *zone of proximal development*. The level of *actual* development is the point wherein students can function on their own without assistance. The level of *potential* development is the point that students can reach with the assistance of a teacher. The zone between the actual development and the potential development is the zone of proximal development.

Not all questions need to be higher-order ones. There is a time and a place for all kinds of questions. Often there is good reason to ask a convergent, lower-level question. Yet, is important to note that the effective teacher makes informed decisions about the questions posed and is cognizant of the purposes and effects of those questions. Whether or not students think on deep levels is not happenstance. It is determined to a large degree by the types of questions the teacher asks and by the manner in which they are asked. Teachers should know whether they want students to simply recall information or to think creatively and should ask accordingly. If divergent questions are used, wait time and probes will encourage student reflection.

3. My students are animated and involved in our discussions. They are so motivated and excited! Again, student motivation is not an uncontrollable mystery; teachers have great influence over it. One consideration is that students of all ages thrive

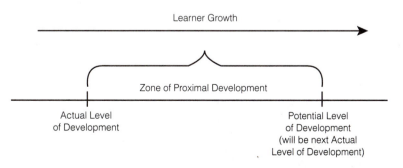

FIGURE 7.1 Vygotsky's zone of proximal development.

on the approval of their teachers. The ways that a teacher responds to students' comments can either motivate them to participate or discourage them altogether. But what is motivating to students? This is a complicated question because different students may prefer different rewards. For example, while one student may thrive on public praise from the teacher, another more inhibited student may be embarrassed by the same public praise. Experienced and sensitive teachers can adjust their feedback accordingly once they know their students. In general, however, the teacher should make all students feel positive about participating in order to increase their motivation.

Feedback given for convergent questions needs to convey whether or not the answer is correct. Some teachers may feel reluctant to tell students that they are "wrong" for fear of harming their self-esteem. Although this kind of sensitivity is admirable, it is truly doing the students a disservice to let mistakes go undetected. For example, if in a third-grade class a student remarks that there are mountains in Houston and the teacher does not correct the student because the teacher is reluctant to hurt the student's feelings, this is obviously poor judgment on the teacher's part. The comment needs to be corrected lest the whole class be misguided. Furthermore, students deserve to know that they made a mistake, why they may have made the mistake, and what they need to do to improve (Kindsvatter, Wilen, & Ishler, 1996). In this case, the teacher could find out on what basis the student made the comment. Does the student misunderstand what a mountain is? Does the student think that since he or she has not seen all of Houston, there also may be mountainous parts of the city? Did the student just say it because he or she wanted to participate to feel part of the class? Once the reason for the error is determined, the teacher can help the student improve.

As for harming egos, research has indicated that the manner in which the feedback is given is more powerful than the feedback itself. **Nonverbal messages** take precedence over **verbal messages** (Sadker & Sadker, 1994b). If a teacher says, "Sue, this was one of the best student essays that I have ever read," but says it with a frown and in a harsh tone, the student would probably give more credence to the negative body language than to the positive verbal message and would interpret that as negative feedback. So even if a student stands to be corrected, the manner in which the correction is made determines how the student feels about it. Another point is that the teacher should be evaluating the idea, not the student. This makes corrections less threatening. For instance, the comment "you are illogical" is much more damaging to a student than the comment "your idea is illogical." Furthermore, students should feel appreciated for participating, even if their answers are "wrong."

Giving feedback for divergent questions is another matter, since there are no right or wrong answers. Here teachers should be open to original thinking on the part of their students. By no means should teachers limit their praise to ideas that conform to their own. Students need to get credit for contributing creative answers, even if they are so creative that they challenge the teacher's beliefs.

Kindsvatter, Wilen, and Ishler (1996) include an extensive section on feedback and praise in their introductory text. In their discussion on praise, they point out that criticism seems to be more prevalent in classrooms than praise, although praise is motivating and criticism is discouraging. They also point out that the most effective praise is specific rather than generic. A student will be more rewarded with a comment like, "Good, Sue, that shows you have taken into account economic aspects that we talked about last week," than "Good, Sue, interesting point." The former shows that the teacher listened to the answer and the appreciation is credible. Giving specific praise will prevent teachers from overusing reinforcement words, a practice that detracts from motivation. Expressions that are overused and general, like "good," "right," and "OK," become empty and nonmotivating in the students' eyes. Teachers should be cautious not to overuse certain words and to be as specific as possible. One effective technique is for teachers to ask each student to select a favorite word or phrase to be used for praise. Students can even write their chosen words on decorated index cards to be placed on their desks. With this technique, not only are the words reinforcing, but the classroom environment becomes a warm, supportive place with small signs of "terrific," "right on," "good thinking," and so forth displayed throughout the room.

Another way to motivate students is to incorporate their answers and comments into the class discussion. Their ideas can be applied to new concepts, compared to similar examples, or used in the closure of the lesson. The teacher can also paraphrase the idea for the class to better understand the student's intent. These practices are considered to be effective for increasing motivation (Kindsvatter, Wilen, & Ishler, 1996).

Asking divergent, thought-provoking questions in itself motivates students to participate. It is much more exciting to think about questions that do not have clear-cut answers than to address those that have only one correct answer. If teachers ask questions to which they already know the answers, the questions are not authentic ones. It is no secret that the teacher is primarily interested in finding out if the students have learned the material, not in finding an answer to the question. These questions are artificial and are unique to classrooms and learning contexts. Yet, when teachers ask questions to which there can be new answers, learning becomes more dynamic for everyone. Consider the teacher that asks, "Do people in our community receive acceptable medical care? Are services available? Do residents take advantage of the services that are offered?" These are authentic questions that the teacher and students can ponder together. Students understand that the teacher is learning along with them and is genuinely interested to hear the responses. Learning becomes authentic and exhilarating. Thinking and problem solving, which are inherently enjoyable and stimulating, permeate the classroom.

4. My students listen intently to one another during class discussions. Teachers also impact how intently their students listen to one another. First of all, the teacher imparts this through **modeling**. Sokolove, Sadker, and Sadker (1994) maintain that, "Students consciously and unconsciously imitate their teachers' styles of behavior, and often accept the attitudes and values projected by their teachers as their own" (p. 191). Johnson and Johnson (1994) concur: "Because there is evidence that students are most likely to imitate the person with the greatest power and control over the distribution of rewards, the teacher's behavior will have a powerful influence on student behavior" (p. 189). Therefore, when the teacher listens with respect to students' ideas and gives each student's contribution thoughtful consideration, he or she conveys the value of student ideas in the learning process. It also follows that students' creative thoughts should never be ridiculed or censured by the teacher. Students, in turn, will listen to each other respectfully and not ridicule each other. Once it is clear that the teacher believes that student answers are important for learning and that students as well as the teacher express important thoughts, then the students will value each others' responses and listen to each other as they model their teacher.

The seating arrangement of a classroom can encourage or discourage students from listening to one another. A classroom that is set up so that all desks are in rows facing the front of the room sends the message that students will communicate with the teacher, but not with each other. Indeed, it may be physically difficult for students to hear one another when seated in this fashion. If, on the other hand, the desks are arranged in a semicircle or with one half of the students facing the other half, the implicit message is that students will converse with each other and exchange ideas. Seating students in groups conveys a similar message. In these arrangements, students see each others' faces rather than the backs of their heads. Naturally, this is conducive to student-student communication.

Another technique to encourage students to listen to one another is for teachers to diminish their own presence in class discussions. The teacher can refrain from commenting on a student idea and ask another student to react instead. Consider this example:

Teacher: What would have motivated a young man in the 1400s to join an exploratory sea voyage?

Joey: Maybe the adventure and a chance to leave home.

Teacher: Sharon, what do you think of Joey's idea?

Sharon needed to have listened carefully to Joey in order to answer the question. The teacher did not repeat Joey's idea, but assumed that all the students listened to him. When conducting a class discussion, it is common for all responses to filter through the teacher. However, there are alternatives. Discussions can proceed with students commenting on student ideas, with teacher remarks only haphazardly dispersed among the students' interactions. Teachers who implement this kind of exchange encourage students to value each other's ideas and to listen intently.

In addition to modeling and to using the indirect techniques already mentioned, above, teachers can directly teach listening skills as part of their classroom curriculum. In fact, productive communication skills should be taught especially in classrooms that rely on good student-student interaction, classrooms that use group work and discussion extensively. Teachers should not just take it for granted that students will instinctively acquire these skills. Listening to others without interrupting, checking for understanding, treating others with respect, understanding how others feel, and controlling emotions are often addressed directly (Aronson & Patnoe, 1997), as are building and maintaining trust, providing leadership, and managing conflicts (Johnson & Johnson, 1994).

Johnson and Johnson (1994) point out that such skills are vital to the learning process in order to engage in effective **cooperative learning**. They are also valuable in and of themselves for future workplace and social interactions. Teachers implementing cooperative learning will often work on team-building and interpersonal skills before they even begin to teach the academic subject matter. Johnson and Johnson recommend an eight-step approach for the direct teaching of these skills:

1. Ask the students what skills they think they will need in order to cooperate (compete, work individually) successfully.

2. Help the students get a clear understanding of what the skill is, conceptually and behaviorally.

3. Set up practice situations.

4. Ensure that each student receives feedback on how well he or she is performing the skill.

5. Encourage students to persevere in practicing the skill.

6. Set up situations in which the skills can be used successfully.

7. Require that the skills be used often enough to become integrated into the students' behavioral repertoires.

8. Set classroom norms to support the use of the skills. (pp. 188–190)

Another technique that builds expertise in interactive skills is for students to engage in self-evaluation of those skills. This type of activity heightens students' awareness of their behavior and helps them realize on what they need to work for improvement. **Group processing** (Johnson & Johnson, 1994) is a popular way to accomplish this. Here students discuss their strengths and weaknesses as a group and determine goals for working together more effectively in the future. The processing can be accomplished in numerous ways. For instance, students can assess individually or in groups, orally or in writing. Students may complete an assessment form on themselves and on each group member. The form may include questions concerning the quality of the student's work, how much the student contributed to the group learning, how dependable the student was about completing assigned tasks, and whether the student asked for help when necessary. Group members can then compare their ratings and discuss discrepancies. Through **self-assessment** the students become less dependent on their teacher for evaluation and more empowered in understanding what to do in order to work together productively.

5. My students follow directions easily and I do not have to waste time repeating instructions. Another important skill for communication in the classroom is clarity in giving directions. In addition to explaining concepts and ideas relating to the subject area, teachers need to be good communicators when it comes to explaining classroom procedures. If teachers give clear, understandable instructions, students will be able to meet their expectations. But ambiguous directions can result in nightmares for teacher and students alike. Imagine being a student of the teacher who says, "When your group finishes the project, answer questions 1 to 5 on page 53." On the surface this sounds clear enough, yet as the students proceed, they may wonder if they are to work in their group or individually, or whether they should write the answers or prepare them orally, or whether it is permissible to talk about the answers with fellow classmates. Students generally want to please their teachers, but teachers sometimes unwittingly make it difficult for their students to do so by not communicating well.

When teachers prepare important yet complicated directions, for example, for a new activity, they should visualize the students going through each stage of the activity so that they do not overlook any detail. As they communicate the directions, they should do so orally as well as in writing. In this way they are accommodating different learning preferences, and the students can refer back to the written instructions if they do not recall some of the details. If appropriate, graphic representation or modeling of what is expected might also be of value. If a teacher is introducing a group activity, the directions should be explained in whole-class format before the students divide up into groups because if clarification is in order, it is easier to do so when the class is still in whole-group format. Asking students to repeat directions is a good way to ensure that the directions have been communicated well. Reiteration of important steps is also advisable. Remember that clear directions add to a positive class climate because with them students feel safe. They can concentrate on the task at hand rather than expend energy wondering what they are supposed to do. Students are able to please the teacher when they understand what is expected of them (Thompson & Kushner, in press).

Communication Pertaining to Class Climate

In addition to knowing how to communicate when teaching, effective teachers also know how to communicate with their students in noninstructional situations. Students appreciate teachers who make them feel valued, respected, and comfortable. Teachers who can develop positive relationships with their students are often those to whom students turn in times of confusion. Those teachers are the ones who frequently become role models and mentors. Because of the positive interpersonal groundwork built by these teachers, students often look to them for guidance and support. They are the ones of whom students will often say in later years, "She changed my life." Positive interpersonal communication also has an effect on learning, since learning well is generally tied to good feelings and to strong emotional bonds with those involved. Following is a selection of concepts teachers should consider as they reflect upon developing effective teacher-student communication.

Expectations Teachers who expect a lot from their students usually get a lot. Likewise, teachers who expect little, get little! We cannot underestimate the power of teacher expectations on students. Imagine being in a class in which the teacher says, "This is a very difficult story. I don't think that you will understand the plot or theme because your potential is limited and your reading level is too low." Students in that class probably would feel deflated and might believe what the teacher has said about their abilities. Yet, the students to whom a teacher says, "I know that you will be able to read and understand this material. Even if there are difficult words in the text, they will not bother you because you are bright and you'll be able to figure out the meaning," probably would feel motivated, would work hard, and would make great strides.

As Oakes and Lipton (1999) point out, teachers usually do not explicitly convey their expectations to their students, but rather they implicitly communicate them. For example, regularly asking higher-level thinking questions of a select group of students communicates high expectations. The teacher believes they can answer those difficult questions. Repeatedly asking low-level questions of a select group of students can imply just the opposite—that these students cannot handle the hard ones, so the teacher is giving them the easy ones. A biased teacher may convey low expectations of minority students and high ones for nonminority students, sending a very damaging message. The strength of teacher expectations was clearly examined in the study *Pygmalion in the Classroom* by Rosenthal and Jacobson (1968), a study that has been replicated many times. This research showed that students met teachers' expectations even when teachers were given wrong information about the ability of their students. Teachers of low-achieving students were told that they had the accelerated class while teachers of high-achieving students were told that they had the remedial class. After several weeks, the "slow" students were performing at an accelerated level and the "gifted" students were performing poorly. In light of this phenomenon, it is apparent that effective teachers believe that their students can learn, and they communicate this belief to the students. Effective teachers set high expectations and do not give up on their students.

Active Listening Of course, communication is a two-way process. Just as we, as teachers, need to be aware of what we are saying to our students, both with words and body language, we need to be sure that we understand what our students are saying to us. Sokolove, Sadker, and Sadker (1994) explore the skill of **active listening** in detail, as do Johnson and Johnson (1994). Some of their most important points are discussed here.

Think about all of the nonverbal actions that say that someone is really listening and interested in what another person is relaying. Direct eye contact, a relaxed posture, leaning forward, and being physically close are all signs that a person is intently listening to another. Of course, the opposite is also true. We would not feel compelled to share our thoughts and feelings with someone who would not look at us, or who would stand as far away from us as possible with arms folded on chest. Most of us would tend to end the conversation with this kind of response. Verbally, we can encourage the other to continue talking by being quiet. Our silence tells the other person that we want him or her to talk. In addition, occasionally summarizing, or paraphrasing, what the other person has said keeps both participants on track. If a summary is inaccurate, it provides an opportunity to clear up misunderstandings and improve communication. These summaries should be nonevaluative and noninferential. They should reflect back the speaker's message without our opinion attached. For example, saying, "So, with your mom's new job she is not at home when you leave for school in the morning. You're saying that mornings are more difficult for you now," is better than, "So, that is really sad that your mom isn't home in the mornings. How could she have taken a job with those kind of hours? It is irresponsible."

As we listen, we should also pay attention to nonverbal messages. They can be reflected back to the speaker in order to give the speaker more self-knowledge. For example, one might say, "As you talk about your new morning schedule, you keep flipping the pages of your book." It also may be helpful to determine if there are discrepancies between the verbal and nonverbal messages. Usually, nonverbal messages are more genuine than verbal. We can carefully share our observations and interpretations with the speaker to see if they concur with our reading of the message. One might say, "As you talk about your new morning schedule, you keep flipping the pages of your book. Do you feel nervous or uncomfortable talking about it?"

If a teacher practices the techniques of active listening, the chances of students sharing ideas and concerns increase. Teachers who wish to have close interpersonal relationships with students outside the academic environment should consider practicing these skills. Active listening will encourage students to confide in the teacher.

Realness This quality, defined by Rogers (Rogers & Freiberg, 1994), relates to the way that the students perceive the teacher. Rogers believes that students should be able to see their teacher as a real person with strengths and weaknesses rather than as an unapproachable, perfect, authority figure. When students view their teacher as a real human being, they can identify with him or her more. They may think, "Even the teacher has good days and bad days. It's OK for me to have a bad day once in a while too!" When a teacher is willing to admit to imperfection, there is more honesty in the classroom environment. The teacher who insists on being viewed as a flawless authority gives students a false impression about human nature and is less approachable than a "real" teacher. Students should learn from their teachers that, just as we all have special talents, we all also have faults that we need to recognize and deal with. For example, teachers may reveal that they, too, sometimes fall into the trap of procrastinating and not managing their time wisely. They may admit that they too end up working all night at times to meet a deadline, although they wish that they could prevent this tendency. Teachers are not people playing interchangeable roles, but are genuine and unique human beings, and students should recognize them as such.

Acceptance Rogers (Rogers & Freiberg, 1994) maintains that by accepting students, teachers create a strong feeling of trust in their classrooms. Teachers who "accept" students have a basic belief in the goodness and well-meaning intentions of the students even though some of their behaviors may find disfavor in the teacher's eyes. There is also a distinction between the students and their behaviors, so that the teacher may disapprove of the students' actions, but never of the students themselves. A student whose teacher displays "acceptance" knows that the teacher trusts him or her, believes in him or her, and that even if the student does something foolish, that trust will not be shaken. This quality is reflected in the comment, "Maria, your constant chattering during class is annoying," which is quite different from the comment, "Maria, you are annoying." The former comment communicates rejection of the behavior but not the student, while the latter does not differentiate between student and behavior and implies a personal rejection. With teachers exhibiting acceptance, students still have to suffer the consequences for their poor behavior, but deep down their teacher's belief in them as good and worthy human beings will not be damaged. Students whose teachers "accept" them in this fashion gain a strong sense of security, which facilitates learning.

Empathic Understanding According to Rogers (Rogers & Freiberg, 1994), this quality adds to a student's feeling of well-being in the school environment. Teachers who exhibit empathic understanding are able to see through their students' eyes. They recognize that their students experience the world through perspectives different from their own and can glimpse what that is like. This ability makes the students feel that someone understands them, a feeling that increases security and improves their learning environment. Those teachers with empathic understanding do not evaluate or critique student perspectives; they simply try to get a deeper understanding of how their students perceive reality. In opposition to empathic understanding is egocentrism, which is the "embeddedness in one's own viewpoint to the extent that one is unaware of other points of view and the limitation of one's perspective" (Johnson & Johnson, 1994, p. 66). As our classrooms become more multicultural, practicing empathic understanding becomes more crucial.

Cultural Sensitivity The best teacher communicators understand that they need to take the cultural norms of their students into account in their teacher-student interactions. The diversity in our schools is great, and it is constantly growing. The probability of a teacher instructing students from cultures different from his or her own is very high. It is probably impossible for a teacher to be an expert on the communicative norms of every single culture represented by the students in our schools. Yet, the teacher at minimum should acknowledge that cultural differences exist and that it is his or her responsibility to try to understand students better in order to communicate better with them.

Researchers have investigated many multicultural aspects of education upon which teachers should reflect. For example, students may be comfortable with different cultural norms than those of the teacher and of the school culture. Norms are defined as behaviors and habits that permeate an environment and that are so taken for granted that the members of the culture may not even be conscious of them. Just as fish may not know that water exists until they are taken out if it, many people are not aware of their cultural norms until they are immersed in a different culture. It is the responsibility of teachers to heighten their own awareness of cultural norms so that they do not impair communication with their students.

Many examples of nonmainstream cultural norms can be found in educational writings. Not acknowledging them can lead to harmful misunderstandings. For example, the use of eye contact is one such norm that could interfere with communication. Some cultures use indirect rather than direct eye contact as a sign of respect. Conversely, in our North American culture, direct eye contact is a sign of respect. If a culturally insensitive teacher converses with a student who will not look the teacher directly in the eye, that teacher may unjustly come to the conclusion that the student is acting disrespectfully. The wiser teacher would consider that there may be a cultural misunderstanding at play and would be less likely to misjudge the student. Similarly, the distance that people place between themselves and others is also culturally bound. North Americans prefer more distance than South Americans, for instance, and females prefer less distance than males. In addition, some cultures are comfortable with physical touch and others are not. In some cultures, conversations between students and teachers about personal subjects are accepted, and in others they are not. Questioning authority is valued in some cultures, while in others it is disfavored.

Master teacher communicators are aware that these cultural discrepancies exist, even though they may not know about each of them specifically. Such teachers are not quick to judge students; rather, they explore the possibility of cultural misunderstandings before jumping to conclusions. When a teacher is feeling negatively about a student, one of the first questions that the teacher needs to ask is if there is a cultural difference at play and if that difference is affecting the relationship with that student. For example, suppose a student did not participate at all in a class activity wherein feelings about family were discussed. A sensitive teacher would consider numerous possibilities for this behavior. Maybe the student was being obstinate to attract attention, or maybe the student was just shy, or maybe there was a cultural element at play and perhaps it is against the cultural norms of the student to talk publicly about something so personal. The sensitive teacher includes culture as a variable to consider in the analysis of student behavior. In this instance, the lack of participation could have been due to any of the possibilities considered. The crucial point is that the teacher included culture as a variable to consider.

In addition to impacting student-teacher communication, cultural norms can also impact student achievement. When there is a difference between communication patterns used in school and those used at home, learning may suffer, especially with young children. Consider, for example, the asking of questions. In White cultural interaction patterns, parents often ask children questions to which they clearly already know the answer. They may ask, "What animal is this?" or "What color is the balloon?" In Black culture, this kind of questioning is not customary. These questions would not be asked because it is clear that the adult knows the answer. Since patterns like the former are used in school, children who are accustomed to this mode of questioning will have a high comfort level, as they will understand what is expected of them. Yet these kinds of questions might be unfamiliar and confusing to children who are not used to such patterns (Heath, 1990). Other varied communication patterns that could lead to misunderstanding in the school environment include the use of praise, corrections, clarification, and the ways of calling on students (McGroarty, 1990). Effective teachers need to be aware of these cultural norms as well and not discriminate against students who need to be acculturated into the world of school.

Respect A positive classroom environment presupposes mutual respect between teacher and students. But what does it really mean for a teacher to respect students? One point is that the teacher has responsibilities toward students just as students have responsibilities toward the teacher. For example, teachers expect their students to come to class prepared, with assignments completed and with materials ready. Teachers should likewise come to class with well-prepared lessons, assignments graded within a reasonable time frame, and so on. Teachers who value their students' time are also showing respect. Assigning busy work with little instructional value indicates a level of disrespect on the part of the teacher. Fairness toward students is another aspect of respect. Students deserve rules that are well-explained with consequences that are consistently carried out. Examinations should not be constructed to trick students, but should be valid evaluation instruments.

But perhaps most important, respectful teachers do not make fun of their students. A student may resent a teacher for a lifetime if that student is humiliated in class. Making a joke at the expense of a student is inexcusable. Teachers who sincerely respect their students do not belittle them outside of the classroom either, not even in the teachers' lounge. Likewise, teachers who manage their classes by intimidation techniques are abusing their power. Students who behave for fear of erratic outbursts and degradation harbor resentment, not respect, for their teacher. Teachers should avoid using sarcasm with students, even if it is well-intentioned, as it can be easily misconstrued and become hurtful. For example, a teacher may joke with a very bright graduating student by saying, "So, where are you going next year, the local community college?" Both may know that this is not the case, but the teacher, as the authority figure, may put a slight doubt in the student's mind about his or her ability. In addition, other students or teachers who overhear the comment may not be privy to the sarcastic intent and the relationship between that student and teacher. False impressions may result. For these reasons, although humor is much appreciated, sarcasm should be avoided. Classrooms that emanate mutual respect are safe places for students; classrooms without it are frightening places that impede learning.

RECOMMENDED CLASSROOM FEATURES

Effective communication on the instructional and interpersonal level paves the way for teachers to incorporate student-centered instruction. Elements of student-centered instruction include three classroom features noted in Competency 7 that are discussed in the following text.

Community of Learners

On what basis could one judge a classroom to be or not to be a **community of learners**? We know that not all classrooms fit into this category and that it may not even be the norm in many of our schools. But what exactly is meant by this phrase, and why is it so desirable? Johnson and Johnson (1994) include terms like "caring," "meaningful goals," "personal relationships," "a sense of belonging," and "extended family" in their discussion of learning communities (pp. 263–264). Classrooms that fit this category connote those same terms.

Teachers have the power to create a community of learners within their class-rooms no matter where they are employed. Granted, some school atmospheres are more congruent to this concept than others, but the teacher still has control over the climate in his or her individual classroom. In a community, all members have a sense of belonging. It then follows that learning students' names as soon as pos-sible should be a priority of the teacher, even in high schools where a teacher may have well over 100 students each day. The teacher likewise initiates activities that ensure that the students learn each others' names and get to know and appreciate each other. Students learn to trust and support one another. "Support is the com-municating to another person that you recognize his strengths and believe he has the capabilities needed to productively manage the situation he is in" (Johnson & Johnson, 1994, p. 195). Implementing cooperative learning models is one way to achieve these goals. In a community, students are not anonymous or alienated. They belong to a caring group, and each member is valued by the group for his or her unique qualities. The teacher employs methods and strategies to bring this about so that the teacher knows the students and the students know one another.

A community also implies that all members have something important in common. Here the commonality is learning. Everyone in the community is learning, students and teacher alike. Students may learn from the teacher, students may learn from fellow students, and the teacher may learn from the students. Nobody has a monopoly on ideas and knowledge, not even the teacher, even though the teacher is the community leader. Student input is taken into account when planning instructional goals and objectives, making the curriculum mean-ingful to students. Due to this purposeful learning environment, positive and productive group norms develop. These norms, or shared expectations, are main-tained largely by group pressure. Doing homework, staying on task, and bringing required material to class become group expectations of its members because these behaviors will help the group succeed. Nobody wants to let the group down. The teacher is also expected to abide by these norms and to put forth full effort toward the teacher's responsibilities. Students feel proud to be a member of the group because they know each other well and appreciate one another and because they share common goals, those of learning.

How can we explain why creating a community of learners facilitates learning? Abraham Maslow constructed a theory about human needs that may shed light on this question. According to Maslow, a hierarchy of needs exists for all human beings. There are seven levels to the hierarchy, and a person must have one level satisfied before he or she can move up to the next higher level (see Figure 7.2). The first four levels are called "deficiency needs," while the upper three levels are called "growth needs." Education is primarily connected to the first growth need of intellectual achievement, but is also ideally connected to the next two higher needs of aesthetic appreciation and self-actualization. However, these growth needs

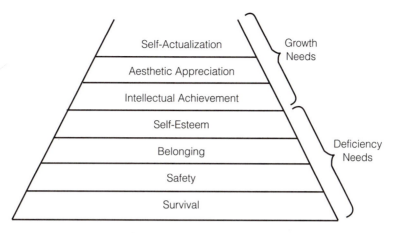

FIGURE 7.2 Maslow's hierarchy of needs.

are unattainable unless the deficiency needs are fulfilled (Eggen & Kauchak, 1994). By creating a community of learners, teachers are making headway in answering these deficiency needs. For example, the supportive atmosphere of trust and respect allows for a feeling of psychological safety for students who are part of a learning community. The feeling of belonging, the third level, is also addressed as efforts are made to make all students feel an integral part of the class. Finally, self-esteem is nurtured as students in a community of learners recognize and build on each oth-ers' strengths and talents. Sadly, students often come from home environments that do not satisfy deficiency needs. Many of our students grow up in neighborhoods where physical and psychological safety is questionable. In addition, many come from dysfunctional families where feelings of belonging and self-esteem cannot be taken for granted. The teacher who can create a community of learners in the classroom can compensate for difficult backgrounds and help these students thrive.

Active Inquiry

Imagine that eighth-grade history teacher Mr. Meltzer and his students have come to the topic of United States immigration at the turn of the century. Mr. Meltzer and his students have brainstormed a list of questions about this topic that includes:

- Why did people from Europe want to come to the United States at that time?
- What were the differences between the people who immigrated from Europe and those who chose to stay in their homelands?
- What was the budget of a family in the United States at the turn of the century?
- What were the best-paying jobs in Europe and in the United States?
- Which immigrants got good jobs in the United States?
- Were there restricted laws about immigration then? Could anyone come?
- What were the hardest things to get used to for immigrants coming from Europe to the United States?

- In what ways is the situation today for immigrants from South America, Central America, and from the Far East the same or different as it was then?

Mr. Meltzer and his students learn about this topic by investigating these and other questions that students have initiated. Students work in pairs or in groups on the questions that interest them the most and answer other questions that come up during their work. The students figure out ways to find information. Some students interview the adult children of immigrants from this time period. They construct a questionnaire for this purpose. Others use the Internet for information about current immigration policy. Some use their computers to make graphs and charts that compare information on prices and costs of living. Some use the textbooks and other library resources that describe conditions in Europe and the United States at that time. As students search for answers, Mr. Meltzer makes suggestions about how to find valuable information and guides students through their research. After several days, students share their information and then draw conclusions based on synthesizing what the class has discovered.

Mr. Meltzer is using aspects of active inquiry in this setting. Let us examine what they are. With this framework, students analyze problems and questions in a systematic way, often employing the scientific method. For example, students in one group may hypothesize that immigrants came to the United States primarily because of financial reasons. Through their reading and interviews they would determine whether to accept, reject, or alter this hypothesis. Answers and solutions are derived from the reflection of the students. The process of learning is as important as the actual knowledge that is gleaned. Learning how to learn and how to think about a problem or question is considered as important as the body of knowledge itself. The curriculum is built around questions that are real and meaningful to the students. Students generally have choices in the learning process. They may choose what content to concentrate on and/or what methods to use in their investigation.

Mr. Meltzer is following Dewey's (1966) vision of the learning process wherein school learning models real-life learning. In real-life learning, an authority does not hand us all the answers; we have to search for them ourselves, usually through collaboration with others. In many problem-solving instances, two heads are better than one. In addition, subjects are not naturally differentiated from one another as they are in school where we may concentrate only on math for 50 minutes and then on nothing but grammar for the next 50 minutes. In genuine inquiry, subjects flow together so that the group working on the economic questions will be using computer and math skills along with reading and writing and historical critique. In Dewey's view, students should learn how to learn rather than memorize stores of information. The emphasis is on the process, not the product. Students learn the way experts in the field learn, through investigations and research and hypothesis testing. Knowledge becomes dynamic rather than static. Students in Mr. Meltzer's first-period class may have experiences and ideas that are very different from those in his second-period class.

Active inquiry also supports the views of the Brazilian philosopher Paulo Freire (1993) and is diametrically opposed to what Freire called banking education. Freire criticizes our school systems for teaching in a way that makes students passive and that divorces them from the natural and empowering quest for knowledge. In his metaphor of banking education, knowledge is like money, a desirable but stagnant commodity. The students are like the banks, passively waiting for money to be deposited into them. The teachers are the depositors of money, or knowledge, which goes into the banks, or the students. Note that the teachers are the only active participants in this process. They decide when to deposit, what to deposit, and how much to deposit.

Banking Education

teacher = depositor

knowledge = money

student = bank

To Freire, the banking education model is dangerous for future generations. It encourages passive learning and does not equip students with the tools for independent learning, as students are dependent on their teachers. Active inquiry challenges the banking model and is more aligned with Freire's idea of transformative education, where students take control of their own learning with the guidance of their teachers.

One might wonder why inquiry learning is not more prevalent in our schools, and perhaps why we as students did not experience more of it. Let us consider some reasons why teachers may be reluctant to implement this kind of student-centered learning, and then reflect on whether we might be affected by these same thoughts. How much do we value active inquiry? What might we do to ease its implementation with our own students in our own classrooms?

There are a number of reasons why teachers are reluctant to implement active inquiry. First of all, teachers tend to teach as they were taught, and many teachers experienced mostly teacher-centered instruction in their own K–12 years. Furthermore, students themselves may be conditioned to more teacher-centered learning and, if so, would have to get used to this alternative approach. Teachers may be reluctant to take the time and energy to wean students from their established mindset. Another consideration is the loss of predictability. Of course, we never have total predictability in teaching, but when the teacher controls the learning experience, as with teacher-centered methods, the teacher knows what questions will be asked and answered, what information will be shared, and how much time will be spent on various topics. Teachers can maneuver the lesson so that they remain in their comfort zones, especially regarding content knowledge. On the other hand, some teachers may feel uneasy with active inquiry as predictability decreases. Teachers have less control over the questions, the information discovered, and the time invested. As students become active learners, teachers cannot anticipate what ideas their students may formulate nor what aspects of the content they may uncover. This may threaten some teachers who fear a loss of authority. However, in the true spirit of inquiry and learning communities, teachers are also learners and are not expected to know everything. Although this type of environment is stimulating for many teachers, some may find it disconcerting. Finally, accountability criteria may be a deterrent for using active inquiry. If teachers are expected to teach their students specific material, they may feel the need to "give" them the needed information. They may feel that the varied and unique learning experiences available in active inquiry are more powerful than direct learning, but that standardized tests do not validate those gains. Although we acknowledge these teacher concerns about using active inquiry, most educators believe it is the most effective way to learn and that we should try to overcome barriers to its implementation.

Collaborative Exploration

Is the teacher responsible for only the academic achievement of students, or is the teacher also responsible for the students' social and psychological well-being? Does learning take place individually, or is learning best carried out through inter-action with others? Those who tend to agree with the latter parts of these state-ments have beliefs that are congruent with the philosophical underpinnings of cooperative learning. Cooperative learning is a well-developed and popular strat-egy that is often used as a synonym for collaborative learning, although coopera-tive learning may refer to more specific models. Teachers whose beliefs coincide with those of this strategy tend to implement it more often and more effectively with their students (Cohen & Tellez, 1994).

Those teachers who feel that learning is an individual enterprise might find it difficult to depend on collaborative groups for the learning of new material. If they tend to believe that the teacher is the sole source of knowledge, they might feel reluctant to delegate this responsibility to the group. However, those who believe that students learn best through collaboration would view group work as a valuable teaching resource. They would view the role of the teacher as facilita-tor, not disseminator of knowledge. Similarly, those who view the role of the teacher as broader than just academic would be willing to teach social skills with no hesitation. However, those who see their role as purely academic in nature would view this task as a waste of time and energy and might be inclined to gloss over it or even neglect it altogether (Rich, 1990).

Johnson and Johnson (1994) advise that by teaching social skills, planning for individual accountability, and structuring group interdependence, teachers can avoid the common pitfalls of group work. In fact, these are crucial components of cooperative learning that distinguish it from just grouping for instruction. When using cooperative or collaborative models, teachers need to invest class time on directly teaching the social skills necessary for productive group work. Neglecting to do so can result in ineffective learning, as students may become par-alyzed by conflicts and nonsupportive interactions. In addition, unless everyone in the group is held accountable, some less-motivated students may slip into the woodwork and let the others do the work. Finally, if the teacher structures the task so that the group cannot succeed without a contribution from every group member, the teacher ensures total participation through interdependence. A clear example of interdependence is evident in the jigsaw model where every member holds a unique piece of an intellectual puzzle without which the conclusion is unattainable. See Chapter 8 for more details on this and other models.

Teachers need to be aware of the philosophy underlying the collaborative approach. In order for collaborative learning to be used effectively, teachers need to feel personally comfortable with its basic principles. Collaborative exploration is a natural complement to a community of learners where active inquiry is prevalent.

SUMMARY

This chapter addresses the importance of communication to effective instruction. The value of communication is discussed regarding three areas of the learning experience: instruction, classroom climate, and classroom features. The teacher's expertise in communicative skills greatly enhances these aspects and, in doing so, facilitates learning.

Teachers can employ communicative techniques in their instruction that result in more student involvement and deeper thinking. Students learn more when they are encouraged to participate in class and to think creatively and deeply. Teachers have the ability to inspire and stimulate students through expert communication. Active listening is modeled and taught by teachers who use their communicative skills to enhance learning. The ability to give clear instructions also helps students.

Communication skills affect the classroom climate. A positive classroom climate is one in which the students feel favorably toward their teacher, fellow students, subject matter, and themselves. Unfavorable feelings characterize a negative classroom climate. Teachers can create a nurturing environment by conveying high expectations of all students and by practicing humanistic interpersonal skills such as active listening, realness, acceptance, and empathic understanding. In addition, sensitivity to cultural differences is crucial. Finally, teachers who respect their students and who encourage their students to respect each other enhance the climate.

This chapter highlights three classroom features that are advocated in Competency 7 and that depend on expert communication. First, a *community of learners* should be established. This term refers to a group whose members all share the desire to learn and who support one another in reaching their goals. Members recognize and value each others' strengths and talents and draw on these for the benefit of group learning. All members contribute to the learning process, students and teachers alike. Second, active inquiry is recommended. This is a strategy whereby students engage in systematic problem solving in order to learn. The teacher's role is that of a facilitator. Students generally follow steps, such as those in the scientific method, to reach conclusions. Finally, collaborative exploration is stressed. Here the teacher is not considered to be the main source of knowledge, but rather, it is assumed that students learn from each other as well as from the teacher and they are encouraged to do so.

SUGGESTED ACTIVITIES

1. Communication Pertaining to Instruction

- Observe a classroom for a number of lessons. Evaluate the classroom for each of the following:

   Quality of student participation

   Quality of student answers

   Student-student interaction

   Clarity of teacher explanations

   Types of teacher feedback

- Analyze the teacher's actions that contributed to what you observed.

- Considering your observations, discuss in what ways you would use this teacher as a model and in what ways you would deviate from his or her techniques in your own classroom.

2. Communication Pertaining to Class Climate

- Discuss any instances of cultural misunderstandings or cultural sensitivities that you have seen during your school observations.

- Develop an activity that may help future students become more sensitive to cultures other than their own.

- Do you see effective interpersonal communation skills between teachers and students at your school? Explain your answer by giving specific details.

3. Recommended Classroom Features

- Survey teachers regarding their opinions about implementing active inquiry for their students. What are their attitudes about this approach? To what do you attribute these attitudes?

- Interview students at your fieldwork school to discern if they have experienced banking education, active inquiry, or collaborative exploration in their school years. What are their opinions on these types of learning? Which do they like best? Which helped them learn the most?

- Choose a topic that you may teach during your career. Design two lessons for this topic, one that uses active inquiry and one that uses the banking education model.

PRACTICE DECISION SET

Ms. Frank's students are working on a project in which they are investigating how many residents use the medical services offered in their neighborhood. After dividing the general topic into subtopics, students chose specific areas for small-group investigations. The students constructed questionnaires that they will use to interview residents about these topics. They will learn the mathematical concepts necessary to analyze their data and will make recommendations about these services based on their results. Ms. Frank suggested that her students embark on this project because they expressed concern that few children in the neighborhood were getting any preventative medical care.

1. This project should be an effective learning experience because it

   I. Allows students choices in their learning

   II. Integrates content areas in a natural fashion

   III. Teaches students the process of learning

   IV. Ensures equity in student participation.

a. I and II only
b. I and IV only
c. II, III, and IV only
d. I, II, and III only

2. Ms. Frank notices that Dan, one of her students, seems troubled and distracted in class. After school he comes to the classroom to turn in an assignment. He begins to tell Ms. Frank what is really bothering him. In order to encourage Dan to continue, Ms. Frank might

   a. Maintain eye contact and listen without interruption
   b. Respond in the midst of Dan's story to tell him about her own similar experiences
   c. Immediately give Dan advice because she really doesn't have much time and she wants to help him
   d. All of the above

3. Ms. Frank notices that during the project work, some of the students are not working well together. Some are quarreling with each other, and some are ridiculing the ideas of their peers. To most effectively help her students, Ms. Frank should

   a. Observe the students carefully and reward those who are behaving well with attractive stickers
   b. Observe the students carefully and call the parents of those students who are not cooperating to alert the parents of the situation
   c. Share her concerns with the class and develop a list of important skills that they can work on together
   d. Be patient and wait for the students to work out these conflicts by themselves

Answer 1: The teacher is using an active inquiry approach to learning through this project. As advocated in this approach, she is giving students choices in their learning (I). Students are drawing on many content areas such as language arts (the questionnaire), math, science, and computer skills (II). They are also learning research techniques as they investigate (III). However, there is no assurance that all students will participate equally (IV). In order to accomplish this, the teacher should assign roles or structure tasks that ensure interdependence. There is no evidence in the description that this was implemented. The answer is *d.*

Answer 2: Maintaining eye contact is an effective way to encourage communication and is a skill of active listening for North American culture (*a*). Allowing a person to talk without much interruption is another technique. By relaying her own personal experiences, the teacher is hampering communication (*b*). In order to work with students on an interpersonal level, teachers need to devote time and be nonjudgmental when possible. By quickly offering advice, this teacher is doing the student a disservice (*c*). The answer is *a.*

Answer 3: It is the teacher's responsibility to teach students social skills needed in collaborative learning. We should not assume that students already have these skills or that they will acquire them without teacher guidance (*d*). Rewarding desirable behavior puts the students in a passive role and does not intrinsically motivate them (*a*). Calling their parents takes the responsibility away from the students (*b*). Teaching these skills by first discussing the importance of them with students and by then developing a list with student input is effective because the students are empowered and should understand the rationale behind the upcoming skill lessons. The correct answer is *c.*

WEB LINKS

Remember that website locations may change. If any of these sites have moved or cannot be located, use the Terms to Know in this chapter to search for further information.

http://ericir.syr.edu/virtual/InfoGuides/alpha _list/Gender-bias07-98-html#2B
This site provides an annotated bibliography of Eric documents related to gender bias in teaching. Areas include communication, teaching strategies, materials, curriculum, and expectations.

http://ericir.syr.edu/virtual/InfoGuides/alp ha_list/Appropskill12_97html#indepth
This site contains resources concerning the creation of positive classroom environments. Practical strategies and plans as well as research articles for new and experienced teachers are included.

http://www.ersnational.org/
This site provides innovative curriculum materials and teaching training programs that focus on peacemaking and conflict resolution. Information on the social, emotional, and ethical development of the child is addressed.

http://ericir.syr.edu/virtual/InfoGuides/alpha _list/selfesteem12_97.html
This site provides resources for testing and improving the self-esteem of young students.

REFERENCES AND SUGGESTED READINGS

Aronson, E., & Patnoe, S. (1997). *The Jigsaw classroom.* New York: Addison Wesley Longman.

Cohen, M., & Tellez, K. (1994). Implementing cooperative learning for language minority students. *Bilingual Research Journal, 18*(1&2), 1–19.

Dewey, J. (1966). *Democracy and education.* New York: Macmillan.

Eggen, P., & Kauchak, D. (1994). *Educational psychology: Classroom connections.* New York: MacMillan College.

Freire, P. (1993). *Pedagogy of the oppressed.* New York: The Continuum.

Ginott, H. (1971). *Teacher and child.* New York: Macmillan.

Heath, S. B. (1990). Sociocultural contexts of language development. In Bilingual Education Office, California State Department of Education (Ed.), *Beyond language: Social and cultural factors in schooling language minority students* (pp. 143–186). Los Angeles: Evaluation, Dissemination and Assessment Center.

Johnson, D. W., & Johnson, R. T. (1994). *Learning together and alone.* Boston: Allyn & Bacon.

Kindsvatter, R., Wilen, W., & Ishler, M. (1996). *Dynamics of effective teaching.* White Plains, NY: Longman.

McGroarty, M. (1990). Educators' responses to sociocultural diversity: Implications for practice. In Bilingual Education Office, California State Department of Education (Ed.), *Beyond language: Social and cultural factors in schooling language minority students* (pp. 299–334). Los Angeles: Evaluation, Dissemination and Assessment Center.

Oakes, J., & Lipton, M. (1999). *Teaching to change the world.* Boston: McGraw-Hill College.

Rich, Y. (1990). Ideological impediments to instructional innovation: The case of cooperative learning. *Teaching and Teacher Education, 6*(1), 81–91.

Rogers, R., & Freiberg, J. H. (1994). *Freedom to learn.* New York: MacMillan College.

Rosenthal, R., & Jacobson, L. (1968). *Pygmalion in the classroom: Teacher expectations and pupils' intellectual development.* New York: Holt, Rinehart, & Winston.

Sadker, M., & Sadker, D. (1994a). *Failing at fairness.* New York: Touchstone.

Sadker, M., & Sadker, D. (1994b). Questioning skills. In Cooper, J. (Ed.), *Classroom teaching skills* (pp. 115–152). Boston: D. C. Heath.

Sharan, Y., & Sharan, S. (1992). *Expanding cooperative learning through group investigation.* New York: Teachers College.

Sokolove, S., Sadker, M., & Sadker, D. (1994). Interpersonal communication skills. In Cooper, J. (Ed.), *Classroom teaching skills* (pp. 189–231). Boston: D. C. Heath.

Thompson, S. J., & Kushner, S. N. (in press). *Decision making in teaching and learning.* New York: Addison Wesley Longman.

Vygotsky, L. (1987). *Thought and language.* Cambridge, MA: MIT Press.

ABOUT THE AUTHOR

Myrna D. Cohen is assistant clinical professor at the University of Houston—Downtown. Her areas of interest include teacher education, second language education, and student-centered strategies such as cooperative learning. In addition to university-level teaching, Dr. Cohen has had 15 years of classroom teaching experience encompassing grades 2–12. Dr. Cohen is coeditor of the *Texas Teacher Educator Forum* and is the president-elect of the Texas Directors of Field Experience.

8

✳

Instructional Strategies and Roles

JANICE L. NATH
UNIVERSITY OF HOUSTON

T his chapter will address Competency 8 of the Examination for the Certification of Educators in Texas (ExCET). Competency 8 falls under Domain II, Enhancing Student Achievement, a domain Texas considers most important for its teachers to know and use.

Competency 8: The teacher uses a variety of instructional strategies and roles to facilitate learning and to help students become independent thinkers and problem solvers who use higher-order thinking in the classroom and the real world.

The teacher uses an array of instructional strategies to actively engage students in learning, and constantly monitors and adjusts strategies in response to learner feedback. The teacher understands principles, procedures, advantages, and limitations associated with various instructional strategies (e.g., interdisciplinary instruction, cooperative learning, discovery learning) and appropriately chooses among alternative strategies to achieve different purposes and meet different needs. The teacher can vary his or her role in the instructional process (e.g., instructor, facilitator, coach, audience) in relation to the content and purposes of instruction and the levels of need and independence of the students. The teacher knows how to make instruction relevant to students' own needs and purposes and helps students acquire strategies and skills (including higher-order thinking skills, such as comparison, analysis, evaluation) that will be useful to them in the real world.

TERMS TO KNOW

Bloom's taxonomy

Higher-order/level thinking skills
  analysis
  synthesis
  evaluation

Rationale

Instructional strategy

Discovery learning

Inductive/deductive strategies

Cooperative learning

Interdisciplinary instruction

Convergent/divergent questions

Teacher roles
  Instructor
  Facilitator
  Coach
  Audience
  Guide

Monitor

Risk-free environment

Wait time

Halt time

> Increasingly we will move away from defining
> educational success exclusively in terms of the quantity
> of information mastered. Instead to a large extent, we
> will define educational success as the ability among
> students to generate, question, combine, categorize,
> recategorize, evaluate, and apply information.
> Secondary will be the content of the information;
> primary will be thinking skills.
>
> KAGAN
> (1992, CH. 11, P. 1.)

A new teacher has many things on his or her mind—settling students, selecting activities, getting through a lesson on time, and a host of other decisions. Teacher educators who work with preservice teachers also may concentrate on those elements that are felt to be "developmental" in getting a new teacher started—designing a good lesson, how to handle classroom management, and so forth. Perhaps many believe that if teachers-to-be can just begin with the basics, they can gradually grow in important areas necessary to become a master teacher. However, in Texas that is no longer an option. A new teacher is asked not only to be aware of but also to apply many of the behaviors and strategies once expected of more experienced teachers. One such area that has, in the past, often been addressed as "something on which to work" is bringing higher levels of thinking into the classroom. Thus, a new teacher must now be completely aware of Competency 8 of the ExCET that requires students to be working at higher levels of thinking.

This chapter will examine several areas that will bring awareness to the teacher-to-be and offer ways to easily apply higher levels of thinking to the classroom. This will be addressed in four specific areas: through lesson plan design, through various strategies and models of instruction, through direct questioning techniques, and through creating an environment where students know that creativity is valued and will risk diverse thinking. As with all the competencies, this one is interlaced with many others such as planning, assessment, creating a positive environment, equity for all learners, and so forth.

There are many definitions of higher levels of thinking given by educators. First, you may hear this type of thinking, as defined in **Bloom's taxonomy,** referred to as the upper levels of analysis, synthesis, and evaluation. You will also hear that higher levels of thinking are involved in forming conclusions, critical thinking (making assessments and judgments), problem solving, creativity, probing, inquiry, and logical decision making. Each of these could be broken down or defined further, perhaps, but this type of thinking is certainly *more* than just acquiring and remembering facts or being able to use certain skills. Your students must clearly acquire a base of knowledge and facts, but they must go several steps further. They must use this base to investigate further and logically and to reflect upon the accuracy and worth of what they have found. Then, students must use that reflection to solve complex problems, make good decisions that are well supported, select logical pathways to follow, or create new ideas. The state of Texas emphasizes this to us because these thinking skills *can* be taught and, thus, are able to be mastered by our students over time and with practice. The reason for helping students learn these skills is obvious. Students will grow to be far more productive and fair-minded members of this state (nation and world) who can think independently and who will continue intellectual growth throughout their lives. Of course, the trick is, "How do I go about doing this, as a new teacher?"

INCORPORATING HIGHER LEVELS
OF THINKING INTO A LESSON PLAN

This competency is intricately interwoven with the competency on planning. It is very difficult to teach a lesson in which students are involved in higher-level thinking without a considerable amount of lesson preparation by the teacher. A teacher who is successful in Competency 8 cognitively plans ahead for students to participate in active learning through activities at higher levels of Bloom's taxonomy, prewrites questions at upper levels in lesson plans, and includes all parts of a good lesson that actively engage students with rationale and scaffolding.

There are several ways to go about planning a lesson: (1) preparing a totally teacher-directed lesson, (2) arranging a lesson that includes partial student control, or (3) designing a format in which students are responsible for their own learning. The most *constructivist* approach involves those classrooms where the teacher plans for students to be *active learners* with some ownership or control over their own learning; thus, they participate in building their own knowledge rather than the teacher delivering all. It is in these situations where students become better thinkers, creators, problem solvers, and lifelong learners (Brooks & Brooks, 1993).

In addition, teachers may plan for activities that involve higher-order thinking and critical thinking skills. From data, information, or evidence collected (given or observed), students form conclusions in **higher-order thinking skills**, while they make assessments and judgments with **critical thinking.**

Writing Objectives for Critical Thinking

Let us look at writing a good lesson plan with Competency 8 in mind. Writing a lesson plan is truly a continuously changing process—discursive in nature. Few parts of the lesson plan are not revamped as the teacher writes, then reflects and rewrites, throughout the writing process. A first step is selecting an overall goal for students (for example, "I want them to learn how to develop a character in their writing," or "I want students to know what it takes to be a great leader and president so they can vote in a more educated way when they are of age"). Thoughts continue as to what would work best to attain that goal, as the lesson begins to develop. Perhaps several activities for students may have already flashed into the teacher's head. Designing a plan involves visiting and revisiting various parts of that plan throughout the writing process, usually in no particular order. However, there is a beacon that guides us throughout this process. Effective teachers know clearly what learning they want students to accomplish (Berliner, 1985). The beacon used in planning is the statement of those particular *objectives* that the teacher wants students to accomplish either for learning content or for performing skills. Therefore, a major step in ensuring critical thinking for students would be for the teacher to choose some objectives for each lesson that come from the *upper* levels of Bloom's taxonomy. Each lesson, thus, should include an objective(s) from **analysis, synthesis,** and/or **evaluation** levels—those that are listed at higher levels of thinking.

Levels of Thinking in Bloom's Taxonomy (Bloom et al., 1956)

Evaluation (Highest Level)

Synthesis (High Level)

Analysis (High Level)

Application (Low Level)

Comprehension (Lower Level)

Knowledge (Lowest Level)

Unfortunately, teachers most often select objectives only from knowledge, comprehension, and application levels that require only acquisition of knowledge or skills rather than *real* thinking by students.

In Texas, the state gives teachers many objectives that students must master. When creating lesson plans in each subject area, a Texas teacher should also consult the TEKS (Texas Essential Knowledge and Skills) for his or her grade level and subject area. The TEKS are state-mandated curriculum guidelines *required* for students in Texas. Children are tested on these skills on their TAAS (Texas Assessment of Academic Skills) tests, and Texas teachers are accountable for teaching these skills. A complete listing of these skills for specific grade levels and subject areas may be downloaded from the Internet (see Web Links at the end of this chapter); much information can also be obtained by simply typing in "TEKS" for a search. For example, by going to the third grade social studies TEKS, the teacher may find an expectational objective that the student must create and interpret timelines. That objective must be included in the teacher's lesson plans at some point during the third-grade year. In high school government, the student is expected to analyze and evaluate the consequences of a government policy that affects the physical characteristics of a place or region. Armed with a list of these TEKS, the teacher can be sure to include all required objectives for the students, along with those objectives that help support and round out a lesson and lead to higher levels of thinking. At first it seems like a daunting task to combine all these elements. It is certainly a puzzle with many pieces. However, as with many skills, writing objectives becomes very easy with practice.

Creating Objectives Through Bloom's Taxonomy   Let us take a moment to examine why we should see evaluation, synthesis, and analysis as "higher levels" of thinking. What if an objective for a lesson was, "Students will tell who was the first president of the United States"? How much thought does that take? Very little, really. The student must only memorize and recall a quick *knowledge*-level answer—George Washington. This is important as a base, however, as the student now has some basic recall concepts, vocabulary, or facts with which to deal. These can be referred to as cognitive concepts, or "simple knowledge" and knowledge of a process (Cangelosi, 1992). The student either "knows it or does not." However, what if another objective was added to the plan to *identify* or *distinguish* the first president of the United States from pictures of other presidents? The student would have to first recall who the first president was and then distinguish his features from those of others. This would be a *comprehension*-level objective. What if an added objective would be to *list and classify* traits of the first president of the United States? Now the student must first recall who that was, list all the important features of that president, and then classify and name those features in each category; now the student would be thinking on the *application* level. So far, only lower-level objectives have been used in the plan.

Let us examine how higher-level thinking can be built into this plan by adding one idea on top of another. "The student will *analyze* the reasons our first president of the United States was seen to be a good model for other national leaders" is another objective for this lesson. This means that the student will take apart components to see how they are interrelated. What does the student have to do now? First, the name of the first president must be recalled as well as positive attributes listed. Then, descriptions of other leaders and situations in which they did or did not adhere to the same attributes must be made, classified, and compared to identify Washington as a good model. Finally, students must support their answer with evidence. This is quite a distance, in terms of thinking, from the first objective of "telling who was the first president."

What thoughts are needed if the objectives are at the *synthesis* level? Note the objective: "Predict what type of person would be the most successful president for the United States today." What are the thought processes required here? Now the student must: (a) recall who other successful presidents were, (b) list traits that made each successful, (c) compare each by analyzing all possible failures with all positive traits remembered by the American people, (d) consider the difference in time and issues facing the nation today, and finally, (e) create a *new* image for a successful candidate today.

The highest level of thinking from Bloom's taxonomy is the *evaluation* level. The following objective is at this level: "Recommend the best nominee from the current candidates who would be likely to have the most successful presidency." Again, let us look at the thought processes needed: (a) recall those presidents most remembered as successful and list their traits; (b) classify successful traits and events that contributed to the presidents' success; (c) keeping those traits in mind, develop a "model" for a president in this era; (d) considering events and concerns in our times, determine what type of person would be even more successful; (e) compare that model to all candidates on the horizon; and finally, (f) make a judgment as to which candidate might fit that model in the best manner.

One can see that there is a world of difference in the thought processes from the recall/knowledge level to the evaluation level. If we cognitively work toward designing objectives *and* activities in lower *and* upper levels of thinking, students will form solid thinking skills needed in *all* subject areas to be successful. These types of objectives can and should be written in every field.

What problems hinder this process for teachers? One problem occurs when teachers do not keep a Bloom's taxonomy chart as a part of their plan book. Often that means that they do not follow a plan that is inclusive of *various* levels of objectives. Also, teachers may not have a good understanding of the terms under each of the categories. Texas has included questions in the ExCET that require a working knowledge of Bloom's taxonomy. The state firmly believes that teachers must have a working knowledge of the terms and activities (as shown in Table 8.1) that are a part of each of Bloom's levels in terms of formulating objectives and asking higher-level questions. Table 8.1 shows a list from Bloom's taxonomy of many terms and activities related to critical thinking. To use the table easily, take a term from the first column and match it to an appropriate activity in the second column.

There are other reasons higher-level objectives sometimes are not used more in the classroom. Many believe that younger children cannot react to higher-level objectives and questions. The objectives, however, can be modified for younger children. Using our previous example, objectives for younger students might be:

1. The student will tell who the first president of the United States was and recognize his picture.

2. The student will orally compare a picture of the first president with a picture of our current president, giving at least one trait the two have in common and one trait that is different.

3. The student will, in writing, give two examples of why the first president was a good president and will think of someone they know who has those same character traits.

Table 8.1 Terms and Activities Related to Critical Thinking

Analysis
(Taking Apart to Interpret Relationships to a Whole)

TERMS TO USE (THE STUDENT WILL . . .)	ACTIVITIES
analyze	a questionnaire
classify	a part of a propaganda statement identified
examine	a syllogism broken down
survey	an argument broken down
research	a survey
compare	a conclusion
contrast	a model
point out	a report
distinguish	a graph
investigate	
subdivide	
differentiate	
infer	
separate	
select	
construct	
take apart	
show the interrelation	
break down	
diagram	
evaluate the relevancy of information	
recognize unstated assumptions	

Synthesis
(Putting Together or Applying New Concepts in a Different Setting)

TERMS TO USE (THE STUDENT WILL . . .)	ACTIVITIES
combine	an article
role-play	a play
hypothesize	a plan with an alternative course of action
speculate on	a song
add to	a game
invent	formulation of a hypothesis or question
decide what if	an invention
rewrite	a report
plan	a poem
formulate	a rebus story
create	a set of rules, principles, or standards
organize	a cartoon
develop	
design	

TERMS TO USE (THE STUDENT WILL . . .)	ACTIVITIES
produce	a book
originate	a theme
construct	a short story
rearrange	a plan
compose	a new scheme
devise	
generate	

Evaluation
(Judging the Outcome or the Merits)

TERMS TO USE (THE STUDENT WILL . . .)	ACTIVITIES
apprise	conclusions
compare	self-evaluation
recommend	a recommendation
critique	a group discussion
weigh	a court trial
solve	a survey
evaluate	an evaluation
criticize	a compared standard
summarize	an established standard
relate	valuing/value of a work
consider	an editorial
judge	
conclude	
justify	

4. In groups of three, students will decide what attributes might make a good president and tell why orally.

5. The student will design, write, and illustrate a short flip book showing the life of George Washington (the student must decide on the events he or she will use), including at least four events of George Washington's life with at least one sentence per page.

6. In an oral question/answer session, the student will recommend a person in *their* family who would make a good president and give at least two reasons why.

Thoughtful teachers of all levels and subjects can find higher-level objectives for their students. They may, however, have better success with higher-level thinking by keeping objectives as close to the young child's "world" as possible. For example, in these objectives, we asked students to compare a figure from history to their own family members rather than to another political figure whom they would probably not know well.

Finally, higher objectives require more time. Therefore, success for students in higher-level thinking requires that "thinking time" during the lessons be built into the teacher's plans.

Other Parts of a Lesson Plan That Are Important
for Critical Thinking

There are three other important areas mentioned in Competency 8 that can be written into a good lesson plan. One of these is the **rationale** of the lesson plan. In forming rationales, teachers engage students in reasons why the lesson and/or skills are important. "Necessity is the mother of memorization (or acquisition)" is a phrase that teachers should keep in mind. If there is a *reason* to know, students will be much more inclined to interact with the knowledge or skills. Think about how many times *we* have sat in class as students and wondered, "When will I ever use this?" When we see the relevance, we want to gain the information or skill much more. "You will need to know this" or "It will be on the test" is not an answer that engages students; teachers may say instead, "There is a need to know this or be able to do this *because . . .*" or "It is tested *because . . .*". A rationale should have solid substance in the real world. There are several ways to engage students in a rationale. A teacher *may simply tell* students why the material is important to them. Or the teacher may design the lesson to help students *discover* that information for themselves. For example, a class project may be for students to find "50 Ways to Use Math in Real Life." Finally, teachers may ask students to *predict* when the information or skills may be used either now or in their futures and then help them to verify or encourage the logic of their predictions. Basically, we are trying to "beat students to the draw" on the question that will certainly be asked if we do not bring it up first: "Teacher, why do we have to learn this stuff?"

Relating content to the need for having the information or skill(s) and *to the real world* is closely knit with the rationale for providing for **interdisciplinary studies.** When schools departmentalize by having one teacher teach only one or two subjects, these subjects often become totally disconnected from others in the school. This even occurs when elementary teachers say, "It's time for math now, boys and girls." Science and language arts rarely meet in schools, for example, and the same with mathematics and social studies. Yet, in the real world, topics overlap continuously. Statistics and experiments play a huge part in health; social studies depend on graphs and mathematical skills, while language arts are essential for communication in the sciences. Again, to engage students in seeing connections that each subject area has in the real world, Texas asks teachers to cross over the boundaries that have been long established in subject specialization. Teachers should plan to make connections with other subject areas somewhere within each lesson or within integrated thematic units. In upper grades, collaboration between various departments can increase the relevance of curriculum for students, so that when, for example, students are studying the Elizabethan period in history, they are reading poetry of that era in their English course; in their Spanish class, they are briefly referencing what was happening in Spain and its colonies during that same period for cultural interest; and in mathematics they are offered some problems dealing with elements of navigation. In addition to strengthening these real-world connections, the lessons will turn out to be much more interesting for students.

This is all closely related to *touching on the community* and/or "bringing the subject matter into the realm of students' interests." A teacher is asked, somewhere in the lesson, to relate the information or skills to the *child's* world and what the student already knows. The best place to start is in students' homes or neighborhoods. If the information or skill cannot be seen there, move to the city or state in which the student lives, and finally, the nation or the world. In other words, think of the information or skill in terms of how closely a student can already relate to it. Trying to make the skill or information a *concrete* reality to them is our goal. For example, when the child begins to learn subtraction skills, teachers can talk about the corner store (by name) where students often go to purchase after school snacks. If a student is beginning to learn about force, teachers use tapes of a *local* flood to show damage to a neighbor in their town or city. Again, this is a part of showing the relevance to the real world of the student.

Relating to students' interests is also an important element for lessons. Younger children are interested in the latest toys and movies. Teachers can use examples in lessons from these areas. Older students who are learning test-taking skills, for example, can relate much better by having the teacher note the use of those same skills in driver's license testing or by relating poetry to current song lyrics. Research shows, for example, that exemplary teachers working in inner-city schools emphasized the appreciation of cultural diversity and enhanced students' self-esteem by providing opportunities for students to relate personal experiences to the content being learned (Cabello & Terrell, 1994).

Planning for *authentic activities* also helps to support real-world connections. Will a student learn more about operating in a democratic society by just reading about democracy or by participating in activities that simulate democratic principles? Will a child learn more about the reason for knowing addition and subtraction facts correctly by doing sheets of problems or by keeping his or her own "checkbook"? Will a student be more motivated to write a "form" friendly letter to be only turned in for a grade or to write a real pen pal on the Internet? Searching for real-life applications will help us to become experts in Competency 8.

All of these areas work with *scaffolding* the information so that students can work upward in their thinking processes from *what they know* to what they *will know*. Bruner's approach to learning states that knowledge is constructed by relating incoming knowledge to a store of knowledge that has already been acquired—or a person's unique model of his or her world. As new information enters, it is categorized based upon what the person already knows (Rosser & Nicholson, 1984). This was also covered in Chapter 1, where children who have attained a category for "a bird" as something with feathers and a beak can easily add a parrot, for example, to the category the first time they see one. If there is no category, there is great difficulty identifying and retaining the new knowledge. Our job as teachers is to try to provide a link to students' known categories so knowledge can be better attained and retained. Much of this can be done in advance if teachers think about ways to scaffold throughout the writing of their plans.

Vygotsky, whom you also learned about earlier, noted that children are not left alone in the world to make discoveries and construct their knowledge—discovery is assisted by social engagement in language with family members, teachers, and peers (Woolfolk, 1998). Indeed, for Vygotsky, language is the most important element in learning, and it occurs between the teacher and the student, the student and his or her peers, and the student and him- or herself. As the child develops, he or she mutters aloud to solve problems, later transitioning to mostly silent, private, inner speech that is still an extremely important part of problem solving (though many people of all ages think aloud in solving problems). Many teachers expect quiet rooms when higher-level thinking and problem solving are in progress, but Vygotsky tells us that cueing or prompting and giving feedback and encouragement by teachers, peers, and even by one's own cognitive self-instruction (talking oneself through a task) are necessary to the process of learning. Plan for talking! As in construction of a building, if the frame of thinking is strongly assembled, students can continue to create solid upper-level thoughts. Brophy (1992) notes that present research is focused on the role of the student. "It recognizes that students do not merely passively receive or copy input from teachers, but instead actively mediate it by trying to make sense of it and to relate it to what they already know (or think they know) about the topic. Thus, students develop new knowledge through a process of active construction" (p. 5). Teachers who put special notations in their lesson plans about how and where they will scaffold, or help students to make these relationships, will aid students in their ability to take the information and go on to higher levels more quickly.

At this point, reviewing Chapter 6 on planning will help to illustrate how these higher-level factors contribute to a valuable plan for students. The lesson plan shown in Figure 8.1 may also act as a guide to show where higher levels of thinking may be incorporated to accomplish teachers' objectives.

STRATEGIES AND MODELS OF TEACHING
THAT INVOLVE HIGHER LEVELS OF THINKING

Instructional Strategies

Another way to bring higher-order and critical thinking into the classroom is through **instructional strategies** and models of teaching. A *strategy* involves selecting a way of instructing that will meet the needs, goals, and objectives of learners. After the teacher has decided what must be taught, the choice of instructional strategies is the "Now, *how* will I teach that?" component. In making choices for "how," we must always remember to keep in mind the reasons behind those choices. The teacher should ask, "*Why* should I teach it that way? What are the strengths of the strategy I am considering and the fit to the content?" And particularly important, "*For whom* am I making these choices today?"

Strategies can be viewed within several different frameworks. For example, there are *teacher-centered strategies* and *learner-centered strategies*. In direct instruction,

---

Lesson Plan Format

Integrated Subjects: Remember that all thematic lessons should include at least three subjects within the same lesson. Select, for example, math, language arts, and music, or science, art, and social studies.

Objectives:

—Should be stated in "Bloom's terms" and should be product and action oriented."

—State "The student or learner will . . . because we want to know exactly *what* the student will be doing in this lesson.

—*Do not* use words such as *TLW (The learner will) learn, TLW understand, TLW appreciate,* and so forth. These concepts cannot be seen (are not observable) or measured, and we must be able to see our objectives and to measure them.

—Low-level only objectives are *not acceptable*. Combine lower and higher objectives.

—Put all objectives in the order in which they will happen in the lesson.

TEKS: What essential knowledge/skills will be included here from Texas lists?

Focus or Set Induction: An event that creates interest and ties into the lesson to be presented.

—Should *entice* students into the lesson (questions *only* for discussion are not usually acceptable unless they are very high-level and will open a broad discussion).

Scaffolding: (Touch on prior or future learning.) How will you tie what students know to what they will learn today?

Touch on Community and Student Interest:

—Where would you find this learning around the student? Begin nearest to student first—in the students' home, then in his or her neighborhood, city, state, and so forth.)

—What does the student like right now? What does the student do in his or her free time? What are favorite hobbies, favorite games, TV shows, movies, songs, stars, etc.?

Rationale: What good reason should a student have for learning this lesson?

—State in *students' terms* (*not* "It's going to be on the TAAS test").

—Answer the question, "Teacher, why do I have to learn this stuff?"

Materials: List everything you need to teach this lesson (*students' needs* and *your list* of things you need for this lesson).

Activities (Instructional Input):   What will you do to get students through the objectives listed?

—List steps *you* will follow, teaching skills and strategies you will use. Identify how you will model what is to be done, monitor, and adjust.

Guided Practice: What will *students* do as you "hold them by the hand" to get them started through the materials to be learned? List the steps: Teacher will. . . .

Independent Practice: What will *students* do all by themselves to exhibit that they have learned the objectives?

What will students do who finish early?   Tell exactly what you want them to do.

FIGURE 8.1 Lesson plan format.

Evaluation: List not only the *activity* you will evaluate, but also ask: "how will I
be able to tell *if* a student "got it" and *how well* he or she "got it"? What
does a student have to do on an activity to get an A, B, C, D, F, or S/U (What is
the criteria)? What are your expectations for the student to achieve the grade
he or she desires? What is passing? How will you grade it? (Tell students the
criteria in advance for objectivity and student success.)

Closure: How will you reinforce what students have learned one last time? (Or,
for mini-closures, how/when will you close on information given throughout
the lesson?)

Modifications for Special Learners:

FIGURE 8.1 continued.

teachers provide and/or explain information, model skills and expectations, and
then give students an opportunity to practice with evaluation and/or feedback.
The learner's role is as the "receiver" of knowledge. The teacher has a very visible
role in teacher-centered strategies. On the other hand, by using a cooperative
learning strategy, students are more active and interactive in their learning.

Strategies can also be defined as deductive or inductive. A **deductive strategy**
begins with "knowns" and moves to conclude with "unknowns," such as in a lecture or in a "direct teach" where the teacher gives definitions or steps for skills and
students follow with guided and independent practice. An **inductive strategy,**
such as an inquiry or a discovery lesson, begins with curious events, scenarios,
"unknowns," or questions and moves to "knowns" or to finding the answers. Such
a strategy is more student-centered; the student actively searches for knowledge.

Strategies can also be classified by grouping. At times, a more fruitful plan is a
lesson that addresses the class as a whole. *Whole-group* or *whole-class* instruction
gives the teacher time to impart information to all members of the class, to have
everyone see a demonstration, or to participate together with all members in a discussion. *Small-group* instruction allows pairs or groups of students to interact more
with each other, to be more active learners, and allows the teacher to supervise more
closely in the role of a facilitator. *Independent instruction* may allow students to work
alone—it may be either completely teacher-directed, or students may choose a
project. Mastery learning, learning centers, and computer-assisted programs are
types of independent instruction.

All strategies can be used—at different times—with consideration for different
learner goals. At times, we need to deliver information in a more direct manner,
while at other times, the goal is to have students think more for themselves, as in
discovery. At another point, we may be more interested in social development
through small-group instruction. A lesson should contain a variety of strategies in
order to provide motivation and to match the goals and objectives that are a part
of the lesson. However, when our goal is higher-level thinking, strategies that
involve *students being the more active thinkers* are desirable. Our job as teachers is thus
to **monitor,** or constantly gain feedback from students as to how their learning is
progressing, and then to make adjustments or changes in our instructional strategies
when needed to help them grow. Monitoring students may be done through

questioning (individually or as a class), by having students give a visual signal such as a "thumbs up," by observing students at work, and so forth. It should be done more during the process than after a product has been completed, though we may also monitor class grades, for example, prior to the six-week examination to determine if our strategies are working. Thus, we may begin with one strategy and discover through monitoring that we must change to another in "midflight" or over a longer time.

Models of Teaching

Models of teaching offer a clear plan for instruction that can help in the goals that teachers select. For each type of strategy, there may be many models. What is a model of teaching? Think of a model simply as an empty building. A building can be filled with many different types of things, as can a model of teaching. The best known of these are probably the many types of models used under the heading of cooperative grouping, such as Jigsaw II, STAD, Numbered Heads, and so forth. A teacher knows that a cooperative grouping model can "be filled" with language arts, science, social studies, mathematics, and other subject areas, just as a building can be filled with apartments, offices, or storage rooms. Besides cooperative models, there are other models of teaching that are "empty buildings" waiting for instruction—many of them offering opportunities for students to work at higher levels of thinking. Each model comes with instructions for the teacher and rules for students to follow during the learning process. A crucial part of each of these models is that, as students complete the model, teachers ask students for reflection on their thinking processes or ask them to use their metacognitive skills to look back on what happened during the learning process. What, for example, led students to come up with answers quickly, or what led them astray? How could the process be better refined next time? Such models and processes are at the evaluative level of thinking.

Inductive Models of Teaching Earlier, deductive and inductive strategies were introduced. Both encompass models of teaching that can help students gain information. In *deductive* lessons, teachers give students background information and then "lead" them to deduce or make conclusions at the end, such as in a lecture. The teacher is the most active player, while students more or less passively listen to receive the information. In *inductive* models, however, students are given pieces of information and must actively form conclusions on their own—or "build their own learning." This is a very *constructivist* notion, where the teacher acts as a guide. A deductive model, such as lecture, often sets the stage, while inductive models take students to much higher levels of thinking. Both deductive and inductive strategies have a place in teaching.

There are some areas to consider with inductive strategies to make sure that they are being used correctly. First, teachers need to be sure that induction is proper for the goals they wish to accomplish. For example, if students have no "tools" on the subject with which to think, they will only be frustrated in trying to determine what the teacher is asking. Student level and student background are important in designing inductive strategies. Next, teachers must be careful to truly act as guides rather than as intellectual manipulators. Some teachers blend into the background during inductive teaching, refusing to help students at all—even during roadblocks. This leaves students lost or completely off track, wasting valuable learning time. The teacher *must* participate, stepping in to help when needed. This will be discussed later in the material on setting up a correct environment for critical thinking.

Concept Attainment Concept attainment (Gunter et al., 1995; Joyce et al., 2000) is an inductive model that is very simple to use and offers students a "gamelike" atmosphere to determine a concept. It can be employed as a wonderful *focus* activity that certainly draws students into the subject matter of the day. It can be used with pre-K through high school, depending on how teachers "fill" the model. As a note, the objective of the lesson should be stated after playing, so that the teacher does not give the concept away. The teacher presents, *one at a time*, examples and nonexamples of the concept either in writing, in pictures, or with concrete items. An important rule for students is *not* to call out an answer that is the *actual concept* during the process of the game. That is left to the end. Instead, during the beginning of the game, students must "test their hypothesis" by suggesting an item as an example or a nonexample, which the teacher then confirms by placing it in the correct category area. The student compares and contrasts each of these examples or nonexamples in an effort to determine the essential attributes that make it belong to the hidden concept.

To show students how this works, the teacher may want to play a simple practice game with a simple concept, listing each word one at a time:

Examples	*Nonexamples*
apple	carrot
pear	rock
orange	
peach (and so forth)	

When asked for examples or nonexamples, students may offer grapes, bananas, and so forth as examples and corn and peas as nonexamples. When most of the class has a good hypothesis of the concept, the teacher switches modes to show an example/nonexample and then asks students to tell in which category it should be placed. When it is obvious that most of the class has a clear idea of the concept, the teacher asks someone to name it (fruit). If the correct answer is given, then more examples are asked for until all possibilities that students know are enhausted. The teacher may also contribute examples to help expand the students' knowledge.

At this point, the teacher will know the entire body of knowledge that the class has on this concept—a valuable piece of knowledge for a teacher! The teacher can then continue the lesson with confidence, rather than wondering about what students know (and which student knows what) and without covering material students have already learned. The class then discusses what attributes make up the concept and sets rules for the concept. Finally, the class discusses strategies that helped in obtaining the concept. This model has been shown not only to help students develop clearer concepts but also to help them retain information. Most importantly, the teacher will have students who are actively involved in thought!

Let us examine a quick "game" at the lower-elementary level using either concrete items or pictures rather than words (though words can be used). First, the teacher presents several examples and nonexamples, separating them from each other. For example, using plastic toys, the teacher might present:

Examples	*Nonexamples*
a horse and buggy	a basket
a dog sled	a telephone
a person on ice skates	a bowl
a hang-glider	a table
a tank	

Students *may not* guess the concept, but they may test their hypothesis by offering an example or a nonexample. For example, the teacher may ask at this point, "Who can give me an example?" Marissa, when called on, offers, "A boat." The teacher immediately adds the boat to the area where "examples" are being placed. If Marissa says, "A glass," the teacher immediately places a glass on the nonexample side. If what is named is not clearly an example or a nonexample, the teacher leaves it in the middle and comes back after the game is over to discuss why it was placed in the middle. The group process can also be used at times in this game. When students appear to be having difficulties "getting" the concept, the teacher can have the class do a few minutes of group discussion to generate ideas.

Students eventually will have a "good guess" as to what the concept is (often evidenced by their excitement). At that point, the teacher switches to the mode of holding up an item or picture and having students tell if it is an example or a nonexample. Then it is put in the correct place under examples or nonexamples.

Item:	*Categories*
a picture of an airplane (or a plastic one)	an example
a picture of a book (or a real one)	a nonexample

After several items have been shown or words/concepts given and students have categorized them correctly, the teacher asks one student or the class as a whole to announce the concept. If the answer is given correctly (transportation), then students are asked to generate other examples, to give attributes of the concept, and to give a definition. Finally, students analyze their thinking strategies to determine what helped them best to understand the concept.

This example game was designed for young children, but it is easy to see that the same process could be modified for students of any age in mathematics or language arts, in high school science areas, or in middle school social studies—in fact, in every subject area and at every grade level. In the middle grades, for example, concepts such as metaphors, similes, and so forth could be used along with very complex concepts. When there are concepts to be learned, this "game" is a way to actively involve students in determining understanding. How much more thinking is done by the student in this game rather than if the teacher just gave students the definition of the concept followed by several examples?

Discovery Lessons Another effective inductive model is **discovery learning.** There are several terms used to refer to some type of discovery. One author, article, or book may use the term *inquiry* or *inductive learning,* while others use *discovery lesson* or *problem solving.* All of these mean that the teacher does not give the information to the student in an explicit way, but instead, students must find out for themselves through active involvement in learning experiences of some type. A discovery lesson may look very much like the one for older elementary children shown in Figure 8.2.

Inquiry Lessons An inquiry model is a very easy and quick way to bring students into higher levels of thinking through guided discovery. Many of us remember playing the game "Twenty Questions" as a child because it was so mentally stimulating. One such inquiry model, developed by Richard Suchman (1962), has the teacher select a puzzling situation. Again, because it is an instructional model, it can be used for any subject area or grade level. Extremely student-active, this model teaches problem solving through discovery and questioning. A teacher could use this model in many ways: as a focus activity to draw students into the concept of the day, as an activity that may take a good portion of the class period, or as a closure to apply the concept of the day to a real situation or bridge into the next session.

After presenting a situation or an experimental phenomenon in an inquiry, the teacher then allows students to gather information about the answer by asking questions that can be answered by a *yes* or *no* only. The burden is on the student to formulate questions that will gain information leading to the answer. This is a fine time to teach students how to ask "umbrella" questions that help them quickly narrow to the answer rather than taking "pot-shot" guesses (putting forth one guess or hypothesis after another). Look at the difference in thought processes if we were to say, "I'm thinking of a vegetable," and students responded with the following sequences of questions.

Pot-Shot Questions	*Umbrella Questions*
Is it a potato?	Does the part we eat grow above the ground?
Is it an onion?	Is it round?
Is it a carrot?	Is it green?
Is it a beet?	Do we eat it cooked only?
Is it beans?	

The umbrella questions indicate a much higher level of thinking than does the "pot-shot" approach. As the process goes along, the teacher is allowed to "feed"

A Discovery Lesson

Integrated Subjects: Science, history, language arts

Objectives: In groups, students will (A) predict orally and (b) discover: (1) how much weight it takes to sink a vessel, through an experiment in tanks of water in which they place weights in a vessel until it sinks, and (2) how dispersing weight can affect the vessel in "rough seas," by moving the weights around in the vessel and then stirring the water.

Each student will write the results of the experiments in complete sentences.

Students will listen to a historical story.

Focus or Set Induction: Students will participate in predicting "formulas" for the experiments.

Scaffolding: Students will be reminded of the cause-and-effect paragraphs they wrote last week in language arts. They will be asked to try to determine how this experiment might relate to cause-and-effect. Through questioning, they will also be reminded of the filmstrip they watched yesterday in science about the scientific expedition that discovered the Titanic below the ocean. The class will discuss what they already know about weight and about boat design.

Touch on Community and Student Interest and Rationale: Remind students that Texas has some major ports in the United States where ships of many kinds bring goods to us from around the world. Both Houston and Corpus Christi are large port cities. There are even large cruise ships, such as the Titanic, that sail from Houston.

There are many jobs in Texas that people do both on land and on the sea with regard to these ports and ships. One of those is ship/boat safety. Most students will go out on some type of boat or ship. Science helps us to know about ship safety. It is important to know about this concept in order to protect yourself in a ship or boat.

Materials:

Teacher: Water tanks, play boats, weights, experiment form, group role cards. Students: Paper and pencil

Activities:

Guided Practice:

Teacher will ask students to predict the results of experiments.

Teacher will divide the class into groups and assign roles.

Teacher will give experiment rules and demonstrate.

Teacher will do one example together with students and fill out one area of experimental form as an example.

Teacher will read a story about the Titanic survivors in lifeboats after the sinking of the Titanic.

Independent Practice: Students will individually complete a short paragraph on the results of their experiment in at least four complete sentences.

What will students do who finish early? Students will go to the class library and take out a book on the Titanic.

Evaluation:

Participation: Students must participate in their group by fulfilling the jobs that come with their roles (group points).

Group: Groups must complete their experiment form together as a group, and each student must sign it (group points).

Individual: Each student must complete a short paragraph of at least four sentences stating the results of the experiments.

FIGURE 8.2 A discovery lesson.

A = Student has at least four sentences that are complete and states results correctly.

B = Student has three sentences with results or four sentences with slightly less clear results.

C = Student has two sentences with results or three to four sentences with unclear results.

D = Student makes an attempt.

F = Student does not make any attempt.

Closure: The teacher will ask questions that determine how well students were able to understand the material, for example: How much did each small weight actually weigh? How many did it take to sink your boat? What was the least safe way to arrange your weights in "rough seas"? Why? What was the safest way to arrange for high seas? Why? Why is this concept important? Who are some of the people whose lives may depend on this concept? What important cause-and-effect relationship have you discovered today that relates to boating disasters?

Modification for Special Learners: A = Two sentences, etc.

FIGURE 8.2 continued

whatever information is necessary to have students stay with the "game." In addition, students may ask or be directed to caucus or talk together in small groups about what they know or need to know, before returning to the inquiry. After students develop and test their hypothesis through the question-answer inquiry, rules can be developed that explain the theory. Finally, they may analyze the process and evaluate the results of participation.

For very young children, the inquiry may be very simple, such as the one just illustrated, or it may be presented through the use of the *mystery box*. This box can be a simple box (or even a sack) containing an item that is held by the teacher during the process of inquiry. We ask students to see if they can guess what is inside (remembering again to teach "umbrella" questions). There are other ways to use this concept. In the case of a "feelie box," a hole is cut in both ends, and tube socks (the toe is cut out) are attached. The top of the box is held down with a jumbo rubber band. Students put their hands through the tube socks so they are only able to feel (and not see) a concrete item. This adds a kinesthetic sensory input. For example, a teacher may begin a unit on birds. In each of several boxes, the teacher places an item that is connected with birds (a feather, a small nest, an egg, and so forth). Boxes are then rotated among students' tables, and questions are asked for a focus discovery on the topic of the day. For older students, the inquiry may still use a box (for example, to deal with metaphors on textures or for the introduction of various rocks, such as those with glassy surfaces, large crystals, sandy, etc.

In science classes, inquiry is most often seen when teachers show the class an experiment that seems amazing in some way to the particular age of student. Making clouds or rain or collapsing a can after heating/cooling are typical examples in elementary schools. This triggers the curiosity of students, increasing the chances that they will engage in finding out "why" through experimentation and questioning.

Inquiry can be more complicated, involve much more information, and use a step-built-upon-step process. For example, the teacher may introduce the interaction of engineering and science through a questioning inquiry dealing with difficulties of extracting oil. The inquiry could begin with, "In one rich oil field, the weather is so harsh that lives are often lost and the environment is often damaged with conventional rigs. Scientists and engineers began to try to solve this problem. How were they able to do this?" First, students would have to determine *where* this event took place by, again, asking *yes* or *no* questions *only* (in the North Sea). Students would then ascertain what (a solid structure the size of the Empire State Building), and how (built in a deep fjord and towed to the oil field). The inventions by students that come from this process are usually wonderfully creative (submarine rigs, flexible rigs, balloons, barge-type structures that leave with bad weather, and so forth).

History is rich with ideas for discovery/inquiry, too. For example, a teacher may want to introduce the study of Egyptian religion with an interesting focus inquiry. Following the focus activity, the teacher would continue with all the remaining parts of the lesson plan. Again, the answer to the inquiry would be developed by the class asking questions that could be answered only with *yes* or *no*. During the process, when we see that students may need more help, we direct students to use their groups to see what we have already discovered and to generate some more questions. After a few minutes, we would return to the whole-class format. This may be done several times during the process, depending on the length of time we wish the class to spend on this activity. An example of such a focus inquiry is:

> A city in Egypt was besieged by Persians. Though the city had enough water and food to last for a long time, the people threw open their city gates and surrendered. Why would they have done that? (The Persians were lobbing cats over the walls of the city, and the Egyptians, who believed cats were gods, could not stand the sacrilege.)

Beginning *yes* or *no* questions from students might be: Were they ill? Were they tricked into opening the gates somehow? The teacher should support students' ideas with encouraging remarks such as, "That is a good thought because history shows that in a siege, that is often the case."

Also, an artifact (either real or a picture) might be introduced: To whom did this shoe (pen, book, tool, or whatever) belong? How would we know? Why would it be important? What would it tell us about a particular person, author, poet, civilization, and so on?

Mathematics, reading, and health also are rich in areas that can offer puzzling situations. Inquiring minds want to know! What could be more exciting than watching a scientific experiment in front of your eyes with a puzzling outcome or being presented with an age-old question about an archeological mystery? Rather than being told all about it, students unravel what is known in the scientific exploratory tradition. At times, there is not an answer to a real-world problem or situation, so students have the opportunity to hypothesize with current knowledge and the latest theories. This entire process is one in which students shift from extrinsic to intrinsic rewards of learning (Gunter et al., 1995). It is the same concept that kept the television series *Unsolved Mysteries* in reruns for many years—people are caught up in wanting to know, and they love the process of trying to attain the answer or solve the mystery. This sort of inquiry definitely involves a higher-level thinking process!

Cooperative Models Cooperative learning has been highly recommended to teachers for many reasons. One is that grouping really aids in developing thinking skills. Many cooperative groupings that are more teacher-directed models are discussed in another chapter. However, several **cooperative learning** models that involve students working at higher levels of thinking will be discussed here. The most student-centered of these models is known as the *group investigation* process.

Sharan and Shacher (1988) found that in group investigation, disadvantaged students, as well as nondisadvantaged students, achieved academic gains over twice those in whole-class methods. In this model, originally formulated by John Dewey, problem-solving groups are organized to take on a set of inquiries. Acting as a "mini-society," students identify related problems, analyze what is needed to solve these problems, identify and fill the roles needed for solving these problems, then act, and finally, evaluate their progress toward solutions. Negotiations used in a real democratic society are extremely important to this process. One result of students who are working together to actively participate in meaningful learning is that the teacher moves from a disseminator of information to that of a learner and a facilitator of learning (Brodhagen, 1995). When students are working and learning on their own, the teacher in the role of a facilitator and coach aids students only when they need help rather than controlling each part of the learning process.

Jigsaw II is another way of grouping students that *can* lead to higher levels of thinking. Students are placed in an original or core group. From there, each member goes away to become a member of a second "expert" group. In the expert groups, all the new group members concentrate only on a part of the whole assignment task, literally becoming experts on their piece of the "jigsaw puzzle." Their task is to learn the material, design new ways to creatively help the rest of their groups learn and remember the material, then return to provide their original group with their piece of information or new skill(s). Each member of the group cannot be successful unless all are, as no one member of the core group has all the pieces.

It is apparent that this model *could* be very teacher-directed with little high-level thinking. Let us look at a way, however, that teachers can use it at the synthesis and evaluative levels. In a classroom of 24 students, there may be 6 core groups of 4 students each. Each table numbers off, and all the "ones" reposition to one table together, the "twos" to another table, the "threes" to a third table, and the "fours" to still another area. If, for example, the topic was "The Rain Forest," the new "ones" grouped at their expert table might concentrate on learning about the animals of the rain forest, while the other tables might be assigned topics such as the destruction of the rain forest, the makeup of the rain forest, and the environmental effect of the rain forest. The teacher would help facilitate this by being sure that each group judges or determines the most valuable main points given in the information, formulates a creative way to teach the information to others, and designs a visual or other method(s) to aid this effort. All experts would then return to their original core group, and in an orderly manner, each expert would give a presentation based on knowledge gained from the expert group.

Think-pair-share and other types of small-group discussion models give students an opportunity to generate their own thoughts as the teacher poses a divergent or open-ended question. Students are given a moment of silence to think about their opinion, and then they are directed to share their interpretations with another or others in a group. Often, they go to evaluative levels of conversation almost immediately.

TEACHER ROLES

When investigating strategies for students to use in creative thinking areas, we usually ask students to become explorers, authors, designers, teachers, and performers as they *produce* knowledge. This often requires teachers to change their roles rather than remain as the direct instruction leader or "the sage on the stage" who only delivers information. This role has a place in lessons, but there are other teaching roles that help students become more active as thinkers. During the authoring or designing process, teachers often move into **facilitator roles,** providing opportunities for students to work collaboratively and helping when there are questions or stumbling blocks in a rich learning environment. Facilitators lead rather than direct and tell, often using an exploratory approach where students make decisions in their learning (Fradd & Lee, 1999). Teachers would move into the role of **audience,** however, as a product is completed, then shown, explained, or performed. For example, if a student created a book report that is a "news flash" and recorded it on videotape for viewing by the class, the student would be involved in a higher-level synthesis activity, and the teacher would first be a facilitator during the process, then later an audience member. The teacher-as-audience role also would come after the teacher had a group write a skit on the progression of food through the digestive system. As the group performed that skit, the teacher would be an audience member, rather than giving a lecture on the process. We also see this trend during a lesson on why geometry works in bracing construction, as students are given materials such as straws and tape to see which group can create the highest structure that will stand on its own. First, groups or individuals are facilitated during the construction, then watched (audience role) as students explain their structures and rationales for their buildings to the class. A **guide's role** comes in mediating and adjusting to help students obtain information (such as in Suchman's inquiry), while also

deling. A teacher's **coaching role,** very closely related to the
ves giving immediate feedback and encouragement to students
skills.

g any one of these models as a part of a lesson, we can ensure that
thinking at upper levels. There are many more instructional models
g that involve higher levels of thinking: concept development, other
s of cooperative groupings, conflict resolution models, synectics, class-
.iscussion models, and so forth. Two texts that explain these very well are
s of *Teaching* (Joyce & Weil, 2000) and *Instruction: A Models Approach* (Gunter
e. d., 1995). Kagan's *Cooperative Learning* (1992) also explains cooperative grouping in detail.

Sometimes local universities teach courses in models of teaching. Such courses
would be a wonderful professional development activity in which to enroll. Most
teachers who have taken such courses feel that these are some of the most valuable
courses in education for boosting their students' thinking.

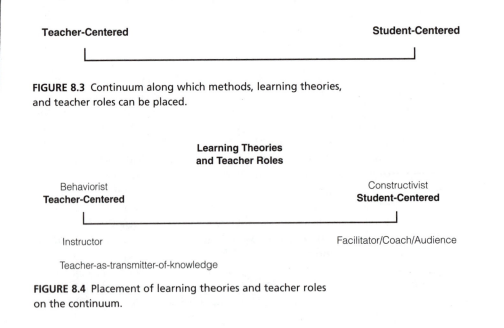

LEARNER-CENTERED VERSUS
TEACHER-CENTERED INSTRUCTION

To gain more perspective on how Texas would like to see teachers teach, it may
be helpful to think about models and other methods, learning theories, and
teacher roles in terms of their teacher-centeredness or learner-centeredness. For
example, if we construct a continuum like the one in Figure 8.3, where would the

Teacher-Centered   **Student-Centered**

FIGURE 8.3 Continuum along which methods, learning theories,
and teacher roles can be placed.

**Learning Theories
and Teacher Roles**

Behaviorist   Constructivist
Teacher-Centered   **Student-Centered**

Instructor   Facilitator/Coach/Audience

Teacher-as-transmitter-of-knowledge

FIGURE 8.4 Placement of learning theories and teacher roles
on the continuum.

teacher role of facilitator and that of coach be placed? Where would bel constructivist learning theories be placed? Would group investigation teacher-as-the-center-of-action or student-centered? What about course, there are no clear-cut points in the placement of these con continuum. However, most educators would place the learning theor teacher roles in the fashion shown in Figure 8.4.

The placement of models on such a continuum is more diffict each model can be modified, thus moving it to one side or the other. For example, although most educators would agree that lecture fits best on the teacher-centered side of the continuum, there are some lectures that are more student-centered, such as an interactive lecture, and some that are more teacher-centered, like the "talking-head" model. Along the same lines, cooperative learning, in general, would fit more toward student-centered, but STAD (Student Team Achievement Divisions, where individuals' test scores, homework, etc., are combined for a group score and then placed in running competition among groups) is more teacher-centered than is group investigation. Likewise, inquiry can be open (more student-centered) or guided (more teacher-centered). Any model can be implemented in a more teacher-centered or more student-centered way. Yet, taking that into account, one way to place the models would be in the fashion illustrated in Figure 8.5. Readers should consider whether they agree with this arrangement.

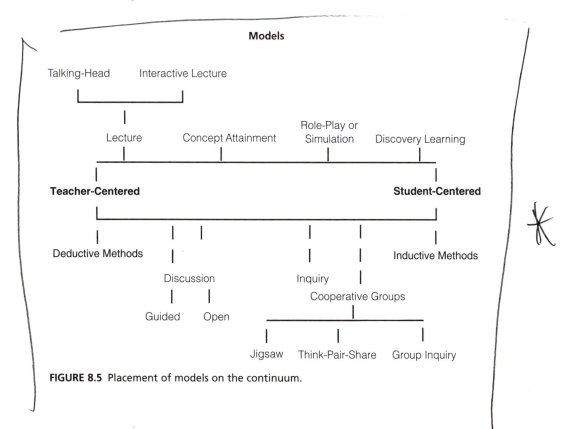

FIGURE 8.5 Placement of models on the continuum.

Table 8.2 Advantages and Limitations of Various Models

Model	Advantages	Limitations
Cooperative Learning in General	Synergy generates more intrinsic motivation. Members learn from each other. Interacting produces cognitive and social complexity and increases intellectual activity. Increases positive feelings, reduces alienation and loneliness, builds relationships, and provides affirmative views from others. Increases self-esteem. Builds "working together" skills the more it is done. Provides support for mainstreamed students or lower achievers. Allows the teacher to become a facilitator. Fits cultural styles of some groups. Increases efficiency in positive interdependence. Increases academic achievement (except with the top 5 percent of students—the very gifted).	Takes strict organization to work well (teacher cannot expect results by saying, "Get in a group and work together"). Using 100 percent of the time does; not allow for other individual learning styles.
Group Investigation	Very student-centered. Provides an experience-based learning situation. Teaches democratic procedures by simulating an ideal society. Teaches scientific methods of inquiry. Extremely constructivist. Positive effects on student learning in all domains. Inquiry is higher-level thinking. Effective group process and governance. Teaches respect for all through negotiated rules and policies. Teacher functions as facilitator and academic counselor.	Teacher must have a high level of interpersonal and instructional skills and must be flexible. Cumbersome and slow. Schools are organized to support basic instruction in academic subjects and are unwilling to change format. (Dewey suggests that the entire school should be organized for group investigation.) This also requires a great amount of resource support. Models based on the democratic process assume outcomes of any educational experience are unpredictable.
Jigsaw II	Students teach students—very student-active. Can involve much creativity. Teaches a great amount of interdependence.	Can be completely teacher directed and involve little creativity.

Model	Advantages	Limitations
Concept Attainment	Higher-level thinking and inductive reasoning activity.	Teacher must thoroughly prepare with clear categories.
	Can combine individual and group thinking.	
	Helps students in concept-building strategies.	Teacher must set rules of game carefully and maintain those rules.
	Increases awareness of alternative perspectives.	Can be frustrating at first for students who have no training in this type of thinking.
	Can be an engaging focus for the "concept of the day."	
	Active thinking.	
Inquiry/ Discovery	Develops independent learners who can problem-solve.	Teacher must be supportive to all students' ideas.
	Builds the idea that all knowledge is changing.	Can be time-consuming.
		May be completely teacher-directed.
	Builds the idea that views of others can enrich our own thinking, and knowledge is facilitated by help and ideas of colleagues.	Students may be frustrated at first who have no training in this type of thinking.
	Natural inquiry occurs when students are puzzled, so intrinsic motivation to learn is more likely.	Teachers must learn to be active listeners and directors of questioning.
	Mimics real-life scientific inquiry.	
	Creativity is often generated.	
	Students learn questioning strategies and use scientific language of inquiry.	
	New thinking strategies can be built, analyzed, and taught.	
Interdisciplinary Learning	Students learn that knowledge is interconnected rather than isolated in the real world.	Teacher must struggle at times to make connections.
	Students become "experts" on concepts.	Planning takes time, especially in a departmentalized school.
	Students see teacher colleagues working as a team.	
	Thematic units are often more motivating to students.	

The importance of understanding this for the ExCET is that Texas believes that learning should be mostly student-centered and constructivist—that is, students should be active learners rather than just passive listeners most of the time in the classrooms. The chart shown in Table 8.2 lists the advantages and limitations of each of the models.

ASKING QUESTIONS AT HIGHER LEVELS
OF THINKING

Unfortunately, research shows that most teachers ask a high percentage of knowledge-level and comprehension-level questions. Why? Three reasons are that (1) higher-level questions are harder to think of while standing on one's feet in the classroom; (2) teachers do not plan for them or write them ahead of time when preparing lesson plans; and (3) they take more time for students to answer. There is knowledge, preparation, and skill required for this area of teaching.

Some educators classify questioning into two categories: **convergent questions** and **divergent questions**, which are easy to remember by thinking in terms of what *converge* and *diverge* mean. *Converge* means that all answers must come together—in other words, there is only *one* response or one type of response, and that narrow response can be anticipated. This one true and correct answer can be memorized and recalled. *Diverge,* however, means to go away from or push apart—the responses can take many different directions or broader ways; these answers are open-ended. Among the latter type of responses are opinions, hypotheses, and evaluations—all of which require higher-level thinking. With divergent questioning, a student's answer cannot be anticipated because the student takes factual information and makes it his or her own in some manner. There is another type of question that is divergent in nature—the productive question (Moore, 1998). These questions have unpredictable answers that students create or produce imaginatively; in other words, the students synthesize their own unique answer.

Scaffolding and sequencing have much to do with a plan of questioning. If we lay a solid foundation of convergent, knowledge-level questions, then the student is better able to move into divergent questioning. In other words, if a teacher is able to move from lower-level Bloom's taxonomy knowledge through several levels to evaluation, the student will have an easier time answering those questions at higher levels because the language and tools needed for application will be in place.

How should teachers prepare for higher-order questions? First, teachers should prepare questions in advance—writing them into the lesson plans will guarantee that the teacher has thoughtfully worded them. The teacher should note whether the questions match the lesson objectives. In a more constructivist manner, teachers can plan to have students write their own questions at different levels, particularly at interpretative (opinion) and evaluative (judgment) levels, for classroom discussion.

Questioning at higher levels can be used in sections of the lesson plan. For part of a focus, for example, an engaging higher-level question can draw students into the lesson to come. For example, "What will happen to Africa if a cure for AIDS cannot be found?" might open a health class, or a question like "What do you think will happen when I put this balloon over heat and this one over ice?" might open a science class. In a literature class, the teacher might ask, "The Shelleys and Lord Byron all decided to write the same type of story before they retired one stormy night after discussing Darwin's theories. The result was one of the most famous novels in history, due to dreams that kept the author awake. What novel do you think was the result of this night?" (The answer is *Frankenstein*.) For closure, a teacher might also ask students a higher-level question to generate dialog over the lesson at the end.

A RISK-FREE ENVIRONMENT
FOR CRITICAL THINKING

Have you ever offered a "far-out" creative idea in a group or class and had it scoffed at, or have you intrinsically known that a teacher thought your answer was really "weird"? How many additional responses did you offer in that situation? The answer is probably, "None!" The importance of an open environment is crucial for critical thinking. The teacher—the most visible person in the room, the one who controls the rewards in the classroom, and the person who is seen as the learned person—is a model for acceptance of divergent thinking.

"Learning is enhanced by challenge and inhibited by threat," emphasize Gunter et al. (1995, p. 9), explaining that challenge can always be seen as a risk to one's self-esteem or success. When faced with new learning, mistakes usually occur. Teachers can set the stage for a learner to "take a chance" or not. In what ways can a teacher do this? First, teachers should *model respect* for the answers of *all* students (unless, of course, the answers are inappropriate in language or subject matter, or students are attemping to create management problems). Students are able to understand intuitively if the **environment** is **risk-free** and open, or if the teacher will threaten them in some way for their responses. The teacher's tone of voice or the way a question is "pressured" on to students can intimidate them, especially in critical thinking. No one wants to look or feel like he or she is less than bright in front of peers—students are no exception. Encouraging students' questions (not just their answers) in an open manner also increases the atmosphere of openness for thinking. Formative support should be given often during the process of critical thinking rather than always formative grades, and credit for effort during the process will also help to demonstrate to students that teachers are interested in the learning and thinking process. Using encouragement for improvement rather than just rewarding a correct answer or giving a high grade helps promote cooperation (rather than competition), and students will take more of a chance in learning.

Using *teachable moments* also indicates respect for students' thoughts. A teachable moment occurs when a student veers from the lesson plan with a thought or question that, though not on the topic, is truly valuable for all students—and the teacher follows. The teacher leaves his or her plan and directs the lesson to the thought introduced by the student, returning to the plan when appropriate. Many times it is in teachable moments that higher-level thinking is generated because the information is of so much interest to students—they, not the teacher, raised the question.

In asking questions, an open environment is one in which questions, particularly higher-level questions, are never used to embarrass a student. Questions should not be asked prior to the teacher having taught enough for students to be able to respond. **Wait time** and *really* listening to the answers also have much to do with the environment. Giving three to five seconds of silence after a question is asked increases the chances that more students will volunteer and that the same students do not always answer. Answers will also be more thoughtful. If this is hard for a teacher, he or she can ask a question and walk to another spot in the room before taking an answer. **Halt time** is another important strategy—that is, stopping the forward motion of the lesson to give students time to digest the material (Moore, 1998). This period follows a time when students have been heavily engaged in complex material. The teacher simply pauses for a time, so the class has a moment to collect and reflect on that material without pushing forward. We might compare this to an intense physical workout where we stop for a moment to "shake it out." Students need time to mentally "shake it out" when the concepts are difficult and at higher levels.

Another important environmental area in higher-level thinking is listening and *reacting to students' responses*. How the teacher reacts shows value for students' thoughts. By repeating the main points of a student's answer, the teacher lets the student know that the teacher is listening well. Unfortunately, most students have already been trained to expect that teachers want a quick answer, so training ourselves and students to react to longer, higher-level questions and their answers may take some time. Students of all ages sense when teachers are trying to rush through a questioning session. Nonverbal teacher behavior is important in critical thinking questions, as students may sense when teachers are impatient for students to finish so the discussion can move on. Teachers must be careful not to exhibit "impatient" body language that tells the student clearly to "hurry up and think and then get finished." Students also sense when teachers consider their own opinions to be much more important and are not particularly interested in what they have to say; they know when teachers are manipulating them into the "correct" answer. For example, particularly in divergent questioning, teachers may have a tendency to say, "Yes, but. . . ." This tends to stop further divergence.

Authentically rewarding students for thoughtful answers increases the chances they will try again. Praise words such as "Good," or "Great answer," may not spur students on. Phrases such as, "Your answer was so thoughtful. It really has added another dimension to this topic," "I'm impressed with the depth of your answer," or "Wow! Look how this relates back to what Raul answered earlier. You are really making some great connections here," will be much more meaningful. Critique is also important in helping students reach higher levels. Studies show that teachers do not give enough effective criticism of answers. Specific feedback allows students to reach the teacher's expectations much more closely. For example, a teacher might say (or write a comment) to a student that, "If you will go back and look at your second argument more closely, I think your proposal would then have clear merit," or "You have done some exceptional thinking in this paragraph. Your ideas are crystal clear!" This is much more specific than, "Good" or, worse still, just putting a grade on a paper with no feedback.

Probing is another way to increase levels of questioning and can be seen as a reward for many students, as the teacher is "staying with" their ideas. Probing questions follow a student's response by asking that student to think more deeply and thoroughly about what he or she just said. However, teachers should be careful to do this equally with students rather than just one or two of the "smarter" ones. If a teacher continuously interacts orally with only a few (even though at higher levels), the rest of the class loses interest. Rewarding students for higher-level thinking is critically important. Students are rarely spurred to think when there seems to be no challenge or encouragement for their ideas.

Even *management* sets the stage for higher-level thinking in several ways. First, if the teacher is a model listener and requires the class be quiet to hear an answer, students will vicariously see that their answers, when called on, will be important also. Teachers must be careful to make sure that students with soft voices are still heard when they are answering. In contrast, in recognizing that talking all at once in group work is often part of the process, teachers' management techniques must change to ask students to talk in "six-inch voices" (rather than "twelve-inch voices") so that neighboring classes are not disturbed, *but talk is allowed*. With students whose home language is not English, it is important to remember that they may gain much more during this process by speaking in their native language.

Modeling a think-aloud process for students is also an effective strategy for cueing students on divergent thinking. For example, there are many times teachers could give a simple knowledge answer to student questions. "Why is there so much air pollution here, teacher?" asks one student. The teacher could answer with a quick reply like, "Because it's expensive to have antipollution equipment." But a teacher interested in modeling deeper intellectual thinking might show his or her thought processes by responding with the following: "I've often thought of that same question, Keisha, when I'm driving downtown. It seems like I can almost taste pollution in the air. I ask myself, what are all these people doing on this freeway in their own cars? They are all going to work at different places, and each car is using gas and putting emissions into the air, which means that we need lots of refineries. Sometimes I see those refineries that provide us with gas and oil for our cars putting smoke into the air, too. Why don't they fix this? Well, one answer might be a mass transit system. Oh, but what would be the cost of having trains or monorails all though the city? Very high . . . and the same for installing pollution prevention on factories . . . very expensive. We will always need to work to make money, and cities offer jobs for so many people, so I suppose that the answer to part of your question is expense. Can you think of other reasons?"

Equity issues associated with Competency 3 can also be linked with higher-level questioning. For example, teacher-questioning behaviors that are associated with low-achieving students have been identified. These are: asking low achievers lower-level questions most of the time or exclusively; giving them less wait time and eye contact; assessing their answers and work differently; and interacting with them less overall. Langer et al. (1990) found that cultural minorities often lost confidence in the fast-paced, convergent question-and-answer sessions that teachers often employ, while divergent, or open-ended, questions encouraged confidence. However, a teacher must be careful to provide nonnative English-speaking students with enough support for them to be able to understand the question or engage in a strategy and to answer (Fradd & Lee, 1999). In other words, building up to these type questions and strategies is a need. For all students, divergent questions are much more likely to captivate interest for participation. It has also been found that teachers often ask boys rather than girls questions that call for more complex, abstract, higher-level thinking, and boys' responses most often receive the teacher's active attention. In addition, teachers may only engage a *few* of their top students academically in higher levels of activity. Teachers may need to go so far as to keep a note card, marking off names of students as they answer high-level questions. Another strategy is to have a mental grid of the classroom and to direct high-level questions to seat numbers to make sure all students are covered.

Teachers' expectations about students' responses have much to do with student responses. If the teacher sets expectations for careful, thoughtful answers for *all* students, then the likelihood of that happening increases. *Failing at Fairness* (Sadker & Sadker, 1994) addresses many of these issues in depth. If a teacher expects all students to be able to deal with higher levels of thinking and uses strategies for making sure that the entire class participates in questioning at higher levels, then the whole class becomes engaged. Thus, setting an environment where high expectations are the norm will most likely produce high achievement in thinking.

LINKING HIGHER-LEVEL THINKING
TO ASSESSMENT

Higher-level thinking can also touch on assessment. Teachers can design assessment instruments to be at thoughtful, higher levels or simply at the recall/knowledge level. Tests that offer only knowledge- or application-level, fill-in-the-blank, short-answer, true-or-false, or lower-level matching questions do not stretch students into deeper thinking. Though essay questions are time-consuming to grade, they do offer the student an opportunity to think at higher levels. Careful construction of multiple-choice can provide higher levels of thought as well, while student portfolios offer a chance for students to engage in evaluative thinking, as they must critically judge which works they will retain in the portfolio and why. In terms of observation, teachers' rubrics for grading can include areas noted for higher levels of student thinking. Authentic assessment, where students simulate a more real-world scenario, is a place where students also can be assessed for using more logic and creativity. Linking higher-level strategies with lower-level assessment is not an effective or fair measurement for student abilities. Teachers should try to make this connection during lesson planning. Chapter 10 discusses assessment in more detail.

THE LANGUAGE OF THINKING

Using the language of thinking is also an important part of setting the stage for critical thinking. "Just as the colors on an artist's palette influence the painting that emerges, the words we have available to us influence the way we think about the world, including the inner world of our own mental life," state Tishman and Perkins (1997, p. 371). If metacognition is "thinking about thinking," then the vocabulary of *thinking words* is the tool that guides, assesses, and evaluates the process. This language, according to Tishman and Perkins, creates a disposition or an invitation for thinking in a certain way.

Many teachers ask students generic "think" questions but do not use specific terminology to help students process more. By using the language of thinking, teachers can extend and guide the thought processes and theory building of students. For example, a teacher might ask, "Do you think there was a conspiracy in the assassination of President Kennedy?" One student might answer, "No"; then the teacher might turn to another student and ask, "How about you, Yi-Ling?" However, by using the language of thinking, the teacher could deepen the thought process for the students. Examine how the teacher uses that language in the following scenario (noting words in italics):

Teacher: Does anyone have a *theory* on the conspiracy to assassinate President Kennedy?

Student: I really think that Cuba was behind it.

Teacher: What reasons do you have for thinking that? Is there any *evidence* to support that?

Student: Well, President Kennedy was involved with the Bay of Pigs and the Cuban missile crisis.

Teacher: Can you tie any other *evidence* to that *theory?*

Student: Well, I know that Cuba and the USSR were tight, and Lee Harvey Oswald had been to the USSR. They might have recruited him there.

Teacher: That's an interesting *theory.* What would you need to know to *prove your hypothesis?*

Student: Well, now that the USSR is opening up all its old records, it would be interesting to see if there are any records of Lee Harvey Oswald being in the USSR at the same time that Cuban officials like Castro were there, and if there were any records of meetings.

Teacher: That would certainly strengthen your *theory,* wouldn't it? Does anyone else have another *theory?*

Note how the teacher's use of the language of thinking in this dialog increased the likelihood that students will go deeper in their thought processes.

SUMMARY

In this chapter, we have looked carefully at the emphasis on higher-level thinking skills (analysis, synthesis, and evaluation) and examined a variety of ways to incorporate those into our teaching. Educational researchers (Eggen & Kauchak, 1996) continue to recommend that practicing thinking skills is extremely important for internalization. Rather than being considered as a separate skill ("It's time for critical thinking now, class!"), these skills should be *integrated* into the curriculum often. That way, students are practicing with all subject areas at the same time. Competency 8 also reminds us to think of authentic situations in teaching and relate our lessons to the real world. Only then will students understand the relevancy of subjects to real life. In addition, we need to vary our own roles in the classroom as we monitor and adjust our instruction to student needs.

Four areas in this chapter have been examined closely in helping us to become more adept at teaching higher-level thinking: lesson plan design, selection of various strategies and models of instruction, direct questioning techniques, and creation of an accepting environment for taking risks in learning. By reviewing Bloom's taxonomy in terms of inclusion of higher-level thinking each time we design instruction, we can ensure that students will be able to face the world ready to evaluate situations, solve problems, and become creative members of society by the time they leave school.

Competency 8 asks us to embrace the philosophy of teaching thinking and to apply it often in our classrooms. One reason teaching is such an engaging profession is that *we* as teachers do so much higher-level thinking each day as we go about designing creative lessons, solving problems, and evaluating many areas of our practice. Our students deserve the same stimulating situations.

SUGGESTED ACTIVITIES

Process/Data Collection

1. Observe how often cooperating/mentor teachers use higher-level questioning, and document what type of children (high achievers, low achievers, ethnicities, genders) receive high- and low-level questions.

2. Collect lesson plans and methods that have various higher level activities embedded within them.

3. Find an Internet site that focuses on higher-level skills.

Application

1. Design lesson plans that include:
   - Rationales for the "real world"
   - Questions at higher levels that are likely to appear as a natural flow of the lesson
   - Activities using various models of teaching that encourage critical thinking
   - Touching upon the community and interests of the student

2. Generate a list of 50 real-world uses for mathematics, language arts, social studies, and so forth.

3. Tape a lesson that you teach and mark how many higher-level questions you asked, noting also the frequency in levels of achievers, genders, and ethnicities.

Reflection

1. Examine the teachers' editions of your students' textbooks and note the percentages of lower- and higher-level questions. Evaluate the questions that you find for relevance. What does that mean to you as a new teacher?

2. Reflect on strategies you plan to use to increase the amount of higher-level questions that you will ask.

PRACTICE DECISION SET

1. Mr. Farran teaches in an urban Texas school. Most of his students are on free lunch. The parents of his students are not well educated; in fact, some are illiterate. Mr. Farran opens his class each day by having his students read a short story. Today, for example, the story focused on a neighborhood setting in which two Texas students live near their grandparents, who live right across the border in Mexico. Then, as the class sits casually in a circle, Mr. Farran asks questions such as the following: Can you tell me . . .

   > Who are the main characters in this story?
   >
   > Where did the story take place?
   >
   > When did the story take place?
   >
   > What happened first?
   >
   > What happened last?

   Mr. Farran's principal overheard a couple of these opening lessons while walking through the classroom and was dismayed because:
   a. The questions were always the same.
   b. The principal was worried that students were not at their desks.
   c. All the questions were at low levels of thinking.
   d. The students could not answer the questions.

2. In order to include some interdisciplinary areas, Mr. Farran decides to add some mathematics and social studies into the story. "Let's say you are going to drive from where this story takes place to Illinois for a vacation. How long do think it will take you to get there?" However, this focus question does not motivate his students, and several become distracted and inattentive as he tries to get answers. If you were to advise Mr. Farran, you might tell him that:
   a. Map skills are not an appropriate area for inner-city students.
   b. It is important to take into account the background of the students to make instruction relevant.
   c. He should not worry about it; he did fine. These kids often do not pay attention.
   d. In order to motivate these students, he should give one of the disruptive students detention to show the class he means business.

3. In today's story, the grandparents have no electricity. Mr. Farran continues to integrate his lessons today with the story, so in science class, he has students work together to discover concepts about electrical current. He does very little talking

and has groups work through the project on their own in discovery, as he walks around the room, smoothing out a few small problems here and there. His main role in this lesson as a teacher is:

a. Instructor
b. Facilitator
c. Coach
d. Audience

Answer 1: The questions that Mr. Farran asked are always opening questions for a reading assignment, which are important for students to know. It would only be a personal preference if students were not in their chairs for reading. Many teachers in all grade levels allow for a more relaxed environment during reading. It is likely that at least some of the students would be able to answer these basic questions. However, all of the questions are knowledge-level questions, requiring little thought. The answer is *c,* all the questions were at recall/knowledge level (a lower level of thinking).

Answer 2: Map skills are very much a need skill for inner-city students, and it is the teacher's job to make sure that students do pay attention. One way to go about this is to take into account the background, interests, and *daily* lives of the students so that learning has meaning and relevance to them. Many can relate to time elements in their neighborhood, city, or state rather than a place so far away (and for a vacation of which few could conceive). The answer is *b.*

Answer 3: The teacher uses a variety of instructional strategies and roles to facilitate learning and to help students become independent thinkers and problem solvers who use higher-order thinking in the classroom and the real world. The teacher is varying his role in the instructional process (e.g., instructor, facilitator, coach, audience) in relation to the content and purposes of instruction and the levels of need and independence of the students. Mr. Farran is not giving out content information or teaching skills, so he is not instructing and he is not watching (audience). He may be doing some encouraging and giving feedback as a coach, but mostly he has set up a situation for students to discover and is facilitating that purpose. The answer is *b.*

WEB LINKS

Remember that website locations may change. If any of these sites have moved or cannot be located, use the Terms to Know in this chapter to search for further information.

Search Tip: If you type in critical+thinking+teaching, you will have a long list of sites that offer theory, activities, materials to purchase, and so forth. You may also want to try inquiry+teaching and/or cooperative+groups+teaching. There may be other search combinations that will help you gain more information.

http://7-12educators.miningco.com/msub 17.htm

This very helpful site offers some critical thinking lesson plans, definitions, articles, and other pathways to help understanding in this area.

http://www.bus.indiana.edu/isweb/teachln /collab.htm
A huge amount of information is offered here on using cooperative groups.

http://www.excel.net/~ssmith/cooplrn.html
This site offers information on teaching with cooperative groups.

http://www.geocities.com/"tdkest/crit1.html
This site offers help in understanding critical thought and links to topics such

as "Teaching Critical Reading Through Literature," "Critical Reading Strategies," and many more.

www.gsu.edu/~dschjb/wwwcrit.html
This site gives further definitions of critical thinking from a master teaching program along with information on cooperative groups (with a few activities for critical thinking in the classroom).

www.epcc.edu/Projects/IVALP/active.htm
This site presents active learning techniques, dimensions of learning, indicators of engaged learning, and a section that discusses the rationale for critical thinking in the new millennium.

www.criticalthinking.org/ncect.nclk
The National Council for Excellence in Critical Thinking provides a list of their principles and pedagogical implications for critical thinking.

http://ublib.buffalo.edu/libraries/projects/tlr /thinking.html
Here you will find articles and links for critical thinking.

http://libr21.ntu.edu.sg:8002/biblio/ thinking/thnk-toc.htm
"Thinking: A Select Bibliography" offers an excellent listing of books in various areas of thinking, in different subject areas, and so forth.

www. tea.state.tx.us/teks
This is a gateway to the Texas Essential Knowledge and Skills (TEKS) for various subject areas and grade levels.

http://www.tcta.org/QAteks.htm
This site lists questions and answers about the Texas Essential Knowledge and Skills (TEKS).

REFERENCES AND SUGGESTED READINGS

Berliner, D. (1985). *Effective teaching.* Pensacola, FL: Florida Educational Research and Development Council.

Bloom, B. S., Englehart, M. D., Furst, E. J., Hill, W. H., & Krathwohl, D. R. (Eds.). (1956). *Taxonomy of educational objectives: The classification of education goals, handbook I: Cognitive domain.* New York: David McKay.

Bransford, J., Goldman, S., & Vye, N. (1991). Making a difference in people's abilities to think: Reflections on a decade of work and some hopes for the future. In L. Okabaki & R. Sternberg (Eds.), Directors of development (pp. 147–180). Hillsdale, NJ: Erlbaum.

Brodhagen, B. L. (1995). The situation made us special. In M. W. Apple & J. A. Beane (Eds.), *Democratic schools* (pp. 83–100). Alexandria, VA: Association for Supervision and Curriculum Development.

Brooks, J. G., & Brooks, M. G. (1993). *In search of understanding: The case for constructivist classrooms.* Alexandria, VA:

Association for Supervision and Curriculum Development.

Brophy, J. (1992). Probing the subtleties of subject-matter teaching. *Educational Leadership, 49,* 4–8.

Cabello, B., & Terrell, R. (1994). Making students feel like family: How teachers create warm and caring classroom climates. *Journal of Classroom Interaction, 29*(1), 17–23.

Cangelosi, J. S. (1992). *Systematic teaching strategies.* New York: Longman.

Eggen, P., & Kauchak, K. (1996). *Strategies for teachers: Teaching content and thinking skills* (3d ed.). Boston: Allyn & Bacon.

Fradd, S., & Lee, O. (1999). Teachers' roles in promoting science inquiry with students from diverse language backgrounds. *Educational Researchers, 28*(6), 14–20.

Gunter, M. A., Estes, T., & Schwab, J. (1995). *Instruction: A models approach.* (2d ed.). Boston: Allyn & Bacon.

Joyce, B., & Weil, M., with Calhoun, E. (2000). *Models of teaching* (6th ed.). Boston: Allyn & Bacon.

Kagan, S. (1992). *Cooperative learning.* San Juan Capistrano, CA: Resources for Teachers, Inc.

Langer, J., Bartolome, L., Vasquez, O., & Lucas, T. (1990). Meaning construction is school literacy tasks: A study of bilingual students. *American Educational Research Journal, 27,* 427–471.

Moore, K. D. (1998). *Middle and secondary school instructional methods.* Boston: McGraw-Hill College.

Rosser, R. A., & Nicholson, G. I. (1984). *Educational psychology.* Boston: Little, Brown.

Sadker, M., & Sadker, D. (1994). *Failing at fairness: How our schools cheat girls.* New York: Simon & Schuster.

Sharan, S., & Shachar, H. (1988). *Language and learning in the cooperative classroom.* New York: Springer-Verlang.

Suchman, R. J. (1962). The elementary school training program in scientific inquiry. Report to the U.S. Office of Education, Project Title VII (Urbana: University of Illinois Press, 1962).

Tishman, S., & Perkins, D. (1997). The language of thinking. *Phi Delta Kappan, 78*(5), 368–374.

Woolfolk, A. (1998). *Educational psychology.* (7th ed.). Boston: Allyn & Bacon.

ABOUT THE AUTHOR

Dr. Janice L. Nath, Ed.D., teaches at the University of Houston in the Curriculum and Instruction Department. She is also the Coordinator for Elementary Education, Director of PUMA TRACS (Teachers Receiving Active and Collaborative Support) post baccalaureate certification program, Assistant Director of the Internship Program, and has headed one of the university's Professional Development School (PDS) sites for several years.

Teacher education is her main area of interest and research, along with technology in teacher education, action research, and others. She has been actively involved in field-based teacher education for many years and is currently the president of the AERA (American Edu-cational Research Association) Professional Development School Research Special Interest Group (PDSR SIG).

9

✳

Instructional Materials
and Resources

MARY E. PARKER

WEST TEXAS A&M UNIVERSITY

This chapter addresses Competency 9 of the Examination for the Certification of Educators in Texas (ExCET). Competency 9 falls under Domain II, Enhancing Student Achievement, of those domains Texas considers most important for its teachers to know and use.

Competency 9: The teacher uses a variety of instructional materials and resources (including human and technological sources) to support individual and group learning.

The teacher knows how to enhance learning for all students through the appropriate use of instructional materials and resources (e.g., computers, CD-ROM, videodiscs, primary documents and artifacts, AV equipment, manipulatives, local experts) and helps students understand the role of technology as a learning tool. The teacher evaluates the effectiveness of specific materials and resources for particular situations and purposes; selects appropriate materials and resources to address individual students' strengths and needs, learning styles, preferred modalities, and interests; understands the value of using multiple resources in instruction; and manages the logistics of individual and collaborative use of limited materials and resources.

TERMS TO KNOW

Instructional resources

Manipulatives

Technology-related resources

Specialized area resources

Technology

Print resources

Audio resources

Learning centers

Computer-assisted instruction (CAI)

Visual materials

Human resources

Instructional strategies in Competency 9 relate directly to instructional materials and resources—that is, materials and resources that are necessary to implement or enhance the lesson. However, those same materials and resources can be instructional strategies themselves. Teachers who use materials resourcefully can use those same objects to teach relevant skills for life, and the student so taught will become a higher-order, independent-thinking problem solver (Competency 8).

Competency 9 of the ExCET proficiencies states that the teacher uses a variety of educational resources (including people and technology) to *enhance* both individual and group learning. Although, at first glance, this competency seems very simple, the word *enhanced* carries with it an admonition to the classroom teacher. Teachers should use **instructional resources** as tools to extend or widen the learning process, rather than as a replacement for quality instruction. In other words, good lessons or required objectives should be made better rather than having technology or other resources being offered to students as the lesson itself. Teachers who cannot scaffold their technology into the scheme of learning are creating a "fluff" day. Also, teachers should judge if the addition is really appropriate to the subject, age level, and so forth. Just because benchmarks of learning sometimes include using a resource, the resource may be a waste of learning time for students because it does not correlate with the subject matter. In some cases, a purchased resource may not turn out to be as advertised, yet having spent the money, a teacher feels compelled to use it even though it is not an addition to the lesson.

That having been said, the following information may be helpful to the new teacher trying to create a more exciting classroom. Certainly of concern to a new teacher is establishing the classroom and its equipment. If a new teacher is replacing a teacher and "inherits" the room, he or she may have many items provided. If the new teacher is entering a brand-new school, he or she will have lovely desks, nice chairs, and shiny floors. New schools ordinarily have monies set aside for teachers to order the necessary equipment; new teachers should ask relevant questions during their interview with the school principal about what is available and when to and how to order materials and supplies.

Aside from the overall standard equipment a district provides, a teacher should consider in the planning phase of every lesson what "materials" will be necessary to the production of that lesson (Competency 6). Every new teacher soon discovers that materials and resources do not miraculously appear, nor do they pay for themselves. Sometimes, the school provides a budget for each teacher; but, more often than not, teachers provide for materials out of their pockets. Sometimes teachers can apply for grants for materials, but these resources are seldom available immediately; the teacher often must apply for such funding six months to a year in advance. It is very questionable whether a teacher should "go to the community" to secure funding for projects without prior approval by the school principal. The best policy is to ask first. Teachers who wish to have one of their classes participate in a program (e.g., "Apples for Students" sponsored by a food chain or others) should make sure to secure approval from the principal before proceeding, especially if they intend to involve students' help for a time-consuming, lengthy project.

TEACHER RESOURCE BEHAVIOR

Teachers, when thinking about materials and resources, seem to "take on" certain characteristics. Few teachers really leave the school behind when they exit the building at the end of the day. Instead, they are usually thinking about tomorrow's lesson or about something that will help Johnny learn a concept. Those thoughts filtering through the reflective process might be used to describe teacher resource behavior in these ways: teacher as hunter-gatherer, teacher as researcher, teacher as seer, teacher as innovator, and teacher as technologist.

Teacher as Hunter-Gatherer

Experienced or new, teachers frequently take on the characteristics of the "hunter-gatherer." Such teachers are always on the lookout for free or sale items that can be incorporated into the classroom. Garage sales (especially those of retired teachers) are wonderful. I once went to a garage sale and quite unexpectedly came across "stacks" of bulletin board items, seasonal items, and so on, which the owner proudly gave me without cost. She wanted a "teacher" to have them. I used them in my classroom until I left, at which time a lucky replacement (one of my former students) received my largesse. It may be worthwhile for new teachers to find out which teachers are retiring at the end of the year and ask whether they might buy some of those teachers' instructional materials. Half-price bookstores are also wonderful resources for building a classroom library.

If a teacher decides to ask for donations, he or she should remember that students can ask for donations more easily than teachers can in some cases—especially those students who work at the local grocery store, carpet and tile store, or appliance store. Stores, large and small, often discard magazines and books after a certain time. In approaching any source for a donation, a teacher has about a fifty-fifty chance of getting something he or she wants (or needs). Most importantly, students will benefit from having concrete items to use as manipulatives. Problems to foresee, however, include taking advantage of situations and making sure not to connect students' grades and extra credit points to donations. Remember, a good teacher is never "off-duty" where supplies are involved.

Teacher as Researcher

Teachers should contact the local Chamber of Commerce when they arrive in a new town to learn about the community where they will be teaching (Competency 14). During this discovery process, teachers should be alert to listings of organizations that might respond to educational needs. Teachers can talk to people in the community and let them know their needs, as many organizations are looking for "worthwhile" projects to fund. Teachers also can learn which times of the year organizations make their monetary commitments for the following year, as this process can provide a wealth of resources for the classroom. For example, my competitive speech team once wrote letters to every community club and organization listed by the Chamber of Commerce volunteering to provide programs— humorous, dramatic, readings of prose and poetry, and so forth. Because students wrote these letters early in the spring *before* program committees met, the response was phenomenal. In return, the clubs donated to the speech team's travel budget. Many communities also have museums that offer free resources (as well as resources that can be purchased), and often teachers can check out special subject-area kits or have expert speakers come to the classroom.

Teacher as Seer

New teachers must learn to view things through a "teacher's eyes." A cotton ball is no longer a household item used to remove makeup; it is the tail of a rabbit, or a cloud in the sky. Newspapers become dragons (Grindle), and hats create new characters (role-playing). Class projects from the year before become models and new bulletin board enticements for lessons to come. Planning ahead for the year will certainly result in better accumulation of resources. Believe it or not, I have been collecting toilet paper rolls for students who utilize them for scientific experiments!

Teacher as Innovator

Teachers should become innovators. Just because they "did it that way last year" does not mean they should do it the same way this year. As a matter of fact, there is an old adage that says, "There are those teachers who have taught 20 years one time; and there are those teachers who have taught one year 20 times." If a teacher is a reflective practitioner (Competency 12), he or she is eager to find new resources every year. The popsicle sticks used to build a log cabin with this year might be used to make Jamaican worry dolls next year. The pictures of people illustrating historical periods last year become studies in human emotion this year. The novel recorded last year for the class becomes enrichment study for students this year in a learning center.

Teacher as Technologist

Technology is defined as a scientific process that produces replicable solutions for educational tasks. This process involves the use of tools, techniques, and procedures; for example, a pencil or a pen is a tool that teachers use to accomplish a task. A common example of technology would be the use of computer technology in the classroom. Teachers should become computer-literate and stay that way. If this is, indeed, the age of technology, the teacher is a part of it, so the teacher needs to be a competent part. A particular campus may have state-of-the-art computer labs, or little or no access to computers. Teachers must find a way to adapt to the level of technology on their campuses; they can begin by learning what is available. I was ecstatic when my students introduced me to AutoCAD, a program used in the drafting classes on campus. The student council produced an award-winning scrapbook with assistance from the drafting teacher and other students (human resources)—the first in the state to do so. Technology skills also enable teachers to find resources for themselves. Hundreds of websites exist that tell teachers how to teach every subject, often providing detailed lesson plans. Through newspapers.com, for example, a teacher can find every online newspaper in the United States. Teachers should take advantage of those valuable resources and bookmark them for repeat visits.

Teachers who master this competency have learned the difference between the art of teaching and the science of teaching and know how to integrate the two. Therefore, a teacher's competency with instructional resources may have a lot to do with how much his or her students learn.

A new teacher-graduate recently secured her "dream job" in a school noted for its high academic achievement. Not only did she get the school and principal she desired, but she also got the "first pick" of classrooms that had become available. The very day of being hired, she got the key to her room. About two days after her contract had been signed, she told me she could not sleep at night for thinking about how she wanted to supply her classroom. Among those things on her wish list were classroom sets of books, a computer, various supplies for learning centers, and a CD player. What this young woman worried about was what instructional materials and resources the district would provide and what she would be expected to provide for her own room. A large part of her thinking was about the content within Competency 9. This teacher was also already beginning the "planning" part of her academic year (Competency 6). Soon, the principal called this new teacher to come to a grade-level meeting designed for the purpose of ordering supplies and materials for the upcoming year. Depending on when a teacher's teaching contract is signed, such a meeting may or may not be possible, but teachers should remember that it is never too late to ask for consideration.

Preservice teachers frequently say, "I want to make my classroom fun! I want my students to enjoy learning." Adding to the knowledge that teachers have today of learning styles and diversity, the new teacher will want to become aware of practical resources that help them address those human differences in abilities and motivation. Teachers should recognize the student diversity that manifests itself in auditory, visual, and kinesthetic learning styles (Competency 4). Knowing that such diversity exists should motivate teachers to explore instructional strategies that lend themselves to diverse learning styles. Instructional materials and resources provide a very good place to begin motivating that seemingly unmotivated child.

MATERIALS AND RESOURCES

This chapter continues by examining the many resources a new teacher should know about and utilize in the quest to vary and enrich lessons for students. In general, materials and resources include both physical enhancements and technology-related resources.

When the principal issues a key and "walks" the new teacher to his or her new domain, there may be some despair over the blank, freshly painted walls and scrubbed desks as the empty room is first seen. The institutional (physical) environment of the classroom is both daunting and exhilarating as one imagines the possibilities. Physical enhancements involve bulletin boards, seating arrangements, wall decorations, and the teacher's desk and students' desks. A quick survey will show whether pencil sharpeners, water fountains, bathrooms (often in kindergarten rooms), and room numbers are in order. In many classrooms, a computer(s) is standard equipment. When this is the case, the teacher will need to plan for easy access and usage. When setting up the computer, the teacher must consider screen glare from windows along with placement for use by small groups or partners when equipment is limited. Posting and practicing rules for computers will help avoid incidents and damage to machines, particularly when more than one student is assigned to a computer. If the Internet is available and unfiltered, the teacher will want to make sure he or she has an easy view to students who may be working on the computers as the teacher is working with others. On this note, teachers should be aware of any school policy regarding Internet use. Normally, acceptable use policy (AUP) forms will go home to parents granting or denying Internet use at school. These must be honored by teachers.

Teachers have certain resources to make learning centers, bulletin boards, and walls come alive. Not only will the school district have resources in the the media center, library, or in a "resource closet" at your school, but resources are also available from the Region Service Center (RSC). Throughout the state, each school district is assigned to a Region Service Center, although the RSC may not be located in the same town. The cost for materials and supplies is often free at the district level and nominal at the Region Service Centers. Also, new teachers may find commercial businesses such as the local teacher or school supply store to be invaluable resources for exciting and colorful enticements for their classrooms. Teacher and school supply stores may be found on the Internet as well. Although materials from these businesses tend to be very expensive, most of these stores offer discounts for teachers.

Sometimes, new teachers are offered seed money ("start-up" money or stipends) to enable them to purchase some initial supplies. Depending on the resources in the district and community, teachers are eligible to apply for competitive grants and stipends to support classroom projects through the district.

In addition to physical enhancements, teachers need to be aware of technology-related resources. Today's students comprise the first generation of students who have been raised in the computer age. The cartoon depicting a father asking his very young child to "make the blinking go away" on the VCR comes to mind!

Teachers may be a little intimidated by all the technological advances of the 2 century; but intimidated or not, they must participate in this revolution or be left behind in their own classroom.

Perhaps the first term with which new teachers should become acquainted is **computer-assisted instruction (CAI)**. Computer-assisted instruction is divided into two distinct parts: (1) drill and practice, and (2) instruction (tutorials). A third use of the computer for instruction is the rapidly growing online instruction (distance education), but it has not yet reached the public schools to a great degree.

Classroom resources available to teachers are extensive, varied, and sometimes very task-specific. The following categories of resources—print resources, visual resources, computer resources, technology-related resources, media resources, audio resources, human resources, manipulatives, specialized area resources, and learning centers—reflect representative samples of kinds of materials available to teachers.

Print Resources

Print resources—whether from a book, a photocopied handout, or a periodical—can still provide the basis for most instruction. Figure 9.1 lists print resources that might be used in the classroom to enhance instruction. School libraries or media centers, city/county libraries, and college or university libraries are good sources of other print resources to use with students.

Textbooks	Manipulative books	Colored overlays
Dictionaries/thesauri	Advanced organizers	Pamphlets
Atlases	Restaurant menus	Diaries
Periodicals	Organizational newsletters	Abstracts
Postcards	Flyers/informational circulars	Student journals
Thematic booklets	Government reports	Flipcharts/books
Trade bulletins/catalogs	Day calendars	Newspapers/youth pages[a]
Graphs/charts	Educational comic books	Online newspapers
Timelines	Microfiche	Telephone books
Transparencies	Websites	Pen pals
Advertising	Children's magazines	Manuscripts

FIGURE 9.1 Print resources.

[a]Newspapers in Education (NIE) is an international program, and most major newspapers support this program through an organizational department devoted to NIE. This program is directed primarily toward contributing in a tangible way to the literacy of the population. By accessing newspapers.com, teachers can locate newspapers all over the world with many international newspapers printed in their own language. These sites usually provide free lesson plans in many subject areas. Syndicated pages like the Mini Page (or other youth pages) have ready-built activities that teachers can use on a weekly basis in the classroom or in a learning center. Teachers can also contact their local newspapers to find out about how to order newspapers for the classroom and how to receive training on using newspapers with students.

Visual Resources

...he classroom environment (Competencies 2 and 11) initially
...eans, and students' first impressions of a teacher come through
...t. **Visual materials** and print resources overlap, for most visual
...lassroom gain primary attention through color appeal and offer
...ages that may be in print. Teachers need to recognize that many
...imarily visual learners and need to diversify lessons by adding a
...mpact in their classroom and to their lessons. Some visual resources
include ... listed in Figure 9.2.

Computer Resources

When one thinks of technology resources today, it is very common to think first
and only of computers. Students and teachers alike may erroneously categorize
all of technology into the computer resource category; but for clarity, computer
resources do not include all of the technology available to teachers. Some technology resources that are available to teachers today are shown in Figure 9.3.

Teachers should remember to thoroughly and critically evaluate software before
using it with students. One determination teachers should make is to ascertain what
level of thinking the software presents. Programs can be lower-level recall, skill and
drill, or designed to include high-level, problem-solving activities. Furthermore, there
is little reason to make an investment in a number of expensive software packages that
are usable by only one or two children at a time if they are essentially parallel to pen-
cil-and-paper tasks. Some of the graphics and gimmicks found in educational software
may be motivating for a time to students, but a teacher must ensure that software is
promoting higher-level thinking.

Technology-Related Resources

The category of **technology-related resources** is quite large. Some of the items
mentioned in Figure 9.4 are very discipline-specific but are mentioned here to
illustrate the enormity of resource possibilities for the teacher.

Billboards	Mobiles	Transparent coins/dice
Eye-cue puzzles	Cartoons	Graphic organizers
Geo-boards	Observations	Electronic bulletin boards
Primary artifacts	Charts	Sentence strips/word walls
Artwork	Scrapbooks	Paintings
School plays/programs	Collages	Clocks
Flannel boards with stories	Posters	Manipulatives

FIGURE 9.2 Visual resources.

Internet	Satellite classes	Virtual museums/simulation software
E-mail	Chatrooms	Video conferencing
CD-ROMs	Browsing libraries	Take-home laptops
Hyper Studio	Digital cameras	CAI
Virtual library	Software	TENET (Texas Education Network)

FIGURE 9.3 Computer resources.

Neon/digital signs	Hectograph machines	Microscope/scales
Camcorders	Overhead projectors	Telescopes
Laser writers and printers	Graphing calculators	Reaction plates (athletes)
Slide shows	Student broadcasts	Laser pointers
On-screen touch devices	Automated grade books	Digital cameras
LCD units	Dry-erase boards (dust-free for high-technology areas)	Document cameras

FIGURE 9.4 Technology-related resources.

The use of technology in teaching has brought mixed blessings. In days gone by, a teacher could film students doing simulated newscasts and weather reports, record original short stories, and do a host of other special projects. In addition, a teacher was able to film the entire class for reflective-teaching purposes. Today, confidentiality issues, parental custody issues, and lawsuits have changed this media activity. Now some school districts require that teachers have a parental consent form returned before filming any students in the school. Teachers should be sure to ask about this prior to planning a lesson in which students will be filmed.

Media Resources

Some students are aware of the old filmstrip projector and the record player. These tools are probably still in the library's media center, but things have changed significantly with the role the media center plays in teacher's lives today. Both technology resources and human resources come together in the form of one of the most valuable resources available to teachers: the media center director or librarian. New teachers should ask their school librarians for a list of resources at the school and the district that are available for classroom use.

School librarians always encourage students to tour the library to learn about its resources and how to access research materials. They provide tours for students and work diligently to meet the specific needs of the classroom teacher. It is certainly worth some of the new teacher's time to see what is available prior to the start of the new school year; and experienced teachers should see what new resources arrived over the summer.

In most schools, teachers check out VCRs and televisions from the media center or utilize the Channel 1 monitor in their classrooms (if it is available) for video showing. Many school districts subscribe to Channel 1, which is an educational news program produced and announced by young people. These daily newscasts normally last about 10 minutes. When I sponsored the student council, we utilized the Channel 1 monitors for live announcements each morning. Students were able to make nomination/acceptance speeches, do skits to advertise projects, and otherwise "jazz up" the daily monotony of school announcements.

The media specialist will assist teachers with graphics and research via the Internet and will provide CD players, tape players, videos, filmstrips, and recordings for classroom use. Many librarians will assist students with film making by providing instruction in the use of camcorders, editing processes, and copying videos. A digital camera is sometimes available to make color photos of each student or to integrate photos into classwork. Teachers may also check out overhead projectors from the media center, as well as secure materials for making overhead transparencies. Teachers can, if a computer and color printer is available, make color transparencies.

On the more practical side, most media centers have: (1) a die-cut machine for making letters, symbols, and pictures; (2) borders for bulletin boards; (3) a laminating machine; (4) and rolls of wide, colored paper for bulletin boards and projects. It is apparent from this discussion that the school librarian or media center director is an invaluable resource for teachers and students.

Audio Resources

The traditional audiovisual (AV) equipment of yesteryear is still around. However, with the proliferation of technology, some specialized kinds of **audio resources** that help students develop listening skills and produce multimedia projects with music and voice components have found their way into the classroom. Some of these audio resources are so specialized that they might not be available in the typical school media center. Figure 9.5 presents examples of some of the audio resources that are available.

Human Resources

Often called the "overlooked resource," **human resources** are invaluable to the teacher. Those resources may be categorized into three parts: (1) school/professional resources, (2) community/business resources, and (3) school/university collaboratives.

1. *School/Professional Resources.* Exchange students, other teachers, principals, curriculum directors, technology specialists, paraprofessionals, nurses, secretaries, and other support personnel provide invaluable resources by speaking with students about cultural issues, leadership roles, and careers. Many of these individuals have academic areas of specialization that can be utilized for content-area knowledge.

Microphones	Interactive ed (computer-based)	Speakers
Mixers	Teacher-made tapes	Sound systems
Amplifiers	Musical instruments (rhythm/piano/guitar)	Tape recorders
Books with tapes		CD players
Listening kits	Films	
Books on tape	Record players	

FIGURE 9.5 Audio resources.

2. *Community/Business Resources.* Museums, zoos, discovery centers, nature centers and parks, police and fire stations, and local businesses are popular places to take students for educational field trips. Community members from different cultures, ministers/pastors/priests (no indoctrination topics), medical and dental profes-sionals, business professionals, local government officials, family members, and retired citizens can provide the classroom teacher with "voices of authority and experience." By inviting experts into the classroom, subject matter will become more relevant and exciting to students.

3. *School/University Collaboratives.* Public and private schools often collaborate with colleges and universities to bring many resources into the schools. Teachers can benefit by matching older student tutors with younger students who need help, getting supplies for programs and projects, collaborating on grant-writing activities, and creating positive working relationships with future teachers.

Inviting guest speakers into the classroom and taking students on field trips are two ways to bring the curriculum alive for students. However, some caution must be heeded with both practices. Before inviting a guest speaker, a teacher should be sure of the school policy regarding visitors to the campus and clear the visit through the principal. If special rules are applied for visitors on campus to check in through the office, the teacher should inform the visitor of those rules and arrange for him or her to be greeted at the office and shown to the classroom. Some problems may arise in the scheduling of outside speakers or events. Teachers should always be prepared for no-shows, late-arrivals, or "surprise" presentations. Teachers should always stay in the room during guest presentations, as they are responsible for the content the human resource brings to the class. Teachers should also prepare students to be good listeners and to ask relevant questions.

Field trips are an excellent way of using the resources of the area. Careful preparation will, indeed, *enhance* the experience, as students often remember these trips as highlights of their year. Again, it is the teacher's job, as with a guest speaker, to prepare students with information first so that students will be able to get more from their experience. A typical sequence of events might be: (1) sending home permission slips informing parents of the field trip; (2) making sure all permission slips are returned, as a student cannot go without one; (3) arranging for parent volunteers; (4) preparing and teaching several lessons related to the field trip; and

ng on the experience with students after the field trip. Finally, dis-
's and appropriate behavior before the trip will help make the visit a
for all involved.

Manipulatives

Research clearly shows that students who are tactile-kinesthetic learners prefer
hands-on activities. Lists of **manipulatives** and hands-on materials are quite
lengthy and extensive. To give a representative listing of manipulatives, some of
the objects included in Figure 9.6 are specifically elementary while others are
specifically secondary. Teachers can collect all kinds of everyday objects such as
buttons, beans, and bottle caps to use in the classroom as manipulatives.

Purchased manipulatives can be very expensive, while teacher-made manipulatives can take time to make. Schools often buy limited sets of manipulatives
for teachers, and teachers may have time to construct only enough for groups.
Teachers who are planning to use manipulatives with groups of students must
use good cooperative learning techniques. Students should each have a role in
the group that serves to enhance social-skill development. When students take
their roles seriously, the task of sharing goes more smoothly. Finally, using a
timer to help students remember to pass the manipulatives around will help to
ensure that each student has access to the manipulatives at some point during
the group time.

Specialized Area Resources

Most academic and elective subject areas have instructional resources specifically
for that discipline. Usually, the school will provide a budget for specialized areas

Cubic Mania	Wooden alphabet blocks	Poetry magnets
Snap cubes	Alphabet rubber stamps	Skeletons
Lacing cards	Jigsaw puzzles	Chips
Beads 'n baubles	Magnetic letters/numbers and boards	Pasta
Tactile blocks	Slide rules	Algecans
Counting blocks	Marbles	Picture grids
Maps	Puppets	Animals
Shaving cream	Index cards	Dominos
Unifix cubes	Brain maps	Post-It notes
Tiles	Dice	Berculator/pieculator
Magna-Doodle	Abacus	Cuisenaire rods
Felt letters	Floor puzzles	Scrabble
Erector sets	Legos	3-D models

FIGURE 9.6 Manipulatives.

that covers the costs of materials and supplies. The teacher must be very aware of filling the needs of the department by planning ahead and ordering supplies in a timely manner. Figure 9.7 shows resources related to the specialized area of art. Besides needing a specialized room, an art teacher will need to gather many resources for the classroom. A teacher who is in an elementary school that has no art teacher for the teacher's grade level will be expected to teach this subject. Such teachers will need to obtain some of these materials as well. Other content areas that need specialized resources are music, theatre arts, and industrial arts.

Learning Centers

Learning centers are small spaces the teacher creates within the classroom. These small spaces contain specific materials and resources that are commonly used to reinforce basic skills or extend classroom lessons. Learning centers can be designed to accommodate a variety of learning styles (Competency 4). Often teachers set up permanent learning centers around the classroom and designate the centers to meet the learning needs of the class. Learning centers are commonly called by a number of different names: Library/Reading Center, Writing/Journal Center, Science Center, Spelling Center, Social Studies Center, Computer Center, Listening Center, Creative Thinking Center, Puzzle Center, and Dramatic Play Center. These centers are a perfect place for including manipulatives that will enhance tactile-kinesthetic learning.

SUMMARY

In summary, there is a great deal of knowledge Texas teachers should have regarding instructional resources. This knowledge includes what resources are available and how to use them with students. Connecting instructional resources to learning activities is critical; using "cute" materials does not necessarily indicate that learning is taking place even though high interest and curiosity may be present. By clearly defining lesson objectives and choosing instructional resources that support and enhance the lesson, teachers can ensure that the students are truly learning.

Color wheel	Colored pencils	Easels
Transparent color paddles	Brushes	Inks
T-square	Potter's wheel	Oils
Stencils	Canvases	Clay

FIGURE 9.7 Specialized art supplies.

SUGGESTED ACTIVITIES

1. List manipulatives that you might use for each of the following subjects: mathematics, reading, science, social studies, and writing. Describe how you would use these in the classroom.

2. What are some of the limitations to using human resources in your classroom? What are some of the legal issues concerning using human resources in your classroom?

3. Write a paragraph connecting constructivist theory (Competency 4) to using resources in the classroom.

You may also choose to include discovery learning/hands-on learning in the discussion.

4. Draw a picture of your "dream" classroom. Be realistic about measurements so that you represent empty space (what is left over after desks and chairs are placed) accurately.

5. Explore the websites in this chapter.

6. Answer these questions: What technological resources still "scare" you? How can you become familiar with them during your fieldwork?

PRACTICE DECISION SET

1. An example of a manipulative is:
   I. Modeling clay
   II. Jigsaw puzzles
   III. Base ten blocks
   IV. Dominoes
   a. I
   b. II and III
   c. I, III, and IV
   d. All of the above

2. What is the main purpose for using resources in the classroom?
   a. To enhance student learning
   b. To give the students a change of lesson presentation
   c. To give the teacher added support in the classroom
   d. To provide an interesting lesson that will aid in classroom management

3. Manipulatives are most effective for which age group?
   a. All ages of students, provided they are age-appropriate
   b. Elementary school-age students
   c. Preschool students

   d. Middle school and high school students

4. Ms. Smith wants to have Mr. Bob, the local weatherman, come talk to her third-graders about earthquakes. She should first:
   I. Call all of the students' parents and ask permission
   II. Write a letter inviting Mr. Bob
   III. Notify the principal of her plans to have a guest speaker
   IV. Send a note home with students advising parents of the visit
   a. I
   b. I and II
   c. I, II, III, and IV
   d. III

5. Miss Mays has invited a guest speaker to visit her class. She does all of the following *except:*
   a. Put away all distracting materials
   b. Add relevant information when the speaker pauses
   c. Observe the speaker with alertness

d. Carry out an activity related to the topic afterward

6. Several students independently conclude that recycling could be a solution to the problem of waste. During a class discussion, Mr. Jeung asks these students to talk about recycling to the rest of the class. Soon many of the students in class become enthusiastic about the whole school having a recycling project. Following the discussion of a possible recycling project, Mr. Jeung arranges for his students to take a guided tour of a recycling plant. Which of the following are most likely to be key benefits of Mr. Jueng's use of local resources?

   I. Helping students understand and visualize procedures in recycling
   II. Promoting students' sense of control with regard to their learning
   III. Enhancing student motivation to pursue the project they have been discussing
   IV. Encouraging students' conscious use of self-assessment during the learning process
   a. I and II
   b. I and III
   c. II and IV
   d. III and IV

7. Miss Taylor's class is planning a business project. They invited the bank president to discuss lending practices because the students will need to borrow money from the bank as start-up money. They intend to plan everything about the business in detail, including the amount of money they expect to invest in the business and their projected profit. Which of the following computer applications would

be best for the class to use for record keeping?
   I. Database
   II. Graphing
   III. Simulation
   IV. Spreadsheet
   a. I and IV
   b. IV only
   c. All of the above
   d. None of the above

Answer 1: The correct answer is *d*, all of the above. These are all examples of manipulatives.

Answer 2: The correct answer is *a*. The teacher must understand the purpose of using resources.

Answer 3: The correct answer is *a*. The correct answer hinges on "age-appropriate." The correct answer might also include lesson objective–appropriate.

Answer 4: The correct answer is *d*. Although it would be nice to call each parent and/or send a note home, it is not necessary. Before writing the letter to Mr. Bob, it would be better to ask the principal or check school policy.

Answer 5: The answer is *b*. The teacher should prepare the classroom for a visit, be attentive and appreciative of the speaker, and relate the speaker's comments to the topic for relevancy. The teacher should refrain from interrupting any speaker, pause or no pause.

Answer 6: The correct answer is *b*. Although students may have voted to tour the plant, they are not "in control" of this activity. Students are not likely to self-assess during this activity.

Answer 7: The correct answer is *b*. The spreadsheet is the correct choice for keeping records. Although the other choices may be used at some time during the project, the question calls for record-keeping usage.

WEB LINKS

Remember that website locations may change. If any of these sites have moved or cannot be located, use the Terms to Know in this chapter to search for further information. *Note:* The following websites contain resources such as lesson plans, information on technology, graphic organizers, freebies, black-line masters, glossaries, and most importantly, ideas.

www.csun.edu/~vceed009/index.html
This website contains helpful resources for all ages of students and all subjects. Each subject has various options such as lesson plans, strategies, resources, geography, multimedia, ancient worlds, museums, and organizations. You can even tour the White House on this site.

www.teachnet.org
This website stresses that teachers know that technology is a useful learning tool, but it is not an end in itself. This site correctly defines technology to include video and audio recording and playback devices, fax machines, copiers, printers, cameras, scanners, and projection devices.

www.educationindex.com/educator
This site provides lesson plans, classroom resources, teacher experience stories, and much more.

www.teachers.net
This site provides opportunities for teacher chat in addition to lesson plans and resource listings.

www.lessonplans.com
This site includes lessons that offer resource suggestions as appropriate.

www.execpc.com/~dboals/boals.html
This page is useful in locating and using Internet resources in the classroom. Its purpose is to encourage the use of the World Wide Web as a tool for learning and teaching.

www.capecod.net/schrockguide
This site contains more than 1,000 links to websites for educators. It contains specialized resources such as special education and search engine instructions for education.

www.loc.gov
This site has a large collection of text, photographs, sound recordings, movies, and maps of historic events (with lesson plans). This information occurs in the American Memory Collection.

www.nationalgeographic.com/resources/
This website is interactive and provides material suitable for downloading.

www.pbs.org/learn/
The main purpose of Public Broadcasting Service (PBS) is to provide information on using video as a tool for learning in the classroom.

www.si.edu/
The Smithsonian Institution site includes a huge photography database that can download photos. There are classroom activities and active-learning lesson plans.

www.gcdsd.wednet.edu/
Of interest on this site (in addition to plans) is access to test forms, grade books, and calendars.

www.teacher-zone.com/free.html
This site contains four pages of free items such as stickers and posters from NASA.

www.esc16.tenet.edu/
This site refers to the Region 16 Service Center. Substitute your own Region Service Center location for more information.

www.mathprep.com/basicskill.html
This site provides interactive mathematics lessons.

http://ericir.syr.edu/Virtual
ASKERIC. The Educational Resources Information Center (ERIC) is a

federally funded national information system that provides a broad range of education-related issues through its 16 subject-specific clearinghouses.

www.scholastic.com
This site provides excellent classroom activities and games, curriculum programs, and materials, software, and film and video information. You may also access reproducibles, articles, and lesson plans.

www.sdcoe.k12.ca.us/score/actbank/torganiz.htm
This site provides 12 examples of graphic organizers that can be used in the classroom.

www.tea.state.tx.us
This is the Texas Education Agency site that every teacher should bookmark. At this site, you can research TEKS, Regional Service Center resources, and much more.

www.csu.edu.au/education/library.html
This site for Charles Stuart University provides a plethora of information including a resources link.

www.enchantedLearning.com/
This website is committed to early childhood. It contains a learning dictionary and studies on dinosaurs and sharks, and it provides connect-a-dot puzzles and many more high-interest programs with exciting graphics.

www.newspapers.com
This site contains listings of online newspapers from around the world.

www.parenting-qa.com/
This site offers multiple age-level activities and development tips.

www2.rbs.org/ec.nsf
This site is the Eisenhower Consortium, which focuses on science and mathematics education.

www.teacherhelp.com
This excellent, multifaceted resource contains all kinds of information related to professional development.

www.eskimo.com/~user/kids.html
This resource offers links to all known gifted resources (or so it claims).

REFERENCES AND SUGGESTED READINGS

Blackhurst, A. E. (1997). Perspectives about technology in special education. *TEACHING Exceptional Children, 29,* 41–48 (Council for Exceptional Children).

Blatzheim, B., & Bowen, S. (1997, November). How to strengthen the use of centers in the classroom. Paper presented at Kappa Delta Pi Convocation, St. Louis, Missouri.

Brooks, J. G., & Brooks, M. G. (1993). *In search of understanding: The case for constructivist classrooms.* Alexandria, VA: Association for Supervision and Curriculum Development.

Burns, M. (1994). Arithmetic: The last holdout. *Phi Delta Kappan, 75,* 471–476.

Butzin, S. M. (1992). Integrating technology into the classroom: Lessons from the Project CHILD experience. *Phi Delta Kappan, 74,* 330–333.

Edinger, M. (1994). Empowering young writers with technology. *Educational Leadership, 51,* 58–60.

Ladewski, B. G., Krajcik, J. S., & Harvey, C. L. (1994). A middle grade science teacher's emerging understanding of project-based instruction. *The Elementary School Journal, 94,* 499–515.

McKenzie, J. (1998). Grazing the net: Raising a generation of free range students. *Phi Delta Kappan, 80,* 26–31.

Sellers, J., & Robichaux, J. (1996, May). Frequently asked questions for schools. Request for comments. [Memo posted on the World Wide Web]. Retrieved May 30, 1999, from the World Wide Web: http://www.it.kth.se/docs/rfcs/rfc1941.txt.

ABOUT THE AUTHOR

Mary E. Parker, Ed.D., is an Assistant Professor of Education at West Texas A&M University in Canyon, Texas, where she teaches Educational Psychology. Dr. Parker taught American literature and communications in public school for many years before completing her doctoral work. Her research involves the historical aspects of early education on the Llano Estacado, collaborations with math and science elementary education and field experience, professional portfolio development, and online teaching. In addition to handling the recruiting efforts of the Division of Education, she is the Kappa Delta Pi counselor of an award-winning chapter and copresents the Division of Education's ExCET Reviews twice a year.

10

※

Formal and Informal Assessment

PAM LINDSEY
TARLETON STATE UNIVERSITY

This chapter describes the key vocabulary and knowledge base needed for Competency 10 of the Examination for the Certification of Educators in Texas (ExCET). Competency 10 is the fifth of six competencies that fall under Domain II, Enhancing Student Achievement. This competency deals with the foundation of an effective learner-centered classroom, assessment and evaluation of student performance.

Competency 10: The teacher uses processes of informal and formal assessment to understand individual learners, monitor instructional effectiveness, and shape instruction.

The teacher understands the importance of on-going assessment as an instructional tool and employs a variety of formal and informal assessment techniques (e.g., observation, portfolio, teacher-made classroom tests, student self-assessment, peer assessment, standardized tests) to enhance his or her knowledge of learners, monitor students' progress in achieving outcomes, and modify instructional delivery. The teacher is aware of the characteristics, uses, advantages and limitations of different types of assessments; understands assessment related issues such as those related to bias, reliability, validity, and grading; and knows how to select or construct and use assessment instruments for various purposes.

TERMS TO KNOW

Evaluation	Grade-equivalent scores
Assessment	Formal assessment
Standard score	Curriculum-based assessment (CBA)
Teacher-made tests	
Test bias	Percentile ranks
Domain	Criterion-referenced
Observational data	Summative data
Standardized test	Formative data
Portfolio	Norm-referenced
Reliability	Age-equivalent scores
Validity	Informal assessment

> Assessment means the process of gathering
> information. For teachers, assessment is conducted
> for the purpose of deciding which skills to teach or
> re-teach (Choate, Enright, Miller, Poteet, & Rakes,
> 1995). An effective assessment process should play
> a positive role in how students learn.
>
> BROWN, RACE, & SMITH
>
> (1996)

TEST, ASSESSMENT, AND EVALUATION: WHAT IS THE DIFFERENCE?

The keys to structuring an effective classroom assessment process are embedded in the language of Competency 10. Often the word *assessment* is used as a synonym for test or evaluation. **Assessment** of student achievement or progress, however, involves much more than testing and is less encompassing than an overall evaluation of students' level of mastery for a specific grade or course. Specifically, a **test** may measure a small amount of knowledge in a very specific way, like a unit test or end-of-course exam, while an **evaluation** process typically means the formal methods schools use to measure overall student progress (e.g., TAAS, ITBS, ExCET).

Assessment means, as Competency 10 suggests, an appraisal process that is ongoing and dynamic. Assessment involves the measurement of students' skill acquisition, fluency, maintenance, and generalization on a specific set of objectives or lessons. A powerful assessment process also acts as an evaluation of teachers' instructional techniques. Assessment necessitates data collection from several sources, both formal and informal. Therefore, assessment includes tests, observations, student conferences, work samples, and projects that allow the student to demonstrate what he or she has learned. In addition, an appropriate assessment process is continuous and ongoing; that is, teachers collect assessment data daily, weekly, and sometimes hourly to constantly monitor their students' understanding and progress.

The purpose of an active assessment procedure is to make curricular, program, and placement decisions based on hard evidence, not serendipitous speculation (Choate et al., 1995), and to provide information to students, parents, and teachers concerning the student's progress and effectiveness of the teacher's instruction. The assessment process also provides information for sorting students based on their skill level and for evaluating teachers in terms of accountability for student progress (Slavin, 1997).

Evaluation typically refers to all means used in schools to formally measure student performance. Therefore, it includes formal, informal, and observational data collected before, during, and after instruction. Evaluation data are generally used to make curricular and program decisions such as referral for special education or gifted education assessment.

This chapter offers the preservice teacher an explanation of the assessment process, specific definitions of important assessment terms, and descriptions of various types of assessment data sources. The chapter also defines the characteristics of valid and reliable assessment instruments. In addition, a discussion of teacher-made tests based on Bloom's taxonomy will help the new teacher construct tests and other assessment instruments that evaluate his or her students' higher-level thinking skills.

THE ASSESSMENT PROCESS

The assessment process involves two main data sources: **formal assessment** (norm- or criterion-referenced, standardized tests) and **informal assessment** (interviews, observations, alternative assessments, curriculum-based assessment). Accurate (valid), dependable (reliable), and sufficient formal and informal data collection allows teachers to make appropriate instructional and program decisions about their students (Sattler, 1994).

For informal data, such as interviews, **validity** refers to the truthfulness of the information. In the case of a test, validity means that the test measures what it purports to measure. For example, in order for a teacher-made test to have validity, it must cover the skill or content of the teacher's instruction; that is, it must be directly tied to the content objectives (Arends, 1998; Sattler, 1994). If over half of the class fails a test, a teacher should analyze the validity of the test, not the lack of intelligence of the students. Although this outcome could be linked to lack of student preparation for the exam, it is more likely a result of inappropriate format and/or content of the test itself—specifically, the exam was not aligned with the classroom instruction.

Reliability relates to the dependability of information. In a standardized assessment instrument or teacher-made test, reliability refers to the consistency of results over time. In other words, a reliable test is one that yields similar results time after time when administered to the same group or level of students and under the same conditions (Arends, 1998; Sattler, 1994). For example, if an "A" student scored a 95 on a math test first period, we would expect other "A" students in similar classes to score close to 95 in following periods if the test has reliability. In the case of informal data, reliability would involve such concerns as teacher bias, disrupting events, student motivation, and appropriateness of an assignment to demonstrate the skill or content assigned.

In addition to reliability and validity factors, assessment data must be as free from bias as possible. **Test bias** refers to the fairness of the test. Because assessment data, especially test data, have become increasingly important and widely used to make crucial decisions about students, it is critical that teachers and other professionals be aware of the bias of tests toward certain individuals or groups of students. For example, Torres's (1991) study suggested that approximately 5 million students in the United States each year are inappropriately judged using standardized test data. This and other studies suggest that students are mismatched with an assessment that is culturally or linguistically biased against them. In addition, studies have suggested that age- or grade-based data are often misinterpreted by teachers or parents and that misinterpreted data result in inappropriate placements and/or programs for students (Torres, 1991; Ward & Murray-Ward, 1999). There are many who would argue that the TAAS has a cultural bias (Lawton, 1997). For example, how likely is it that a school in the Texas south valley would score competitively on the TAAS with a school in an affluent Dallas suburb? Another example of predictive bias would be the translating of an American-normed test into Spanish for an immigrant student from Mexico. There are items on a typical intelligence scale that are American culture–specific (like the colors in the American flag or America's first president). The immigrant student would be unlikely to know the correct answer in Spanish *or* English. Some tests also contain items that ask for information typical of the region in which the test was developed that are atypical in another American region. Some examples might be sleds, silos, toboggans, and snowsuits. Some Tex-Mex terms may equally puzzle transfer students from northern regions.

Other types of test bias typically discussed in assessment literature are predictive bias, inflammatory bias, true or statistical bias, and inherent bias. Predictive bias refers to the ability of a test to predict future performance. For example, SAT, ACT, and GRE scores are often used as predictors of an individual's college grade-point average (GPA) or success in an undergraduate or graduate program. However, Wilder and Powell's (1989) study indicated that a female student's math SAT score may significantly underpredict her college GPA and success in college-level math classes. In fact, recent data suggest that the best predictor of college success is a student's high school GPA, not his or her SAT or ACT scores (Arends, 1998).

Inflammatory bias occurs when items are included on the test that stereotype certain individuals or groups. For example, an item that references an Asian person running a laundry or a blonde female being forgetful and unorganized would have inflammatory bias because it would be offensive to a certain group or individual.

True or statistical bias occurs when variations of scores on certain test items are not related to the knowledge required to answer the item correctly. For example, if an item on a math test is related to the scoring of a specific kind of sport (like calculating baseball batting averages) in order to solve the problem, the item would have true bias because anyone unfamiliar with the sport would be unable to answer the question regardless of his or her fluency with mathematical computations (Ward & Murray-Ward, 1999).

Inherent bias usually is found when using interview or teacher-made test data (Arends, 1998; Sattler, 1994). Interview data, as will be explained later in this chapter, provide important information to the teacher. The inherent bias in interviews is, of course, in the validity and reliability of the information provided, especially secondhand information. Because people tend to interpret behavior in relationship to their own perceptions rather than what is factual, interview data must be considered informal and be interpreted with caution. In addition, teacher bias in grading also must be carefully analyzed as a source of inherent bias. Specifically, teachers often allow their personal feelings or a student's past performance to influence the grading of a subjective assignment like an essay question on a test. Ways to prevent this type of grading bias are discussed later in this chapter in the section describing the construction of teacher-made tests.

In summary, a dynamic assessment process provides purposeful, timely information that can be used for several instructional and evaluative purposes. Because assessment data are used to formulate hypotheses and plan instruction, to evaluate students' skill acquisition and progress, and to judge the effectiveness of teachers' instruction, it is important that teachers understand the different types of assessment data they need to gather and the purposes for each type.

FORMATIVE AND SUMMATIVE DATA

The two main types of assessment information gathered by teachers in classrooms are **formative** and **summative data**. These data may be gathered through formal or informal means. Formative data sources are those that *formulate* or express precisely an evaluation or judgment about the student's current skill or knowledge level. Formative assessment provides the teacher with feedback about the student's progress "along the way" to the end of the instruction or intervention. Formative assessment data are collected before or during instruction and can be used for planning instructional goals and objectives and/or adaptations of instruction. One use of such data is to plan modifications for students with special needs or those who are struggling with traditional grade-level material. Formative assessment is also used to diagnose student strengths and weaknesses. Prior to instruction, diagnostic formative data sources would include pretests, student and/or parent interviews, past report card grades, learning styles inventories, and/or class discussions.

Diagnostic data could also include discussions with the student's previous teacher. However, the reliability of these data must be carefully considered.

Formative data gathered during instruction is usually in the form of quizzes, class discussions, and guided and independent practice activities. During instruction, formative assessment data should be gathered frequently, and feedback should be immediate. Formative evaluation should be part of each day's lesson plan and be considered an evaluation of the student's prior knowledge and skills related to the class or lesson content, but should not be used to make judgments about the student's work (Arends, 1998; Slavin, 1997). For example, one simple way to collect formative data is to ask the students evaluative questions. In an elementary classroom, the teacher could ask each student, using a round-robin technique, to tell the most important point they had learned during a specific lesson. The teacher would record each student's responses. Later the teacher would review the students' statements to ascertain if the students' learning reflected the objectives of the lesson. This information could be used in several ways: for planning reteach or remedial lessons, modifying lessons or extending or expanding concepts of a lesson, and/or planning summative (overall) judgment of the students' learning. At the secondary level, the same technique can be used; however, the teacher would request that the secondary students write their comments on a half sheet of paper. In addition, the older students would be asked to comment on any point that remained unclear. Again, the teacher would analyze the students' comments and plan modifications or emphasis points for the next day's class. In other words, teachers should be collecting formative data as they go along through a course or unit to "form" the student more toward the desired end result. By reporting the formative feedback to the student, the teacher provides students with the opportunity to use it to form their study or project goals in order to successfully complete or master the course or content objectives.

Summative assessments can be formal and/or informal and are intended to be more or less judgments about the student's progress through the curriculum or instructional activities. The purpose of summative evaluation is to summarize how well the student, group of students, or a teacher has performed on a set of learning goals and objectives. Summative data are gathered after instruction and include such things as unit or chapter tests, curriculum- or criterion-based tests, cooperative or individual learning projects or products, term themes, or other activities that answer the question, "In the end, how well did you do?" Summative data typically compare students' progress with that of other students to determine grades or mastery of skills or content. The Texas Assessment of Academic Skills (TAAS) is a summative evaluation tool because it measures each student's progress against a specific curricular standard and compares one student's skill mastery with another. In addition, TAAS scores give teachers diagnostic information to plan instruction. Summative data are usually not gathered as frequently as formative data. However, both should be closely tied to the course or curriculum objectives and have reliability and validity (Arends, 1998; Slavin, 1997).

FORMAL ASSESSMENT

Formal assessments are typically standardized and either **norm-** or **criterion-referenced.** A **standardized test** is usually commercially generated and given to particular groups or individual students. For example, when a student is referred for special education assessment, formal data are gathered through precise diagnostic instruments, namely, intelligence and academic achievement tests. Standardized assessment instruments must meet rigorous statistical standards for reliability and validity.

Norm-Referenced Tests

One type of formal assessment is a norm-referenced test. A norm-referenced test is one that has been standardized on a clearly defined group called a norm group. The scores are reported in **standard scores** or **percentile ranks,** which compare an individual student's performance with that of his or her norm group (Choate et al., 1995; Sattler, 1994). For example, the WISC-III is a norm-referenced intelligence test. A student's score compares his or her performance with others in the same norm sample or age group and reflects his or her rank within the norm group. Because the mean or average score for the WISC-III is 100, a score of 100 indicates *average intelligence* within a particular age group or norm sample. Standard scores express the individual's distance from the mean or average score in terms of the standard deviation of the norming sample (see Figure 10.1); so this score could also be reported as being in the 50th *percentile,* which means the individual scored *as well as or better than* 50 percent of the norm sample.

A good way to remember the elements of a norm-referenced test is to think of it as a test that seeks to identify how close to a theoretical "normal" test taker an individual scores. We could also see what is a "normal" score for a very large number of test takers and how a specific test taker compares to that large group. Scores are related to the theoretical score distribution or bell curve, where the majority score at or close to the average or mean score, and the others score at a significant distance from the mean. An individual's score is reported in standard deviations from the mean and as positive (+) or negative (-), depending on the direction from the mean. Using our previous example of an IQ of 100, a student whose score was 115 would be reported as scoring one standard deviation above (+) the mean, while a student with an IQ of 85 would be reported as scoring one standard deviation below (-) the mean. Most students score at or about 100, with a much smaller number scoring significantly different, either considerably above or below 100.

Norm-referenced tests are typically used to categorize students for special or gifted education placements. Normative data are important because they provide information about the student's performance in comparison to a large number of his or her peers as well as information about the student's developmental, academic, physical, and social changes. A norm-referenced test, however, provides little information about how students learn or the success or failure of instruction.

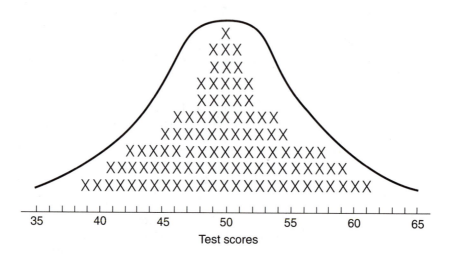

FIGURE 10.1 Frequency of scores forming a normal Bell curve.
If 100 people take a test and the score for each is marked by an x on a graph, the result could suggest a normal curve. In a normal distribution most scores are at or near the mean (in this case, 50) and the number of scores further from the mean progressively decreases.

Therefore, other types of assessment sources must supplement norm–referenced data (Choate et al., 1995; Sattler, 1994).

Other ways to report normative data are by **age-** or **grade-equivalent scores.** This type of reporting is often misleading and should be avoided as much as possible. Because age- and grade-equivalent scores are based on developmental norms, reporting such scores assumes that all children of certain ages have developed skill levels or all children in certain grades have received uniform instruction. For example, a child in fourth grade who obtains a grade-equivalent score of 6.9 in mathematics cannot be assumed to have mastered the arithmetic process taught in sixth grade. Rather, the child's score was determined by his or her superior performance on *fourth*-grade arithmetic problems.

Criterion-Referenced Tests

Criterion-referenced tests are also standardized measures and are used to provide information about a student's mastery level for specific skills or content. A student's scores are reported as mastered skills in areas such as arithmetic operations, mathematical reasoning, written language, reading comprehension, and word decoding. Criterion-referenced tests use absolute standards to answer specific questions about student achievement (for example, does Angelina read beginning third-grade material with 70 percent accuracy?). Criterion-referenced scores provide information useful in formulating instructional objectives, thereby assisting the teacher to know where to start and how to sequence classroom instruction. The TAAS and ExCET are examples of criterion-referenced tests and are scored in percentages of 100. To pass, a student must receive a predetermined percentage of 100. For the ExCET, that percentage is currently 70.

CURRICULUM-BASED ASSESSMENT

Curriculum-based assessment (CBA) is defined as the process that determines a student's instructional needs within the classroom curriculum. Therefore, CBA is the foundation of an effective learner-centered classroom. Curriculum-based assessment may be formal or informal in design and collected before, during, or after instruction so that it can be used as both a formative and/or summative assessment source. Regardless of the method, CBA is generally criterion-based, with a standard designated within a set of objectives to an indicated mastery (Choate et al., 1995). In other words, a curriculum-based assessment process is designed by the teacher to assess the student's mastery of the content and is based on a percentage or passing score. Typically, and unfortunately, the standard percentage for mastery is 70 percent, which is given as the student's grade in the course or content area. This arbitrary 70 percent, of course, does not make sense for some functional skills like telling time or counting money. Some skills need 100 percent accuracy to be functional; however, the teacher cannot require 100 percent mastery if the school's or test's criteria for "passing" is set at 70 percent.

Curriculum-based assessment helps teachers make decisions about the type, pace, and effectiveness of instructional strategies. When an effective CBA process is in place, both the learner and the teacher are well informed about student progress and the efficacy of instruction. Curriculum-based assessment may include teacher-made tests, chapter tests, portfolios, performance assessment, quizzes, and/or work samples. Curriculum-based assessment can be accomplished through traditional assessment procedures (e.g., teacher-made tests) or alternative assessment measures (e.g., portfolios) as long as the measure is a valid standard for evaluating a student's progress.

Just as CBA may use a number of data sources, it may be accomplished in several different ways. It may be achieved by setting course objectives, testing the objectives, teaching, and retesting. This method would obviously involve a pretest to determine the student's current skill level and a posttest to determine if his or her skill had improved (Blankenship, 1985). Another type of CBA uses observational data related to the student's academic learning time (ALT), that is, the percent of time the student engages in task-related behaviors, the number of items attempted, and task comprehension (Gickling & Thompson, 1985).

Curriculum-based assessment has many advantages over the use of standardized or group achievement tests. Curriculum-based assessments help the teacher determine what to teach by providing information about the exact skills in the curriculum the students have not mastered. This process is popular with schools who "teach to the TAAS." Teachers may teach a unit or skill, and then give a posttest designed in the TAAS format. Those students who do not pass will receive special support through remediation and/or reteaching of the nonmastered skill.

Using a curriculum-based assessment process is efficient because the teacher may use several data sources, including daily student improvement charts, to illustrate students' progress toward mastery and completion of short-term instructional objectives. Curriculum-based assessment facilitates evaluation of student progress, program effectiveness, and educational research. Reports from CBA are easy for parents to understand because the student's progress may be graphed or charted daily or weekly, thereby demonstrating even very small increments of improvement. Unlike standardized and annual group achievement tests, CBA allows the teacher to evaluate the effectiveness of an instructional strategy by providing him or her with precise, timely information. In addition, curriculum-based assessment is both valid and reliable because (a) it uses material from the student's own classroom; (b) it is brief; and (c) performance samplings are repeated frequently. Further, curriculum-based assessment increases student achievement because it matches the assessment process to classroom instruction. Obviously, when what is taught relates to what is being assessed, student achievement increases.

Because CBA assessment data are collected frequently, these data help teachers make decisions about the severity of a particular student's skill deficits. For example, classroom teachers initiate special education referrals based on a student's lack of progress. In order to identify a student who may have specific learning problems, the classroom teacher must have precise information about the target student's skill level and rate of progress. This kind of information gives a clear indication of the nature and severity of the student's educational need for specialized services.

Finally, CBA complies with the requirements of the Individuals with Disabilities Education Act (IDEA) because it specifies the student's present skill levels or competencies within the curriculum. Because the latest revisions of IDEA strongly suggest that students with disabilities be included in or progressing toward the regular curriculum goals, compliance with the law is important to both the classroom teacher and the special education teacher. Curriculum-based assessments allow both teachers to evaluate the degree to which the special needs student's instructional objectives stated on his or her individualized education program (IEP) are being met (Choate et al., 1995).

Teacher-Made Tests

One type of CBA is a teacher-made test. **Teacher-made tests** are probably the most common way used to assess student progress in a specific content area. Teacher-made tests, like all other assessment data sources, must be reliable and valid. The construction of a reliable, valid teacher-made test is a laborious process that involves thoughtful planning. The test must relate directly to the course objectives and classroom instruction. Most instructional objectives cover a range of behaviors and cognitive processes such as important facts, major concepts, and vocabulary about a topic, as well as critical and analytical thinking and problem solving about course content. Therefore, when planning a test, the teacher must first decide how much of the test will be devoted to each behavior or process, what weight will be given to each section, and which information will be included in the test. Obviously, a six-week test cannot include every bit of information covered during the time period. A table of specifications is often useful to organize the planning process. The table of specifications allows the teacher to predetermine the content of the test (Arends, 1998; Slavin, 1997). (See Figure 10.2.)

Once the teacher has decided which topics and behaviors to test, the second step is to decide the format of the test, specifically, whether the test will be objective, essay, or a combination. There are advantages and disadvantages to all three formats.

An objective test (e.g., multiple-choice, true-false, fill-in-the-blank) can be scored objectively, that is, relatively free from bias. There is typically one correct answer, and a great deal of content can be covered. The disadvantage of this type of test is that it is difficult to write objective items that assess the student's higher cognitive functions and problem-solving skills. Another disadvantage is that a valid, reliable objective test is very time-consuming to construct. In addition, there is the element of student guessing to be considered, especially with true-or-false items. Finally, objective tests can measure only a limited range of understanding and skills (Arends, 1998; Slavin, 1997).

Essay tests tend to do the best job of assessing the students' higher-level thought processes and creativity. In addition, essay items take less time to construct; however, good, clear questions do take some thought and planning, including sample answers and grading criteria. Criticisms of essay tests include teacher bias in grading and limited covering of content. Both of these criticisms may be addressed through careful construction of questions, use of sample questions and answers, and designation of specific grading criteria through scoring rubrics. A scoring rubric is a tool that helps eliminate teacher bias in scoring essay answers (see the example in Figure 10.3). The teacher provides the student with an outline of expected content and number of points each **domain** (or common area) is worth. In this way, the

Unit covered: Prehistoric times Three-week topic: Dinosaurs Anticipated time to take the test: 20 minutes Student behaviors and cognitive processes		
Topic/Content	Recall Questions	Higher-Level Thinking Questions
Physical characteristics	3	1
Names	5	1
Extinction	2	3
Total Number	10	5

FIGURE 10.2 Example: Table of Specifications.

Domain	Number of Points
Grammar, spelling, and mechanics; uses complete sentences	5
Content: describes the dinosaurs using adjective words like *color* and *size*	10
Accuracy: descriptions are accurate in detail; habitat is accurately described; food is accurately reported	10

FIGURE 10.3 Example: Scoring rubric.

student has a clear understanding of the teacher's expectations of an acceptable answer. Teachers may also use a holistic scoring procedure to reduce bias in grading. Holistic scoring involves skimming through all the essays and selecting samples that could be judged as poor, average, and outstanding. These samples then become the models for judging other papers (Arends, 1998; Slavin, 1997).

Another consideration when planning a teacher-made test is the actual administration. Teachers in learner-centered classrooms must consider several things as they plan when and how the test will be administered. For example, the students' level of text anxiety must be heeded. Although test anxiety is a normal part of the testing situation, overanxiousness is not healthy or productive. When test takers' stress or anxiety levels are very intense, their ability to think constructively and recall learned information is significantly diminished (Jensen, 1998). The teacher must find ways to lessen test anxiety by making sure the students know what is expected of them. Using humor before the test and giving the students a few minutes before the test to simply take a deep breath are good ways to create a more relaxed testing environment.

The teacher must also organize the learning environment to be conducive to test taking. For example, the students should have ample room to work so that opportunities to share their work are minimized. Other considerations include sufficient time, appropriate support for students with special needs, environmental considerations like lighting and temperature, and specific test-taking routines and instructions. One common error made by beginning teachers is the lack of carefully developed classroom test-taking routines and clear instructions. A good routine to follow includes: (a) passing out the tests face down and asking students to wait until everyone has a test to turn it face up; (b) instructing students not to begin until they are told; (c) reviewing instructions for each section of the test; and (d) providing students with guidelines about how long to spend on each part. If a new test format is being introduced, the teacher should explain the procedures and expectations of the format. In addition, preparing and scoring a "freebie" question in each section often lessens test anxiety and promotes student success. Finally, it is imperative that each student understands the tasks he or she is asked to perform; therefore, the teacher should provide time for students to ask questions prior to beginning the test (Arends, 1998).

Grading the test is the final step in the process. Teachers may grade on a curve or grade to criterion. Grading on a curve is typical for secondary and university classes. Using this method, teachers follow strict interpretations of grading-on-a-curve concepts, which give 10 percent of the students As, 20 percent Bs, 40 percent Cs, 20 percent Ds, and 10 percent Fs. With this grading system, even students with a high degree of mastery may fall into the lower grading areas, and vice versa.

Grading to criterion or mastery may be used by teachers at all levels. The approach defines precisely the skills and objectives for the class and then measures student performance against that criteria. Typically, a percentage of correct answers determines the student's grade. For example, a spelling test would be graded to criterion if a student needed to score 90 to 100 percent correct in order to earn an A (Arends, 1998; Slavin, 1997). In theory, therefore, all students taking the test could earn an A.

In summary, the guidelines for effective teacher-made testing procedures include providing clear instructions to students about what they will be tested on. It is also important to test frequently so that students have an opportunity to be successful and the teacher has the opportunity to reteach. Finally, it is essential that teachers be specific and explicit about their grading procedures. When students understand the expectations of the teacher and see the fairness in the grading system, they are more likely to accept judgments made about their work (Arends, 1998).

Constructing a Teacher-Made Test

As mentioned previously, an objective test has advantages and disadvantages, but it is probably one of the most-used data sources in the classroom. To construct a reliable and valid objective test takes planning. Each item needs to be clear and concise as well as contain information based on classroom instruction. In addition, clear, concise instructions for completing each section of the test should precede the group of test items.

Multiple-choice items are probably the best kind of objective item and the most difficult to construct, especially if the teacher wishes to tap thinking skills such as analysis, application, and/or synthesis (Slavin, 1997). A good multiple-choice item has a stem with enough contextual information so that the test taker completely understands the problem or question being posed. The stem should be straightforward and specific. The item also must be written so that the correct answer is not easily revealed; that is, all distracters must be plausible yet clearly recognizable as wrong by students who really know the content. Distracters should also be grammatically consistent with the stem and of approximately the same length and should not be identifiable by *a* or *an* (Arends, 1998; Slavin, 1997). For example:

____ A dinosaur was a prehistoric animal that

(a) ate only plants and seeds.

(b) had wings, fangs, and claws.

(c) laid eggs and became extinct.

This is an example of a well-constructed multiple-choice item. In contrast, the following is an example of a poorly constructed item:

A dinosaur:

(a) prehistoric animal that ate only plants and seeds

(b) wings, fangs, and claws

(c) became extinct.

In this example, the distracters are of unequal length and are not grammatically consistent with the stem.

In order to test students' higher-level cognition, multiple-choice items must be carefully thought out and worded. The ExCET has many application-based multiple-choice items. (Also see the items in the Practice Decision Set at the end of this chapter.) Typically, this type of item sets up a situation or scenario and poses several multiple-choice questions based on the described situation.

True-false items are useful if the content of a lesson requires the student to compare alternatives, learn definitions, or distinguish fact from fiction. They are also a good alternative to multiple-choice items if the instructional objective does not lend itself to several distracters. True-false items must be written so that the choice is clear. For example, "Prehistoric means before written history" is clearly a true item, but "Prehistoric animals lived in ancient times" is an ambiguous item because the word *ancient* means old, but not before written history. The use of words like *always* and *never* are also confusing or giveaways in true-false items. The obvious drawback of using true-false items is that the student has a 50 percent chance of guessing the correct answer; therefore, this type of item should be used sparingly (Slavin, 1997). In addition, it is a good idea to have the students write out the words *true* or *false* or to have *true* and *false* printed beside each item for the students to circle. This prevents the argument over whether the letter is a T or an F based on the student's or your perception of the student's handwriting skills.

Matching items are helpful in measuring large amounts of factual information. In a matching item, students are provided with two lists and asked to select which items closely match. Experts caution against using lists that are too long. Most agree that a list of six to eight items is preferable. Matching items assess basic factual recall. As with true-or-false items, matching items have a guess or process-of-elimination factor that sometimes adversely affects their reliability.

Fill-in-the-blank items are very popular with classroom teachers because they are easy to write and do a good job of measuring students' recall of facts. The element of guessing is virtually removed using this format unless a bank of answers is provided for the student. Like other test items, fill-in-the-blank items must be clearly written, avoid ambiguous wording, and have only one correct answer. For example, "Dinosaurs lived in _____" is a poor item because there is more than one correct answer. Students could provide answers like prehistoric times, jungles, swamps, and so on. A better format would be "Dinosaurs lived in _____ times, or before written history." For this item, there is clearly only one correct response. Also, for easy grading, it is helpful to have blanks to the left of the questions (e.g., "____ Dinosaurs lived in _____ times"; however, this format is often difficult for students with reading disabilities.

Because these students often use context cues and sequencing to ascertain the correct response, they need to have the sentence sequenced with the blank appearing in the natural flow of written language.

Constructing Essay Questions

As previously stated, teachers often like to write essay tests because they believe essay questions are easy to create. Essay items allow students to express in their own words, and often creatively, the concepts they have learned. Short-answer items often require students to synthesize and apply information, evaluate concepts, or think at a higher level than typical objective test items. The difficulty with essay items has to do mostly with the fairness or lack of bias in grading and the amount of time needed to accurately and fairly grade each essay.

An essay item, like an objective item, should be clear in purpose. Essay items should also approximate the amount of detail needed to answer the question and have an expected length of the response. An essay response can range from one sentence to a page or two. It is important for the student to know precisely what is expected. As previously mentioned, a scoring rubric is helpful in making the teacher's expectations clear. Further, an essay item should be tied directly to instructional objectives and classroom instruction. For example, "Discuss dinosaurs" is a poor essay question because it has no parameters or any indication of what is to be discussed. A better item would be "Describe three different kinds of dinosaurs and tell where they lived and what they ate. Write one paragraph with at least 5 sentences for each one." This item gives the student a clear notion of what he or she needs to discuss and how much discussion is required to answer the question.

Essay items are considered reliable and valid if the teacher can answer three critical questions about the item:

1. Does the item measure content required in an instructional objective?

2. Can the student answer the question well during the testing time?

3. Does the item have language specific enough for the student to understand what he or she is being asked to write about?

To answer the first question, the teacher must refer to the course objectives he or she envisioned and wrote before instruction began. For the second question, a good method is for the teacher to practice writing a response before the test is given. The teacher can then estimate how much time it will take students to complete the assignment. Slavin (1997) suggests that students take about four times longer to answer an essay question than does the teacher who constructed the test. Finally, as the third question indicates, specific, descriptive language is essential for a good essay item. It is better to use words like *compare, contrast,* and *define,* rather than generic, global ones like *discuss, tell all you know,* and *give your opinion.*

The use of a scoring rubric for essay questions minimizes teacher bias in grading and helps students understand the expectations of the grading system. Using the rubric, the teacher provides a standard for himself or herself and one for the students (Arends, 1998; Slavin, 1997). In addition, giving the rubric to the students will help them adhere to the teacher's expectations. Rubrics are also appropriate for grading projects and written papers such as term themes and research papers (see Figure 10.3).

Another way to minimize teacher grading bias is to have the students write their names on the back of the paper so that the teacher is unaware of the student's identity until after grading his or her essay. Having another teacher evaluate the essay also reduces the likelihood of grading bias and adds reliability to the assigned grade.

INFORMAL ASSESSMENT

Informal assessment includes such things as work samples, portfolios, and projects as well as other traditional and nontraditional ways of measuring students' understanding and progress. Informal assessment is the critical element for planning, modifying, and pacing instruction as well as a key factor in determining a student's progress. Informal data may be formative or summative in nature, with an ultimate purpose of evaluating the appropriateness of a teacher's instructional techniques and accuracy of a student's performance or depth of his or her understanding. For example, informal assessment in a mathematics class could include class work samples, student interviews, error analysis, and demonstration or cooperative learning projects.

Many assessment experts suggest informal data should be organized and individualized using assessment planning checksheets or informal inventory worksheets (e.g., Choate et al., 1995; Taylor, 2000; Ward & Murray-Ward, 1999). These organizing tools help the teacher and student assess such areas as strengths, weaknesses, patterns of errors, and appropriate instructional strategies. (See Choate et al., 1995, or Taylor, 2000, for examples of these tools.)

Student Interviews as Informal Assessment Data Sources

Student interviews or conferences provide the teacher with invaluable information regarding the student's perceptions about his or her learning. Individual conferences with students should be an integral part of any classroom assessment process. These interviews or conferences should focus on the student's understanding of the class's curricular objectives and his or her learning styles and preferences. Because an interview is an exchange of information, the teacher must be willing to listen creatively and empathetically (Sattler, 1994). In addition, the interview must be a nonthreatening, ungraded situation that allows the student to "speak his or her mind" in an appropriate manner about his or her progress through the curriculum. Although the interview should be informal, the teacher must have a clear purpose for the appointment and a tentative set of questions or topics about which he or she wants information. It is critically important, too, that the student has been apprised of the purpose prior to the interview session. The teacher should also restate the purpose at the beginning of the interview.

Student interviews allow students time to reflect on their learning. Interviewing students also gives them a sense that the class is a reciprocal, respectful learning environment.

Some tips to remember when interviewing students are:

1. Avoid yes–no questions.
2. Ask direct questions.
3. Avoid long, multiple-answer questions.
4. Give students ample time to answer and elaborate. (Sattler, 1994)

An example scenario might be:

Teacher: Thanks for coming in today, Josh. I wanted you to help me by discussing your experiences with the Texas History class this past six weeks.

Josh: OK.

Teacher: I'd like you to tell me the three most relevant or interesting points you have learned about Texas History during these six weeks.

Josh: Well, I learned more about the Alamo, and that was exciting. I always thought Sam Houston was there as the general, but it was Travis. I also learned something about how brave those guys were to stay when they knew they were going to die. I think that's why the Texans beat the Mexicans—because they were so mad about the Alamo. I never thought about that before.

Teacher: Great, I'm glad you liked that part. What do you remember about the Republic of Texas after Texas won its independence?

Teacher Observations as Informal Assessment Data Sources

Effective teachers are accurate observers of students' academic and social behavior; that is, they are good "kid watchers." *Observation* is defined as careful watching and recording for later reflection. Because events happen very rapidly in a classroom, it is often difficult for a new teacher to be a reliable observer (Arends, 1998; Sattler, 1994). Although **observational data** are very important in a learner-centered assessment system, the reliability and validity of such data should always be highly suspect. Observational data should never be used as the sole source for making decisions about students or instructional techniques because such data typically have a high degree of bias.

Being a good observer takes practice and self-knowledge. A reflective observer understands his or her own values, attitudes, and prejudices. For example, if a teacher has negative feelings about including students with disabilities in his or her classroom, accurate observations of these students may be adversely affected by the teacher's negative views. In addition, it is always good to have someone else, such as a colleague or administrator, observe the situation. Paired observation often helps to validate accurate or inaccurate assessments of a situation. If a paired observation is used, the observers must be sure to focus their observations on the behavior that is of concern and attend *only* to the targeted behavior(s). A common mistake of observers involves the interpretation of motives behind the behavior rather than the occurrence of the behavior only. For example, an observer may tally the number of sound insertions or deletions a student makes in reading a passage aloud, but should not make judgments about why the student made these (e.g., the student was bored with the passage, he was nervous about reading aloud, etc.) (Sattler, 1994).

Alternative Assessment Procedures
as Informal Data Sources

Alternative assessment procedures have gained popularity over the past decade. Alternative assessments include portfolios and performance-based assessment. Performance-based assessment is often referred to as authentic assessment because the student's skills are evaluated by having him or her demonstrate a specific skill by constructing a product or solving a problem that could be generated from a real-life situation (Arends, 1998; Choate et al., 1995). However, some experts would disagree with the two terms being used synonymously (Slavin, 1997). Slavin defines performance assessment as student demonstration of a skill such as playing a song or painting a picture, while authentic assessment requires the student to perform the skill in a real-life setting. For example, writing a letter to a potential employer or giving an introduction for a guest speaker would be an example of an authentic assessment. Authentic assessment results may be interpreted according to the thinking patterns of the student, that is, how he or she chose to solve the problem, as well as the correctness of his or her solution (Choate et al., 1995). In this chapter, the terms *authentic* and *performance assessment* will be used synonymously to mean assessment that requires the student to demonstrate his or her skill level by producing a product or performance. The teacher should also keep in mind that the product or performance should mirror a situation found in real life as much as possible.

Because performance-based assessment allows students to demonstrate their skills, talents, and problem-solving skills through creating a unique product, it may be individually tailored to the student's particular learning style or strength (Choate et al., 1995). Specifically, performance-based assessment strategies fit well with the theories of multiple intelligences (Armstrong, 1994; Gardner, 1983) and learning styles (Dunn & Dunn, 1999). Both of these theories suggest that students have specific ways of learning that are often ignored in the traditional classroom setting. Both theories also assume that a learner-centered classroom is one that is sensitive to the diverse ways children and adolescents learn and one in which this sensitivity manifests itself in instructional strategies geared toward individual rather than group success.

Gardner's (1983) model proposes that there are eight ways of "being smart" (musical, mathematical, linguistic, visual-spatial, naturalistic, interpersonal, intra-personal, and kinesthetic). He suggests that when students are allowed to express their knowledge through their preferred intelligence, learning will be significantly enhanced. For example, instead of a multiple-choice test over dinosaurs, the musically smart student might write a song incorporating the important concepts about the topic, while the visual-spatial student might paint a mural or draw illustrations for the linguistic student's storybook. All these activities would be considered authentic or performance-based assessment products. The emphasis, then, of performance assessment is testing procedural rather than declarative knowledge (Slavin, 1997).

Another example of performance-based assessment can be found in the learning styles research of Dunn and Dunn (1999). This well-researched instructional model suggests that students have environmental needs that enhance the learning process such as lighting, temperature, intake, movement, and teacher involvement. In addition, the Dunn and Dunn model describes students in terms of cognitive styles and perceptual strengths that should be accommodated in the learning environment. Learning styles research indicates that when students are taught and assessed through their learning styles or preference, significant gains are made in academic achievement (also see Chapter 4). For example, one instructional strategy created by the learning styles research is the contract activity package (CAP). The CAP is a performance assessment measure. The CAP is designed to allow the student a choice or menu of activities that he or she may use to demonstrate his or her knowledge about class content. The CAP is set up to allow the student to make choices, create a product, and demonstrate his or her creation to a friend, group of peers, parent, or teacher (Dunn & Dunn, 1999).

In theory, performance assessment (PA) is superior to standardized or traditional assessment procedures because it allows the student to demonstrate a broader and deeper understanding of the subject matter. Because of this, many states are now including PA items on their state assessment programs (e.g., Vermont, Kentucky, Maryland). In addition, performance-based assessment strategies provide all children with opportunities to demonstrate what they know in a variety of contexts and allow them to engage in a continual process of self-reflection (Armstrong, 1994). Although these measures are still very controversial, they have merit in preparing students for their life after school. After all, how many of us take many multiple-choice tests after we complete our formal education?

The difficulties in using performance-based assessment items are the time involved in developing valid items and the expense of administering and scoring the items. Most experts agree, however, that the expense is well worth it in terms of improving the teaching-learning process (Shepard, 1995; Slavin, 1997).

Portfolios are also an informal alternative assessment tool. Portfolios have long been used as an assessment and summative presentation of a body of work for such disciplines as the visual arts, architecture, and photography. It has just been during the past decade that the portfolio has been used by public schools and colleges of education as a summative evaluation of a student's performance. A portfolio is closely related to performance assessment techniques because it shows student progress through specific examples or products.

A *portfolio* is defined as a collection and evaluation of samples of student work over an extended period of time (Slavin, 1997). A portfolio tells a story of the student's effort, progress, or achievement for a certain time period (Arter & Spandel, 1992). The portfolio, then, is not just a notebook with random selections of a student's work, but rather a structured collection of that student's work that demonstrates progress in some way.

Some schools (e.g., in Illinois and Kansas) use student portfolios to assess and report student achievement. In these schools, the portfolio encompasses sample artifacts and reflections that demonstrate what the student has done or can do across all subject areas (Arends, 1998). For example, a portfolio may be structured around a set of questions that the student answers in a variety of ways including essays, video or audio tapes, visual illustrations, computer discs, and/or reflective journal entries. Typically, in those schools that use portfolios as a major portion of their summative assessment, the portfolio is kept and passed on from grade to grade so that the student and his or her parents can compare such things as writing ability and depth of knowledge from year to year. In addition, the portfolio is refined year to year with items being discarded and others added. The purposes of portfolios are for (a) the student to reflect on his or her learning and (b) the teacher to assess student improvement over time and in many different contexts.

For a portfolio to be considered a valid and reliable assessment tool, the teacher must structure it so that it is a true reflection of student progress and not just a collection of student work. Obviously, advanced planning by the teacher is a required element. Experts agree that the creation of a purposeful portfolio system entails several steps. Initially, the teacher must define his or her purpose for the portfolio. For example, a portfolio may be used as a showcase for the student's best work, a documentation of progress, or an evaluation tool. It is possible for a portfolio to have more than one purpose; however, if this is the case, it should be divided into sections that document each purpose (Ward & Murray-Ward, 1999).

The second step in designing a portfolio is to determine the skills and content to be assessed. Like other curriculum-based measures, portfolio artifacts must be closely tied to the instructional objectives of the course content. Therefore, teachers and students must be careful to choose items that reflect student progress toward mastery of those objectives. These items could include teacher-made tests, student reflections, and/or projects or assignments that reflect the student's depth of knowledge about a specific instructional objective.

The third step is to determine how to assess the contents of the portfolio and who will assess them. For schools that use portfolios as an assessment tool, it is imperative that they also determine at what grade levels the assessment will take place. Typically, the assessment process uses a rubric design so that objectivity in grading is maintained.

When the structural decisions have been made, it is critical to determine how students will be involved in the process. One of the major strengths of a portfolio system is the high degree of student involvement. The student should be involved in decisions about the content and organization of his or her individual portfolio. In addition, a student journal and self-reflections should be required items. In order for the student to participate in a meaningful way, however, he or she must be trained and have time to select the work and reflect on it. One criticism of using a portfolio system is the time required to organize and evaluate it, although most users agree the benefits of an effective portfolio are extensive.

Finally, a process by which assessment results are communicated to parents and students must be designed. The very nature of a portfolio lends itself to conferences rather than traditional letter-grade interpretations. However, when assessment results are tied to retention and/or graduation requirements, a specific process must be in place for informal conferences and standardized results. For these reasons, the use of portfolios as a major component of a school's assessment program is very controversial. Although a few schools use the process exclusively, it is more common for a particular classroom or school district to use portfolios as one piece of the formative and summative assessment process (Cheong & Shively, 1991; Mumme, 1990; Nitko, 1996; Ward & Murray-Ward, 1999).

SUMMARY

To design an effective classroom-based assessment process takes teacher planning and creativity. The process must incorporate and be closely tied to the instructional objectives of the course content as well as the needs and strengths of a particular student population. As Competency 10 suggests, teachers should be aware of and use many different assessment techniques to ensure that all students have the opportunity to demonstrate their understanding and progress. In addition, teachers must collect assessment data frequently to evaluate the effectiveness of their instructional strategies and the depth and breadth of their students' understanding.

SUGGESTED ACTIVITIES

Process

1. Collect data about the assessment process used by the cooperating teacher, specifically, (1) what types of formative and summative assessment data he or she uses and why; (2) how often assessment of student understanding takes place; (3) teacher effectiveness at delivering instruction; (4) whether there is a formal, planned process; (5) whether there are any performance-based or authentic measures used; and so on.

2. Collect articles describing alternative assessment measures. Plan how you could incorporate them in your future classroom.

3. Design a brochure for parents describing the relationship between TAAS objectives and your classroom-based assessment program. Be sure the brochure gives parents an indication of the difference between formal and informal assessment practices and the purpose of each.

Application

1. Design a teacher-made test over the content of this chapter. Include one set of matching items, five true-false items, five multiple-choice items that assess application or analysis skills, and three essay questions that assess higher-level

cognitive skills. Design a scoring rubric for your essay items.

2. Design a multilevel assessment process for your future classroom. Designate what types of formative and summative data you will collect, how you will accommodate for student diversity in learning, and a schedule for data collection. Describe how you will use the information to improve instruction as well as evaluate student progress.

3. Make a collage of the different types of assessment practices used to evaluate student progress. Your collage should demonstrate the definition and use of each assessment practice. Present your collage to three of your classmates and see if they can interpret the point you are trying to illustrate.

4. Gather a collection of teacher-made tests (including one of your own). Evaluate them for test bias.

Reflection

1. Reflect on your personal experiences with assessment practices in school. What kinds of activities did you like best or feel were a true reflection of your understanding and knowledge? Which ones did you feel threatened by or less competent with? Write your thoughts as a reflective journal entry or letter to the editor of an educational publication.

2. Make an audio- or videotape of your reactions to such assessment practices as portfolios, standardized tests, teacher-made tests, and/or grades. Share your tape with a peer and ask for his or her reactions.

3. Design a survey for your classmates requesting input about their experiences with assessment processes in school. Collect the data and analyze the results to share with the class.

4. Think back on a test or other assessment technique you felt was unfair. Try to determine from your knowledge now why it did not seem to be fair.

PRACTICE DECISION SET

1. Ms. Jenkins teaches high school English. Each year she has her students keep a notebook of their work. Ms. Jenkins has specific questions that are tied to the course objectives that each student must answer by incorporating work samples in his or her notebook. She has weekly conferences with each student to determine if he or she is keeping up with the notebook and choosing appropriate artifacts to include. At the end of each grading period, Ms. Jenkins collects the notebooks and evaluates each student's mastery of the objectives she covered during the six weeks. The student's grade is determined solely by the workbook collection. Ms. Jenkins is using the students' workbooks as

a. Formative and summative evaluation data
b. Traditional and criterion-referenced evaluation data
c. Standardized and curriculum-based assessment data

d. Formal and curriculum-based assessment data

2. Mr. Rodriquez has three students in his third class that he feels need special attention and methods. Therefore, he would like to refer these students for special education assessment. He has kept samples of their work, including in- and outside-class assignments, pretests and test grades, daily and weekly quiz grades, and an anecdotal journal of each child's response to classroom instruction and teacher-student conferences. Mr. Rodriquez can expect the special education assessment process to

   I. Increase his knowledge about these students' skills in comparison to national norms

   II. Provide him with a basis for better instructional strategies to help the target students in his classroom

   III. Provide him with reliable and valid standardized, formal assessment data

   IV. Make an eligibility determination for special education services

   a. I, II, and IV only
   b. I and III only
   c. I, III, and IV only
   d. I and IV only

3. Ms. Simpson constructed a six-week test for her ninth-grade American History students. Her class is 50 minutes long, and the students were required to complete the test within the 50-minute period to receive full credit. Of her 25 students, only 8 were able to complete the test, and 60 percent of the class failed the test. To compensate, Ms. Simpson simply raised the highest grade of 80 by 10 points and adjusted all the rest of the students'

test grades accordingly. In doing so, her final distribution of grades was acceptable, that is, three students made As; eight made Bs; ten made Cs; three made Ds; and one made an F. Ms. Simpson's test would be described as

a. Reliable and valid
b. Reliable, but not valid
c. Valid, but not reliable
d. Neither reliable nor valid

Answer 1: a. Because Ms. Jenkins meets her students individually on a regular basis to discuss their progress, she is gathering formative data that directs her teaching and the students' learning. In addition, she uses the notebooks as a summative evaluation of the students' progress during a specific grading period, that is, she uses the notebooks to determine each student's six-week grade.

Answer 2: c. Special education assessment uses an individualized assessment process that gathers standardized intelligence and achievement data. These data provide information about a student's ranking within a norm sample or in relation to a specific group of students. The purpose of the special education assessment is to determine if the student qualifies or is eligible for special education support, rather than to help the teacher target areas for instruction.

Answer 3. If the majority of the students can neither finish nor pass the test, Ms. Simpson should consider the test as invalid and unreliable *(d)*. Either the test was not closely related to the instructional content of the course or the wording of the items was not precise enough for the students to interpret them correctly. In addition, the test was obviously too long for the students to complete in the time allotted.

WEB LINKS

Remember that website locations may change. If any of these sites have moved or cannot be located, use the Terms to Know in this chapter to search for further information.

http://www.tea.state.tx.us/student assessment
This site provides information about TAAS objectives and other information regarding the assessment of Texas students. It also provides information about assessment topics relevant to teachers and students in Texas.

http://www.ed.gov/databases/ERIC-Digests/ed286938.html
Definitions of key terms and evaluation procedures such as criterion-referenced tests and teacher-made tests are included in this site.

http://www.indiana.edu/%7Eteaching/sfcats.html
This site has practical suggestions for classroom-based assessment procedures.

It also explains why classroom-based assessment is important for teachers and students. In addition, it has some really good suggestions for collecting formative assessment data that are quick, easy, and valid.

http://www.indiana.edu/%7Eteaching/formsum.html
This site has very good definitions of summative and formative evaluation. It is a one-page summary with examples.

http://www.lgu.ac.uk/deliberations/assessment
This site provides an excellent discussion of the purposes of assessment and why it should be a positive, helpful experience for students and teachers.

http://www.edweek.org/ew/1997/08taas.h17
Information about controversy over TAAS exit exam and discrimination is provided at this site.

REFERENCES AND SUGGESTED READINGS

Arends, R. I. (1998). *Learning to teach* (4th ed.). Boston: McGraw-Hill.

Armstrong, T. (1994). *Multiple intelligences in the classroom.* Alexandria, VA: Association for Supervision and Curriculum Development.

Arter, J. A., & Spandel, V. (1992). Using portfolios of student work in instruction and assessment. *Educational Measurements: Issues and Practice, 11*(1), 36–44.

Blankenship, C. S. (1985). Using curriculum based assessment data to make instructional decisions. *Exceptional Children, 52,* 233–238.

Brown, S., Race, P., & Smith, B. (1996). *An assessment manifesto.* http://www.lgu.ac.uk/deliberations/assessment/manifes.html.

Cheong, J. I., & Shively, A. H. (1991). *Issues and reflections on implementing portfolio assessment systems, K–12.* A paper presented at the annual meeting of the California Education Research Association at Santa Barbara, California.

Choate, J. S., Enright, B. E., Lamoine, J. M., Poteet, J. A., & Rakes, T. A. (1995). *Curriculum-based assessment and programming* (3d ed.). Boston: Allyn & Bacon.

Dunn, R., & Dunn, K. (1999). *The complete guide to the learning styles inservice system.* Boston: Allyn & Bacon.

Gardner, H. (1983). *Frames of mind: The theory of multiple intelligences.* New York: Basic Books.

Gickling, E. E., & Thompson, V. P. (1985). A personal view of curriculum based assessment. *Exceptional Children, 52*(1), 205–218.

Jensen, E. (1998). *Teaching with the brain in mind.* Alexandria, VA: Association for Supervision and Curriculum Development.

Lawton, M. (1997). Discrimination claimed in Texas exit exam lawsuit. *Education Week, 17*, http://www.edweek.org/ew/1997/08taas.h17.

Mumme, J. (1990). *Portfolio assessment in mathematics.* Santa Barbara, CA: University of California at Santa Barbara.

Nitko, A. J. (1996). *Education assessment of students.* Englewood Cliffs, NJ: Merrill.

Sattler, J. M. (1994). *Assessment of children: Revised and updated* (3d ed.). San Diego: Sattler.

Shepard, L. A. (1995). Using assessment to improve student learning. *Phi Delta Kappan, 52*(5), 38–43.

Slavin, R. E. (1997). *Educational psychology: Theory and practice* (5th ed.). Boston: Allyn & Bacon.

Taylor, R. (2000). *Assessment of exceptional students: Educational and psychological procedures* (5th ed.). Boston: Allyn & Bacon.

Torres, J. (1991). Equity in education and language minority students. *Forum, 14*(4), 1–3.

Ward, A. W., & Murray-Ward, M. (1999). *Assessment in the classroom.* Belmont, CA: Wadsworth.

Wilder, G. Z., & Powell, K. (1989). *Sex differences in test performance: A survey of the literature* (College Board Rep. No. 89-3). New York: College Entrance Examination Board.

ABOUT THE AUTHOR

Dr. Pam Lindsey teaches at Tarleton State University and is a member of both the graduate and undergraduate faculty. She is also the director of the Educational Diagnostician program at Tarleton State. Prior to her tenure at Tarleton State, she directed the Diagnostician program at Texas Tech University and was instrumental in reinstating the undergraduate special education teacher training program.

Dr. Lindsey was a classroom teacher in special and general education for 13 years and a full-time educational diagnostician for 5 years. She continues to work as a diagnostician for several local school districts. Because of her extensive background and interest in assessment issues, she has accumulated a wealth of expertise emphasizing the important link between effective assessment strategies, program planning, and student learning.

11

✳

Managing the Classroom Environment

DIANE CLAY
TERRY BRANDT

UNIVERSITY OF ST. THOMAS—HOUSTON

The last area to be considered in Domain II, Enhancing Student Achievement, is Competency 11, which deals with managing the classroom environment.

Competency 11: The teacher structures and manages the learning environment to maintain a classroom climate that promotes the lifelong pursuit of learning and encourages cooperation, leadership, and mutual respect.

The teacher knows how to promote student ownership of and membership in a smoothly functioning learning community whose members are responsible, cooperative, purposeful, and mutually supportive. The teacher facilitates a positive social and emotional atmosphere in the classroom, establishes and maintains standards of behavior, manages routines and transitions, maximizes the amount of class time spent learning, and creates a physical setting that is conductive to the achievement of various goals.

TERMS TO KNOW

Active learning	**Risk-taker/taking**
Constructivism	**Routines**
Cooperative learning	**Schema**
KWL	**Student ownership**
Independent learner	**Transitions**
Learner-centered community	**Transaction-orientation**
Metacognition	**Transmission-orientation**
Passive learners	

CREATING A LEARNING COMMUNITY

A teacher may be a brilliant scholar and have outstanding preparation in a particular field of study and yet fail to teach well unless he or she possesses an understanding of the importance of developing a community of learners within the classroom. The importance of knowing how to create an environment where each learner feels empowered to be a risk-taker and encouraged to become an independent learner and thinker cannot be overstated. Recognizing this fact, the Texas Education Agency has prepared *Learner-Centered Schools for Texas—A Vision of Texas Educators: Proficiencies for Teachers* (State Board of Education, 1995). All of the ExCET competencies emanate from this document. It identifies the following areas as crucial for the development of successful classrooms:

- Learner-centered knowledge
- Learner-centered instruction
- Equity in excellence for all learners
- Learner-centered communication
- Learner-centered professional development

At first glance, structuring and managing the learning environment bring to mind arranging desks and making sure the lighting and temperature are conducive to learning. Indeed, these are important factors in creating an effective learning environment. Physical comfort and the ability to see and hear well make significant contributions to students' learning and cannot be neglected or overlooked. However, a careful reading of both *Learner-Centered Schools for Texas* and Competency 11 emphasizes the importance of developing an effective and nurturing atmosphere in the learning environment. Effective teachers, not curricula, teach students. Creating optimum conditions for each student's learning requires extraordinary interpersonal skills on the part of every teacher. This discussion of Competency 11 provides suggestions for creating a supportive, nurturing environment that focuses on students' needs and enhances learning.

LEARNING COMMUNITIES

The importance of creating community in the classroom is not a recently developed concept. John Dewey (as cited in Lickona, 1991) wrote that education fails when it neglects school as a form of community. Donald Graves (1991) speaks for many experts when he says that learning how to become a community is an essential achievement in any teacher's or student's survival tool kit. The most well-planned lessons will fail unless students feel invited into the learning community.

The Center for the Study of Community in Santa Fe, New Mexico, suggests that a learning community possesses the following identifying characteristics:

- Sense of shared purpose—Teachers and students have a common understanding that their goal is learning.

- Respect for difference—Each member of the classroom recognizes and appreciates diversity.

- Acceptance—Everyone is welcome.

- Participation—All students willingly contribute to learning tasks and share in classroom routines.

- Trust—Students feel it is safe to share ideas and opinions.

- Communication—Teachers and students accept responsibility for the effective transmission of information and the exchange of ideas.

- Collaboration—Students enjoy working together on common tasks.

- Commitment—Students have a common interest in doing their best.

- Reciprocity—Students support each other and share responsibilities.

- Conscious choice—Teachers and students select procedures and tasks that advance commonly agreed-upon knowledge and skills.

- Accountability—Students understand expectations and eagerly accept responsibility for their performance.

- Efficacy—Students feel empowered to learn.

- Equity—All students are considered as equal partners in learning.

- Perceived skill—Teachers and students believe that they "have what it takes." Everyone believes that all students can learn.

- Openness—Teachers and students are receptive to new ideas and opportunities.

- Cohesion—Teachers and students work together toward common goals.

In such places, each member is encouraged to contribute something that he or she feels especially able to give, something that he or she is good at. "The gift from each member is valued by the whole community and all gifts are unique and individual. The gift that the community gives back to each member is that of a role and a connection" (Margarson, 1999, p. 2). Peter Senge (1990) underscores this belief when he describes a learning community as a place where people are continually discovering how they create their reality and how they can change it.

Developing communities of learners requires certain prerequisites (Kohn, 1996; Lickona, 1991):

■ *The class has a group identity.* Harwayne (1992) and Smith (1992) suggest that teachers should strive to create a community of learners within each class in order to optimize learning. Since learning is a social process (Smith, 1992), students who have a sense of belonging to a learning community have the advantage of identifying with other learners. Students in these classrooms do what students do naturally and effortlessly. They learn from each other. Learning and the desire to learn are enhanced because the students are socially acceptable to the group.

■ *Each individual feels that he or she is a valued member of the group.* Several factors must be in place for this to occur. The teacher must model acceptance and celebrate diversity and individualism in all students. Teachers set the social and emotional tone in the classroom, and students follow their lead. In order for students to feel that they are valuable members of the group, they need to feel successful. Students in learner-centered classrooms should not meet failure and frustration on a daily basis. Routines, schedules, and assignments should be planned and executed so that all students experience some measure of success during the class period or school day. Finally, in order to feel valued, each student should be verbally and personally recognized daily. Effective teachers know their students' strengths and weaknesses, interests and needs. Teachers must take the time to let all students know in some way that they are important and valued. These messages can be transmitted verbally or in writing through notes or journals.

■ *Individuals feel responsible to and for the group.* Establishing group identity in the class and creating an atmosphere where each individual feels that he or she is a valued member of the group lead to this third characteristic of communities. Students who see themselves as valued members of a classroom will naturally feel responsible for maintaining the integrity of the group. Creating classrooms that focus on cooperation among members rather than competition helps to establish this sense of responsibility for the group's welfare.

■ *Students have large amounts of time to spend together.* Authentic communities require time to develop. As teachers plan activities, they should reflect on the amount of time that is teacher-centered as opposed to student-centered. Students can only form trusting, supportive communities when time for interaction and cooperative activities is specifically planned.

■ *The teacher is a part of the adult community within the school.* Teachers who collaborate with peers are more likely to encourage collaboration among students in their classroom. McLaughlin (1996) found that teachers who excel at engaging students in **cooperative learning** opportunities tend to be part of a collegial community of fellow educators.

Many well-meaning teachers work hard to develop lessons and teach students effectively, yet fail to develop classrooms that are communities of learners. Teacher-centered classrooms—classrooms where all curriculum and learning decisions emanate from the teacher—usually fail to develop communities of learners. Also, academic learning cannot be the sole focus of a classroom seeking to develop a community of learners. Students' social and emotional needs must be important considerations in the planning and implementation of curriculum. Students must see that learning is a social activity rather than an isolated process.

Classrooms that seek to develop a community of learners empower students to be **risk-takers** and encourage them to be independent learners. Teachers and students work together to shape curriculum and activities. Students work together in cooperative groups to learn. Most importantly, students feel like significant, contributing members of the classroom community, because they are encouraged to make decisions and take responsibility for their own learning.

STUDENT OWNERSHIP/MEMBERSHIP
IN THE LEARNING COMMUNITY

A major goal of all instruction should be the development of **independent learners** and thinkers (Vacca, Vacca, & Gove, 2000). Teachers have the responsibility of planning and providing instruction that students need. Students, however, also have a responsibility in the learning environment. Students need to take responsibility for their own learning (Pappas, Keifer, & Levstick, 1999). Moffett and Wagner (1992) address the importance of student ownership in the learning environment when they say, "As soon as others want the results of learning more than the learner, the game is over" (p. 22). In order for students to care about the outcome of instruction, several conditions must be met.

Teachers must be aware of students' needs in order to provide effective instruction. William Glasser (1992) contends that human beings are born with five basic needs built into their genetic structure: survival, love, power, fun, and freedom. He goes on to assert that if what students are asked to do in schools does not satisfy one or more of these needs—or if the students do not care for the teacher—then students will do the work poorly or not at all. Teachers can consider students' needs in several ways. At the beginning of a term or course of study, teachers can ask students the following questions: What are your expectations for this course or study of this topic? What are your expectations for yourselves as learners? What are your expectations for the teacher? At the elementary level, students can reflect on what they expect and want to learn during the year.

Compiling a list of answers to these questions and referring to them frequently sends important messages to students. They immediately see that their thoughts and desires have a powerful effect on teaching and learning. Asking students to clarify their personal expectations encourages the development of independent learners. It also demonstrates to students that their needs and interests contribute to the learning process. Asking students to identify their expectations for the teacher reinforces the idea that the classroom is a **learner-centered community.**

Another activity to foster and enhance a sense of community is for teachers to spend a few minutes each class period asking students for suggestions on how they could learn more and how the class could be more enjoyable (Glasser, 1992). If students have no control over what they study and how they do their work, they feel powerless. Accepting students' input and suggestions about the school environment empowers them and makes them stakeholders in the learning process.

Teachers can enable students to become responsible for their own learning in many ways. Nancie Atwell (1998) based her successful work with adolescents on providing students with three essentials: time, choice, and ownership. In this section, we will look at the results of providing choice and ownership to students. (Time will be discussed later in the chapter.) Many teachers worry that allowing students to make choices about learning is unwise because students cannot be trusted to know what is best for them to learn. However, students who have no input regarding instructional decisions can easily see no need to take responsibility for their own learning.

An excellent strategy for encouraging choice and ownership for *all* students—elementary and secondary—is the **KWL** (also mentioned earlier). Teachers begin the unit of study or the lesson by asking students what they know (**K**) about the topic. Students brainstorm, and the teacher records everything already known about the topic. Two important things occur during this part of the activity. The discussion and ensuing organization of what is already known about a topic activate prior knowledge for students with some understanding for the topic and contribute to the building of new understanding in those who have little or none. Activating prior knowledge and building new understanding are both essential for a successful learning experience to occur. All learners store and organize information in their minds in a way that makes sense to them (Reutzel & Cooter, 1999). The results of this organization are cognitive structures referred to as **schema.** The importance of schema to learning is critical. The schema that learners bring to the learning task enable them to learn and comprehend new information. Discussing what is already known about a topic activates prior knowledge for students who have some prior experience with the concept or idea. Listening to a group discussion can help students with little or no prior knowledge begin building schema. This method also provides teachers with an understanding of what the students know and how they process information and enables them to enhance learning.

The second part of the activity requires that students create a list of things they want (**W**) to know and learn about the topic. To further encourage choice and ownership, teachers can invite students to decide which of the ideas in the "want list" will be studied by individuals, groups, or the entire class. Once students determine the areas for study, the students can also be included in the decision as to how to learn the information. Textbooks represent just one resource available to students. They may also choose to examine trade books, video resources, the Internet, primary sources, interviews, and reference materials. Allowing students choice in how they will learn contributes to the making of enthusiastic, independent learners.

The last part of this activity is having students determine what they have learned (**L**). Traditionally, students have been given tests to determine what they have learned. Commercially prepared and teacher-made tests serve important roles in assessing and evaluating students. However, many other means of assessment exist. In addition to tests, students can be given the opportunity to decide how the learning will be demonstrated. A class of elementary students composed a KWL similar to the one shown in Figure 11.1 when they chose to study mummies.

Properly aligned instruction begins with a set of performance objectives that describe what the students should know and be able to do at the end of the lesson. The method of assessment should reflect both the objectives and the activities in which the students participated during the lesson. Effective teachers use a wide range of teaching strategies that lead to a variety of student products. Outcomes, such as those listed in Figure 11.2, offer the students a multitude of ways to express personal style and interest and provide the teacher with alternative means of assessment.

Today's classroom may be filled with students who possess a number of learning styles and processing preferences. By varying activities and assessments, the teacher may not only empower students to discover effective ways to learn and demonstrate understandings, but also add a feeling of excitement and anticipation to the classroom.

Another aspect of promoting **student ownership** of learning is ensuring that students in the classroom are active rather than **passive learners.** Involving students in decision making contributes to **active learning** because it helps to shift some

K	W	L
What we know	**What we want to know**	**What we learned**
People in Egypt made mummies a long time ago.	Why did Egyptians begin this process?	The students and the teacher complete this section at the end of the unit of study.
The purpose of making mummies was to preserve people's bodies after they died.	Did people in other countries mummify their dead? after they died.	
The bodies were wrapped in cloth and buried in pyramids.	How did mummification take place? What were the steps the embalmers used?	
Mummified bodies still exist and can be seen in museums.	Why did they stop mummifying bodies?	

FIGURE 11.1 A KWL for an elementary class studying mummies.

Advertisement	Flip book	Poetry
Animated movie	Game	Political cartoon
Annotated bibliography	Graph	Pop-up book
Art gallery	Hidden picture	Press conference
Block picture story	Illustrated story	Project cube
Bulletin board	Interview	Prototype
Bumper sticker	Journal	Puppet
Chart	Labeled diagram	Puppet show
Choral reading	Large-scale drawing	Puzzle
Clay sculpture	Learning center	Radio program
Collage	Letter	Rebus
Collection	Map	Recipe
Comic strip	Maze	Riddle
Commemorative stamp	Mobile	Role-play
Computer program	Model	Science fiction story
Costume	Mosaic	Sculpture
Crossword puzzle	Mural	Skit
Database	Museum exhibit	Slide show
Debate	Music	Slogan
Demonstration	Needlework	Song
Diary	Newspaper	Sound
Diorama	Oral defense	Survey
Display	Oral report	Tapes (audio/video)
Drawing	Painting	Television program
Editorial	Pamphlet	Timeline
Etching	Pantomime	Transparency
Experiment	Paper mache	Travel brochure
Fact tile	Petition	Venn diagram
Fairy tale	Photo essay	Web page
Family tree	Plaster of paris model	Write a lesson
Film	Play	Write a new law

FIGURE 11.2 A variety of student outcomes offers students personal expression and offers teachers alternative means of assessment.

of the responsibility for learning from the teacher to the students. Not only does active learning encourage interest in the topic, it also empowers students to develop independent study skills that can be useful in future learning.

Active learners are curious about many topics and ideas. Students involved in active learning create and test their own hypotheses (Pappas et al., 1999). Effective teachers encourage active learners to seek out areas of study and answers to their questions. Students in these classrooms are learning more than facts and concepts. They are learning how to learn. It is important for teachers to structure activities that require students to analyze, synthesize, and evaluate. Readers familiar with Bloom's taxonomy will recognize that these three activities require higher-order thinking skills.

Active learners learn how to monitor their cognitive activity. This ability to monitor and regulate one's understanding and comprehension of a learning task or to actively think about one's own thinking and learning is referred to as **metacognition.** Metacognition involves self-knowledge, task knowledge, and self-monitoring (Vacca et al., 2000). Self-knowledge requires that students understand the purpose for the learning activity and be aware of their strengths and weaknesses as thinkers and learners. Task knowledge refers to students' ability to analyze a learning task, reflect on the understanding required, develop purposes and plans for the learning, and evaluate progress as the activity unfolds (Vacca et al., 2000). Self-monitoring allows students to be aware of their comprehension and understanding as the learning activity progresses. To be most effective in their learning, students need to have a clear understanding of the objectives of the lesson and the methods by which the learning will be assessed. Experienced students understand that the type of assessment required will guide their preparation. The more the teacher relies on paper-and-pencil testing, the more the students tend to rely on the ability to memorize. The result is often that learning is reduced to short-term recall. This may lead both the learner and the teacher to a false understanding of the extent to which real learning has taken place.

A final consideration for teachers when assessing whether students in their classrooms are active or passive learners is the concept of "learned helplessness." Teacher-centered classrooms encourage passivity in students. When teachers make all decisions regarding curriculum, assignments, class activities, and evaluation, students quickly learn that their ideas and interests are not important. They also perceive that their contributions are not valuable or worthwhile. Students in these classrooms find it difficult or impossible to work independently because they have internalized the message that only the teacher can make effective decisions about learning. Graves (1991) suggests that teachers are often very effective at pointing out what students do not know and cannot do. The result is that students avoid taking risks for fear of being seen as incompetent. Graves says that teachers are too effective in helping students to know what they cannot do to the point that students fear responsibility because it seems designed to display their incompetence.

Another factor that fosters student ownership in the learning environment is the teacher's theoretical orientation to instruction and learning. Teachers who have a **transmission-orientation** to learning believe that teachers have the major responsibility in making decisions about curriculum, planning, instruction, and evaluation. Teachers with a **transaction-orientation** have a more collaborative style of teaching. They involve students in all areas of learning and teaching. The Texas Learner-Centered Proficiencies emphasize transaction-oriented classrooms. The chart in Figure 11.3 compares these two theoretical orientations.

Transmission-Orientation	**Transaction-Orientation**
• Based on the behaviorist model of stimulus/response learning from behavioral psychology (Strickland & Strickland, 1993).	• Based on the cognitive/social model, which is based on research in developmental psychology, linguistics sociology, and anthropology (Strickland & Strickland, 1993).
• Learning is bottom-up or part-to-whole. Students' learning is based on a sequence of skills or managing individual pieces of information.	• Learning is top-down or whole-to-part. Learning begins with concepts or meaning before incorporating skills. Learning follows constructivist theory.
• The teacher's role is to dole out information—usually through lecture (Strickland & Strickland, 1993). Teachers see students as empty vessels or blank slates to fill.	• The teacher's role is that of facilitator. Teachers demonstrate the desired learning for students (Strickland & Strickland, 1993).
• Students tend to be passive learners sitting in desks, taking notes, filling out worksheets, completing assignments, answering when called on.	• Students are active participants in the learning process and are included in decisions regarding instruction and assessment.
• Students view successful learning as answering questions correctly and making high grades.	• Students are encouraged to be risk-takers. The *process* of learning is as important as the *product*.
• Teachers and administrators make decisions regarding curriculum and instruction.	• Students are part of the decision-making process regarding curriculum and instruction.
• Competition among students is encouraged (Farris, 1997). Students often work independently.	• Cooperation among students is encouraged (Farris, 1997). Students often work together in pairs or groups.
• Teachers evaluate primarily by grading assignments and tests (Strickland & Strickland, 1993).	• Teachers observe students and evaluate progress based on observation (Strickland & Strickland, 1993). Students' work is often used for assessment and evaluation.
• The classroom is book-centered. The student must fit the book (Farris, 1997).	• The classroom is student-centered. Instructional materials must fit the student.

FIGURE 11.3 Two different teacher orientations to instruction and learning.

RESPONSIBLE, COOPERATIVE, PURPOSEFUL, SUPPORTIVE STUDENTS

Successful learning environments have responsible, cooperative, purposeful, supportive members. How do teachers go about developing students with these characteristics? Several factors are necessary to create such a learning environment. First, teachers must model support for individuals, positive attitude, and encouragement for their students. Teachers' attitudes and actions set the tone for students' behavior. One aspect of supporting students involves helping them develop independence in the classroom. Teachers should not do anything for students that they can do for themselves (Graves, 1991) but, instead, should delegate to students all the tasks and procedures that they can do for themselves. The teacher must instill in the students the idea that an efficient and successful learning environment is the responsibility of every member of the class.

Teachers also develop responsible, cooperative, purposeful, and supportive students by allowing them to collaborate in all areas of the learning process from planning to assessment. Students who participate in decision making experience a sense of power (Glasser, 1992) and self-actualization and are more likely to strive for the establishment and maintenance of a successful learning environment.

Another important factor is the development of a sense of interdependence and cooperation, rather than competition, among the members of the class. Part Three of Stephen Covey's 1989 book, *The Seven Habits of Highly Effective People: Restoring the Character Ethic*, addresses interdependence and offers three habits that contribute to successful interaction among members of any successful community. The first is to think "win/win" (Covey, 1989). For Covey, the focus of effective group interaction is cooperation, not competition. One student's success does not diminish or preclude another student's chances at success. All members contribute to decisions and are committed to mutual goals and outcomes of instruction and learning.

The second habit is to seek first to understand, then to be understood (Covey, 1989). Successful learning environments depend on caring, nurturing relationships and interactions. Cooperative communities require that all members genuinely seek the welfare of all the other members and listen to each other. Students and teachers must be open to divergent thinking and diverse opinions. Classrooms should be tolerant, accepting, inclusive environments.

The final habit necessary for developing interdependence is synergy. According to Covey (1989), synergy "means that the whole is greater than the sum of its parts" (pp. 262–263). Synergy occurs when differences are valued, strengths are built on, and weaknesses are compensated for. The first step occurs when students perceive that the environment is safe enough for them to listen and learn from each other. Secondly, creativity blossoms through brainstorming, imagining, and "intellectual networking" (Covey, 1989, p. 265). Finally, an excitement for learning fills the class and ignites each student.

Cooperative learning assignments provide teachers with effective ways to achieve the environment and community being described. Cooperative learning occurs when small groups of students work together to accomplish a common task. Several factors contribute to the success of these assignments. The task must be clearly stated or explained, and each member of the group should understand his or her responsibility for the assignment. Students must also understand their responsibility to the group and feel a sense of interdependence. Teachers must ensure the success of cooperative learning activities by teaching and modeling the necessary interpersonal and small-group skills required for successful interaction. The planning and training of students necessary for the development of successful cooperative learning groups is well worth the expertise and effort required. According to Slavin (as cited in Armstrong & Savage, 1998), research supports the fact that not only does cooperative learning increase all student achievement in grades 2 through 12 except for the exceptionally gifted, it also has a positive effect on race relations, self-esteem, attitudes toward school, and acceptance of students with disabilities.

In addition, learning in groups contributes to students' need for belonging and power (Glasser, 1992). Cooperative learning experiences also increase incidences of constructive student interaction among students (Brozo & Simpson, 1995). In order to complete an assignment successfully, students must simultaneously work toward accomplishing academic goals and developing social skills.

Cooperative learning assignments contribute to both active and constructivist learning in students. The importance of active learning has already been addressed. According to Kamii (as cited in Vacca et al., 2000), **constructivism** learning theory holds that students construct meaning in their heads while interacting with the environment rather than internalizing information from the outside. Constructivist learning requires that students accept more responsibility for their behavior and learning. It also requires that teachers and students respect the often creative and divergent thinking that occurs when students construct their own learning (Armstrong & Savage, 1998).

Finally, much evidence exists that learning is a social process (Armstrong & Savage, 1998; Smith, 1992; Wiseman, 1992). Cooperative learning satisfies students' need for socialization because it provides them with opportunities for social engagement while they are learning. Working together to achieve common goals while seeking success for a group fosters the growing sense of cooperation and mutual respect identified in this competency.

CREATING A POSITIVE SOCIAL AND EMOTIONAL ATMOSPHERE

Competency 11 recognizes the important role that a positive social and emotional atmosphere plays in a successful learning environment. Teachers who are effective leaders are able to build positive relationships with students and communicate effectively with them. They strive to build a positive physical, social, and intellectual environment that is conducive to learning and motivating for students (McCune, Lowe, & Stephens, 1995). Purkey and Novak (1984) call this concept invitational learning. They say, "[I]nvitational education is the process by which people are cordially summoned to realize their relatively boundless potential" (p. 3). The responsibility for creating a learning environment where all students feel they are valued members of the group falls mainly on the teacher. Indeed, the teacher's responsibility in creating an inviting learning environment cannot be overemphasized. Purkey and Novak (1984) underscore the crucial role of the teacher in learning:

> In looking at what actually happens when teaching occurs, a growing body of research points to the teacher—his or her attentiveness, expectations, encouragements, attitudes, and evaluations—as the primary focus in influencing students' perceptions of themselves as learners. There is ample

research evidence that these teacher characteristics increase or decrease the probability of student learning. (p. 3)

If Purkey and Novak (1984) are correct in saying that the atmosphere created by the teacher is a great determiner of students' success or failure, what do teachers need to understand and do regarding invitational learning? Invitational learning is based on the following concepts:

- "People possess untapped potential in all areas of human development.
- People are able, valuable, and responsible and should be treated accordingly.
- People, places, policies, procedures, and programs all invite people to realize their fullest potential." (Wong & Wong, 1998, p. 62)

Based on these concepts, invitational education employs the following assumptions:

- "Opportunities are everywhere, but little happens until invitations are sent, received, and acted on.
- A positive self-concept is the product of inviting acts.
- One inviting act can make a positive difference even if everything else is disinviting.
- Human potential is always there waiting to be discovered and invited forth.
- To maintain a consistently inviting stance is the essence of an effective teacher." (Wong & Wong, 1998, p. 62)

Everyone who has spent much time observing and working in classrooms has observed students who come to school day after day knowing they will be neither welcomed nor successful. Research validates what we already know. There is a significant relationship between students' low self-concept and misbehavior in the classroom (Purkey & Novak, 1984). And students who are misbehaving are not learning.

What can teachers specifically do to create a positive social and emotional atmosphere? Purkey and Novak (1984) offer the following suggestions:

- Initiate contacts with students before school begins if possible. If students' names and addresses are available, send postcards welcoming students to the classroom. Tell them you are looking forward to the new school year. Introduce yourself and welcome them to *our* classroom. Many teachers begin the school year by displaying a poster or bulletin board that introduces the teacher to the class. This activity allows students to see teachers as unique individuals with many and varied interests.
- Whenever possible, make students a part of the decision-making process. Involve students in setting rules and expectations. Let them make decisions regarding topics and units to be studied.
- Create activities that ensure that students get to know something about each other. Designate a "Star of the Week." Let this student prepare a poster or bulletin board that allows other students to know him or her better. Have students prepare graphs that illustrate students' birth order, dominant hands,

learning styles, and so on. Use colored pins to designate the states and countries where class members were born or have lived.

- Divide the class into triads or groups of three for research or study projects. This allows students the opportunity to get to know classmates better and breaks down barriers in the classroom. Consider each assignment with regard to dyads and triads. Consider multiple-grouping techniques for research and other learning projects.

- Make sure that all school-to-home communication is not negative. Send home positive messages whenever possible. In fact, attempt to make a positive school–home communication for each student during the first week of school. Consider using e-mail and the telephone in addition to sending written notes.

- Learn to lower your voice to get attention rather than raising it. This should be done with intent so that students learn you will not compete with classroom noise. Teach students to use "inside voices," especially for group activities.

- Let students see that you are human—that you do not know everything, and that you make mistakes. You encourage **risk-taking** in your students when you do so. Be willing to admit that you make mistakes and do not know everything.

- Avoid responding to a situation when you are angry or upset. Respond to the behavior, not the person. Refer the student's attention to the class rules and expectations. Ask the student which rule was broken. Define the student's behavior and compare it to the rules and expectations established by the class. (pp. 107–109)

These suggestions, while no means exhaustive, highlight the fact that teachers must be proactive in creating a positive social and emotional atmosphere.

ESTABLISHING AND MAINTAINING STANDARDS OF BEHAVIOR

Even though establishing standards of behavior and maintaining discipline are not instructional activities, learning does not occur until they are in place. Many of the instructional practices of effective teachers reinforce good behavior. In addition, maintaining discipline in the classroom enhances learning. Student achievement is "directly related to the degree to which the teacher establishes good control of the classroom procedures in the very first week of the school year" (Wong & Wong, 1998, p. 4). Preservice teachers often hear the admonition not to smile until Christmas. Although that advice may be a bit extreme, it is imperative that students know what is expected of them and what is acceptable and unacceptable in the classroom.

Ultimately the goal is for students to exercise self-discipline. However, teachers cannot assume that students know what constitutes proper behavior, and students do not automatically understand what teachers expect of them. Every teacher has different expectations for his or her students. Students need to understand specific expectations, classroom rules, and the rewards and consequences that accompany them. Experienced teachers learn to give explicit and specific directions to students regarding expected behavior before expecting compliance. Elementary teachers might say, "Raise your hand if you can tell me. . . ." or "When I call your name, line up quietly." Secondary teachers might say, "When you are ready to make your report, let me know by . . ." or "If you should need assistance, you may do one of the following. . . ."

The following suggestions can serve as guides for teachers as they begin the important task of establishing and maintaining standards of behavior:

- Students need a warm, safe, supporting, inviting environment. The importance of the teacher in creating such an environment cannot be overstated. Students are much more likely to respond appropriately when the teacher respects them as individuals and truly cares about their well-being.

- "Rules imposed by external constraint remain external to the child's spirit. Rules due to mutual respect and cooperation take root inside the child's mind" (Piaget in Lickona, 1992, p. 112). Many students walk into classrooms on the first day of school and find the rules for classroom behavior already posted. However, teachers who agree with Piaget's philosophy immediately begin building a sense of community by allowing students to participate in establishing behavior guidelines for the class. Giving students the opportunity to discuss and choose the rules for the classroom is another way to allow them a measure of power and freedom in the classroom. Ideas to consider when developing rules and expectations with students include: (1) State rules in a positive format, for example, "Listen when others are speaking"; (2) Limit rules to five or fewer; (3) Guide students' thinking and decision making so that they select broad categories for rules, for example, "Move safely through the school" covers many behaviors including not running in the hall, not pushing, staying in line, and not bumping into others; and (4) Discuss and explain rules and expectations during the first class. The teacher must consistently enforce all rules and expectations.

- Discussing rules and procedures with students is important, but it may not be sufficient to obtain the desired behavior. Be certain that students under-stand exactly what is expected of them. Explain the desired behavior. Model what is expected. Then have students practice the behavior until it is apparent that they all understand. Spend as much time as necessary ensuring that everyone understands what is expected of them. Occasionally, it might be necessary to reinforce or reteach the desired behavior. Never think that the time spent developing an awareness of what is expected is wasted or could be put to better use. Teachers who clearly explain expectations at the beginning of the year do not have to continually remind and train students.

- Once a system of rewards and consequences has been established and the students understand it, the teacher must enforce this system consistently and impartially. Students have a strong sense of what is fair and unfair. Teachers who appear inconsistent and capricious in dealing with rewards and consequences will not command the respect of their students. It becomes impossible to build and maintain a strong sense of community in such an environment.

- Encourage students to practice self-discipline. Allowing students choice and input in the establishment of rules is one way to help students develop self-discipline. Another way is to teach the life skills necessary for students to succeed in this area (Elias et al., 1997). Goleman (1997) contends that students need to be taught emotional-awareness lessons in order to succeed in school and later in life. Among the areas included in emotional-awareness are learning to control impulses, recognizing one's feelings, monitoring what the students and those around them are feeling, and recognizing hostility in others.

- Remember that the best way to maintain discipline is to maintain interest. Students who are actively involved in learning activities seldom become discipline problems. Many discipline problems can be avoided with careful planning and preparation. When students come into the classroom and find assignments ready and when routines and procedures are familiar to them, they are much more likely to begin working.

- Students who experience success in the classroom are less disruptive. Knowing students' strengths, interests, and needs enables teachers to plan instruction and activities that invite success, provide positive reinforcement, and validate students' worth as individuals (Elias et al., 1997).

- It is important to maintain a safe, inviting learning environment that encourages risk-taking. Oftentimes the classroom is the only place in students' lives where they experience a sense of acceptance and self-worth. When students need discipline, be certain that they understand it is the behavior that is unacceptable, not the student.

- Be proactive rather than reactive in your system of discipline. In addition to planning and preparation, observe the behavior of the students carefully. Walk about the room so that students are aware of your physical presence and realize that you are noticing theirs. Oftentimes your physical presence near a student who is disruptive or off-task will be enough to redirect his or her behavior.

- Learn to distinguish between minor distractions and truly disruptive behavior. Calling attention to minor disruptions draws attention to the student and away from the learning environment. However, overtly disruptive behavior requires immediate attention.

- Reinforce desired behaviors. All of us want to be successful and accepted by others. Students are no exception. By acknowledging and praising positive behaviors, teachers reinforce them and increase the chance that students will repeat them.

MAXIMIZING LEARNING TIME

A smoothly running classroom is the result of much planning and preparation on the part of the teacher. The effective teacher maximizes the amount of time spent on instruction by developing a sense of order and a learning routine that are understood and followed by all students. The school day may be filled with many barriers to teaching and learning: grading, report writing, taking attendance, record keeping, students taken out of class, equipment not working, forgotten books or school supplies, interruptions, and so forth. The effective teacher takes a proactive position by anticipating and minimizing. **Routines** are carefully planned. Students are taught to become independent learners. Momentum and pacing are maintained, and dead time is eliminated. The following suggestions can serve as guides for maximizing learning time:

- Plan ahead. Prepare an instructional plan for the semester, for each six- or nine-week period, and for individual weeks. Planning well enables the teacher to gather needed resources and materials before a lesson begins. Having well-prepared lessons to teach increases the likelihood that students will stay on-task and that learning will be enhanced.

- Begin immediately. A teacher who is ready to begin teaching the lesson when students arrive eliminates a lot of off-task behavior and many disruptions. Students will develop the expectation that they are to come to class prepared to work and learn.

- Facilitate the handling of materials. Have papers and materials needed for a lesson ready for immediate distribution. Develop a routine so that students know how to quickly and efficiently obtain what they need. You will consider the time that this preparation takes well spent. The same suggestion applies to turning in materials. Identify specific routines and places for students to turn in work or projects. Take the time to teach, model, and practice until students understand what is expected.

- Make sure students know what they are to do when work is finished. Students can brainstorm a list of suggestions for activities to do until instruction resumes or another activity begins. These suggestions can be posted in the room or in students' work folders so they can be easily seen and reviewed.

- Reduce the number of **transitions** and interruptions that occur. Each time students stop one activity and begin another one, valuable teaching time is lost. Identify the transition periods in the instructional day and determine ways to minimize the time spent on noninstructional tasks.

- Have specific procedures for transition periods. Make students aware of the importance of smooth and efficient transitions. This is another area where students' input and suggestions are valuable. Rather than telling students how you want them to move from one activity to another, allow them to propose suggestions for transitions. The same suggestions for developing standards of behavior apply to teaching transition procedures. Determine the desired action. Specifically teach it to the students. Model the desired behavior for the students. Have students practice the transition procedure until everyone understands what to do. Remember that you may have to review or reteach from time to time.

- Do not begin any transition or give instructions until you have the attention of every student. The confusion that results when some students do not know what is expected lengthens the time needed and encourages off-task and disruptive behavior. Effective teachers have some signal that alerts students that their attention is needed. Choose one signal that means you are ready for students to return their attention to you. Examples often used are blinking the lights on and off, raising your hand and waiting for students to raise theirs and give you their undivided attention, clapping a rhythm that students are to repeat, or having a phrase such as "One, two three. All eyes on me."

- Select assignments and activities to enhance the learning or understanding of students rather than to fill up the school day or to keep students continually busy. Students quickly learn to discriminate between meaningful activities and "busy work" and appreciate the difference.

- Once students begin an assignment or lesson, they should have adequate time to complete it. Encouraging creative thinking and enthusiasm for learning requires that students have adequate time during the school day for independent and group study. Blocks of time should be scheduled to allow for divergent study and the extension of assignments to meet students' needs and interests.

- Make students aware of the daily schedule so that they know what to expect and can be prepared for the next subject or activity. Another suggestion is to set time limits for routines and activities. Knowing exactly how much time is available helps students to plan and manage their activities.

- Arrange the room and materials so that students can quickly and easily get what they need. For example, students' work folders can be conveniently filed together in plastic containers where students can easily access them. Extra pens, pencils, papers, and other supplies can be kept in an accessible place. Devise a procedure so students who have been absent know how to collect assignments, handouts, and notices. Designate a bulletin board or folder where students can check upon returning from an absence.

To ensure the success of group work in the classroom, it is essential that the teacher develop in the students the skills that will be employed. These skills fall generally into two categories, social and task. Among the social skills are cooperation, listening, providing support, and effective communication. Task skills include clarification of roles and responsibilities, sharing workloads, organization, and record keeping. Students must be taught such things as an "inside" voice. They should be shown how to maintain a vocal level that is effective within a single, small group while not being disruptive to nearby groups. Effective group work requires that students learn to divide their labor and to assume such roles as group leader, scribe, timekeeper, and resource person. In order for students to become effective group workers, the teacher should take the time to explain the skills and roles required and give students ample opportunities to practice.

One of the most important considerations in group work is the time allotted for each activity. Students respond best when they know the amount of time allotted. Besides the classroom clock, effective teachers often use cooking timers with five-minute and two-minute warning tones. Digital timers, which may be used with an overhead projector, are highly effective tools. These devices can be set to "count down" the minutes of time remaining, and some have tones that sound when time is running out.

SUMMARY

Competency 11 places emphasis on the development of a classroom climate that encourages cooperation, leadership, and mutual respect. The purpose of such an environment is the promotion of a lifelong pursuit of learning. In order to accomplish that goal, students must come to feel that they are actively participating in their learning and that learning is an enjoyable and socially stimulating activity. Learning is not an automatic consequence of pouring information into a student's head. It requires the learner's own mental involvement and response/action. As students learn, they create schemas, or understandings, through which they construct their views of the world and make connections. In addition, students have a deep human need to respond to others and to operate jointly with them toward an objective. By placing students in groups and giving them tasks in which they depend on each other to complete the work, teachers provide the means to capitalize on the social needs of learners. Students tend to become more engaged in learning because they are doing it with their peers. Once involved, they also have a need to talk about what they are experiencing with others, which leads to further connections.

In order to meet both the needs of active learning and social engagement, the teacher must strive to create a community of learners. In such a community, students are taught to collaborate and take responsibility for their learning and actions. The teacher shifts focus from solely transmitting knowledge to encouraging the students to transform their knowledge in useful ways. Students move from being passive learners to risk-takers and from dependent to independent learners. They study ideas, solve problems, and apply what they learn. Learning becomes fast-paced, varied, fun, supportive, and personally engaging.

SUGGESTED ACTIVITIES

To reinforce or expand on the information presented in this chapter, the teacher may consider the following activities.

1. Visit at least two classrooms. Observe the environment and interactions among the students and between the teacher and the students. Make note of the presence or absence of the following:

    - Classroom management practices
    - Routines that maximize teaching/learning time
    - Evidence of active/passive student learning
    - Transaction versus transmission teaching
    - Signs or indicators of inviting classrooms

2. Role-play examples of behaviors one would see in a classroom that is effective and nurturing.

3. Role-play examples of transmission-oriented and transaction-oriented behaviors.

4. Interview a successful teacher. Ask the teacher to identify specific steps necessary to create a classroom that maximizes learning and community.

5. Working in groups of three, research a topic or area discussed in the chapter.

6. Use one of the exercises suggested to foster cooperative learning (see the text following this list of activities) as a review for a chapter quiz, midterm test, or final examination.

7. Arrange to sit in on the planning sessions of the faculties of schools that are known for their outstanding programs.

8. Explore the websites referenced in this chapter. Search for other websites that address related topics.

9. Study both the Texas standards for curriculum and certification standards for teachers.

10. Attend teacher-training workshops on classroom management and cooperative learning processes provided by local school districts and regional service centers.

11. Read books and articles that address the physical, emotional, and psychological characteristics of students at various ages.

12. Meet with university professors and other experienced educators to discuss ideas and concerns regarding creating and maintaining a learning community.

Exercises That Foster Cooperative Learning

The following are a number of generic group exercises that have been used for many years. There are, of course, many variations. Experienced teachers "collect" group exercises in the same way that they keep alert to various possibilities for student products. By making files of exercises and products, the teacher is able to create a large repertoire and produce vitality in lesson design.

Boggle Boggle allows students to recall information and make sense of it.

- Provide a brief amount of time for the students to study and review their notes.

- Provide a few minutes for the students to jot down, individually, as many facts as they can recall.

- Have the students form dyads to discuss what they wrote and to fill in the gaps to create a combined list.

- Each student should check his or her list with a new partner. Special attention should be given to the accuracy and relevance of items not on the new partner's list.

- The teacher should direct a class review of items not duplicated to check for understanding.

Carousel Carousel may be used as pre-assessment, a review, or a summative evaluation.

- The teacher presents topics to the class. This may be done by posting individual topics at different places around the room and assigning a group of students to each topic. Each group then captures on paper as many ideas as it can regarding its topic.

- The groups are then rotated, and the new groups add their ideas to the growing list of each topic. After all groups have had an opportunity to respond to each topic, a final "gallery walk" is done so that each group may see all of the responses to all of the topics.

A variation on the carousel strategy, which is particularly effective for review, is to have all groups respond to the same question or topic, and then have all the groups perform a "gallery walk" so that they may see how the other groups addressed the issue. The teacher may choose the option of assigning each group a different colored marker with which they may make comments on the other groups' papers. This encourages evaluation, recognition, and support.

Mind Mapping Mind mapping is a way to enhance student learning through the use of visuals, color, words, and connectors. It is a very "brain-friendly" activity that helps students to capture ideas and visualize relationships among ideas and topics.

- Provide the students with sheets of blank paper—the larger the better—and colored pens or pencils.

- A topic is then identified for the center of the mind map.

- The students should think of a picture, symbol, word, or phrase that captures the essence of the topic and place it in the center of the paper.

- The students then brainstorm key ideas about the topic and represent them with pictures or words around the main topic. It is important that the students understand that there is no order to which the ideas are placed around the center topic.

- The students may make graphic or verbal connections between or among the key ideas as the mind progresses.

- The students may extend sub-ordinate ideas by creating branches off key ideas.

Mind mapping may be used in a variety of ways. Three common uses are as an advance organizer, as a topic review, and for note taking.

Modified Lecture/Discussion The modified lecture/discussion helps the students to visualize and organize the information as it is being presented by the teacher. It also permits ongoing interaction between the students and the teacher during the lecture.

- The teacher begins with an anticipatory set to gain the attention of the students.

- The teacher uses a visual organizer in the form of an overhead transparency, flip chart, chalkboard, and so on to increase the students' participation.

- The teacher lectures while asking questions during the entire lesson.

- The teacher completes the visual organizer during the course of the lecture as each segment is presented.

- During the lecture, the teacher walks around the room checking students' notes for completeness and understanding.

- When the visual organizer is completed, the teacher may cover it and check for student understanding.

It's a Mystery This strategy can help students to establish understanding of new material. The teacher presents an anticipatory set in the form of a "mystery." This can be an intriguing question, a riddle, a strange occurrence, and so forth. The teacher supplies students with evidence or clues, and the students attempt to decipher the evidence, to establish related patterns, to draw conclusions, or to seek cause-and-effect relationships.

PRACTICE DECISION SET

Maria Sanchez is a new teacher in a school that is on a block schedule. Each of her classes meets for 90 minutes. Her students represent a wide range of ability levels and cultural backgrounds.

1. Ms. Sanchez has decided to divide the long instructional block into shorter blocks. She plans to devote the first 15 to 20 minutes of each class session to direct instruction. Ms. Sanchez can best use the direct instruction segment of the class period to:

    I.   Connect student's prior knowledge with new concepts and skills

    II. Provide an introduction to new concepts and skills

    III. Give students practice applying new concepts and skills

    IV. Review and reinforce concepts and skills previously covered

    a. I, II, and III only
    b. I, III, and IV only
    c. I, II, and IV only
    d. II, III, and IV only

2. During a modified lecture activity, students sit in rows of chairs facing the front of the room. After Ms. Sanchez has finished the lecture, the students move their desks to form groups of four to begin a carousel activity. Later, Ms. Sanchez asks the students to arrange their desks in a semicircle so that representatives from each group may present their group's findings to the class as a whole. Throughout this sequence of events, Ms. Sanchez demonstrates which of the following aspects of effective classroom management?

    a. Establishing consistent routines to minimize student confusion
    b. Varying the pace of instruction to accommodate all students
    c. Establishing high standards of behavior to minimize disruptions
    d. Varying the physical setting to achieve different instructional goals

3. Ms. Sanchez can most effectively ensure that students spend as much time as possible on task during small-group activities by consistently:

    I.   Communicating the goals and purpose of each group activity

    II. Monitoring groups and intervening when necessary

    III. Allowing students to choose members of their own groups

    IV. Maintaining established class routines during group activities

    a. I and II only
    b. I, II, and IV only

c. III and IV only

d. II, III, and IV only

4. The first time students in one of Ms. Sanchez's classes attempted to work in small groups, it took them a long time to get down to business. Once they started work, they frequently interrupted it to ask the teacher for assistance. To ensure that the students make the best use of the time they spend in small groups, Ms. Sanchez should prepare the students for small-group work by:

    a. Clarifying the procedures and requirements for the small-group activity

    b. Allowing students to choose the names for their own small groups

    c. Assigning specific tasks and responsibilities to each member of the small groups

    d. Reminding students that class behavior guidelines also apply during small-group activities

5. Ms. Sanchez has noted on several occasions that students tend to have difficulty expressing their mutual disagreements without becoming involved in emotional conflicts. She decides to have the class work together to formulate guidelines for conducting orderly and productive class discussions. Ms. Sanchez's actions in this situation *best* demonstrate an understanding of the importance of:

    a. Making students aware of standards of classroom behavior

    b. Informing students of the objectives promoted by class activities

    c. Encouraging students to participate fully in class activities

    d. Giving students ownership in the management of class activities

Answer 1: c. Lessons should not *begin* with practice on applying new concepts and skills. Concepts and skills must be developed before they may be practiced.

Answer 2: d. Arranging chairs in rows for direct instruction, small groups for activities, and a semicircle for full-class review are all examples of varying the physical setting.

Answer 3: b. Allowing students to choose group membership will do little to ensure on-task behaviors and may produce just the opposite.

Answer 4: c is helpful, but *a.* For groups to function at their best, they must be very clear on the procedures and requirements of the task presented.

Answer 5: d. Having the class work together to formulate guidelines gives student ownership in the management of the class.

WEB LINKS

Remember that website locations may change. If any of these sites have moved or cannot be located, use the Terms to Know in this chapter to search for further information.

Cooperative/Collaborative Learning
http://www2.emc.maricopa.edu/innovation/ccl/ccl.html
Principles of cooperative/collaborative learning plus models, theories, resources and links. The "lesson and activities" section is rich in lesson designs and descriptions of activities.

The Brain Store
http://www.thebrainstore.com
An outstanding source of books and materials on "brain-compatible" teaching. Many feature the works of noted author and lecturer Eric Jensen.

Maximizing Learning in Small Groups
http://www.cs.ukc.ac.uk/national/CSDN/edu_resources/small_group_learning.html
A guide to effective small-group instruction based on workshops developed for teachers.

Northwest Regional Education Laboratory
http://www.nwrel.org/scpd/esp/esp95_1.html#1.2
Best practices for learning and classroom management presented as a topic outline.

Infomine
http://infomine.ucr.edu/search/k12search.phtml
A library and search engine for scholarly educational resources for grades K–12.

Cooperative Learning Strategies
http://www.ed.gov/databases/ERIC_Digests/ed306003.html
An overview of current best practices in cooperative learning with a helpful list of references.

REFERENCES AND SUGGESTED READINGS

Armstrong, D., & Savage, T. (1998). *Teaching in the secondary school: An introduction.* Columbus, OH: Merrill.

Atwell, N. (1998). *In the middle: New understandings about writing, reading, and learning.* Portsmouth, NH: Boynton/Cook.

Brozo, W., & Simpson, M. (1995). *Readers, teachers, learners: Expanding literacy in secondary schools.* Columbus, OH: Merrill.

Covey, S. (1989). *The seven habits of highly effective people: Restoring the character ethic.* New York: Simon & Schuster.

Elias, M., Zins, J., Weissberg, R., Frey, K., Greenberg, M., Haynes, N., Kessler, R., Schwab-Stone, M., Shriver, T. (1997). *Promoting social and emotional learning: Guidelines for educators.* Alexandria, VA: Association for Supervision and Curriculum Development.

Farris, P. (1997). *Language arts: Process, product, and assessment.* Madison, WI: Brown & Benchmark.

Glasser, W. (1992). *The quality school: Managing students without coercion.* New York: HarperCollins.

Goleman, D. (1997). *Emotional intelligence.* New York: Bantam Books.

Graves, D. (1991). *Build a literate classroom.* Portsmouth, NH: Heinemann.

Harwayne, S. (1992). *Lasting impressions.* Portsmouth, NH: Heinemann.

Kindsvatter, R., Wilen, W., & Ishler, M. (1998). *Dynamics of effective teaching.* White Plains, NY: Longman.

Kohn, A. (1996). *Beyond discipline: From compliance to community.* Alexandria, VA: Association for Supervision and Curriculum Development.

Lickona, T. (1991). *Educating for character: How our schools can teach respect and responsibility.* New York: Bantam Books.

Margarson, E., in Cooper, C., & Boyd, J. (1999). *Schools as collaborative learning communities.* Tasmania, Australia: Global Learning Communities.

McCune, S., Lowe, M., & Stephens, D. (1995). *ExCET: Professional development tests.* Hauppauge, NY: Barron's Educational Series.

McLaughlin, in Kohn, A. (1996). *Beyond discipline: From compliance to community.* Alexandria, VA: Association for Supervision and Curriculum Development.

Moffett, J., & Wagner, B. (1992). *Student-centered language arts, K–12.* Portsmouth, NH: Boynton/Cook.

Pappas, C., Kiefer, B., & Levstick, L. (1999). *An integrated perspective in the elementary school.* New York: Longman.

Purkey, W., & Novak, J. (1984). *Inviting school success: A self-concept approach to teaching and learning.* Belmont, CA: Wadsworth.

Reutzel, D., & Cooter, R. (1999). *Balanced reading strategies and practices: Assessing and assisting readers with special needs.* Upper Saddle River, NJ: Merrill.

Senge, P. (1990). *The fifth discipline: The art and practice of the learning organization.* New York: Doubleday.

Smith, F. (1992). Learning to read: The never ending debate. *Phi Delta Kappan, 73,* 432–441.

State Board of Education. (1995). *Learner-centered schools for Texas—a vision of Texas educators: Proficiencies for teachers.* Austin, TX: Texas Education Agency.

Strickland, K., & Strickland, J. (1993). *Uncovering the curriculum: Whole language in secondary and postsecondary classrooms.* Portsmouth, NH: Boynton/Cook.

Vacca, J., Vacca, R., & Gove, M. (2000). *Reading and learning to read.* New York: HarperCollins College.

Wiseman, D. (1992). *Learning to read with literature.* Boston: Allyn & Bacon.

Wong, H., & Wong, M. (1998). *How to be an effective teacher: The first days of school.* Mountain View, CA: Harry K. Wong Publications.

ABOUT THE AUTHORS

Diane Clay, Ph.D., is an associate professor of reading and language arts at the University of St. Thomas in Houston, Texas, where she also directs the Center for Professional Development and Teaching. Her main areas of interest and research are emergent literacy, teacher modeling, and children's literature. She is a coauthor of the assessment monograph for the Restructuring Texas Teacher Education Series published in 1998 for the Texas State Board for Educator Certification.

Terry Brandt, Ph.D., is the coordinator of undergraduate teacher education and director of gifted education at the University of St. Thomas in Houston, Texas. Before joining the faculty of St. Thomas, he was a teacher and administrator in Texas schools for thirty-two years. Dr. Brandt teaches the introductory course in curriculum and instruction to the undergraduates who are starting their preparation to become teachers, and he teaches theories of learning to graduate students who are seeking to broaden their understandings of effective teaching practices.

✳

Understanding the Teaching Environment

12

✳

Becoming a Reflective Practitioner

DONNA CUNNINGHAM

TEXAS WOMAN'S UNIVERSITY

COLLEGE OF PROFESSIONAL EDUCATION

This chapter will deal with Competency 12 of the Examination for the Certification of Educators in Texas (ExCET). Competency 12 is the first of four competencies that fall under Domain III, Understanding the Teaching Environment. Domain III has fewer competencies than Domains I and II, yet almost 30 percent of the total test includes questions related to this domain.

Competency 12: The teacher is a reflective practitioner who knows how to promote his or her own professional growth and can work cooperatively with other professionals in the system to create a school culture that enhances learning and encourages positive change.

The teacher understands the importance of reflection and self-evaluation and recognizes personal factors (e.g., self-concept, attitudes toward authority, biases, sense of mission) that affect one's role as a teacher and the nature of one's interpersonal relationships with students. The teacher recognizes that he or she is a member of a learning community and knows how to work effectively with all members of that community (e.g., teaching colleagues, a mentor, special needs professionals) to solve problems, deal with stress, explore new ideas, and accomplish educational goals (e.g., planning a new curriculum, working across disciplines, assessing school effectiveness, implementing site-based management plans). The teacher actively seeks out opportunities to grow professionally; knows how to use different sources of support, information, and guidance (e.g., mentor, principal, professional journals and organizations, inservice training programs) to enhance his or her own professional skills and knowledge; and is aware of the value of technology in promoting efficient time use and professional growth.

TERMS TO KNOW

Reflective practitioners   **Self-evaluation**

Reflective teachers   **Site-based decision making**

Reflective teaching   **Special needs professionals**

Reflectivity   **Working across disciplines**

Self-concept

> To learn to be reflective is to learn to be an expert.
>
> PIBURN AND MIDDLETON
> (1997, P. 4)

In order to become a reflective practitioner, a teacher must understand the concept of reflection and why it is so important. This chapter offers an example of reflection and then proceeds to answer several questions: What is reflection? Why is reflection important? What are the benefits of reflection? What are the characteristics of reflective practitioners? How can preservice teachers become reflective practitioners? Finally, it provides exercises to help in developing reflection skills.

AN EXAMPLE OF REFLECTION

Suppose you decided to develop a catering business. When your first client requests your services for a very important and elaborate dinner party, you are anxious—but eager—to show what a good cook you are. You put together a menu and spend endless hours pouring over recipes, deciding upon a theme and color scheme, rounding up the utensils you will need, and selecting only the freshest of ingredients. You follow the recipes exactly and prepare what you think is a delicious meal.

The night of the party, you have all the right bowls, platters, and plates on which to serve the meal, and you make sure it is appealing to the palette as well as the eye. Sure enough, all of your extensive planning and preparation has been worth all the effort. There is no leftover food, and the people who attend the party are very generous in their compliments. You congratulate yourself as you leave the party. Your check is in hand, and with it, there is a list of dates for future parties.

You think about how successful the party was and how proud you are. You also think you will probably use the same recipes you used for this party. Then you begin to think about how some of the same people who were at this party may be at the next party. Since that might happen, you think you had better do something different. You ask yourself questions such as: Should I take a risk and try something new? If I do try something new, will the food be as good as it was this time? How can I make the next party as successful as this one?

Hopefully, that is how the party would transpire. However, what would happen if the party was *not* successful? What if something went terribly wrong? The guests did not seem to react positively to all of your preparations. A great deal of food was left on the buffet table, and what little food was taken remained on the guests' plates. You think about how this party did not turn out like you had planned.

Now, if you intend to be a successful caterer, you will ask yourself several questions: Why didn't the guests like the food? What happened? Where did I go wrong? Did I not plan well enough? Was the food inedible? Was the menu inappropriate for this event or this particular group of people? Did I prepare more of what I would like, rather than what the guests would like or with what they would be comfortable sampling? And, most of all, you will ask the all-important question: What can I do so that this situation will not occur again? You will replay the event over and over in your mind.

If you do not arrive at some answers about how to prevent the disaster from happening again, you may continue to make the same mistakes over and over again and experience the same negative results. Your business and your reputation will suffer. If, however, you step back from the situation, look at it from various perspectives, and pour over your countless notes and lists you made for the party, you will be able to make decisions that will be of use to you in the future. You will grow personally and professionally.

Teaching is much like catering in that both involve planning, preparing, and serving a product. Teachers are "salespersons" who also think about the success and failure of what they do. Whatever subject teachers are responsible for teaching becomes a "product," and the student is the "customer." What happens if the customer does not want the product? The teachers may think about how they can entice their customers to buy the product. Teachers, too, review their sales statistics and evaluate the success of their salesmanship. As a result, teachers who want to be successful in their profession devote time and energy to examining and reviewing the different aspects of the teaching and learning process. These teachers also devote time and energy to developing the skills of **reflectivity** where they review what occurs and understand the effects of these occurrences.

WHAT IS REFLECTION?

The process that the caterer and the teacher go through—the process of thinking, questioning, problem solving, and decision making—is called **reflection.** There are so many interpretations of the term *reflection* that it is difficult to arrive at a single definition (Borko et al., 1997; Gore, 1987; Moallem, 1997). For this reason, it may be easier to understand reflection by considering three different meanings of the term itself.

One of the first examples that may come to mind is found in the children's book about Snow White. When Snow White's stepmother looked into a mirror, she asked the question, "Who is the fairest of them all?" The stepmother gazed intently at the mirror hoping to see a *reflection* or likeness of herself. A second example may be found in photographs of a clear pool of water. The water often acts as a *reflecting* surface, which throws back the image of a tree growing on the edge of the bank. A final example is related to the carnival fun house filled with mirrors. How entertaining and relieving it is to know that we are seeing our real images become distorted *reflections*. All three of these examples describe different versions of the same term.

The term *reflection* as it relates to education offers yet another interpretation. Reflection, in this context, means to ponder, to contemplate, and to meditate about the specifics of the problems, questions, and matters that are of concern to educators. Simply put, *reflection* means to think seriously about, or to "put one's thinking cap on" to consider, educational issues, themes, events, circumstances, or topics. Reflection inspires teachers to think *deliberately* and *carefully* about issues and practices. It also inspires teachers to ask not only *what* happened but also *why*.

For example, if teachers are unable to reach their goals, they are not always willing to accept failure without asking why they failed. Teachers are ambitious, and their intentions are to find out what went wrong and what they can do in the future to make their objectives more attainable. When teachers *are* successful in reaching their goals, they will ask themselves what went right, what they can do to make things go right the next time, and how they can make it even better. The information they gain about why they were able to succeed in whatever they were trying to accomplish will be added to their reservoir of positive actions and behaviors that can be applied to subsequent teaching and learning situations.

THE CYCLE OF REFLECTION

Reflection is cyclical in nature. It involves developing and refining the skills to (a) think, (b) question, (c) reflect, and (d) act. The four components, or steps, in the cycle of reflection are connected to each other. Each of the four steps occurs in sequence and leads to the next. Eventually, the sequence repeats itself. (See Figure 12.1.)

An example of a teacher engaged in the cycle of reflection is illustrated in the following description of a lesson being conducted by Ms. Jacobsen:

> Ms. Jacobsen begins by reading a poem about spring to her first-grade class. She wants the students to participate in a class project in which they will illustrate each verse of the poem and make a book. Ms. Jacobsen explains that each illustration can include different background details (flowers, eggs, baskets, grass, trees, etc.) so that the students can add their individual personal touch. She does, however, want the bunny to look the same in each of the illustrations. She decides to have a contest to decide which bunny to use in the illustrations. All of the students are to take turns

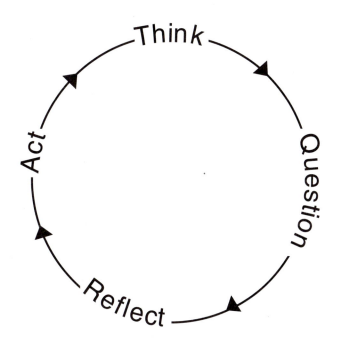

FIGURE 12.1 The cycle of reflection.

drawing their version on the chalkboard. The class will then vote on which one bunny they want to use.

John, one of the students in the class, asks if he can draw his version of the bunny on paper because he can draw better that way. Ms. Jacobsen allows the class to vote on whether they will draw the bunny on the chalkboard or on paper. Since only three students want to draw their bunnies on paper and the rest of the class wants to draw their bunnies on the board, John is outvoted. He begins to cry, puts his head down on the table, and refuses to go to the chalkboard when it is his time to draw. Although Ms. Jacobsen asks him several times, John will not draw his bunny on the chalkboard.

The other students draw their bunnies on the board and, after a class vote, choose the one bunny that will appear in all of the illustrations. One child's bunny gets only one vote, while others get several votes. However, some children's did not get any votes and they also begin to cry. As a result, several children will not participate in the rest of the project.

That afternoon, Ms. Jacobsen began to *think* about the lesson. She feels that something just is not right. Something seems out of sync. She also thinks about how to conduct this lesson next year when she uses it again. Or, perhaps, she thinks she does not even want to do this lesson again. Thus, reflection can occur "in flight," after the fact, and even prior to teaching and acting again. At first, she thought the lesson went well. She was concerned, however, about John and how he had not been included in the class project.

As she began to mull over the project, she began to wonder just how successful the lesson had been. She began to *question* what she had done. For instance, why did the bunny have to be the same in each illustration? Why had she decided there had to be a contest? Why was it so important that the bunnies be drawn on the board? These questions prompted her to reflect about how she had, unintentionally, excluded one child from an activity that was to be a group effort. Other children had drawn their bunnies on the board, but when their bunnies were not chosen, their feelings were hurt and they, too, would not participate. While it had not been her plan to embarrass or damage her students' self-esteem, that was exactly what had happened. She began to *reflect* about the outcomes of the activity. Ms. Jacobsen came to the conclusion that she needed to make some decisions about how to continue the activity.

She realized she had to take some action that would make the activity a total group effort. She knew that everyone had to be included in classroom activities. She also knew that she had to *act* quickly to make sure that each student could make a contribution. The next day, Ms. Jacobsen told the class that the bunny that had been chosen by the class would be on the cover of the project. She also announced that there would be a different bunny in each illustration. By doing this, Ms. Jacobsen could make sure that each child would have a bunny on a page.

As the students clapped and everyone became involved, Ms. Jacobsen began to *think* again about the decisions she had made and *question* whether these decisions were the right ones. And so the cycle began again.

Think

As the example about Ms. Jacobsen illustrates, the cycle of reflection begins when teachers *think* about issues and concerns associated with teaching and learning. It is difficult, if not impossible, to separate the terms *reflection* and *thinking*. In fact, most definitions of reflection contain the word *think* (Cruickshank & Applegate, 1981; Ross, 1989; Tsangaridou & O'Sullivan, 1997).

The concept of reflection, for teachers, may seem simple and uncomplicated. After all, teachers are required to think on a regular basis. They are thinking automatically without thinking they are thinking. There are, however, levels of thinking.

Some thinking remains at a surface level; that is, little deliberation or contemplation is involved. For instance, it takes very little effort to think about how much you would like to get a soda and maybe something to eat from a vending machine, especially if you have a pocket full of change.

Thinking may become more purposeful, however, when you have only a small amount of change. You want to make sure you get what you want. Since you will not have any more money if you make a bad selection, the decision you make has to count. Will you get a soda or will you get a bag of chips? You cannot have both.

Still more thought may be required if you have to decide to spend the money you have at the vending machine or pay back your friend the dollar you borrowed last week. You have to weigh your options: food or friendship? The thought process and the related decision become more complicated.

What is involved here is the *depth* of thinking that is required. If you are alert, you begin to monitor your thinking and the procedures involved in your thinking. You begin to think about *how* you are thinking and the strategies you use to process information. *Metacognition* is a term that relates to these procedures and processes of thinking about your own thinking. As the thinking or cognitive processes become more complex at the vending machine, the depth of the metacognitive thought becomes more involved.

Teachers frequently begin their cycle of reflection by recalling their experiences and events that occurred during the day. They review conversations they had with students, parents, or other teachers. They replay things they heard in the lounge during lunch. Teachers will remember student chitchat they heard in the hall between classes. They may also want to make a mental note about the recent announcements of schedule changes for the next day. In addition, teachers might suddenly remember that they are to begin a new unit the first of next week. In these situations, their thoughts may flit in and out of their minds. Little deliberation is involved.

As teachers begin to examine, to reason, and to become more intentional in their thinking, their thinking becomes more involved. For instance, they may become more engaged in thinking and focus on specifics. They may even have some of the following thoughts:

- I can't believe the students liked the activity so much. I was afraid it wouldn't go over very well.

- I don't understand what happened.

- I'm confused by the low test grades; I thought the students understood the material.

- There's more to this situation than I first realized.

- There must be something I'm not aware of.

- I was surprised by the student's outburst.

- I enjoyed talking with the student's parents today. I believe we can help each other.

Reflective Thinking At this point, teachers become more serious and pensive in their thinking. Thoughts that would normally dart through their minds remain. At first, they may question why they are even *thinking* about a particular topic. Nonetheless, they become more focused, devote more mental activity, and even "rack their brain" about how they will teach the new unit they are to begin the first of next week. They think about what they said or did not say. They think about something that might happen and the consequences if it does or does not happen. In other words, they are turning something over and over in their minds.

This kind of thinking in which something is given "serious and consecutive consideration" is what John Dewey (1933) referred to as "reflective thinking" (p. 3). It was he who really introduced the concept of reflective thinking (Canning, 1991). When teachers are thinking reflectively, they begin to probe, to inspect, to study, and to examine educational issues and practices. For them, the purpose of reflective thinking is to convert a predicament that is confusing, conflicting, or disturbing to a situation that is clear and comprehensible (Dewey, 1933).

As the earlier example of reflection draws a parallel between a caterer and a teacher, a teacher also can be compared to an investigator. That is, a teacher who thinks reflectively reconstructs events, replays conversations, uncovers relationships, and questions what was done and why. Just like an investigator, teachers pore over what they *are* doing and what they *anticipate* doing, and they attempt to *predict* the consequences of their actions. The teacher, like an investigator, experiences suspense and the need to search for answers (Dewey, 1933). Both the teacher and the investigator who are stimulated by a problem take out a magnifying glass and search for clues and seek explanations. Baffled, the teacher is on a "scavenger hunt," collecting bits and pieces here and there in an effort to gather information, facts, and documentation that will reduce the bewilderment. Like the investigator, the teacher wants to have a total picture of how all the puzzle pieces fit together. In the end, the teacher arrives at a list of possible solutions.

Reflective thinking is critical to *all* teachers, but especially for the preservice teacher who wants to develop teaching skills that are examples of best practices. If, in the earlier example, Ms. Jacobsen had not practiced reflective thinking about what she had done in the classroom, she would have alienated some of her students and created a sense of failure in others. By not carrying out reflective thinking, Ms. Jacobsen would have continued to make the same mistakes and prevented some of her students from experiencing success and a sense of accomplishment.

Once teachers develop the skills of **reflective teaching**—or examining, evaluating, and improving the way they teach—their minds become tumblers. A tumbler is a machine that polishes stones by tossing, whirling, mixing, shuffling, stirring up, and jumbling them against each other. At the end of the tumbling process, there is a beautifully polished product. When teachers "tumble" their thoughts, they are able to refine them and round out their rough edges.

Question

Solutions are not always apparent immediately. After teachers begin to think more deliberately or reflectively, they start asking themselves questions. By asking questions, teachers are attempting to distinguish between pertinent and irrelevant information. They are also trying to determine the significance and importance of the questions and what the answers might be. They begin to ask questions that may not have answers readily available. They may ask: I wonder why . . .? What if . . .? Do you suppose . . .? Could it be that . . .? How can I avoid . . .?

Again, as teachers become more precise in their thinking, the questions become more detailed and distinct. At this point, the teacher who is developing the practice of reflective thinking may solicit answers to such questions as:

- What should I have done?
- What can I do next time?

- Why did I react that way?
- What have I learned from this?

As they refine their reflective thinking skills, teachers are able to answer the questions, solve the problems, or resolve the conflicts. The question that initiated the "tumbling in the mind" originally had rough and jagged corners. At the completion of the tumbling, however, the question becomes like a polished stone. It becomes burnished and smooth. Through the process of tumbling—of reflection—the question becomes more understandable and less ambiguous.

Many other professionals also think reflectively about their business decisions and the consequences of their decisions. They think about who will receive a raise, what to do about the drop in production, when they should increase their office space, where to house the new employee, how to resolve a conflict and improve morale, and why overhead costs continue to soar. All of their questions focus on making their business more profitable, their employees more content, and their customers more satisfied.

Teachers are also geared to critically examine their "business." For them, creating and maintaining a learning environment in which each student is able to experience a sense of personal fulfillment and success is crucial. Among other things, teachers think about teacher actions, student actions, interpersonal relationships, activities, methods, instructional planning, and activities.

In other words, teachers think reflectively about anything related to their professional role(s) and responsibilities. They want to know: How can I become more organized? How can I manage my time better? What can I do about a student who does not seem interested in class activities? Why didn't the students make better grades on a recent test? What resources are available to students who need additional professional help? Why do I feel uncomfortable with my classroom management of a particular student?

On some occasions, teachers are able to ask their questions of other professionals. At other times, they ask questions of themselves. When they do this, teachers are having a conversation with themselves. Teachers who talk and listen to their "inner voice" are able to explore the possibilities of any given situation and its related issues (McIntyre & O'Hair, 1996). They are able to debate with, argue with, and exchange private views with their "inner voice." Any issue becomes a subject of investigation as teachers cross-examine their own responses and personal agendas.

Reflect

In order to reflect, teachers must clarify what they are thinking about. Sometimes the teacher must shed light on things after they have occurred. It may be that the teacher does not have a chance to interpret, to delineate, or to comment upon events until after the fact. For teachers, it can be difficult to answer questions or to make things clear in their minds and teach at the same time. Reflection must then be reflection-on-action (Schon, 1983). Reflection-on-action occurs when teachers are able to think and question events, actions, or conversations *after* these things have occurred.

At other times, however, teachers can reflect during the time they are teaching. When teachers are able to do this, they are performing reflection-in-action, or thinking about what they are doing even while they are doing it (Schon, 1983). For instance, sometimes a teacher may be in the middle of a lesson and realize that things are not proceeding as he or she had hoped. The plans, which the teacher had thought were well made, are obviously not working. The teacher will realize that he or she must salvage the lesson by doing something different. So, through the process of reflecting while teaching, the teacher "changes horses in midstream" and goes in another direction. In this sense, reflection has a sense of urgency about it. A teacher must often question, analyze, and act instantaneously, or "think on one's feet."

Reflection is not limited to thinking about what has happened in the past or what is happening at the present time. Reflection is a process that includes the present, the past, *and* the future (Dougherty, 1997). Unless teachers reflect about the future and anticipate what might happen, they become motionless. Unless they reflect about what they "hope to do, [their] future actions will remain somewhat unguided and ineffectual" (Ogden & Claus, 1997, p. 72).

Viewpoints The process of clarifying what is happening, what has happened, or what might happen necessitates that teachers be aware of and allow for different viewpoints. They realize that there are different "sides of the coin." It may be that their personal viewpoint is not the only perspective that should be considered.

For example, when an accident occurs and there are several witnesses, there will always be as many versions about what happened as there are witnesses. By engaging in reflection, the teacher is able to separate and examine the different parts of the situation under study. Through reflection, the teacher is able to appraise, evaluate, think through, reason out, and make the various parts more congruent. Making a harmonious whole of many parts forces a teacher to look at the total picture. To see the total picture, teachers must access all of the available resources. These resources include not only examining their own thoughts but also carefully inspecting what others might be thinking.

Reflection assists teachers in critically analyzing their personal interpretations, assumptions, convictions, and expectations. To see themselves as well-informed individuals and as competent professionals from someone else's point of view means that teachers must be open to new "adventures." Looking at their own educational endeavors from a parent's, a student's, or a colleague's vista, teachers are able to find new significance, new knowledge, and new explanations (Colton & Sparks-Langer, 1993, p. 50).

Frequently, like an artist, a teacher must step back from a "work of art" and observe it from different angles. Walking around the "art," looking at it from the top, from the different sides, from beneath, under different lighting, through a camera lens, and even by placing it in different locations, the teacher understands what it looks like from another person's perspective. Teachers can then begin to "critique" their artistic endeavors.

By critiquing what they do and accepting the viewpoints of others, teachers are able to comprehend how the situation appears to another person. The situation will appear differently to those who were involved and even to those who were *not* involved. The teacher must become an omniscient narrator of events who is able to be more objective, more impartial, more unbiased, and more fair and just. When preservice teachers become more accepting of another's point of view, they are able to broaden their perspectives and become more knowledgeable about themselves and their professional performance (Galvez-Martin, Bowman, & Morrison, 1998).

Decision Making Clarifying events and having a broad perspective assist teachers in making the innumerable decisions that need to be made. Daily, teachers are faced with a multitude of decisions. What can teachers do when faced with these decisions? If the time and situation allow, they can reflect-in-action. If the present time and situation do not allow reflection-*in*-action, teachers must seize opportunities to reflect-*on*-action. The main idea here is to take advantage of all opportunities to think, gather information, and reflect.

Reflection is indispensable in developing teachers who possess determination, decisiveness, and resolve. Diligent teachers who base their decisions upon reflection are likely to make solid and reliable choices. Decisions, then, are not made indiscriminately; they are not a hit-or-miss happening. Decisions based upon reflection are more consistent, well organized, and reasonable. Reflection helps preservice teachers become more effective decision makers (Collier, 1997, p. 1). They can use reflection to make judicious choices and to look at the immediate consequences of their decisions as well as the long-term effects of their decisions.

Carefully considering the point at which a decision needs to be made, the chance events related to the decision point, and the available alternatives allows the teacher to make more informed decisions. While gathering all of the facts related to the possible alternatives, the teacher may find that there is no one, clear-cut solution. In fact, there may be several reasonable options.

Through reflective thinking, teachers will be able to predict what *might* be the results of each possible decision. In the end, a decision must be made. If the decision proves to be less desirable than anticipated, the reflective teacher then asks such questions as: Why did I make this choice? What could or should I have done? How did this decision impact my students? Teachers who think about what they are doing will also ask themselves two *final* questions: What have I learned from this? How can I make a better decision next time?

The schools of the future will require reflective decision makers. Teachers will be required to be selective in choosing their options from a wide selection of alternatives. "We see the teachers of the future as thoughtful persons intrinsically motivated to analyze a situation, set goals, plan and monitor actions, evaluate results, and reflect on their own professional thinking" (Colton & Sparks-Langer, 1993, p. 45).

The ability to make rational choices means that those teachers who are reflective in their thinking improve their ability to teach (Galvez-Martin, Bowman, & Morrison, 1998). Through reflection, teachers can look critically at teaching and student learning, search for a deeper understanding and meaning of classroom events, consider their strengths and weaknesses, identify ways to improve, and formulate a plan for subsequent action.

Act

Part of being a responsible professional is the ability to make decisions and then to shoulder the responsibility for the decisions that are made (Ross, 1989). For teachers, the cycle of reflection is not complete unless they act on the decisions they make. Without the follow-through, the action that should be the result of reflective thinking, questioning, and reflecting remains idle speculation.

After making a decision, the teacher might think: I should have just left it alone—it was really none of my business; or, maybe I should have let someone else handle the problem; or, maybe this was not the right thing to do; maybe I should have made another decision. With such questioning, they are trying to determine if the decision was an appropriate one. Teachers may think about how this was the "perfect" decision and praise their ability to make good choices. Their thinking will then lead them to question: Why was this a good decision? Was it a good decision because I considered all the issues related to the problem? How was I able to make this a win-win situation for everyone involved? In the end, the decision may prove to be well-chosen and pertinent, and then the next problem or question can be addressed.

If the decision does not prove to be a relevant and suitable one, however, teachers will try to figure out *why* the decision was not right. Although they try to predict what the consequences of decisions might be and "play them out mentally," teachers may realize that the choice they made was not appropriate (Colton & Sparks-Langer, 1993). Thinking about why the decision was not fitting will lead to questions: What did I overlook? What if I had done something else? Next time, what should I do differently? What would have been the consequences then? Whether the decision was well-chosen or not, teachers will begin the cycle of reflection over again. They will begin to think, question, reflect, and act. The cycle of reflection will repeat itself until a satisfactory solution is achieved.

WHY IS REFLECTION IMPORTANT?

Reflection and the process of developing reflective educational professionals are prominent themes in education, and their importance in preparing teachers for the schools of the future cannot be overlooked. Reflection is considered a *significant, dominant,* even *vital* part of preservice teacher education programs (Borko, et al., 1997; Dieker & Monda-Amaya, 1995; Galvez-Martin, Bowman, & Morrison, 1998; Kruse, 1997; Pultorak,1993).

Thus, the majority of the teacher education programs responsible for preparing quality teachers include reflection and related reflective activities as part of preservice teacher education professional development. When reflection is included in their professional development, preservice teachers become

reflective teachers who are able to gain knowledge, develop self-confidence, advance personal and professional growth, experience empowerment, link theory and practice, carry out self-evaluation, improve self-concept, and access school support services.

Knowledge

Teachers gain knowledge about teaching in several ways. Typical paths are through (a) traditional, formal academic training, and (b) through actual experiences in the field. There is a great deal of controversy about which of the two is most influential in developing quality teachers. Schon (1983) believes that although teachers gain knowledge from the more traditional approach, most of their knowledge comes from participation in the classroom and reflection about what they are doing there and why.

The best opportunities then should come from combining the theory, the pedagogy, and the field experience activities into a meaningful whole. Reflection is introspective and encourages self-observation. Through self-observation, teachers are able to discern the real purpose of their teaching. They can also gain insight about and proficiency in their ability to teach and become more serious about the events related to their teaching experiences (Pultorak, 1993).

Self-Confidence

Teachers who are reflective tend to develop self-confidence as well as an understanding of what they are doing and a sense of direction (Dougherty, 1997). When teachers know more about what they are doing and where they are going as professionals, their self-image improves and they are more secure in reflecting. They are less frightened about taking stock of themselves, their behavior, and their actions. Through reflection, preservice teachers begin to develop a philosophy and rationale about their professional roles and responsibilities. Teachers are then able to share with and explain to other professionals and parents their reasoning behind their actions (Colton & Sparks-Langer, 1993).

Having self-assurance and a sense of resolution helps teachers to determine a course of action for change and growth. Those teachers who exhibit self-assurance function as individuals having courage, spirit, and conviction. These qualities inspire others to view them as more credible and professional. Professional teachers are knowledgeable about their work and are able to explain the logic and reasoning behind their teaching practices.

At times, teachers isolate themselves in their classrooms and forget that their teaching "world" includes clear, open communication with parents, colleagues, administration, and the community. This "extended classroom" is composed of individuals who need to be assured that teachers are reliable, trustworthy, conscientious, and able to address educational issues with wisdom and good judgment. It is essential, therefore, that teachers present themselves as experienced, well-trained, well-informed practitioners who are adept at providing quality learning experiences for all students. Teachers who are able to present themselves in this manner believe in themselves and are able, as a result, to compel others to believe in them also.

Growth

Growing—changing from a caterpillar into a butterfly, from a tadpole to a frog—is one of the most important aspects of reflection. For a teacher, the metamorphosis that occurs when experience is combined with the ability to practice reflection is phenomenal. The series of changes begins when the teacher moves from the novice who simply "does" things to the professional who asks the "why" of doing. The changes that occur are enhanced by reflection, which motivates growth in teachers (Colton & Sparks-Langer, 1993).

Thinking carefully, being analytical and diagnostic about teaching, provides a basis for future growth (Ayers, 1989). Through reflection, teachers can predict and anticipate their growth as professionals, their students' growth as learners, and the growth of the educational system as a whole. They can be more optimistic that the future can be changed, reorganized, and remodeled, just as our world continues to change. Teachers can then see themselves as agents of change in the process of reform.

These agents of change do not seek change compulsively. Change comes as the result of deliberate efforts to improve teaching and learning. Teachers become more open to new possibilities of what *might be* rather than settling for *what is*. Reflective individuals become inquisitive about new possibilities and, as a result, become lifelong learners (Robinson et al., 1997).

As well as aiding in professional development, reflection can contribute to personal growth. Progress and improvement in one area frequently effects advancement and maturity in the other because it is difficult to separate professional and personal growth. As teachers begin to cultivate self-reliance and self-assurance about themselves and what they are doing in their professional role, a certain amount of enthusiasm, zeal, and spirit is manifested in their personal role. When teachers are excited and enthusiastic about what they are doing, students also become more eager and energized. The students' positive response to the teacher increases the teacher's self-esteem. It is understandable, then, how students who are excited about learning contribute to a teacher's enthusiasm, which, in turn, contributes to the students' reaction.

Reflective teachers see their professional growth and development as an ongoing process. For them, growth is essential. These teachers continue to explore new ideas, try out new techniques, and search for solutions. They actively seek opportunities to participate in professional development activities.

Professional Development Activities Individual school districts regularly provide professional development activities for their faculty. These activities, or inservice training programs, may include workshops in which consultants who have expertise in a particular field are brought to the school district. These consultants may, for example, demonstrate new software or help teachers develop computer skills. Other presentations may relate to providing new techniques in delivering instruction in specific content areas such as English or history. Still other programs focus on providing teachers with tips in self-help topics such as time or stress management.

It is not uncommon for teachers who are teaching in the district to offer workshops for their district faculty. For instance, the technology director may explain how to integrate a new technology program into classroom instruction. Another teacher may describe a successful lesson plan or unit. In addition, some teachers who have been trained in a specific field will, themselves, be responsible for training other teachers in the district.

Inservice workshops may be given during the class day. That is, the students may not be required to come to school on days that are devoted to faculty professional development. At other times, workshops are offered after school hours. Occasionally, substitute teachers may be provided for teachers so that they are able to attend professional development activities during the time when schools are in session.

Teachers may also continue to grow professionally by attending college classes, taking part in distance education, and completing online courses through professional organizations. Professional organizations often have annual state or national conferences as well. At these conferences, there are sessions related to current topics of interest. Teachers attend these conferences to acquire information and to network with other professionals. In addition, teachers also participate in panel discussions, display poster presentations, or present papers.

When teachers present papers at conferences, they may be sharing the results of action research. What is action research? Action research focuses on classroom teachers sharing and solving problems related to teaching and learning and offers an outstanding opportunity to assess school and program effectiveness. The results of action research can contribute to appropriate decision making, reorganization, and reform.

It is common for teachers to work collaboratively with university supervisors, principals, school counselors, and others to conduct action research. These individuals will work together to identify an area of focus, collect data, analyze and interpret the data, and develop an action plan. Those who conduct action research are able to gain a clear understanding of general educational practices, build their reflective skills, recognize what changes can and need to be made, and boost student learning outcomes (Mills, 2000, p. 75).

Teachers are encouraged to join and become active participants in professional organizations as a part of continued professional growth. The opportunities to collaborate, discuss, share information, and take part in the activities of professional organizations are extensive. In addition, membership in many professional organizations frequently includes a subscription to the journals published by those organizations.

Articles published in professional journals are excellent sources of information. These articles address current issues and topics that are of interest to teachers. In addition, the articles allow teachers to remain up-to-date on prevailing trends, methods, and research that can impact teaching and learning.

Empowerment

Not only will the teachers of the future need to be able to make appropriate decisions, they will need to be *"empowered, reflective decision makers"* (Colton & Sparks-Langer, 1993, p. 45). Empowered, reflective decision makers will become an integral part of learning communities that can respond to the perpetual change and reform of education. When teachers feel empowered, they feel they have the power to regulate or exercise authority over themselves and their situation.

Reactive Teachers There are teachers who do not experience a feeling of empowerment, however. Some teachers may feel like powerless victims who are unable to exercise any kind of authority over who they are, what they do, and what happens to them. These teachers are "reactive" teachers who usually lack enthusiasm. They appear indifferent, unconcerned, and apathetic. They may even exhibit a negative attitude. They appear to be simply putting in time on the job. Reactive teachers are eager to escape the classroom when opportunities arise. Rather than reflect about why students are not learning, they simply go through the motions of teaching.

If they are unable to motivate or control their classes, reactive teachers may resort to entertaining the class or simply "baby-sitting" so that the noise level does not get out of hand. Reactive teachers do not feel they are in charge. The reasons for teacher burnout and dropout are often related to this feeling of lack of control. These teachers often develop critical accusing attitudes that prevent them from having a positive influence on others.

Rather than examining their practices, envisioning what might happen, and anticipating new situations, reactive teachers simply react to events as they occur. Their reactions, then, tend to be driven more by emotion than by good judgment. They feel helpless, incompetent, and ineffective. As a result, reactive teachers lack a sense of power that comes from an internal sense of control.

An Example of Reactivity Suppose a teacher is in a school that limits the amount of paper available for classroom use. As a result, copies of handouts and worksheets are stringently controlled. The reactive teacher who is faced with the situation of not having enough paper might become angry, argumentative, and constantly complain that it is impossible to conduct the classroom learning activities properly. This teacher becomes irritable, unfriendly, bad-tempered, and whines and complains incessantly. To this teacher, it is the *school's* fault that the students are bored and not much is being accomplished in the classroom. After all, how can a teacher teach properly if there is not enough paper? In essence, the reactive teacher is inflexible, blames others, is never really satisfied, and makes excuses for why "I can't!"

Proactive Teachers Teachers who feel that they are in control become "proactive" teachers. They come to class prepared and eager to present interesting and engaging lessons. Proactive teachers look forward to contact with students and keep track of students' individual needs and progress. They also take pride in helping students overcome learning difficulties (Brophy & Good, 1974).

Proactive teachers are committed to teaching and become advocates for their students. In addition, they stay current in their field through professional growth (Beasley, 1996). Proactive teachers focus on being a strong teacher, a strong supporter of the school, an encourager of others, and a mentor. As a result, they receive a more positive response from others, and their personal influence on others increases (Martin & Cunningham, 1999).

Proactive teachers design instruction that will help their students succeed. Students in classes with proactive teachers may seem to have a head start in achieving school success (Duke & Madsen, 1991).

An Example of Proactivity   The proactive teacher acknowledges the limited amount of paper but realizes that students still must be provided with meaningful learning experiences. This teacher quickly adjusts and searches for ways of conveying the same information and conducting activities without the use of an unlimited supply of paper. Questions might be written on the board or printed and displayed on an overhead projector. Students may also be given more hands-on activities that reduce the need for paper and offer alternative assessment options to paper-and-pencil items. The teacher might also decide to buy an end roll of newsprint from a local newspaper, the cost of which is usually very cheap. Creativity, imagination, and ingenious ways of presenting information to the students flourish.

The proactive teacher maintains a positive attitude and "makes lemonade out of lemons!" Resourcefulness and inventiveness are characteristics of the proactive teacher. Such a teacher does not find fault and blame others for conditions or situations that are less than perfect. The proactive teacher accepts responsibility, keeps on going, identifies ways to achieve, and enthusiastically declares "I can!"

Proactivity and Reflection   Reflection is an approach that helps teachers feel that they are in control and become proactive. The feeling of being in control is enhanced as teachers implement instructional plans that are thought-through and well-planned. It helps the teacher gain strength and authority. Critical reflection facilitates proactivity, which, in turn, enables teachers to take charge of their lives and their teaching practices. Reflection contributes to self-sufficiency and self-reliance (Kamhi-Stein & Galvan, 1997). The move toward reflection in teacher education is a result of the efforts to grant teachers more self-reliance, independence, and empowerment (Smyth, 1989).

Reflection helps teachers determine how to make an impact upon their students, school, and community. The immediate questions for the reflective teacher are: Who makes decisions in my school? How can I play a decisive role in my school? Empowered teachers have a sense of personal self-control. These same teachers want to experience a sense of professional empowerment that is the result of being involved and making decisions that relate to teaching and learning in their school and district.

Teachers who are reflective become more active, more energetic, and more alive. They set personal goals and identify their objectives. These goals and objectives become a part of their "mission," or their educational pursuit of excellence. This pursuit encourages them to accomplish, to strive for, and to push toward achieving their goals and objectives. Reflective teachers, then, are not teachers who are apathetic and lifeless. Reflective teachers view themselves as being proactive, or in charge. These "in-charge" teachers participate in making decisions that make an impact on their students, school, and community (McIntyre & O'Hair, 1996).

It is natural for teachers to consider themselves among those individuals who know students best because they are often with the students more than any other adult. Because of this close association, they feel that they are able to identify student needs, and they want to be a part of deciding how to meet these student needs. When teachers are left out of making decisions that affect them and their students, they become discouraged, upset, and disheartened. If teachers view themselves as agents of change, they want to be a part of the change process itself. What are the opportunities that exist to enable teachers to have input in making decisions?

Site-Based Management Decision Making A part of the restructuring of schools that allows students, teachers, parents, community leaders, administrators, and other school staff to work together as a decision-making body at the school level is known as **site-based decision making** (SBDM). Other terms that identify this approach are *school-based management, collaborative decision making, shared governance, shared decision making,* or *decentralization.* In the past, decisions related to educational procedures and processes were traditionally made at the superintendent and school board level. Now, however, many decisions are made at the individual school sites.

Site-based decision making in Texas includes the following key ideas:

- The process is ongoing.
- The decisions are made as close to the student as possible.
- The learning outcomes for all students at every campus are enhanced.
- It is a collaborative effort by all stakeholders.
- There is a shared responsibility for results.
- Student achievement is a primary purpose. (Texas Education Agency, 1992, pp. 1–15)

If teachers take part in making the decisions that directly affect them, they are more likely to accept and go along with those decisions. These decisions may relate to the school's goal setting, staff development, budgeting, curriculum, planning, and school organization. Through SBDM, teachers become a part of the process of selecting new teachers and administrators, organizing school schedules, and developing new programs, polices, and procedures.

Rather than having decisions imposed upon them, teachers are able to join in and become members of a team that makes suggestions, solves problems, and improves school operation. As a result of their input, teachers become champions of the solutions that are mutually decided upon by their team members. They will speak out for, campaign for, and plead the case of reform and reorganization. When teachers are recognized as professionals who have the ability to make rational, logical, and reasonable decisions, their morale improves and they become an empowered positive force in creating harmony, consistency, and order within their school.

Theory and Practice

Refining and improving teaching skills are dependent on the ability of the teacher to link theory to practice. Through reflection, teachers are able to make a connection about what and how they have been taught to teach and the true-to-life events related to teaching. Reflective teachers can connect academic theory and textbook training to what is actually going on. Reflection promotes a more realistic approach to teaching. It also makes it easier for teachers to understand theory, and to conceive new ideas and the prospects of new developments in education (Dell'Olio, 1998). Teachers need to develop in themselves the ability to link what they have learned in college with what is happening in the classroom. At the same time, teachers must be able to help their students link their prior knowledge, or what they already know, to new knowledge and experiences.

The real world of the classroom is filled with circumstances and conditions that require the teacher to deal with reality and to apply the concepts of theoretical principles at the same time. Frequently, preservice students are confused by what they have been *taught* should happen in the classroom and what actually *does* happen in the classroom. The perceptions of the "perfect classroom world" may change for preservice teachers when day-to-day, true-to-life experiences are *less* than perfect. Teachers must then find a balance between what *should* and *can* be done. Keeping in mind what is considered to be "best practices" enables teachers to rely on a foundation supported by theory and to adjust to the unique needs of the individual students and educational system.

Theory and practice often appear to be in conflict. For example, a teacher may decide to include a particular topic in the classroom without considering the school locale. That is, discussions of controversial topics, especially, require that teachers understand the culture and societal norms of their school district. There can be a conflict about what teachers perceive as acceptable and what actually *is* acceptable. New teachers, especially, must remember that some decisions are not always entirely up to them. Therefore, it is critical that teachers consider how their decisions will impact the community in which they teach (McIntyre & O'Hair, 1996). Their decisions must then be based on a global perspective rather than just a personal one.

Self-Evaluation

Just as a teacher assesses, analyzes, and examines educational issues and practices, the teacher must also conduct personal self-assessments or **self-evaluation.** As a means of personal self-assessment, teacher self-evaluation is particularly meaningful because it becomes an "evaluation of the teacher by the teacher and for the teacher" (Airasian & Gullickson, 1997, p. 2). By evaluating themselves and their own teaching and learning activities, teachers are able to improve, judge, discover, determine, and more fully understand their own:

- Performance
- Scholarship and convictions
- Attitudes about teaching
- Perceptions of the day-to-day activities of teaching
- Efficacies and deficiencies
- Principles, wisdom, abilities, and capabilities (Airasian & Gullickson, 1997)

Self-evaluation is not something that occurs only on an annual basis. Self-evaluation is ongoing and continuous. The competent and dependable teacher is in a perpetual state of self-evaluation. Teachers are prone to self-assessment especially when events prompt the question: What did I do wrong?

Self-examination, soul-searching, and, yes, even heart-searching need not always be thought of as a negative experience, however. Self-evaluation can also be a pleasant experience, particularly when events inspire teachers to think: That was a fantastic lesson! The reflective teacher will follow up by asking: What did I do right? How can I make sure that I do the same thing next time? Can I make it even better?

If teachers are persistent, self-appraisal becomes an ingrained element in their personal and professional development. They center their attentions on self-improvement and are relentless in their attempts to become better at what they do. Teachers who are committed and totally devoted to teaching develop the attitude of "whole-heartedness" in which "questions occur spontaneously; and a flood of suggestions pour in" (Dewey, 1933, p. 31).

If teachers want to make corrections, revisions, or even repair themselves, self-evaluation will provide opportunities to do just that. As teachers review or "size up" their personal behavior and actions, the process of change can begin. As teachers become introspective and self-observant—that is, reflective—they are actively seeking "the path to change and improvement" (Airasian & Gullickson, 1997, p.15).

Choosing the path to change and improvement—the route or course along which a teacher moves—means that the teacher will not blindly accept what others believe to be true. Through self-examination or self-analysis, teachers will "examine their underlying beliefs and taken-for-granted assumptions and theories" (Moallem, 1997, p. 149).

Self-Concept

Teachers soon realize that the "act" of teaching cannot be accomplished in isolation because teaching is a social experience. There are several different ways of looking at **self-concept**, or how teachers view themselves as persons. The social self-concept relating to teaching—or how well teachers believe they are able to build rapport, form affiliations, and make connections with other people—is very important (Pintrich & Schunk, 1996). One of the major tasks for teachers is to create congenial, cordial, pleasant, and positive connections with students, parents, the business community, and coworkers.

When teachers have a positive self-concept, they have self-confidence and look for opportunities to collaborate with other individuals. They are eager to work side by side, team up, and join forces. Positive self-images encourage teachers to work together, unite, and band together to solve problems, make decisions, and support one another.

Teachers understand the importance of being able to get along with others— of being sincere, agreeable, and responsive to those around them. When teachers are socially responsible and sociable individuals, they are able to concentrate their effort and energy in a positive way. When teachers make a habit of actively seeking to participate in a constructive rather than destructive manner, they become part of the solution, not part of the problem. Teachers who are able to give and take and connect with other teachers have a positive self-concept. They are confident about who they are, their talents, and their abilities. They are able to concentrate on other people around them without focusing entirely on themselves. Reflective teachers who possess a positive self-concept will begin to think more about what they *do* know and the contributions they *can* make and less about what they *do not* know and what they *cannot* do.

SUPPORT SERVICES

When teachers have a positive self-concept, they are able to view themselves in a more favorable light. Possessing self-assurance enables teachers to acknowledge and feel comfortable with the possibility that they do not have all the answers. They still feel good about themselves, and they do not feel that it is bad *not* to have all the answers. They continue to explore issues, pore over possibilities, and scout out answers. These reflective teachers—while they may not know all the answers—still want to *find* the answers. Where can teachers go to find the answers they need?

Mentor Teachers When teachers have concerns and issues that need to be addressed, there are several opportunities for them to request information from one or more individuals in the school. Mentor teachers, professionals who are experts in providing for the unique needs of individual students, and building administrators are three typical sources of support.

It is reassuring, especially for preservice teachers, to know that there is someone who will help guide and "escort" them as they begin their professional journey. New teachers are assigned mentors, or more experienced teachers, who are there to help the new teachers feel more comfortable and to make their teaching experience more pleasant and rewarding.

Mentors offer invaluable assistance in helping new teachers understand how to navigate the sea of policies and procedures, resources, and routines that are in place to make the school run more smoothly. New teachers may ask themselves such questions as: How do I get books for my classroom? Where is the workroom? Where do I get my mail? Will I be given a grade book and a lesson plan book? Who will give me a key to my room? Am I able to make an unlimited number of copies for my students? Do I supply my own stapler, paper clips, and pencils? When and where are faculty meetings? What if I am ill and cannot make it to school the next day? Who do I call if there is an emergency?

These are just a few of the questions that can create anxiety and apprehension for the new teacher. All teachers, especially new teachers, need someone to be a partner and confidant. They need someone who will help them reflect on how to function, perform, and manage the day-to-day demands of teaching. The mentor is there to be a teammate for the beginning teacher.

Although mentor teachers are available to answer routine questions, they are also ready to help the new teachers with more difficult requests for information. When a new teacher needs advice about classroom activities, lesson planning, and classroom assessment, the mentor teacher is there to make recommendations. When new teachers think about why the lesson they taught was not well received by the students, what to do about maintaining discipline in the classroom, how to involve students in developing classroom rules, or how to teach a particular topic, the mentor teacher is there to offer advice.

Mentor teachers, who are already identified as being successful classroom instructors, will be able to share their experiences and firsthand knowledge about how to deliver quality instruction with the new teacher. The mentor is only one of many school staff, faculty, and personnel who are in a position to offer their assistance.

School Professionals There are additional professionals in the school who are able to address the unique individual needs of students. These individuals may include building administrators, a special educator, school psychologist, nurse, resource teacher, or counselor, for example. Each of these professionals is available and responsible for helping teachers with their special concerns.

Often, the new teacher will notice that a student needs additional support or help. As an example, consider what various teachers might think after observing a middle school student eating only an onion during lunch. Observing that the student had a simple, brown paper bag containing this single item, one teacher might think, "That's an odd lunch." The teacher might then dismiss the observation. Another teacher might think something like, "You can never tell about what an adolescent will do!" Another teacher might disregard the scene altogether.

The reflective teacher, however, will think, "That's not what typical adolescents eat. They usually like pizza and hamburgers." One of the distinguishing characteristics of a reflective teacher is that the episode will not be ignored. The teacher will not embarrass the student by making a personal comment to the student. The teacher will, however, make mental notes and think about questions such as: Why is this student eating an onion? Did the student mistakenly grab the wrong bag when leaving home this morning? Does this student eat an onion every day? Does the student sometimes have nothing to eat? Does this student need help? And then there is the final question: If the student *does* need help, how can I get help? The teacher will realize that there are sources of support within the school that will be able to provide assistance to this student. It is now up to the teacher to connect the student with those sources of support.

The reflective practitioner, who is also a keen observer of student behavior, will be alert to the different indications that students need to be connected with school support services. This teacher will be attentive to detail. Should there be changes or alterations in student conduct, reaction, or habits, the teacher will be mindful of these changes. Again, the teacher will begin to recall what the behavior was before and compare it to the present behavior. Not content to just think that the student is "going through a stage," the teacher begins to question and speculate on what the implications of the change mean. Do I need to have a private conference with this student? Is there a relationship between this student's actions and my teacher actions? Is this student experiencing frustration with an activity? Do I understand all of the issues related to this student's behavior?

If there are questions that are beyond the scope of the classroom teacher, there are highly skilled and well-trained experts available in the school. Most teachers are not trained counselors, and there are some issues that are best brought to the attention of qualified professionals. It becomes important for the classroom teacher to identify the point at which the services of these professionals are needed.

Teachers are often reluctant to ask another teacher or professional for help. Admitting to *themselves* that they do not know everything is much easier than admitting to *others* that they do not know everything. However, these "helping hands," when reflective, remember well how it was to be new.

Special Needs Professionals When teachers have questions that remain unanswered, however, there may be serious consequences for the student. This is especially true for the student whose needs are immediate. The **special needs professionals** are those who have special skills in overseeing the needs of students and are able to link the teacher to school resources or to contact other resources outside the school. A student may need, for example, glasses or clothes. There are community organizations and businesses that work with local school districts to provide for the emergency needs of students. Other special needs professionals will be able to guide the new teacher through the process of making referrals for students who may need special testing or modification of classroom instruction. In addition, these professionals are able to provide guidance about how to communicate with parents.

Learning Community Preservice teachers may wonder what their roles and responsibilities are in their school. They realize that they do not have the years of experience that some of their coworkers have. Preservice teachers should realize, however, that they still have many good ideas that need to be shared with their colleagues. The questions here may be: How can I become a more active participant in school activities? What will the other teachers think about my ideas?

When teachers ask themselves these questions, they are acknowledging that they are only a part of a learning community. The learning community includes anyone who, in any way, is involved in meeting the instructional, social, emotional, and even physical needs of students. In addition to mentor teachers and other school professionals who comprise a significant part of the learning community, other teachers can provide assistance.

Other Teachers The learning community includes teachers working together with other teachers to provide for the individual instructional needs of students. As teachers plan together, they are able to coordinate the learning experiences of their students. When teachers **work across disciplines,** teachers from other content areas are able to design activities that enable students to link subjects and concepts. Teachers who plan and work together help students see how different subjects and ideas relate to one another.

A good example of working across disciplines is a history teacher, an English teacher, a music teacher, and an art teacher who plan and coteach a unit on the Civil War. These teachers are able to capitalize on their areas of expertise as they connect the historical events, literary styles, music, and art that evolved during a particular period of time. The history teacher can present, for instance, information about the political figures, battle locations, causes, and results of the Civil War. The English teacher can lead discussions about the newspaper articles, advertisements, propaganda, and reports from individuals who were present at many of the events that occurred at that time. The music teacher might offer examples of the instruments used in the patriotic songs and spirituals that were popular during the Civil War. The art teacher can display the political cartoons, pen-and-ink drawings, etchings, paintings, and photographs that survived this difficult time in history.

All students are not able to see the relationships that exist between different subjects. To some students, history, English, music, and art are separate and disconnected classes they must attend. They may even have a separate spiral notebook for each class! For some students, history may be boring and unrelated to their interests. History, for a student who is interested in art, however, may "come alive" when it is learned in the context of *art* history. Then the pieces fit together; students realize the connections that exist between each subject. Teachers who relate their subjects to other subjects will make learning more meaningful for their students.

Building Administrators Building administrators such as principals and assistant principals, department heads, and supervisors are also essential members of the learning community. It is vitally important that teachers develop professional working relationships that are mutually respectful. Building administrators are there to be facilitators and to assist teachers in achieving their goals. They are available to listen, to talk about teacher concerns, to examine situations and circumstances, and to promote open communication with students, parents, and the community. These administrators are not punitive; that is, their aim is not to inflict punishment on a teacher. They are individuals who are devoted to making sure that quality instruction is provided to all of their students.

Building administrators are also dedicated to the professional growth and development of their teachers. In addition, they pay particular attention to anticipating the needs of their students, parents, staff, community, and faculty. Finally, building administrators are also committed to establishing a safe, risk-free learning environment that will maximize the potential of all individuals in their school. Teachers and administrators should make certain they develop a courteous, amicable, and cooperative affiliation.

SUMMARY OF BENEFITS OF REFLECTION

There are innumerable benefits for the teacher who develops and uses the skills of reflection. From the earlier discussion of reflection, it is evident that teachers who reflect (a) think and question, (b) gain more knowledge about themselves and teaching, and (c) increase their self-confidence. In addition, they are able to (a) grow personally and professionally, (b) become better decision makers, (c) experience empowerment, (d) develop the ability to link theory to practice, (e) expand their skills in self-evaluation, (f) build positive self-concepts, and (g) access school support services.

Along with those benefits identified earlier, reflection also motivates teachers to:

- Equate student learning styles with teaching styles.
- Draw a parallel between teaching techniques/approaches and lesson content.
- Question their own ideals, standards, and code of ethics.
- Determine if they are content with their performance and the results of their decisions.
- Apply theory and test hypotheses.
- Draw conclusions about methods and procedures used in the classroom.
- Become more resilient.
- Enhance their teaching accomplishments.
- Develop and expand their own educational philosophy.
- Reinforce their self-image.
- Acquire personal insight about the world of teaching (Bainer & Cantrell, 1993; Canning, 1991; Colton & Sparks-Langer, 1993; Cruickshank, 1985; Rust, 1988; Valverde, 1982).

Perhaps the main reason reflection is so important is that it is indispensable in developing reflective practitioners. Who is a reflective practitioner? Shulman (1987) refers to **reflective practitioners** as "those who review, reconstruct, reenact, and critically analyze their own and their students' performances, and who formulate explanations with evidence" (p. 15). In addition, reflective practitioners are considered to be those who are:

- Thoughtful problem solvers.
- Able to revise and enrich their knowledge about methods and procedures.

- Capable of understanding the unending succession of past, present, and future events in the classroom.
- Constantly reviewing their performance, the reasons for performing as they do, and the impact and outcomes of their performance.
- Able to take advantage of their reflection to expand their classroom methods and strategies.
- Able to accept new ideas, new possibilities, and new opportunities.
- Socially responsible.
- Looking for relationships (Colton & Sparks-Langer, 1993; Copeland et al., 1993; Dewey, 1933; Kruse, 1997; Shulman, 1987).

HOW CAN PRESERVICE TEACHERS BECOME REFLECTIVE PRACTITIONERS?

There are several ways for teachers to become reflective practitioners. Mentioned here are twelve different strategies used to help teachers develop their skills in reflection.

Field Experience

To become a true reflective practitioner, preservice students need the experience of observing and participating in the classroom setting. Field experiences are invaluable to preservice teachers. Providing opportunities to relate theory and practice is one of the most obvious advantages of being placed in the classroom.

Through these experiences, students replace the passivity of simply recording what goes on in the classroom with activity—hands-on interaction with students. Preservice teachers are then more likely to answer, honestly, the question: Is teaching really for me? The socialization process for preservice teachers develops as they (a) are assimilated into the school as well as the classroom, (b) collaborate with teams of teachers, and (c) acquire professional attitudes and behaviors.

Journal Writing

Field experiences provide the basis for one of the most popular techniques in developing reflection in preservice teachers. Reflective journal writing, a natural extension of being in the classroom, helps preservice teachers apply their writing skills when they write about what they see (Grabe & Grabe, 1998). Journal writing or "journaling requires the teacher to maintain and reflect on a record of classroom events or activities with the intent of recognizing recurring problems, themes, successes, and needs" (Airasian & Gullickson, 1997, p. 16). Through journaling, preservice teachers genuinely contemplate the performance of teachers and students whom they observe as well as their personal experiences in the classroom. Each of these observations provides an opportunity to develop reflective practice. As university supervisors respond to the journals, another avenue of self-awareness becomes available. Effective journaling must move beyond a diary approach in which the writer gives a simple description or schedule of events. Instead, preservice teachers must explore their feelings, relate theory to practice, and evaluate self and others.

Portfolio Development

Portfolio development is another reflective device that provides a uniquely individual portrayal of a preservice teacher's strengths, abilities, talents, and successes. Portfolio assessment is a widely utilized method of appraisal in teacher preparation programs. It allows preservice teachers and others to trace their professional development as they progress through the teacher education program. A possible pitfall of portfolio development is that preservice teachers may simply prepare a scrapbook of experiences without connecting the experiences to reflective practice. Preservice teachers must envision the portfolio as a reflective tool and assemble a variety of indicators of professional growth along with reflection upon their development. The guiding components of a portfolio are a statement of philosophy and goals. These elements provide an opportunity for preservice teachers to examine their own commitment to teaching and to articulate their personal and professional direction, thus creating a blueprint for their development as a teacher.

Oral Debriefing

Oral debriefing is another effective mechanism to develop reflection skills. Debriefing can occur in an individual or group setting. Individual debriefing occurs as university supervisors, preservice teachers, and cooperating teachers discuss classroom performance, areas of concern, and methods for improvement. Oral debriefing can also occur as groups of preservice teachers discuss their common concerns. When meeting in groups, preservice teachers can offer each other objective insights that can further encourage self-awareness and reflection.

Peer Coaching

Peer coaching offers the teacher another avenue of feedback. Here, a teacher selects specific behaviors for another teacher to observe. The teacher who is observing sits in the classroom and takes notes about those behaviors only. Debriefing then occurs when the observer provides specific information related only to the behaviors identified by the teacher. Another peer coaching opportunity is provided when a fellow teacher (participant) models a procedure or way of teaching for the new teacher (observer). The two teachers then reverse roles. The new teacher who was the observer becomes the participant who will try out the new technique in the classroom. The fellow teacher becomes the observer who will provide suggestions, advice, and pointers to the new teacher.

Critiques

Critiques, or positive criticism of lessons taught by preservice teachers, are provided by both university supervisors and cooperating teachers. Also valuable are critiques by peers, although these are used less often. Objective critiques allow preservice teachers to become aware of their strengths, areas of needed improvement, and the relationship of their experience to theories and ideas presented through their teacher education program. Comprehensive critiques provide a basis for change and improvement.

Metaphors

Personal teaching metaphors are another approach to developing reflection. Metaphors offer distinct opportunities for preservice teachers to understand how they view their world. Using imagery helps teachers to comprehend how they really feel about teaching and to identify their areas of concern (Munby, 1986, p. 197).

Metaphors suggest a comparison made between two unlike things without using the words *like* or *as*. One thing is said to be another; for instance, "A teacher is a tour guide who is leading tourists (students) on an adventure." Metaphors help preservice teachers view their roles and responsibilities.

If teachers consider carefully the metaphors they use, they will be able to recognize and understand the implications of those metaphors. For example, what is really meant by the comment, "Well, I'd better get back to the trenches (or the zoo)," made when a teacher is leaving the lounge to go back to class after lunch? Does this teacher believe the classroom is a "war zone" and the students are "enemies"? Are the students really animals in a zoo? Is the teacher outside the "cage" looking in? Is the teacher only an observer who has little personal contact with the students? Or, is the teacher a zookeeper who takes care of, "feeds," nurtures, and provides for the students?

Depending on the teacher's personal perspective, teaching may be laborious, routine, and combative. Some teachers may also feel isolated from their students. Here, the student-teacher interaction may be strained and lack mutual understanding. On the other hand, teachers may be sensitive caregivers who attend, nourish, and protect those under their supervision. Different perspectives affect how teachers approach their job, their responsibilities, and their expectations. Their performance reflects the perspective that they may or may not verbally express to others. Whether or not teachers actually verbalize how they feel, students will be able to sense how a teacher really feels about teaching and about them as students.

Other metaphors may reveal additional information about the attitudes of the teacher. For one teacher, the classroom may be a journey in which the teacher is a conductor and the students are passengers on a train. The teacher may want to examine this metaphor more closely, however. What about those students who "derail" or "jump off" at one stop and, although they are running alongside the train, are unable to "jump back on board"? There are some student passengers who are already on the train and are quite comfortable. There are other student passengers who are left behind. As the train gathers speed, these students get further and further behind. Additional questions might include: Is the teacher an engineer who is always driving the train and are the students simply "along for the ride"? Is the train trip boring? Have the students' trip been worth the price of the ticket?

Similes

A simile is also a comparison between two unlike things. In this instance, however, the comparison uses the words *like* or *as*. An example might be: "A teacher is like a gardener who carefully sows the seeds and nurtures the plants." An effective simile can create a clear, distinct likeness of a person, place, or thing. Similes can also add meaning to and assist in the creation of a picture. Frequently, similes tell more about the person, place, or thing than mere descriptions. Through the use of similes, the teacher is forced to explain and to understand the comparison. In addition, the teacher is forced to ask some specific questions: What qualities does the gardener have that the teacher should also have? What does this simile tell me about a teacher and a gardener? How is being a teacher an example of being a gardener? What does this tell me about being a teacher?

Story Writing

Another interesting technique that inspires and guides reflection for preservice teachers is story writing (Langley & Senne, 1997). Through the narrative, or story process, preservice teachers are able to describe what they have achieved from their teaching experiences. Here, preservice teachers use the basic elements of a story (main character and/or a set of related characters, a problem or conflict needing a solution, and a set of related events) to tell a story about their classroom teaching experiences. Relating their experiences through story writing forces the students to (a) scrutinize their decisions and actions, (b) explore their responses to their concerns, and (c) work within a uniform structure (Langley & Senne, 1997, p. 60).

Ethical Dilemmas

Parkay and Stanford (1998) refer to teaching as "an ethical enterprise—that is, a teacher has an obligation to act ethically, to follow what he or she knows to be the most appropriate professional action to take" (p. 201). Recognizing and responding to students and what is in their best interests should always be given priority. Some teachers, however, are unaware of the numerous ethical dilemmas that they encounter each day (Eberlein, 1989).

Preservice teachers must first identify what an ethical dilemma really is. Once they recognize that they are faced with making a decision based on ethics and values, the decision becomes more complex. Teachers frequently must realize that there are different value systems and that some of these value systems may be in direct conflict with their own personal values. This conflict can make it difficult for teachers to avoid imposing their personal values upon others and to be objective when making decisions. Above all, however, teachers must be role models who exemplify moral qualities and a personal code of ethics.

In making any decision, especially those relating to ethical issues, teachers must remember to conduct themselves in an honorable manner. They will want to gather as much information as possible in order to (a) have a broad overview of the situation, and (b) make an informed decision. Often, there is no completely right or wrong answer to an ethical dilemma. It may be a right-versus-right decision in which the dilemma may pivot around two choices, both of which may be right (Kidder & Born, 1999). If there appears to be only one option, the proper decision seems more obvious. On other occasions, however, there may be several alternatives, each of which are reasonable (Strike, 1988).

When there are several possible and plausible alternatives, a teacher can become confused. The teacher begins thinking about what would be wrong or right in the situation and asking the questions: Can I make an objective decision? What are the alternatives? Will this decision hurt anyone? Which would be the best decision for *everyone*? Are my personal values interfering with my decision?

An example of an ethical dilemma might be one in which a teacher is faced with helping the rest of the class while a special needs student who requires additional help and support is ignored. Does the teacher spend extra time with one particular student while the rest of the class is "neglected"? Or does the teacher give the student crayons and drawing paper and help the rest of the class? The reflective teacher will wonder if there is some way to help both the individual *and* the rest of the class at the same time. What about peer tutoring? What about modifying the class activity so that the student can participate in the learning experience, too? Must it be either/or?

As this situation illustrates, decisions can be complicated, and teachers need practice in addressing ethical dilemmas. They need to use their skills of reflection to understand (a) the responsibilities involved in making decisions, (b) the risks and hazards involved in making decisions, and (c) how to make the right decisions (Strike, 1988).

Sketch Journals

Sketch journals provide the teacher with yet another means of acquiring skills in reflection. They offer a means "to gather information and reflect on learning" (Ernst, 1997). Through drawing or sketching—rather than composing a written narrative about—what they see in the classroom, preservice teachers are able to:

- Focus on classroom and students.
- Reveal the partnership between art and writing.
- Detect ideas for writing and responses to queries.
- Chronicle their thinking.
- Substantiate their learning.
- Merge what they see in the classroom with their thoughts about teaching.
- Understand and interpret the classroom atmosphere (Ernst, 1997, p. 3).

Technology

The use of technology in the classroom is advocated as a key component of meaningful learning. This is not only true for students, it is especially significant for reflective practitioners. Through technology, teachers are able to develop and improve communication skills, manage their time, access resources, and communicate with other professionals.

Word Processing   Word processing, or typing on a computer, can assist the teacher in any of the responsibilities related to teaching (Roblyer & Edwards, 2000). No longer is it necessary for the teacher to use a typewriter to type assignments or activities on purple ditto masters that then must be run off by hand on duplicating machines. Now teachers can use computers to develop a wide array of documents. Parent letters, announcements, and classroom newspapers are some common examples. Because all of the documents can be saved and accessed again at the teachers' convenience, a test or any assignment can be copied and modified for special needs learners.

Resumes, letters of application, and even transparencies can be created on computers and enhanced by graphics, pictures, and unusual fonts (type). By using spelling and grammar checks, teachers can create products that appear more professional and appealing. Word processing packages offer teachers the opportunity to determine margins and line spacing. The ability to draw and insert tables into the document is available. Individual words, lines, and paragraphs can be moved. Pages can be numbered, and words can be written in different type styles, for example, in bold, italicized, or regular print. Teachers can write anecdotal records, lesson plans, and their personal journals. Because teachers are often unable to complete many of these tasks during the day, the computer allows them to complete their journals when they have more time to think and reflect on classroom events.

Database   A database is "used to organize, store, and search for information" (Grabe & Grabe, 1998, p. 177). Not only do databases help teachers manage their time, but they also help teachers reflect.

A database is commonly used by teachers to maintain student grades. When teachers access a database, they are able to enter, sort, and look at the grade averages of individual students and individual classes. The information found in the database will alert the teacher to problems an individual student may be having. The teacher may notice that a particular student's grades are dropping or that there are missing assignments. The reflective teacher begins to ask questions such as: Did I forget to enter the student's grade? Why is this student not turning in homework? Does the student understand the assignment? Is the assignment too difficult? Is there something outside the classroom that is impacting the student's achievement? Do I need to make a counseling referral? When can I talk to the student? How do I contact the parent or guardian? Does this student have similar problems in other classes?

The reflective teacher does not ignore the missed assignments or the drop in grades. For this teacher, bells ring and sirens go off. There is an immediate need to stop the student's downward spiral. The teacher searches for answers, seeks solutions, and develops an intervention plan to rectify the situation.

From the database, teachers are also able to make charts and graphs to visually display the information. By comparing the charts and graphs, the teacher may notice that there are significant differences in the achievement level of students. One class may have a higher average than another class. Again, the teacher begins to reflect about what is making the difference. Why is one class doing better than another class? Did I use different strategies or activities that affected the level of learning? Am I meeting the needs of individual learners? What can I do to help the students achieve? What about the tests I give? Are the tests fair? Do my tests actually cover the material I presented? Are the test questions clear?

Internet Communicating, exchanging information, expressing feelings, and building rapport with other teaching professionals is of primary importance to the reflective practitioner. The opportunities for communicating, asking questions, and reflecting that are available through the Internet are endless. Among other things, the Internet offers teachers a means of:

- Obtaining abstracts and articles related to topics of interest.
- Contacting professional organizations.
- Viewing lesson plans.
- Reading magazines and journals.
- Designing their own web page.
- Participating in distance learning and video conferencing activities.
- Exploring graphics and animation.
- Conducting research.
- Scheduling events and making appointments on calendars.
- Preparing slide show presentations.
- Developing portfolios.

E-Mail E-mail, or electronic mail, assists the teacher in communicating with other individuals such as parents, students, administrators, and other teachers. Maintaining contact with colleagues is important for teachers, especially in developing the skills of reflection. Frequently, it may not be possible for a teacher to contact another teacher at the exact moment a question arises. Later in the day, or even at night, however, a teacher can e-mail another teacher to ask for advice or assistance. Teachers can communicate with each other to discuss concerns or solutions to problems. They are able to exchange ideas and make suggestions about lesson plans and classroom activities. Teachers find it comforting to know that there is someone to listen to them and someone who will be a "sounding board" for their ideas and opinions. Teachers can offer each other clues, hints, and recommendations. They can also understand another teacher's feelings and become good listeners.

During the day, it may not be convenient or even possible for teachers to have "quality time" with another teacher. Once the school day is over and teachers leave the school, they are able to put things in perspective and take the time to reflect. E-mailing another teacher when there is enough time to actually discuss issues from top to bottom and from head to foot makes it possible for each teacher to focus and carry on a conversation without interruptions.

Bulletin Boards There are other opportunities to communicate or "talk" with other individuals on the Internet. This "talk" may occur "among individuals, between an individual and a group, or among groups" (Grabe & Grabe, 1998, p. 195). One way to conduct these conversations is through bulletin boards.

Bulletin boards operate much like the bulletin boards in classrooms. Classroom bulletin boards serve as a place to post information about schedules, announcements, events, and topics of interest. Internet bulletin boards also serve as a place to post messages. They do not allow individuals to carry on actual conversations with one another; however, teachers can post their questions about a given topic and review messages left by other teachers or professionals who have information to share about the same topic.

Chatrooms Unlike bulletin boards where there is no real "live" ongoing conversation, chatrooms are locations where the conversations are "live." That is, two or more individuals may be conversing with each other at the same time. Those who are in the "room" at the same time are able to share in the typed conversation. Chatrooms are more interactive than bulletin boards. A teacher is able to find other teachers who can answer questions, present different perspectives, or suggest other resources.

Why would a reflective teacher be interested in technology? A response from the teacher who is a reflective practitioner might be: Why not? Teachers who practice reflective thinking are never really satisfied with everything they do. They are constantly asking themselves questions: How can I make my teaching more interesting? How can I help motivate my students? How can I learn more about a topic? How can I keep current on issues related to teaching and learning? These teachers are lifelong learners; they are always eager to share what they know.

SUMMARY

Reflection may be easier for the experienced teacher, but it is very profitable for the beginner. The earlier a teacher begins to reflect on educational practice and issues, the better (McIntyre & O'Hair, 1996). For preservice teachers, developing reflective thinking skills should begin early in their careers. The question is: How do preservice teachers reflect?

For Dewey (1933), reflection "commences when we begin to inquire into the reliability, the worth, of any particular indication; when we try to test its value and see what guarantee there is that the existing data really point to the idea that is suggested in such a way as to justify acceptance of the latter" (p. 11). For some, the reflective process originates with a question, a doubt, a misgiving, or an objection. For others, reflection emerges when they are uncertain, lack confidence, or challenge or oppose something. (See Figure 12.2.)

There are as many ways to reflect about teaching and learning as there are teachers (Bibik, 1997). Perhaps one of the best ways for teachers to develop reflection is to access the resources that are available to them. Colleagues, mentor teachers, and administrators with whom a teacher collaborates in the day-to-day life of teaching can be excellent sources of information and support.

One of the most difficult challenges of reflection is actually finding the time to reflect. But when teachers devote time to reflection, there are benefits for both teachers and students. Teachers need to seek opportunities to converse with other professionals in education because "teachers need time to share, reflect, and ultimately learn from each other" (Moreno, 1998, p. 18). The best recommendation comes from Wesley (1998) who instructs teachers to "read, think, write, communicate your questions and ideas, share with colleagues, and publish. Teaching is largely a thinking life—forward to a plan, backward to an evaluation. It is constant reflection" (p. 81).

FIGURE 12.2 The reflective practitioner.

SUGGESTED ACTIVITIES

This chapter explored reflective thinking as a part of reflection. To become a reflective practitioner, a teacher must engage in reflective thinking and reflect through exercises. The following activities, based on this chapter, are creative exercises in reflection. These exercises will motivate preservice teachers to think about what they are doing, what they are seeing, and the interrelationships that exist.

One of the first activities preservice teachers will want to do is to keep observation journals of the things that occur in the classroom. These observation journals will provide the starting point for completing the activities that follow. By selecting events from their personal observation journals and then engaging in the suggested activities, preservice teachers will develop the skills of reflective thinking and begin the process of becoming reflective practitioners.

Using your field experience observation journal, select classroom experiences, and then carry out the following activities.

1. Select at least one sentence to complete—and elaborate on—from the following choices:
    - I was amused by . . .
    - I had to laugh when . . .
    - I was happy to see that . . .
    - I was confused by . . .
    - I was concerned when . . .

2. Observe a classroom and take notes on teacher actions, student actions, and classroom environment. Choose one event that is of particular interest to you and describe, *objectively*, what you saw. Follow the description of what you saw with a *subjective* reflection about what the event means to the teaching/learning process.

3. Write a short article about a classroom event as it might appear in a newspaper. Typical information found in a newspaper article includes "who," "what," "when," "where," "why," and "how." Include a headline for your article.

4. Identify a decision that the teacher had to make. Make a decision tree (Magee, 1964) to plot the decision point, the various alternatives, and the possible consequences of these alternatives.

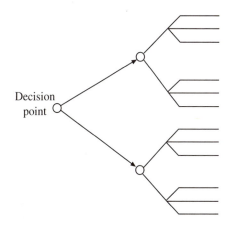

5. Observe a single student who is shy, quiet, and rarely participates in class. Write a soliloquy for this character. In this soliloquy, the student is alone on the stage and makes a speech revealing thoughts and feelings that the audience (teacher or other students) might not know about. Use this soliloquy to discern information that might help others understand more about the inner thoughts of the student and how he or she feels about learning, being in the classroom, or just being a person. Then provide a reflective response to this student's thoughts and feelings.

6. Select an event in which two students had a disagreement. Compare the students to each other by asking yourself the following questions:

   - Why does each student act the way he or she does?
   - How do the other students react to these two students?
   - How does the teacher react to these two students?
   - How is each of the two students to blame for the way people react to him or her?
   - How are other students to blame for the way the two students acted?

7. Experiment with different viewpoints of a classroom incident. Write a short narrative describing the event from the viewpoint of a "fly on the wall." What does this fly see as it flits around the room?

8. Convert a classroom incident into a radio play. Develop the action and characters by using dialog. Include instructions for music and sound and directions for how the actors and actresses should say their lines.

9. Turn one of the classroom events into your favorite soap opera. This could be a scene from a new version of "All My Children" for teachers. Include directions for lighting, music, costumes, and sound effects that will reflect the mood and the character portrayal.

10. Pick out an event that produced a conflict between students. Write a flashback for this event. Imagine what might have occurred earlier—before the conflict—that created the conflict.

11. Identify a situation in which a student was made a scapegoat—that is, the student was blamed for a problem by others who did not have any real evidence. Describe what this student might be saying to himself or herself.

12. Settle upon one classroom episode in which a student was having difficulty with the teacher or another student. Pretend that you are the student and write a "Dear Abby" letter. Then provide a reflective response in which you give advice to the student.

13. You may already know of a school district or even a particular school in which you would like to teach. Using the Internet, go to the web page of the school district. Each school district should have, among other information, its mission statement. Frequently, the mission statement of each individual school in the district will also be given. Look carefully at the mission statements and reflect about how your personal as well as professional teaching philosophy would fit together with those statements. Is your philosophy of education compatible with the school district's mission statement?

14. E-mail your university supervisor about one of the observations in your journal. Divide your message into two parts. The first part will be a description of what you observed. This description will be objective and will not include any of your own interpretations or thoughts about what you saw. The second part will be a reflective discussion of what you saw. Here, you will insert your own thoughts and assign a meaning to what you observed. You will be able to draw conclusions about how the observation impacts teaching and learning. Conclude by identifying specific learner-center proficiencies and ExCET competencies that address the issues related to your observation.

PRACTICE DECISION SET

1. A physical education class for K–3 students is randomly divided into four groups and is taught by a team of four teachers. Each group of students rotates to each teacher every 20 minutes. Each teacher has one sport he or she teaches for the week. The teachers are supposed to meet each morning to discuss the previous day's activities. They also are supposed to meet once a week to decide which new sports will be taught the next week. There is one teacher who does not want to plan with the other teachers and does not want to attend the meetings. As a reflective practitioner, what should this teacher do?

    a. Argue about what needs to be done and how
    b. Go to the meetings but ignore the plans the other teachers make
    c. Tell the teachers that he or she prefers to do his or her own thing
    d. Agree to work cooperatively with other professionals

2. A thematic unit is being used for the four-week science class of thirteen ESL students K–3. The curriculum is complete with daily lesson plans, materials, manipulatives, activities, and videos. The students work in three groups (stations), with each having a leader for the day. One day, the groups wear masks and caps and perform "brain surgery." They work on the brain of a "patient" and discover its functions and importance. After lunch, the groups then experience predicting scents by smelling four food samples and predicting flavors by tasting four food samples. These activities tie in with how the brain theoretically works. Thirty minutes after the class, the teacher reviews what has gone wrong and writes down some steps to be taken to avoid making the same mistakes in the next class session. This review enables the teacher to:

    a. Be better organized
    b. Be more in control of spur-of-the-moment distractions
    c. Develop skills of a reflective practitioner
    d. Use more hands-on activities

3. A middle school history class has spent several days completing a writing assignment on a topic chosen by each student. The assignment was to write a rough draft of a research paper. The research paper was to be six paragraphs written on every other line. One of the girls reported to the teacher that she had successfully completed the required assignment. She was proud of the fact that she had written ten pages and then cut them down to eight pages.

    The teacher looked at the student's paper and began telling the student what she had done wrong. When the student looked at her paper, she saw entire paragraphs marked out with a red pen. She just sat and stared at the paper, never making a mark on it or trying to fix it. The teacher warned the student that she would receive an F if she did not complete the revision. This did not seem to phase the student. The rest of the students were correcting their papers and revising them. This student, however, did not attempt to revise her paper. How would a reflective teacher respond?

    a. Write an F at the top of the student's paper

b. Go back and congratulate the student on what she had done right
c. Threaten to call the student's parents
d. Send the student to the principal's office

Answer 1: The correct answer is *d*. The whole purpose of collaboration is working together with other teachers and professionals cooperatively. Reflective teachers are confident teachers who are always willing to work with and learn from others. Answer *a* is certainly not an example of working together. There should never be arguments; there should be differences of opinions that are resolved collaboratively. Answers *b* and *c* are further examples of teachers not working together as team members to problem-solve and make decisions.

Answer 2: The correct answer is *c*. To become a reflective practitioner, a teacher must constantly examine, review, and revise. In regard to answers *b* and *d,* the teacher's review may allow more control and hands-on activities; however, this is not guaranteed.

Answer 3: The correct answer is *b*. The reflective practitioner would think about *why* the student was not working on the assignment. Before simply making red marks on the paper, the teacher should have praised the student for what she had done right and then explained the things that she had not done correctly. The teacher will come to the conclusion that the student's self-esteem has been damaged. Answer *a*, writing an F on the paper, would simply reinforce the student's belief that she has failed. To the student, there is no hope of saving the paper; nothing she did was right, and all of her efforts were for nothing. In regard to answers *c* and *d,* the student's refusal to work on the assignment was not an act of defiance; sending the student to the principal's office or threatening to call her parents would effectively shut down any rapport the teacher could have established with the student. The student's sense of self-worth and accomplishment has been hurt. As a means of self-defense, the student may actually become defiant and uncooperative in the future.

WEB LINKS

Remember that website locations may change. If any of these sites have moved or cannot be located, use the Terms to Know in this chapter to search for further information.

www.algonquinc.on.ca. /edtech/gened/ reflecti.html
Learning on the Internet: Reflective Thinking

www.ceap.wcu.edu/Houghton/EDELComp Educ/BibReflective.html
Bibliography on Reflectiveness in Teaching and Learning

www.ncbe.gwu.edu/ncbepubs/focus/focus6.htm
Re-Thinking the Education of Language Minority Children Developing Reflective Teachers for Changing Schools

www.sasked.gov.sk.ca/docs/ela/elateach.html
A Teacher's Self-Reflection Questionnaire

www.ed.uiuc.edu/facstaff/m-weeks/ technks.html
Checklist for Teachers

Teaching Techniques: Styles of Teaching: Reflective Discussion Technique

www.lhup.edu/~tbrink/Model/seval.html
The Reflective Teacher in a Changing
Society

*http://ublib.buffalo.edu/libraries/projects/
tlr/reflect.html*
Role of Reflection in the Renewal of
Teaching

*www.extension.usask.ca/programs/IDEV/
philosophy.html*
Developing Your Teaching Portfolio

*www.tamu-commerce.edu/coe/shed/
espinoza/ETEC625/978/shahid/*
Reflective Practice

*www.wmich.edu/english/tchg/lit/adv/
metaphor.html*
Basics of Metaphor and Simile

*www.coe.tamu.edu/~studentteaching/
pro2.html*
Reflective Teaching Practices

www.curtin.edu.au/learn/unit/RefPrac/
Reflective Teaching Practice Web Site

*www.cstudies.ubc.ca/facdev/services
newsletter/90/may90-6.html*
Teaching in Action: Criteria for
Effective Practice

*www.spcomm.uiuc.edu/projects/vta/PSG/
psgl2-ov.html*
Teamworks Module: Reflective
Problem Solving

*www.chepd.mq.edu.au/cpd/macteach/
macteach.htm*
Reflective Teachers Special Interest
Group

REFERENCES AND SUGGESTED READINGS

Airasian, P., & Gullickson, A. (1997). *Teacher
self-evaluation tool kit.* Thousand Oaks,
CA: Corwin Press.

Ayers, W. (1989). Headaches: On teaching
and teacher education. *Action in Teacher
Education, 11*(2), 1–7.

Bainer, D., & Cantrell, D. (1993). The relationship between instructional domain
and the content of reflection among
preservice teachers. *Teacher Education
Quarterly, 20*(4), 65–76.

Beasley, A. (1996). Becoming a proactive
library leader: Leadership 101. *School
Library Media Activities Monthly, 13*(2),
20–22.

Bibik, J. (1997). Metaphors for teaching:
How health and physical education
teachers describe their roles. Washington,
DC: U.S. Department of Education.
(ERIC Document Reproduction
Service No. ED 412 198)

Borko, H., Michalec, P., Timmons, M., &
Siddle, J. (1997). Student teaching portfolios: A tool for promoting reflective
practice. *Journal of Teacher Education,
48*(5), 345–357.

Brophy, J., & Good, T. (1974). *Teacher-student
relationships: Causes and consequences.*
New York: Holt, Rinehart, & Winston.

Bullough, Jr., R. (1989, March–April).
Teacher education and teacher reflection. *Journal of Teacher Education,* 15–21.

Canning, C. (1991). What teachers say
about reflection. *Educational Leadership,
48*(6), 18–21.

Collier, S. (1997, November). *Theories of
learning: Reflective thought in teacher educa-
tion.* Paper presented at the Annual
Meeting of the Mid-South Educational
Research Association, Memphis,
Tennessee.

Colton, A., & Sparks-Langer, G. (1993). A
conceptual framework to guide the
development of teacher reflection and
decision making. *Journal of Teacher
Education, 44*(1), 45–54.

Copeland, W., Birmingham, C., La Cruz, E.,
& Lewin, B. (1993). The reflective practitioner in teaching: Toward a research
agenda. *Teaching and Teacher Education,
9*(4)347–359.

Cruickshank, D. (1985). Uses and benefits of reflective teaching. *Phi Delta Kappan, 66*(10), 704–706.

Cruickshank, D. R., & Applegate, J. H. (1981). Reflective teaching as a strategy for teacher growth. *Educational Leadership, 38*(7).

Dell'Olio, J. (1998). "Hearing myself": Reflection-in-action in experienced teachers' peer-assistance behaviors. *Journal of Curriculum and Supervision, 13*(2), 184–203.

Dewey, J. (1933). *How we think.* Boston: D. C. Heath.

Dieker, L., & Monda-Amaya, L. (1995). Reflective teaching: A process for analyzing journals of preservice educators. *Teacher Education and Special Education, 18*(4), 240–252.

Dong, Y. (1998, April). *Promoting ESL preservice teachers' reflection on learning how to teach linguistically and culturally diverse students.* Paper presented at the Annual Meeting of the American Educational Research Association, San Diego, California.

Dougherty, J. (1997). *Four philosophies that shape the middle school* (Fastback No. 410). Bloomington, IN: Phi Delta Kappan Educational Foundation.

Duke, R., & Madsen, C. (1991). Proactive vs. reactive teaching: Focusing observation on specific aspects of instruction. *Bulletin of the Council for Research in Music Education, 108*, 1–14.

Eberlein, L. (1989). Ethical decision making for teachers. *The Clearing House, 63*, 125–129.

Ernst, K. (1997). Teachers' sketch journals. *Teaching K–8, 27*(5), 70.

Galvez-Martin, B. (1998, February). *Reflection and the preservice teacher.* Paper presented at the Annual Meeting of the Association of Teacher Educators, Dallas, Texas.

Galvez-Martin, M. E. (1997, October). *Who is more reflective? Inservice or preservice teachers?* Paper presented at the Annual Meeting of the Mid-Western Educational Research Association, Chicago, Illinois.

Galvez-Martin, M., Bowman, C., & Morrison, M. (1998). An exploratory study of the level of reflection attained by preservice teachers. *Mid-Western Educational Researcher, 11*(2), 9–17.

Gore, J. (1987). Reflecting on reflective teaching. *Journal of Teacher Education, 38*(2), 33–39.

Grabe, M., & Grabe, C. (1998). *Integrating technology for meaningful learning* (2d ed.). New York: Houghton-Mifflin.

Kamhi-Stein, L., & Galvan, J. (1997). EFL teacher development through critical reflection. *Teachers of English to Speakers of Other Languages Journal, 27*(1), 12–17.

Kidder, R., & Born, P. (1999). Resolving ethical dilemmas in the classroom. *Educational Leadership 56*(1), 38–41.

Kruse, S. (1997). Reflective activity in practice: Vignettes of teachers' deliberative work. *Journal of Research and Development in Education 31*(1), 46–60.

Langley, D., & Senne, T. (1997). Telling the stories of teaching: Reflective writing for preservice teachers. *Journal of Physical Education, Recreation, and Dance, 68*(8), 56–60.

Lunenburg, F., & Ornstein, A. (1996). *Educational administration: Concepts and practices* (2d ed.). New York: Wadsworth.

Magee, J. (1964, July–August). Decision trees for decision making. *Harvard Business Review, 42*, 126–138.

Martin, J., & Cunningham, D. (1999). *Preparing proactive teachers: A strategy for increasing teacher retention.* Unpublished manuscript.

McIntyre, J., & O'Hair, M. (1996). *The reflective roles of the classroom teacher.* Boston: Wadsworth.

Mills, G. (2000). *Action research: A guide for the teacher researcher.* Upper Saddle River, NJ: Prentice-Hall.

Moallem, M. (1997). The content and nature of reflective teaching: A case of an expert middle school science teacher. *The Clearing House, 70*(3), 143–150.

Moreno, E. (1998, May/June). Quality time. *Thrust for Educational Leadership*, 16–18.

Munby, H. (1986). Metaphor in the thinking of teachers: An exploratory study. *Journal of Curriculum Studies, 18*(2), 197–209.

Ogden, C., & Claus, J. (1997). Reflection as a natural element of service: Service learning for youth empowerment. *Equity and Excellence in Education, 30*(1), 72–80.

Parkay, F., & Stanford, B. (1998). *Becoming a teacher.* Boston: Allyn & Bacon.

Piburn, M., & Middleton, J. (1997, January). *The importance of reflection.* Paper presented at the International Conference on Science, Mathematics and Technology Education, Hanoi, Vietnam.

Pintrich, P., & Schunk, D. (1996). *Motivation in education: Theory, research and applications.* Upper Saddle River, NJ: Prentice-Hall.

Pultorak, E. (1993). Facilitating reflective thought in novice teachers. *Journal of Teacher Education, 44*(4), 288–295.

Robinson, E., Anderson-Harper, H., & Kochan, F. (1997, March). *Applying the theory of reflective practice to the learner and the teacher: Perspective of a graduate student.* Paper presented at the annual meeting of the American Education Research Association, Chicago, Illinois.

Roblyer, M., & Edwards, J. (2000). *Integrating education technology in teaching* (2d ed.). Upper Saddle River, NJ: Prentice-Hall.

Ross, D. (1989). First steps in developing a reflective approach. *Journal of Teacher Education, 44*(4), 22–30.

Rust, F. (1988). How supervisors think about teaching. *Journal of Teacher Education, 39*(2), 56–64.

Schon, D. (1983). *The reflective practitioner.* New York: Basic Books.

Shulman, L. (1987). Knowledge and teaching: Foundations of the new reform. *Harvard Educational Review, 57*(1), 1–20.

Smyth, J. (1989). Developing and sustaining critical reflection in teacher education. *Journal of Teacher Education, 40*(2), 2–9.

State Board for Educator Certification. (1993). *Examination for the certification of educators in Texas preparation manual: Professional development.* Amherst, MA: National Evaluation Systems.

Strike, K. (1988). The ethics of teaching. *Phi Delta Kappan, 3*(70), 156–158.

Texas Education Agency. (1992). *Resource guide on site-based decision making and district and campus planning.* Austin, TX: Author.

Tsangaridou, N., & O'Sullivan, M. (1997). The role of reflection in shaping physical education teachers' educational values and practices. *Journal of Teaching in Physical Education, 17*(1), 2–25.

Valverde, L. (1982). The self-evolving supervisor. In T. Sergiovanni (Ed.), *Supervision of teaching* (pp. 81–89). Alexandria, VA: Association for Supervision and Curriculum Development.

Volkman, V., Scheffler, A., & Dana, M. (1992). *Enhancing preservice teacher's self-efficacy through a field-based program of reflective practice.* Paper presented at the annual meeting of the Mid-South Educational Research Association, Knoxville, Tennessee.

Wesley, D. (1998). Eleven ways to be a great teacher. *Educational Leadership, 55*(5), 80–81.

ABOUT THE AUTHOR

Dr. Donna Cunningham is Associate Professor, Director of Student Teaching, and ExCET Trainer in the College of Professional Education at Texas Woman's University in Denton, Texas. She received a bachelor's degree in Education from Baylor University, a master's degree in Vocational Education from the University of North Texas, and a Ph.D. in Vocational and Adult Education from Texas Woman's University.

Dr. Cunningham has been instrumental in designing and teaching the courses in the university's field-based teacher education program. She has been a prominent figure in developing one of Texas's first university-approved promotion, tenure, and merit review policies for field-based teacher education faculty.

Dr. Cunningham's publications include a manual for training Texas professionals and paraprofessionals to provide services and academic programs for at-risk youth, a guide to help parents ensure their children are provided a bias-free education, and numerous articles related to professional teacher education preparation. Her research interests include the teacher concerns of undergraduate and graduate students; minority teacher education preparation; teacher preparation for inner-city schools; mentoring; teacher proactivity; and rural, urban, and suburban district/university partnerships. She has an extensive record of presentations at local, state, and national organizations.

A Texas-certified teacher and Vocational Supervisor, Dr. Cunningham taught junior high and high school English and history for 15 years. Before joining the university, she was director of several teen pregnancy programs as well as several state and federal grants.

13

✳

Home-School
Relationships

JENNIFER L. MARTIN
JOANN ENGELBRECHT
LILLIAN CHENOWETH

TEXAS WOMAN'S UNIVERSITY

This chapter will deal with Competency 13 of the professional development Examination for the Certification of Educators in Texas (ExCET). Competency 13 is the second of four competencies that fall under Domain III, Understanding the Teaching Environment.

Competency 13: The teacher knows how to foster strong school-home relationships that support student achievement of desired learning outcomes.

The teacher is able to establish a relationship of trust with parents or guardians from diverse backgrounds and to develop effective parent-teacher partnerships that foster all students' learning and well-being. The teacher recognizes the importance of maintaining ongoing parent-teacher communication, is aware of factors that may facilitate or impede communication with students' families, and understands basic principles of conducting parent-teacher conferences (e.g., beginning and ending on a positive note, avoiding technical jargon) and knows how to work cooperatively with parents to devise strategies for use at home and in the classroom.

TERMS TO KNOW

diversity

teacher partnerships

school relationships

technical jargon

Types of involvement

Basic obligations of parenting

Communications

Volunteering

Learning activities at home

Decision making and advocacy

Community collaboration

> Despite real progress in many states, districts, and schools
> over the past few years, there are still too many schools
> in which educators do not understand the families of
> their students; in which families do not understand their
> children's schools; and in which communities do not
> understand or assist the schools, families, or students.
>
> EPSTEIN
> (1995, P. 711)

WHY HOME-SCHOOL RELATIONSHIPS
ARE IMPORTANT

Beginning teachers may wonder why building strong home–school relationships is considered one of the 15 most important competencies needed by Texas teachers. While the teacher's most immediate and pressing focus may be planning and actual classroom instruction, the impact of home–school relationships cannot be ignored. **Home-school relationships** encompass all interactions between school and home that support student achievement. Synonymous terms used in ExCET Competency 13 are *school-home relationships* and **parent-teacher partnerships**. The classroom teacher has a major effect on positive home–school relationships; and, in turn, those positive relationships have been shown by an increasing body of research to have major benefits for students, parents, teachers, and schools. No longer can collaboration with the families of students be considered simply a nice enhancement to the teacher's primary responsibilities. Building strong home–school relationships is one of the teacher's chief tasks.

Federal, state, and local policies have supported the effort to involve families through legislation, mandates, and guidelines (Epstein, 1995). For example, the eighth goal of the National Education Goals, as set out in the Goals 2000: Educate America Act, states: "Every school will promote partnerships that will increase parental involvement and participation in promoting the social, emotional, and academic growth of children" (U.S. Department of Education, 1994). Similarly, in the Texas Education Agency's 1995 publication, *Learner-centered Schools for Texas: A*

Vision of Texas Educators, proficiencies outlining the skills and attitudes educators should possess in order to be successful in the coming century were described. Throughout the proficiencies, the importance and necessity of parent-school involvement were stressed. As schools increasingly involve families in their children's education, teachers must be prepared for the role of facilitating home-school relationships. And, instead of viewing this expanded role as a burden, teachers must recognize the benefits of home-school relationships in helping them achieve their primary goal, the educational success of all students.

Many reform efforts have attempted to improve student school performance without complete success; as a result, research continues to focus on a number of variables related to students, schools, and teachers. Research over the last decade has underlined the importance of the home in children's school progress. Studies have shown that a major key to student success is the extent to which families are involved in the educational process (Kellaghan, Sloane, Alvarez, & Bloom, 1993). The family and the school are major influences on a child, and successful learning cannot be attributed to either alone but to their joint efforts (Robinson & Fine, 1994; Seeley, 1982). Both families and schools are highly invested in ensuring student success, and collaborating toward that common goal can relieve the teachers of the burden of academically preparing children alone.

Benefits of home-school collaboration for students include:

- Improved grades
- Improved test scores
- Improved attitudes
- Improved behavior
- More completed homework
- More engagement in classroom learning activities
- Higher attendance rates
- Reduced suspension rates
- Lower dropout rates (Christenson & Cleary, 1990; Comer, 1984; National Center for Education Statistics, 1992)

In summarizing research about benefits for students, Epstein (1990) suggested that students at all levels do better academically and have better attitudes about school when parents are "aware, knowledgeable, and encouraging about school" (p. 105).

Families are also beneficiaries when they collaborate in their children's education. Examples of benefits include:

- Increased parental interactions with children at home
- Better feelings about their ability to help their students
- More positive ratings of teachers
- More understanding of how schools operate
- Better communication with their children, particularly about schoolwork
- Increased level of communication with educators (Christenson & Cleary, 1990; Epstein, 1984; Epstein & Becker, 1982a; Epstein & Dauber, 1991)

Teachers, too, experience benefits as they collaborate with families:

- More positive feelings about teaching and their school
- More positive ratings of teaching ability and interpersonal skills by parents and principals
- More teacher self-confidence
- Willingness to continue and expand practices to involve families
- Heightened expectations of and appreciation for families as educational partners
- Greater job satisfaction
- Fewer transfers requested (Christenson & Cleary, 1990; Epstein, 1985; Epstein, 1992; Epstein & Dauber, 1991; Hoover-Dempsey, Bassler, & Brissie, 1987; Leitch & Tangri, 1988)

This chapter examines the reasons for building strong relationships between schools and the diverse families of today's students. In addition, methods for encouraging and bringing about strong home-school partnerships will be explored. Specific topics include building relationships with parents/families, recognizing family diversity, communicating effectively, conducting parent-teacher conferences, and creating strategies for home-school collaboration.

BUILDING RELATIONSHIPS
WITH PARENTS/FAMILIES

A relationship is "a connection; the state or condition that exists between people or groups that deal with one another" (Barnhart & Barnhart, 1983). Forming positive relationships with the primary caregivers (birth parents, adoptive parents, stepparents, foster parents, extended and fictive family members, and guardians) is foundational to home-school collaboration. For the purposes of this chapter, *parent* refers to anyone who carries the responsibility for raising a child. Recognizing the importance of home-school collaboration, teachers are challenged to create opportunities to build relationships. Positive relationships are built over time and are based on a common interest and familiarity. The central common interest between parents and teachers is the well-being and success of the student.

Some schools attempt to build familiarity with an open-door policy that invites family members to visit the school at any time. Although this is a positive policy, it does not reach out to many families because it is not a specific opportunity and may involve some risk-taking for those unfamiliar or uncomfortable in a school setting (Nielsen & Finkelstein, 1993). Familiarity is best facilitated by personal contact during which the parent and teacher share information about their lives, interests, and hobbies, as well as their interests, goals, and concerns for the student. While teachers are encouraged to maximize informal opportunities that may occur when younger children are dropped off or picked up (Berger, 1996) or during a chance meeting at the grocery store or shopping center, specific opportunities for relationship building should be created throughout the year. Schools that conduct conferences where teachers primarily listen and parents share early in the school year (Nielsen & Finkelstein, 1993) and schools where home visits prior to the beginning of the school year are a common practice are excellent examples of the use of relationship-building opportunities. Recognizing that these practices cannot occur in all situations, schools and teachers can still facilitate the contact and sharing that builds relationships through telephone calls, interest surveys, interactive homework, voice-mail systems, and more traditional strategies such as open houses and newsletters. The specific vehicles used to develop the relationship are less important than the overall understanding of the value of building and maintaining a positive alliance with families.

RECOGNIZING FAMILY DIVERSITY

In order to understand children, teachers must understand families. Children bring their family experiences and background with them to school. Their needs must be considered within the context of family culture, characteristics, and circumstances. Understanding families is an important prerequisite to creating partnerships between families and schools. Only after understanding and appreciating the diversity in families can we create successful strategies for involvement and partnership.

The typical American family today differs from that of a generation ago and from our perception of what is "typical." **Family diversity** today includes: (a) diversity of cultural background, (b) differences in family characteristics and structure, and (c) circumstances or situational differences. These differences result in diverse languages, customs, attitudes, behaviors, and values.

Students today come from a wide range of backgrounds and milieus that may be quite different from those of teachers. It is imperative to become aware of similarities and differences in families in order to reach out and respond in sensitive and appropriate ways. Most parents, whatever their background, want their child to succeed. However, they may possess attitudes that are barriers to involvement in schools. Family members may see teachers as authorities or experts who are not to be questioned. They may feel that the only reason teachers want to talk to them is that their child is in trouble or is having problems. In the past, curriculum was frequently designed with a somewhat meager understanding of cultural differences. Teachers have to be careful to keep from assuming that the way they were raised is the only right way. Practices perceived as functional for one type of family may be inappropriate for other cultural contexts. For example, put yourself into the place of many families who have moved into cultures different from their own. If you moved to another country, would you still want to celebrate the same holidays of your original country or would you adopt new holidays and new practices? Would you prefer to gather with other Americans with similar backgrounds for a "traditional" Thanksgiving or July 4th? Sometimes it is hard to give up and trade the old for new, seemingly strange habits. Culturally sensitive approaches must be developed for families served by each school.

Differences in family characteristics and structure are also important to understand. There have been dramatic demographic changes in families and family configurations. The reality is that the mythical all-American family of an employed dad and a stay-at-home mom with children is a very small percentage of all families today. Married couples with children are less than 25 percent of all U.S. households (U.S. Census Bureau, 1999). Approximately one in four Texas families with children is headed by a single parent (Annie Casey Foundation, 1999). According to the U.S. Census Bureau (1999), the majority of children (more than 84 percent) who live with a single parent live with their mother. About 40 percent of these children live with mothers who have never been married. Most of these households have no other adults present (Lugaila, 1999). Nearly 6 percent of all U.S. children under age 18 live in the household of their grandparents. Many of these children have no parent present (Lugaila, 1999). Teachers need to be aware and accepting of the impact of changes on children such as different roles of fathers, including noncustodial fathers; grandparents or other family members; single parents; cohabiting partners; and blended families.

Family circumstances and situational differences must also be considered in planning partnerships. One example of such a difference is the amount of spendable income available to a family; this difference significantly affects the quality of life and ability of a family to meet the needs of the children. The amount of income makes both obvious and subtle differences. Income influences diet, health care, housing, and child care, as well as other resources available—clothes, school supplies, equipment, time, telephone, and choices. Money may influence family stress, safety, conflict, and feelings of despair or hopelessness. Families living in poverty may develop different rules for daily survival. Some families experience generational poverty, poverty that lasts for two generations or longer. Families of many migrant workers in Texas fit into this category with poverty lasting over long periods of time. Other families experience situational poverty, a condition that lasts for a shorter time period and may be caused by circumstances such as death, illness, or divorce (Payne, 1995). Sometimes, new immigrants to this country experience poverty, even though they are well educated and had excellent jobs in their home country. Both situational and generational poverty occur in all races (Payne, 1995).

Approximately one in four children in Texas live in poverty (Annie Casey Foundation, 1999). Since many families move in and out of poverty, almost 40 percent of all children will experience poverty at some point in their lives (Kacapyr, 1998). Almost 10 percent of all Texas children live in extreme poverty with family income below 50 percent of poverty level (Annie Casey Foundation, 1999).

While families have changed, many of our stereotypes have not changed. We need to change our understanding of what a family is and maybe even what a family does. We may have unrealistic expectations; it is important to examine our personal prejudices and preconceived ideas about families. Acknowledging differences rather than deficits is a crucial step toward accepting diversity.

Our model for working with families must acknowledge that (a) all families have some strengths; (b) different family forms are legitimate for children; and (c) our job as teachers is to reach out and respond to children from all types of families. The model should be a culturally sensitive one that does not attribute the causes of family problems to personal deficiencies. This orientation attempts to facilitate families' expressing needs and goals and then collaborating in the process of achieving success for children. Teachers are challenged to build on family strengths rather than just remediate deficits.

Cultural competence includes the critical elements of self-awareness, knowledge specific to unique cultures, and skills to engage in successful interactions. In developing cultural competence, teachers must first become aware of their own values and assumptions, as well as their own heritage and roots.

To learn about other cultures and contexts, it is helpful for teachers to expose themselves to literature, music, art, movies, and foods representative of other backgrounds. They should create opportunities to interact with persons different from themselves. If possible, they should participate in the daily life and language of a different culture or situation. Teachers must challenge themselves to move outside the familiar. Instead of viewing behavior or beliefs as negative or pathological because they do not conform to their unrealistic expectations, teachers must be open to accepting what other cultures offer. They must be careful not to impose their values and beliefs on others. Teachers can identify the characteristics and circumstances of families being served and design unique opportunities and strategies for collaboration (Powell, 1998).

COMMUNICATING EFFECTIVELY

Teachers have numerous opportunities to devise effective forms of communication to parents and to initiate communication with parents. The major teacher communication task is to design effective school-to-home communications and home-to-school communication opportunities (Epstein, 1995). An imperative of effective communication is that it not be one-way; rather, communication should be redefined to include "two-way, three-way, and many-way channels of communication that connect schools, families, students, and the community" (Epstein, 1995, p. 706). These communications can take many forms such as:

- Teacher conferences
- Folders of student work sent home for review and comments
- Availability of translators for families who do not speak English or have limited English proficiency
- Parent/student report card pickup with teachers present for informal conferences
- Telephone calls, both positive and negative in content
- Newsletters
- Effective information on choosing schools, classes, programs of study, and so on
- Clear information on school policies and changes
- Voice-mail homework hot lines
- Teacher and school e-mail
- Websites with updated information on school activities and opportunities

Importance of Communication

Communication with families has benefits for students, parents, and teachers. Students experience the following positive effects:

- An awareness of their progress and the actions needed to maintain or improve their grades
- An understanding of school policies on behavior, attendance, and student conduct
- Resources to make informed decisions about school programs, courses, and activities
- An awareness of their role in building home-school relationships, that of courier and communicator

At the same time, parents receive these advantages:

- A more complete understanding of school programs and policies
- An opportunity to monitor and stay aware of children's progress
- Information to respond effectively to children's problems
- Interactions with their child's teachers
- Ease of communication with teachers and schools

Teachers also experience positive outcomes when home-school communications are promoted. Included are:

- Encouragement for increased diversity of types of communications with families
- An awareness of their personal abilities to communicate clearly
- Appreciation for and use of family networks for communication
- An increased ability to invite and understand family views on children's programs and progress (Epstein, 1995, p. 706)

Factors That Facilitate Communication

Since parents are more involved when schools encourage involvement (Christenson & Cleary, 1990), it is important for teachers to provide many opportunities for home-school and school-home communication. By using many channels of communication—notes, memos, websites, e-mail, newsletters, telephone calls, and so on—teachers maximize their ability to reach families of their students.

In all communications, consideration needs to be given to the language, literacy level, and special needs of families. For example, translators may be needed for conferences, a native-language or lower-literacy-level edition of memos and newsletters may be necessary, or large print may be required. The readability, clarity, and form of all communications should be assessed. **Technical jargon**, the use of terms and acronyms unfamiliar to those outside the education profession, should be avoided. The quality of communications, which may be an important feature in attracting attention of families, should also be evaluated.

Families are likely to communicate more when the school encourages more communication. Convenient times should be provided for family communication. This may involve occasional evening or weekend opportunities for employed parents. Care should be taken that teachers do not contact families only for crisis situations or negative reports. Equal attention should be given to communications that recognize the positive efforts of students. For example, when an elementary-age child has exhibited cooperative behavior over a period of time, a note or telephone call to families is likely to be highly appreciated. Likewise, the families of secondary students would also appreciate messages describing the positive actions of their youths.

Barriers to Communication

Despite the overwhelming evidence of the benefits of school-home relationships, effective interaction is hindered by many barriers. The obstacles include parental characteristics, attitudes, and life situations; educational traditions; educational environments; and teacher characteristics, attitudes, and responsibilities.

Parental Characteristics, Attitudes, and Life Situations Parents who stay away from schools include racial and ethnic minorities, those with lower incomes, those with limited English-speaking abilities, and those who had bad personal experiences in school (Moles, 1996). We may forget that not everyone remembers his or her school experience fondly, and the "baggage" from less-than-positive experiences may increase the chances that a parent either does not come to school or approaches school interactions in an adversarial manner prior to even knowing the teacher or the circumstances. The quality of early partnership experiences establishes patterns and relationships that encourage or discourage family involvement in later years. Some families may be difficult to reach because of physical, social, or psychological distance; student age; age of parent; parental background; family structure; and family personal problems (Epstein, 1992). In some cases, job and family demands leave little free time for family involvement (Moles, 1996; Shartrand, Weiss, Kreider, & Lopez, 1997).

Parental involvement decreases as students become older (Epstein, 1986; Stevenson & Baker, 1987). Although most parents of high schoolers are interested in adolescents' education, they are affected by not knowing how to respond to youths' desire for greater independence. Older students may be reluctant to have parents involved (Pryor, 1995). When asked why parent involvement drops off at the high school level, over 3,000 parents identified the chief reason as lack of understanding of high school subjects and lack of teacher invitations for involvement (Chavkin & Williams, 1993). Parents are sometimes intimidated by school personnel and feel that they do not possess knowledge and skills to help their children (Riley, 1994).

Unprofitable Educational Traditions Educational bureaucracies tend to resist broad and active parent involvement in education (Cibulka, 1996). Schools may be unwilling to share information with parents or may fear that parents will be troublemakers who might make decisions school leaders oppose (Heckman, 1996). The traditional philosophy of many schools and teachers focuses on needs of children with little attention to their context of family life and circumstances (Burton, 1992).

Educational Environments Some educational environments deter school-home relationships. Middle and high schools may appear to be distant, impersonal settings to families (Epstein, 1992). At the high school level, schools are larger, departmentalized, and farther away from students' neighborhoods. Teachers are often subject-matter experts who may not be trained to work with families (Epstein & Connors, 1992). Less information is given to parents in schools that serve educationally and economically disadvantaged students (MacIver & Epstein, 1990). According to Epstein (1992), "Families who may need the most information in useful forms are presently receiving the least" (p. 1144). Swap (1987) identified three barriers to effective school-home relationships: limited time for communication, ritualized parent-school contacts, and frequency of communication during crises only.

Teacher Characteristics, Attitudes, and Responsibilities Just like parents, teachers' personal responsibilities may limit their availability to meet with families outside school hours (Swap, 1990). Because of increasing ethnic diversity, teachers and families are likely to come from different cultural and economic backgrounds, which can lead to contrasting values and beliefs (Murphy, 1991). Teachers (and administrators) may not understand families with different backgrounds, experiences, and needs (Epstein, 1992). Teachers in environments where they believe their attitudes differ from others at the school report weaker parent involvement programs. Stronger programs are reported when teachers feel they are similar to administrators, other teachers, and parents (Epstein & Dauber, 1991). Some teachers hold negative attitudes toward family involvement (Shartrand et al., 1997), including beliefs that parents are not qualified or interested in involvement in children's education (New Futures Institute, 1989). Moles (1982) stated that many teachers have low expectations about parental commitments to help children with schoolwork. Teachers may also lack confidence to work with families (Shartrand et al., 1997). Epstein (1991) found that many teachers had reservations about whether they could motivate parents to be involved. Teachers want more parental involvement but may be frustrated by the expectation that they should be initiators of activities to solve motivation and achievement problems in students (Pryor, 1995). Teachers may not systematically encourage family involvement, and parents do not always participate even when encouraged (Shartrand et al., 1997). Teachers are sometimes discouraged by their attempts to communicate and work with parents (Epstein & Becker, 1982b). Though there are many teachers whose attitudes block home-school collaboration, many more work toward making positive differences.

CONDUCTING PARENT-TEACHER CONFERENCES

Parent-teacher conferences represent the most common means of family-school communication and can offer a building block for teacher-parent partnership. However, the hearts of many parents and teachers are filled with anxiety and apprehension when it is time to schedule conferences (Gestwicki, 1996). In an explanation of the stress that often accompanies parent-teacher conferences, Barron and Colvin (1984) stated that "conferences between teachers and parents have sometimes been seen as monsters hovering on school calendars to prevent teachers from enjoying their week" (p. 76).

Parent-teacher conferences are usually scheduled to share a developmental overview or focus on a particular issue. In either case, careful attention to all aspects of the conference—preparing, planning, conducting, and evaluating—is critical to building a positive home-school relationship.

Preparing for the Conference

The teacher's preparation begins long before the actual conference is scheduled. Long-term preparation involves awareness of personal attitudes toward cultures and varied family situations and roles. This self-awareness is necessary before educators can communicate with families different from themselves (Jordan, Reyes-Blanes, Peel, Peel, & Lane, 1998). Developing basic relationship or interpersonal skills is also critical to effective conferencing. Basic relationship skills include reflective listening, building rapport, communicating, genuine caring, and empathizing (Perl, 1995).

Planning the Conference

Careful planning reduces anxiety and maximizes the time spent in parent-teacher conferences. Planning involves scheduling, preparing materials, arranging for a translator if needed, and preparing a comfortable location.

Scheduling Whether invitations for conferences are made by telephone, written, or extended in person, they should be friendly, provide information about the purpose of the conference, and reflect an awareness of parents' busy lives. For example, when a scheduling sheet is posted or sent home, it should include abundant choices of days and times, allowing for differing schedules. Teachers need to make it clear that they are anxious to be as flexible as possible in accommodating the needs of parents (Gestwicki, 1996).

Preparing Materials Depending on the purpose of the conference, a list of discussion questions or topics could be sent home for parents to facilitate dialog. For example, questions might include: (a) How does your child view school? (b) What is your child's activity schedule away from school? and (c) How does your child solve problems at home? (Hoerr, 1997). Teachers need to accumulate the necessary resources to guide the conference discussion. If the primary goal is a developmental overview, an array of writing and art samples as well as developmental assessments and photographs can assist the parents in understanding the level of the student's physical, social, emotional, and cognitive development. If the conference is to focus on one academic area, such as mathematics or a behavioral issue, the teacher may have work samples, anecdotal records, and related materials that illustrate concretely the topic or issue to be addressed. Planning in advance to assemble meaningful examples of work or to document behavior, rather than collecting handy materials, will help families recognize your professional commitment.

A brief outline of topics to be discussed helps organize the conference and keep it on track. The outline can be shared with parents at the opening of the conference along with an inquiry as to additions they would like to make. Whether written or oral, the outline should include a clear opportunity for parental input and questions.

Arranging for a Translator If the primary language of the parent(s) is not the same as the teacher's, it is the teacher's responsibility to make arrangements to have a translator at the conference. It is not an acceptable practice to have the student serve as the translator (Trejo, 1999). At the least, student translators are in an awkward and vulnerable position serving as go-betweens for some of the most powerful and important people in their lives. There is a high probability of misunderstanding and frustration as well as the possibility for student translators to purposefully mislead or misinform the parent, the teacher, or both.

Preparing a Comfortable Physical Location Conferences can be carried out in almost any location if the following are available: two or three comfortable, adult-sized chairs; a table on which to spread papers, materials, and beverages; and a door that can be closed and perhaps posted with a sign indicating that "conferences are in progress" (Gestwicki, 1996). Small chairs found in classrooms for preschool and elementary children are uncomfortable for adults and should be avoided if at all possible. Parents and teachers should be at eye level and sitting side by side without a physical barrier such as a desk or wide table separating them. The closed door with a sign indicating conferences in progress conveys a firm impression that the conference is private and confidential.

Schools serving families with limited resources need to prepare for young children who may accompany families to conferences. If child care cannot be provided, a corner where young children can play quietly may need to be prepared. It would be helpful to furnish the corner with preschool play materials and books. Extra chairs should also be provided so families can feel comfortable bringing other adults significant in the child's life to the conference.

Conducting the Conference

Careful planning and a comfortable setting help put anxious parents and nervous teachers at ease. Opening the conference with casual conversation and an offer of a beverage helps create social comfort. A conference can be structured in a variety of ways but should always begin and end on a positive note. Duffy (1997) offered three parts of a conference that can be adapted to various situations and ages of student. Part one involves listening and sharing stories. It is important for teachers to give parents an opportunity to talk about their child, sharing their love, joy, and concerns. Parents are reassured that the teacher does know their child when the teacher responds with a story or anecdote that reflects knowledge and understanding of their student.

The second part of the conference addresses the student's performance level in the educational setting. For regular conferences, the teacher may provide a developmental overview documented with the materials collected prior to the conference. For conferences focused on student behavior or special needs, clear examples should be given as objectively as possible; teacher emotionalism should be avoided.

The final part of the conference prepares for the future by summarizing what has occurred during the conference and developing a plan. This may involve setting goals, scheduling another conference, or developing an action plan (perhaps jointly) to address developmental or behavioral issues.

Documentation of a conference is a wise practice that can take several forms. One simple strategy is to take notes, develop goals, and note any recommendations or agreements. The parents can take a copy, and the teacher has a file copy. In some schools, a standard parent-conference form may be required to provide a format for information such as parent's name, teacher, student's name and age, background information, programs and services discussed, report card explanation, comments, recommendations, and follow-up agreements. In some districts, it is required that both teacher and parent sign conference documentation and that both retain a copy.

Evaluating and Following Up

Within a week after the conference, the teacher should evaluate the conference and follow up with parents. Teachers can enhance their own professional development and build a strong foundation for future parent conferences by reflecting on questions such as: (a) How well did I listen? (b) Did I offer enough specifics? and (c) Was I positive in beginning and ending the conference? (Gestwicki, 1996).

Follow-up strategies include sending a note home or telephoning the parents to thank them for their participation. Depending on the purpose of the conference, the follow-up letter may include goals of the conference, information presented, information gained, and any agreements made. A telephone call is a particularly helpful follow-up strategy when the family needs another conference or referral for other services (Rockwell, Andre, & Hawley, 1996).

Pitfalls to Avoid for Successful Conferences

Gestwicki (1996) identified pitfalls to avoid for successful parent-teacher conferences. These include: (a) using technical jargon or acronyms—"teacher talk," (b) playing the role of an "expert," (c) using negative or destructive evaluations about a child's capabilities, (d) conversing unprofessionally about others by being too personal or taking sides, (e) giving advice—either unasked for or asked for, and (f) trying to solve all problems on the spot or trying to force agreement. A quick review of these common pitfalls associated with parent conferences can be instructive during the planning and implementation phases and also can assist in evaluation of the conference.

Consider the following elementary school conference. Mrs. Chen, a fourth-grade teacher, conducted a conference with the parents of Maria Garcia, who had been exhibiting disruptive behavior during the previous three weeks. Mrs. Chen called Maria's parents on Monday afternoon and asked them to attend a conference on Tuesday after school. As Mr. and Mrs. Garcia entered the classroom, Mrs. Chen invited them to sit in student chairs that she had assembled in a small circle. As she balanced paperwork in her lap, Mrs. Chen launched into a monologue describing the effects of Maria's behavior on her class and on herself. She concluded her diatribe with the remarks that "Maria is driving everyone crazy, and she needs psychological help." The parents appeared shocked and asked for examples of Maria's disruptive behavior. Mrs. Chen replied, "Everything she does is disruptive!" As you can surmise, Mrs. Chen made several strategic conferencing errors. First, she was not sensitive to family scheduling when she asked the family to meet after school the next day. Mrs. Chen did not adequately prepare the physical environment or materials that would provide specific objective examples of Maria's disruptive behaviors. Mrs. Chen's emotional reactions to the situation were not helpful to the parents in understanding what Maria had done to disrupt the classroom. The teacher used emotionally charged language and made a diagnosis that she was not qualified to make.

Here is a positive version of Mrs. Chen's conference about Maria. In preparation for asking the parents to come in for a conference, Mrs. Chen kept an objective log of Maria's behaviors during the three-week period along with a record of school attempts to modify the behavior. She called the parents and inquired if it would be possible for them to come in for a conference at a convenient time in the next week. When they arrived for the conference, Mrs. Chen asked them to sit around a small table in adult chairs. She began the conference by telling them how much she enjoys teaching and how glad she is to have Maria in her class. Next she expressed her concern about the change in Maria's behavior and its effect on Maria's progress and the classroom environment. Mrs. Chen shared specific examples of disruptive situations over the last three weeks and answered the Garcias' specific questions in an objective and caring manner. She suggested that the counselor might join them for the remainder of the conference in order to devise an action plan to aid Maria in decreasing the disruptive behaviors. After the counselor joined them and the plan was made, Mrs. Chen again expressed support for Maria by offering to telephone the Garcias in a week to report on how the plan was working and to find out about their questions and experiences at home. The Garcias expressed appreciation to Mrs. Chen and the counselor as they left. As you can see, this scenario is likely to have a much more positive outcome than the first conference described.

CREATING STRATEGIES
FOR HOME-SCHOOL COLLABORATION

Collaboration is a voluntary relationship based upon mutual goals, shared responsibilities for decision making, and an opportunity for families and schools each to share their expertise and strengths. Collaboration empowers parents to contribute to the academic success of their child (Bempechat, 1992). Success does not come from either the home or school alone but from the combination of the two influences (Seeley, 1982). Collaboration is an ongoing process, not a program of activities; it requires vision, commitment, and continuous effort.

Teachers must see working with families as a crucial part of their job and must broaden their focus to extend beyond the classroom into the home. The Texas State Legislature has stated that the mission for education in Texas is "grounded on the conviction that a successful public education system is directly related to a strong, dedicated, and supportive family and that parental involvement in the school is essential for the maximum educational achievement of a child" (Vornberg, 1998, p. 98).

Involvement is conceptualized as more than PTA meetings or homeroom parent activities. Occasionally families are passive participants, receiving information from teachers, while at other times they are more actively involved. All types of involvement are valuable; parents do not have to be present at a meeting inside the school building for the family to be actively involved or interested in a partnership with the teacher. Involvement is viewed as multidimensional (Grolnick & Slowiaczek, 1994).

Epstein (1992) developed a framework of six **types of involvement**. Consideration of all six types helps a school expand its focus to an integrated view of involvement. Epstein's six types are described in the text that follows.

Type 1: Basic Obligations of Parenting

Schools can help families establish home environments that support children and enable them to be better students. Workshops on guidance and discipline, parent education courses, or family support relative to health and nutrition issues are examples of school-supported or -sponsored initiatives in this category.

Type 2: Communications

Schools can facilitate effective two-way communication between families and schools. Communication features listening to parents as often as telling parents. Involvement might include focus groups, surveys, telephone calls, as well as voice-mail systems for information or questions and personalized notes to parents. Teachers can facilitate numerous opportunities for family feedback.

Type 3: Volunteering

Families can participate in assemblies or functions as well as provide classroom or school assistance. As with the other categories of involvement, families may need specific training on their role as volunteers and the expectations of the teachers. Individuals are more likely to be involved if they are certain about what they are supposed to do. Volunteering includes supporting school goals and children's learning at any place, at any time.

Type 4: Learning Activities at Home

Families can be provided with information and ideas to interact through motivating, encouraging, monitoring, and taking an active interest in school-related activities. Families can be involved in curriculum decisions or participate in interactive homework assignments. Families might be involved in workshops featuring information on appropriate age-level expectations, successful techniques to encourage academic achievement, or subject-matter refresher courses to help families assist with homework.

Type 5: Decision Making and Advocacy

Families are included in school decisions through activities such as committees, site-based management teams, and district task forces. Parents are informed about issues and elections and are helped to develop leadership skills.

Type 6: Community Collaboration

Resources and services from the community are identified to strengthen the school program, family practices, and student growth. Families can be provided with information on health, cultural, recreational, and other support programs, as well as opportunities for service to the community.

Personal contact from teachers increases family involvement in all categories. Teachers should demonstrate the belief that families share their goals for successful children. An open, inviting attitude should be integrated into all phases of the school's program.

The overall atmosphere of the school must be assessed to determine how welcoming it is for families. Clearly marked exterior signs indicating where to park and where to enter, easily followed maps, and welcome displays or exhibits all help schools create trust and willingness to be involved.

An effective strategy is to include opportunities for interaction between teachers and families outside the classroom or school building. Some family members may have less-than-fond memories of their own school experiences and be somewhat intimidated by the school. While home visits by teachers may be beneficial, some school districts do not allow such visits. Teachers should always check with the principal before making a home visit. In some areas, home visits can only be made in teams. Sometimes neighborhood meetings can be held in community centers, parks, libraries, or churches to overcome these obstacles and offer neutral ground for all participants. Schools could sponsor neighborhood coffees or potluck dinners in comfortable, convenient locations.

Involvement also increases when there is a family or parent liaison at the school, someone whose specific job it is to help families or to focus on creating collaboration. This person can personalize invitations to functions, reach out to different families, and coordinate school efforts. A family liaison could also be responsible for training teachers to create partnerships with families. Families may feel more comfortable communicating with the liaison rather than with an administrator or teacher and may appreciate the school's overt effort to increase involvement. Some schools have set aside a meeting room or special lounge for parents and volunteers. Such a place may be more comfortable than a classroom or teacher's lounge.

Families may be more open to involvement during certain "reachable moments." These times include transition periods, such as when a child is entering kindergarten or progressing from elementary to middle school. Another reachable moment might be during school programs such as athletic events or musical concerts, times when families may already be coming to the building or have scheduled time for an activity. A calendar of activities for the semester with reminder notes and/or telephone calls enables families to plan for participation. Conferences or informal teacher meetings can often be planned in conjunction with such nonthreatening, social activities. Teachers and/or administrators could have regular monthly lunches or breakfasts for interaction or informal exchange of ideas. Some schools feature "pancakes with the principal" or "doughnuts for dads" to encourage participation.

Another useful strategy for creating collaboration is to remember the benefits of rewarding those families who are partners with the school. Teachers and administrators need to routinely recognize and acknowledge the contributions of parents. A teacher can say "thank you" to families in many ways. One example would be frequent positive notes to parents to encourage their continued participation.

SUMMARY

Home-school collaboration is a crucial element in the educational success of students because of the many positive benefits to students, parents, teachers, and schools. Key practices that support strong home-school relationships include honoring and respecting the diversity and uniqueness of families, affirming and building on the strengths of the child and family, using positive communication skills, and providing a welcoming school-home partnership. Working with families is not just an optional enhancement to a teacher's job description; it is a critical function that must be considered a primary responsibility for all educators.

SUGGESTED ACTIVITIES

1. Secure a school's site-based management plan, parent handbook, and mission statement. Evaluate the effectiveness of these communications with families.

2. Interview teachers at different levels—early childhood, elementary, middle school, and high school—to determine their perceptions about the benefits of and barriers to home-school relations.

3. Interview several parents concerning their experiences in conferences about their children. Explore whether the guidelines for effective conferences were utilized.

4. Draw a model of each of the following based on this chapter's content:
   a. A family-friendly school
   b. A school-friendly family

5. With a partner, role-play a poor parent-teacher conference. Then role-play the same conference done in an effective manner.

6. Compare the demographics of your classroom with the demographics of school children in Texas. How are they similar and different?

7. Interview a school counselor about stresses on families in your school. Ask about the effects of these stresses on the school's students.

8. Write effective letters to parents for the following purposes:
   a. Welcome letter for a new school year
   b. Letter about a student's behavior problem
   c. Letter praising a student
   d. Letter of invitation to a conference

9. Attend a parent-teacher organization meeting at your school. Critique the meeting for its appeal and usefulness to families.

10. Visit a school. Prepare lists of what made you feel welcome and what intimidated you.

11. Interview a principal, a teacher, and a parent about the types of home-school involvement they have experienced. Compare their experiences with the types of involvement outlined in this chapter.

12. Design an interactive homework assignment that would involve families in their children's school work.

PRACTICE DECISION SET

Ms. Lopez, a first-year teacher in a large urban school, is preparing to hold conferences with each of her students' parents.

1. Another first-year teacher tells Ms. Lopez that he just does not have time to communicate with parents. In convincing her fellow teacher of the importance of home-school relationships, which of the following reasons would be *most essential* for Ms. Lopez to mention?

   a. Parents and families can cause problems for teachers if they do not receive communication from teachers.
   b. Federal, state, and local policies have supported the effort to involve families in their children's education.

c. The extent to which families are involved in the educational process has been shown to be an accurate indicator of student success.

d. Collaboration with families allows teachers to carry less of the burden of educating students.

2. Ms. Lopez is considering several options for arranging conference times with parents. Which of the following strategies is likely to be *most successful* in setting up effective parental conferences?

   a. Sending home with each student an assigned time for the conference

   b. Sending home a note asking parents to indicate several times when they would be available for a conference, developing a list of conference times from the parental input, and then sending home a list confirming a conference time

   c. Sending home a communication indicating times that she will be available for conferences on a first-come, first-serve basis

   d. Spending her preparation period calling parents to set up conference times

3. The school in which Ms. Lopez teaches has great student diversity. Which of the following would be *least important* for Ms. Lopez to consider as she interacts with students and parents?

   a. Most parents of all backgrounds and characteristics want their children to succeed educationally.

   b. Culturally sensitive approaches must be developed for the particular families served by a school.

c. The teacher's job is to reach out and respond to children from all types of families.

d. A primary focus of teachers is to remediate deficits arising from students' family and cultural backgrounds.

4. In preparing for a conference with parents who have limited English proficiency, Ms. Lopez would want to do each of the following *except:*

   a. Arrange to have written information translated and sent to the parents.

   b. Plan extra time for the conference in order to allow adequate opportunity for translation.

   c. Have the student serve as a translator for the conference because the parent will feel most comfortable with this arrangement.

   d. Arrange furniture so she can sit beside the student's parents at a table.

Answer 1: Parents and families are sometimes viewed negatively by teachers, but the main motivation for involving families in children's education is not avoidance of problems with families. Federal, state, and local policies have supported family involvement in schools, and collaboration with families does allow families and schools to work together toward a common goal of academic success for students. However, the primary reason for teachers to focus on home-school relationships is that such relationships are primary keys to student academic success. The best answer is *c.*

Answer 2: Arranging effective parental conferences involves consideration of the needs of parents. In contrast to assigning conference times, strategies that recognize the responsibilities and busy lives of students' families are likely to be most successful in arranging conferences. Many parents are not available during work hours, and drop-in conferences may not provide opportunity for ample preparation and meeting time. Strategy *b* takes into consideration the needs of parents and is, therefore, most likely to result in successful and effective conferences.

Answer 3: A positive view of children and their families will aid teachers in working successfully with both. Most parents do wish for their children to succeed educationally. It is the teacher's job to become culturally aware of her students and their families in order to best respond to them. All families have strengths, and teachers need to focus on student and family strengths rather than

deficits. Therefore, *d* is the *least* important consideration.

Answer 4: In order to be sure that parents are aware of and prepared for conference opportunities, written translated materials need to be made available to parents and families. Plans for a translator other than the student need to be made so that the student is not burdened by being inappropriately placed in an adult role. Extra conference time may be needed for adequate translation, and physical arrangements need to be made so that no barriers are present between the teacher and the parents. Ms. Lopez would want to do everything except *c*.

WEB LINKS

Remember that website locations may change. If any of these sites have moved or cannot be located, use the Terms to Know in this chapter to search for further information.

http://www.aecf.org
The Annie E. Casey Foundation is an outstanding source for current national and state statistics on children. The "Kids Count" data is in understandable form and is updated annually. Other information on the status of children is also found at this site.

http://www.childrensdefense.org
"One Day in the Life of a Child" is just one example of the outstanding data and current information available at this Children's Defense Fund site.

www.cpirc.org
The Colorado Parent Information and Resource Center presents articles on parent involvement, current research, and excellent links.

www.partnersineducation.org
The National Association of Partners in Education is dedicated to providing leadership in developing partnerships. Resources include how-to manuals, recognition ideas, and many other products.

www.nccic.org
This National Child Care Information Center site, part of ERIC, offers information on a variety of topics and links to numerous other agencies and organizations.

www.ncpie.org
The National Coalition for Parent Involvement in Education is committed to strengthening family-school partnerships. This website has ideas for schools, special activities, a database, and a good resource list.

www.tnpc.com
This National Parenting Center site has articles on issues of concern to today's families, book reviews, product ratings, and a chatroom.

www.pta.org
This Parent Teachers Association (PTA) site is excellent. It has guides for parents and teachers on collaboration and a very good list of resources. Articles, such as teachers' best ideas for involving parents, are short and to-the-point. Information on diversity is also accessible through the site.

http://pfie.ed.gov
This site for the U.S. Department of Education's Partnership for Family Involvement in Education demonstrates the federal government's priority in creating partnerships. Excellent online handbooks, examples of successful programs, teacher training materials, and summer home learning ideas are found here.

REFERENCES AND SUGGESTED READINGS

The Annie E. Casey Foundation. (1999). *Kids count*. Available: http://www.aecf.org/cgi-bin/kconline.cgi.

Barnhart, C. L., & Barnhart, R. K. (Eds.). (1983). *The world book dictionary* (Vol. 2). Chicago: World Book.

Barron, B. G., & Colvin, J. M. (1984). Teacher-talk to parents. *Education, 105*(1), 76–78.

Bempechat, J. (1992, Fall/Winter). The role of parent involvement in children's academic achievement. *The School Community Journal, 2*(2), 31–41.

Berger, E. H. (1996). Working with families: Don't leave them standing on the sidewalk. *Early Childhood Education Journal, 24*(2), 131–133.

Burton, C. B. (1992). Defining family-centered early education: Beliefs of public school, child care, and Head Start teachers. *Early Education and Development, 3*(1), 45–59.

Chavkin, N. F., & Williams, D. L. (1993). Minority parents and the elementary school: Attitudes and practices. In N. F. Chavkin (Ed.), *Families and schools in a pluralistic society* (pp. 73–83). Albany, NY: State University of New York.

Christenson, S. L., & Cleary, M. (1990). Consultation and parent-educator partnership: A perspective. *Journal of Educational and Psychological Consultation, 1*(3), 219–241.

Cibulka, J. G. (1996). Conclusion: Toward an interpretation of school, family, and community connections: Policy changes. In J. G. Cibulka & W. J. Kritek (Eds.), *Coordination among schools, families and communities: Prospects for educational reform* (pp. 403–435). Albany, NY: State University of New York Press. (ED 395 718)

Comer, J. (1984). Home-school relationships as they affect the academic success of children. *Urban Society, 16*, 323–337.

Duffy, R. (1997, July–August). Parents' perspectives on conferencing. *Child Care Information Exchange*, 41–43.

Epstein, J. L. (1984). School policy and parent involvement: Research results. *Educational Horizons, 62*(2), 70–72.

Epstein, J. L. (1985). A question of merit: Principals' and parents' evaluations of teachers. *Educational Researcher, 14*(7), 3–10.

Epstein, J. L. (1986). Parents' reactions to teacher practices of teacher involvement. *The Elementary School Journal, 86*, 277–294.

Epstein, J. (1990). School and family connections: Theory, research, and implications for integrating sociologies of education and family. In D. Unger & M. Sussman (Eds.), *Families in community settings: Interdisciplinary perspectives* (pp. 99–126). New York: Haworth.

Epstein, J. L. (1991). Effects on student achievement of teachers' practices of parent involvement. *Advances in Reading/Language Research, 5*, 261–276.

Epstein, J. L. (1992). School and family partnerships. In M. Alkin (Ed.), *Encyclopedia of educational research* (6th ed., pp. 1139–1151).

Epstein, J. L. (1995). School/family/community partnerships. *Phi Delta Kappan, 76*(9), 701–712.

Epstein, J. L., & Becker, H. J. (1982a). Parent involvement: A survey of teacher practices. *The Elementary School Journal, 83*(2), 85–102.

Epstein, J. L., & Becker, H. J. (1982b). Teachers' reported practices of parent involvement: Problems and possibilities. *The Elementary School Journal, 83*(2), 103–113.

Epstein, J. L., & Connors, L. J. (1992). School and family partnerships in middle grades and high schools. *Practitioner (NASSP newsletter), 18*(4), 1–8.

Epstein, J. L., & Dauber, S. L. (1991). School programs and teacher practices of parent involvement in inner-city elementary and middle schools. *The Elementary School Journal, 91*(3), 289–305.

Gestwicki, C. (1996). *Home, school, and community relations* (3d ed.). Albany, NY: Delmar.

Grolnick, W. S., & Slowiaczek, M. L. (1994). Parents' involvement in children's schooling: A multidimensional conceptualization and motivational model. *Child Development, 65*, 237–252.

Heckman, P. E. (1996). *The courage to change: Stories from successful school reform.* Thousand Oaks, CA: Corwin Press.

Hoerr, T. R. (1997). When teachers listen to parents. *Principal, 77*(2), 40–42.

Hoover-Dempsey, K. V., Bassler, O. C., & Brissie, J. S. (1987). Parent involvement: Contributions of teacher efficacy, school socioeconomic status, and other school characteristics. *American Educational Research Journal, 24*(3), 417–435.

Jordan, L., Reyes-Blanes, M. E., Peel, B. B., Peel, H. A., & Lane, H. B. (1998). Developing teacher-parent partnerships across cultures: Effective parent conferences. *Intervention in School and Clinic, 3*(3), 141–147.

Kacapyr, E. (1998). How hard are hard times? *American Demographics.* Available: http://www.demographics.com/publications/ad/98.

Kellaghan, T., Sloane, K., Alvarez, B., & Bloom, B. (1993). *Changes in society and the family: The home environment and school learning.* San Francisco: Jossey-Bass.

Leitch, M. L., & Tangri, S. S. (1988). Barriers to home-school collaboration. *Educational Horizons, 66,* 70–74.

Lugaila, T. A. (1999). Marital status and living arrangements: March 1998 (Update). U. S. Department of Commerce. Available: http://www. census.gov/pressrelease/www/1999/cb 99-03.

MacIver, D. J., & Epstein, J. L. (1990). *How equal are opportunities for learning in the middle grades in disadvantaged and advantaged schools?* (CDS Report). Baltimore: Johns Hopkins University Center for Research on Effective Schooling for Disadvantaged Students.

Moles, O. (1982, November). Synthesis of research on parent participation in children's education. *Educational Leadership,* 44–47.

Moles, O. (Ed.). (1996, August). *Reaching all families: Creating family-friendly schools.* Washington, DC: U.S. Department of Education Office of Educational Research and Improvement.

Murphy, J. (1991). *Restructuring schools: Capturing and assessing the phenomenon.* New York: Teachers College Press.

National Center for Education Statistics. (1992). *A profile of American eighth-grade mathematics and science instruction.* (Technical Report No. NCES 92-486). Washington, DC: Government Printing Office.

New Futures Institute. (1989). *Resource guide series: Vol. 1. Parent involvement in new futures.* Waltham, MA: Brandeis University, Center for Human Resources.

Nielsen, L. E., & Finkelstein, J. M. (1993). A new approach to parent conferences. *Teaching K–8, 24*(1), 90–92.

Payne, R. (1995). *Poverty: A framework for understanding and working with students and adults from poverty.* Baytown, TX: RFT Publishing.

Perl, J. (1995). Improving relationship skills for parent conferences. *Teaching Exceptional Children, 28*(1), 28–31.

Powell, D. R. (1998). Reweaving parents into the fabric of early childhood programs. *Young Children, 53*(5), 60–67.

Pryor, C. (1995). Youth, parent and teacher views of parent involvement in schools. *Education, 115*(3), 410–419.

Riley, R. (1994, February 15). *Prepared remarks for presentation at Georgetown University, Washington, D.C.* Washington, DC: U.S. Department of Education.

Robinson, E. L., & Fine, M. J. (1994). Developing collaborative home-school relationships. *Preventing School Failure, 39*(1), 9–15.

Rockwell, R. E., Andre, L. C., & Hawley, M. R. (1996). *Parents and teachers as partners: Issues and challenges.* Fort Worth, TX: Harcourt Brace College.

Seeley, D. (1982, November). Education through partnership. *Educational Leadership*, pp. 42–43.

Shartrand, A. M., Weiss, H. B., Kreider, H. M., & Lopez, M. E. (1997). *New skills for new schools: Preparing teachers in family involvement.* Cambridge, MA: Harvard Family Research Project, Harvard Graduate School of Education.

Stevenson, D., & Baker, D. (1987). The family/school relation and the child's school performance. *Child Development, 58*, 1348–1357.

Swap, S. M. (1987). *Enhancing parent involvement in schools.* New York: Teachers College Press.

Swap, S. M. (1990). *Parent involvement and success for all children: What we know now.* Boston: Institute for Responsive Education.

Texas Education Agency. (1995). *Learner-centered schools for Texas: A vision of Texas educators.* Austin, TX: Author.

Trejo, F. (1999, May 23). Lost in translation: Kids who must interpret for parents miss part of childhood, experts say. *Dallas Morning News*, pp. 1A, 16A–17A.

U.S. Bureau of the Census. (1999, January 7). Washington, DC. Available: http://www.census.gov/

U.S. Department of Education. (1994). *Strong families, strong schools: Building community partnerships for learning.* Washington, DC: Author.

Vornberg, J. A. (Ed.). (1998). *Texas public school organization and administration: 1998* (6th ed.). Dubuque, IA: Kendall Hunt.

ABOUT THE AUTHORS

The authors of this chapter all teach in the Department of Family Sciences at Texas Woman's University.

Dr. Jennifer Martin, Associate Professor and Chair, has taught high school and college for a total of 24 years. She currently teaches both undergraduate and graduate courses in the Family Studies program, and she has served as a family and consumer sciences teacher-educator for the past 14 years.

Dr. JoAnn Engelbrecht, Professor, teaches undergraduate and graduate courses in the Child Development program. She is also a Certified Family Life Educator (CFLE) who has taught for 28 years in preschool, middle school, high school, university, and adult education settings.

Dr. Lillian Chenoweth, Professor, also teaches in the Family Studies program. She has been active in adult education and university teaching for 28 years. All are involved in research related to parenting education and family-school collaboration.

14

✴

School and Community Connections

JUDITH A. PONTICELL
UNIVERSITY OF NEW MEXICO

This chapter will deal with Competency 14 of the Professional Development Examination for the Certification of Educators in Texas (ExCET). Competency 14 is the third of four competencies included in Domain III, Understanding the Teaching Environment.

Competency 14: The teacher understands how the school relates to the larger community and knows strategies for making interactions between school and community mutually supportive and beneficial.

The teacher is aware of the significance of the school-community relationship and understands the value of working with local citizens to establish strong and positive ties between the school and the community. The teacher knows how to take advantage of community strengths and resources to foster student growth. In addition, the teacher is aware of problems facing the community (e.g., drugs, gangs, racism, crime, unemployment, poverty), understands how these problems may affect students' lives and learning, and is aware of resources and strategies that can help students cope with community problems.

TERMS TO KNOW

At-risk factors

School-community relationship

Demographic characteristics

Community information sources

Community groups

Community-curriculum connections

Service learning

Competency 14 focuses on five basic skills in understanding the **school-community relationship.** These are (1) recognizing challenges facing today's communities, (2) learning about the school's community, (3) effectively communicating with the school's community, (4) connecting with the community in learning experiences, and (5) developing children's sense of responsibility for improving their communities. This chapter will focus on these five skills.

RECOGNIZING CHALLENGES FACING TODAY'S COMMUNITIES

Fordham University's Institute for Social Policy produces the *Index of Social Health for the United States* (Miringoff, 1994). The index uses 16 measures, including infant mortality, teenage suicide, dropout rates, drug abuse, homicide, food stamp use, unemployment, traffic deaths, and poverty among the elderly. The index ranges from 0 to 100 (with 100 being the best condition). From 1970 to 1992, the index showed a decline from 74 to 41. The overall well-being of our society decreased significantly.

Even before the advent of the 1990s, studies were revealing sobering statistics regarding the welfare of our nation's children and youth:

- Over 9,000 teenagers were killed in car accidents annually.

- Suicide had become the second leading cause of death in 15- to 24-year-olds.

- More than 3 million crimes were committed on school grounds each year.

- More than 184,000 students and teachers were injured at school each year.

- Every 36 minutes a child was killed or injured by a gun.

- Approximately 100,000 students reported bringing a gun to school every day. (Harper, 1989)

More recently, Elkind (in Scherer, 1996) reported, "We lose 10,000 youngsters a year in substance abuse–related automobile accidents. We lose 5,000 kids a year in suicide. We have two million alcoholic teenagers" (p. 7). Gabarino (1997) estimated that "about one in five of all U.S. children and two in five among children age 6 and under, live below the officially defined poverty line" (p. 15).

Elkind (in Scherer, 1996) further observed that more common than the tradi-tional nuclear family (two parents, two children, and one parent at home with the children) is the "permeable family—two parents working; single-parent families, adoptive families; remarried families; and so on . . . more fluid, more flexible, and more obviously vulnerable to pressures from outside itself" (p. 4). In 1995, *U.S. News and World Report* noted that 1.2 million divorces occurred, of which more than half involved minor children. Fewer than 49 percent of all children in the United States live with both biological parents.

The Carnegie Corporation report, *Years of Promise* (1996), brought to light the academic effects of the multitude of **at–risk factors** characterizing the lives of today's school-age population. The report described the increasing trend of underachievement by children and youth in the United States:

> Make no mistake about it: underachievement is not a crisis of certain groups; it is not limited to the poor; it is not a problem afflicting other people's children. Many middle- and upper-income children are also falling behind intellectually. Indeed, by the fourth grade, the performance of most children in the United States is below what it should be for the nation and is certainly below the achievement levels of children in com-peting countries. (p. 2)

Beginning teachers enter teaching with wonderful enthusiasm and idealism. They would probably prefer not to know what the *Index of Social Health* or the Carnegie Corporation has to say. However, beginning teachers need to know because kids today are in trouble.

SIGNIFICANCE OF THE SCHOOL-COMMUNITY RELATIONSHIP

Although teachers more often speak of "my classroom" and "my kids," the school is a public entity. Citizens in the community share ownership in schools, even if we do not necessarily see droves of volunteers beating down the school doors. The selection of school board members, the fixing of tax rates, the passage of bond issues, determination of salary schedules, reactions to curricular offerings, letters to the editor—all are indications that the community pays attention to what goes on in schools.

The community definitely has a stake in the school. It is from the schools that the community will get its new workers, its new businesses, its new professionals, and so on. The 30th Annual Phi Delta Kappa/Gallup Poll (Rose & Gallup, 1998) of the public's attitudes toward public schools indicates that 18 percent of the respondents would give public schools in the nation an A or B grade while 49 per-cent of the respondents would give schools a C. When respondents were asked to grade the *local* schools that serve their communities, 48 percent of the respondents would give their local schools an A or B grade while 31 percent would give local schools a C. The grades assigned to the public schools in respondents' communities are higher than the grades assigned to public schools nationally. Communities want to have faith in their local schools.

Understanding the school–community relationship is necessary for (1) promoting the objectives, practices, and needs of the school, teachers, and students; and (2) linking learning experiences to the community's needs and resources and developing students' sense of responsibility for community improvement.

LEARNING ABOUT
THE SCHOOL'S COMMUNITY

It is important for teachers to know about the community they serve. **Demographic characteristics** such as educational attainment, age, gender, occupational patterns, race, ethnicity, and community groups, for example, are important. Educational attainment information can be useful in preparing printed materials. Is the audience comprised largely of adults who finished high school, or who finished college, or who have professional degrees?

Age, gender, and occupational patterns can provide a better understanding of the workforce, of the likelihood of volunteer availability, and of job connections that might be made in the curriculum. Who is at home during the day? Is anyone at home during the day? Are there senior citizens who might be willing to volunteer as readers or guest speakers? What kind of work is typically done in the community? What role models are available? Are there possible job and career mentors who might play a role in classroom projects?

Racial and ethnic characteristics are important to understanding language factors that can influence effective two-way communication and cultural factors that can enrich classroom experiences. What languages are spoken and read in the home? What events or festivals are important in the community? What long-time residents of the community might be tapped for an oral history project?

A number of **community groups** generally show concern for education and often sponsor programs with education connections. Rotary, Kiwanis, and Lions clubs, for example, often sponsor projects that focus on the welfare of school children. There are national organizations with local branches that promote better citizenship and community development.

How does a beginning teacher get to know the community? There are numerous **community information sources.** City directories and telephone books contain the names of organized groups. United States census statistics give detailed information on the population of a community. Information is readily available from the Chamber of Commerce. City, county, and state historical societies and planning commissions have documentary materials that provide insight into the growth of the community. A review of newspaper files, including letters to the editor, will help the teacher to chronicle the events, traditional observances, community efforts, tensions and conflicts, and perspectives on schools in the community. Minutes of school board meetings are rich sources of information on leaders, programs, tensions, conflicts, and relations between the schools and the community.

Schools and school districts keep their own records and reports. The Academic Excellence Indicator System (AEIS) in Texas provides useful information about student characteristics, student achievement, attendance and dropout trends, teacher characteristics, school and district resources, and special needs. Schools and districts often develop their own public relations information in the form of brochures, videos, handbooks, newsletters, program reports, and so on. Today, many schools and school districts maintain their own websites.

Finally, and perhaps most importantly, teachers need to get out there. Increasingly, teachers live outside the communities in which they teach. The image of the one-room schoolhouse, central to the activities and life of the community, has for the most part disappeared. What does that mean for teachers? An important question that teachers must ask is, am I making decisions about what kids would like to learn based upon their experiences or mine? Am I connecting academic content to their experiences or mine?

How do beginning teachers get out into the community of the students they serve? They can drive or walk through the community and talk with people they meet. They can stop in local businesses and attend community group meetings. Attending community events or festivals, volunteering in the community, and making home visits to students are other ways of getting out into the community.

There are many ways through which beginning teachers can learn more about the community in which they teach. Much written material comes in the form of public records, which are readily accessible. There is no substitute, however, for firsthand experience. Knowing more about the community helps beginning teachers to identify experiences and potential resources that might be linked to students' learning activities in the classroom.

COMMUNICATING WITH THE COMMUNITY

Jane Lindle (1989) found that while educators thought parents and community members expected them to be "professional and businesslike," parents and community members wanted the opposite. They did not want educators who were "patronizing" or who "talked down" to people. They wanted educators who were real, who understood how to present information with a "personal touch."

Schools and districts sometimes have a monthly or quarterly newsletter or bulletin that is mailed to parents of school children and to citizens in the community. A newsletter or bulletin can keep parents and community members informed about instructional practices, professional activities, lunch menus, fiscal issues, and special problems facing the school system. Individual teachers sometimes run weekly or monthly bulletins about their own classrooms that often highlight special projects, student accomplishments, volunteer opportunities, guest speakers, classroom requirements and materials, curricular objectives, and so on. These bulletins are good sources of information for beginning teachers. They provide insights into what other teachers, the school, and the district value, and what other beginning teachers are contributing about their own classrooms.

Increasingly schools and districts have annual handbooks to provide ready reference on the school system, the board of education, entrance requirements, attendance regulations, school hours, procedures for telephoning the school, appointment procedures, emergency school closing information, student services, transportation, curriculum offerings, discipline policies, and so on. These handbooks are important resources for beginning teachers, as they provide written expectations that the school and district have communicated to parents and community members. That means that parents and citizens who contact the school or individual teachers will expect to be dealt with in ways prescribed in these handbooks. Granted, beginning teaching is a busy and sometimes overwhelming activity. If a teacher receives such a handbook from the school and/or district, however, it is wise to read it and not just file it in the drawer for later reference.

Many people are using technology to learn about schools. A teacher or classroom home page on the Internet can make information available not only to parents but also to community members. Home pages can include calendars, listings of class activities, special projects, tips for parents and grandparents on how to help with homework or test preparation, calls for classroom participation, and so on.

Many schools have a call-in homework and announcement hot line where a call-in code transfers directly to a teacher's line. A few districts in larger cities may actually have their own television station. The community can watch for district announcements, see school board meetings, or tune in for special program presentations. Students may get homework help through teacher-run or student-run tutorials on television.

The most common form of communication between teachers and the community is communication with parents. Letters and personal notes from teachers can improve relationships between home and school. Gallagher, Bagin, and Kindred (1997) offer several useful suggestions for effective letters to parents. In general, letters should be concise, factual, and to the point. The tone should be warm, friendly, and conversational. Above all, the letter should be "written as though it were spoken directly to the person who reads it" (p. 160). It should be noted that trite business phrases (e.g., *please be advised, regret to inform you, may I call your attention to*) make a letter feel stiff and formal.

There is a tendency among educators to use jargon (e.g., *difficulty establishing rapport, manifests a maladjustment, heterogeneously grouped, engaged in an integrative curricular experience*) in discussing students with parents. Jargon creates a barrier between parents and teachers. It says, "I'm better than you. I know lingo you don't know." Better relationships are established when information presented about students is conveyed in simple, easily understandable common terms. When teachers send notes, letters, or newsletters home, it is important that they know their audience and write for them.

Communications with parents can also improve relationships between community and school because parents talk with each other, with neighbors, and with citizens they encounter on a daily basis. Unfortunately, the most common content in letters to parents and in conferences is report of unsatisfactory work or disciplinary problems. Teachers must beware of such one-sided communication. Better relationships are formed when teachers also report on things students do well. So, if negative observations must be reported, opening and closing observations in a letter, personal note, or conference should describe something positive about the child—superior class work, improvements in study habits, acts of courtesy, special talents, outstanding achievements, or significant behavior changes. Parents who hear positive things about their children generally feel pleased and grateful for the information. They perceive that the teacher cares about their children and sees the good in them. Parents are less likely to react in an angry or hostile manner when they receive negative information if they also receive some positive observations about their children.

Because parents talk, close attention should be paid to vocabulary, grammar, punctuation, and spelling. Principals may even require that all communications that leave the school are screened for errors. When parents read what teachers write and when they talk about it with other parents and acquaintances, they are also likely to talk about any errors they perceive. In the hustle and bustle of the day, teachers may quickly write a note or letter that contains errors. Teachers who have computers in their rooms or in an accessible laboratory or office should use them and use both spelling and grammar checks often.

CONNECTING WITH THE COMMUNITY

Abbott (1995) discussed research done in the United Kingdom in the late 1980s. A study looked at what would most inspire learning in young people. Groups of 17-year-olds were surveyed. Abbott notes that the study came up with a "surprising" conclusion: "What the young people said they needed most was more contact with adults other than parents and teachers" (p. 8). Abbot shared a rather telling observation by one student:

> We know what our parents think—we have heard this many times. We are suspicious of teachers; you are paid to say what you do! But what do *real* adults think? After all it is into their club that we are supposed to be moving, yet we have very little idea of what matters to them and where we might fit. (p. 8)

Increasingly over the last 10 years, schools and teachers of all kinds are using **community-curriculum connections** to link classroom learning experiences to resources and concerns of students' communities. What does this mean? Following are a few examples of schools and teachers who have succeeded in connecting with the community to enhance students' learning experiences at all ages. These examples and others are readily available in education journals and on websites.

Examples of Community Connection

Sulphur Springs School District, Canyon Country, California KBET, a local radio station in Santa Clarita Valley, has a partnership with fourth- through sixth-grade students in Sulphur Springs schools (Winger, 1995). Students give critical evaluations of children's literature selections in on-the-air book reviews. Students are engaged not only in reading the books but also in learning to critique them and to write the scripts for their on-air reviews; in addition, they learn basic broadcasting skills and basic advertising skills. Students who study electricity provide safety and energy conservation tips after the local utility company's advertising spots.

Thomas Jefferson High School, Alexandria, Virginia McFaden and Nelson (1995) told about ninth-grade students' experiences in working as partners with the managers of Mason Neck National Wildlife Refuge about 40 minutes from the high school. Central to the partnership were authentic projects that embedded academic content and skills in English, biology, and principles of technology in actual research projects that reflected the real work of the refuge managers. For example:

> In one project . . . a team of students interviewed a 94-year-old environmental activist, documenting his efforts to establish the area as a national refuge for the bald eagle. They learned from searching the county archives that the refuge was previously used as a dairy farm by Capt. J. A. Hull, a congressman from Nebraska who, in the early 1900s, failed in his attempt to make a profit selling milk to a District of Columbia hospital. The foundations of the old dairy buildings and much of the early equipment can still be found on the refuge. Students surveyed and mapped the location of the old farmhouse, barns, and other outbuildings. (p. 12)

Bluebonnet Applied Learning Academy, Fort Worth, Texas Miller, Shambaugh, Robinson, and Wimberly (1995) described Bluebonnet's efforts to develop curriculum that maintained the importance of academic content but also developed content in applied learning experiences. Health students studied muscular development and physical fitness to design workout equipment kits and video instruction for children at homeless shelters. History students used research to develop scripts and video vignettes of historical events for the Texas Highway Department. Language arts students developed a team of student playwrights to consult with Casa Manana's professional writers, musical director, costume designer, set design and construction staff, makeup artists, business operations staff, stage manager, and director to write and stage their own play.

McCleary Elementary School, Pittsburgh, Pennsylvania What do you do with an ugly lunchroom? McBride (1995) described the transformation of Room G to *Le Stivale Royale* (the Royal Boot) by a fifth-grade class. Students worked with local businessmen in five committees: public relations and advertising, management, art and design, planning and budgeting, and research. The result was (1) a school lunchroom with an Italian theme and connections to a local Italian restaurant, which provided consultation and financial support for decorations; (2) two local discount stores that helped the students understand shopping for supplies; (3) Miss Angie, a community resident, who helped the students translate the school menus into Italian each week; and (4) a local classical music enthusi-ast's consultation on background music.

Skyline Elementary School, Ferndale, Washington   K–1 students in a multi-age class frequently apply academic skills to real-life problems. Morehouse (1995) described her students' in-depth study of airplanes that resulted in students designing and constructing their own student-sized, four-seat, high-wing air-plane. A local building contractor was "hired" by the students who "negotiated to pay the contractor by the hour with 50–100 red wriggler worms from the class compost bin. . . . [T]he students kept close track of the minutes he visited class—they didn't pay him for coffee breaks" (p. 58). From their experience, students learned about tools, materials, management, and safety; collecting, sorting, and classifying; estimating and plan drawing; hammering, sanding, priming, and paint-ing; cooperative decision making; safety inspection; supervision of materials; qual-ity control; inventing, asking questions, and finding answers; and negotiating with the contractor and Boeing Company for "spare parts" for the airplane's interior.

Making the Connection

There are many ways for teachers to tap parents and community members as resources for the classroom. Parents and community members can speak on top-ics about which they have firsthand information. They can loan books, objects, records, videos, historical memorabilia, pictures, clothing, and so on. A Revolutionary War historical heritage group, for example, goes to elementary schools in poor neighborhoods each year. Members of the group dress in period clothing and run discovery stations where children see candle making, musket loading, cloth dying, and so forth. The involvement of the heritage group pro-vides a wonderful extension of social studies for children who may not be able to travel to living history museums around the country to see such demonstrations.

Parents and community members can also help on field trips by serving as chaperones and taking part in follow-up activities in the classroom. Parents and community members can serve as room liaisons. Room liaisons can develop a friendly relationship among parents and neighbors of children in the room. They can encourage parents and other community members to attend classroom func-tions. A room "mom" or "dad" or "grandparent" can help in lower-grade class-rooms, organizing special parties or events.

Parent-teacher associations, neighborhood associations, former student associ-ations, and community groups are also useful resources for the classroom. Parent-teacher associations are often good sources for volunteers. Neighborhood associations are often interested in community improvement. They are good resources for identifying opportunities for special whole-class projects that might focus on making a difference in and a contribution to one's community. Former student associations often sponsor social affairs, are willing to get involved in class-room mentoring, and can provide real-life testimonials as to the importance of school for job and career choices. Schools can also form partnerships with other schools. High school students in a particular subject or extracurricular club, for example, may tutor children or serve as a "big brother" or "big sister" in an elementary or intermediate school.

Community groups are often good sources for contacts within the community. Many citizens groups also have speakers' bureaus that can be tapped for guest speakers regarding the community's history and needs, job and career connections, and special programs for school children and youth. Gallagher, Bagin, and Kindred (1997) provide a useful summary of common community groups:

Civic groups such as the Lions, Kiwanis, Rotary, Jaycees, American Association of University Women

Cultural groups found in the fields of art, music, architecture, horticulture, literature, drama, intercultural education, and racial/ethnic cultural heritage

Economic groups such as labor unions, farm organizations, chambers of commerce, economy leagues, manufacturers' associations, automobile clubs, real estate boards, retail merchants' associations

Fraternal groups such as the Masonic Order, Knights of Columbus, Brith Sholom, Knights of Pythias, Elk, Moose

Government agencies providing services in health, recreation, law enforcement, safety, family life, child care, housing

Patriotic groups like the American Legion, Sons and Daughters of the American Revolution, Veterans of Foreign Wars

Political groups including major political parties, League of Women Voters

Professional groups in law, medicine, dentistry, pharmacy, architecture, engineering

Retired citizens groups such as the American Association of Retired People

Welfare agencies in the fields of health, recreation, child care, and family life

Youth organizations like the 4-H clubs, Future Farmers of America, Boy Scouts and Girl Scouts of America, Junior Red Cross, Police Athletic League

With few exceptions, community groups are anxious to work with schools and to provide support for school activities. A caveat must be offered. Some fraternal groups and youth groups have definite religious affiliations. Similarly, some political groups have very particular agendas. Caution must be exercised in approaching these groups. The school and educators can be limited by constitutional or case law in their relations with these groups. Beginning teachers should always discuss with their principals any ideas they have about using parent, neighborhood, former student, and community groups in the classroom.

Large, national businesses often get involved at the local school level. Businesses frequently provide incentives for reading books or for community service efforts. They can offer discounts or gift certificates, or sometimes products, as school or classroom incentives. There have been some controversies involved, however. In some cases, businesses have asked for advertising time on school district television channels or have proposed offering certain advantages to the school if the school or district will sign an exclusive services contract with the business. A teacher who has an idea for approaching a large or local business to provide classroom incentives should be sure to check with the principal first to determine if the school or district has any special requirements or procedures for contacting businesses.

Finally, teachers should be sure to thank their supporters. Letters or posters from teachers and their students are greatly appreciated. Often community groups or agencies and businesses have places for posting such thank-you correspondence for public view. Their support of schools in their communities is also good public relations for them.

DEVELOPING STUDENTS' RESPONSIBILITY TOWARD THEIR COMMUNITIES

During the 1990s, interest emerged in developing students' sense of responsibility toward their communities. The concept of **service learning** is at the forefront of this interest. Service learning combines the active participation of students in service projects aimed at responding to the needs of the school's community with the development of academic and social skills. Central to service learning projects are the goals of promoting students' self-esteem, developing higher-order thinking skills and problem solving, making use of students' multiple talents and abilities, and providing authentic learning experiences. Following are a few examples of service learning projects. Other examples are available in education journals and on websites.

Examples of Service Learning Projects

Flambeau School District, Tony, Wisconsin In a poor county of five small rural communities and high unemployment, commitment to community education runs high. Thompson (1995) explains:

> In one district program called REAL Enterprises (Rural Entrepreneurship Through Action Learning), students research, plan, set up, and operate their own businesses, filling gaps in the local economy. For example, one girl started her own home-based health care service as soon as she turned 18, while still a senior in high school. She acquired home health care certification. Other examples of REAL Enterprise projects include developing a business plan for a family farm, learning diesel mechanics, and obtaining milk and cheese testing certification. (p. 18)

Thompson further describes the features of the district's efforts. Students work with adult mentors or advisers. They gain real-world experience and make genuine contributions to the community. Finally, the projects are individualized to meet the particular interests or priorities of the students.

Pattonville School District, St. Louis County, Missouri "Reaching out to older people has become a hallmark of the Pattonville Public Schools" (Halford, 1998, p. 50). The focus of the district's efforts is for older community members to get to know children and youth. There is even a dedicated room for senior citizens in the district's community learning center. The district's 55–Plus Club gives members free admission to the schools' sporting and musical events, a discount in the community education program, and use of the district media center. High school students plan and host an annual senior citizen prom.

The Pasqua Yaqui Educational Group Effort (PYEdge) In the Sonoran desert of Arizona, "a patterned mosaic of plants and walkways" emerged (Sandler, Vandegrift, & VerBrugghen, 1995, p. 14). The traditional Native American Yaqui garden was designed, developed, constructed, and maintained by high school students living on the Yaqui Reservation outside of Tucson. Central to the PYEdge curriculum is its student service learning model. Through course work students identify and analyze community problems and needs. They then plan a project that embeds academic content and vocational skills in connections with their own culture and contributions to their community.

EMERGING EFFORTS TO RECONNECT
COMMUNITIES AND CHILDREN

The bottom line is that students return to their communities each day after school. An important part of a teacher's daily lesson planning is thinking about activities that will help students find connections in their communities to the ideas, concepts, and skills that are being taught to them in the classroom. Despite all the challenges facing communities, there is a hopeful side. Efforts continue to increase on the part of communities to reconnect with schools, educators, children, and youth. The following examples illustrate such efforts.

Examples of Community Reconnection Efforts

The Alliance Schools Hatch (1998) described the Alliance Schools as demonstrating the power of community involvement for improving student learning. The Alliance Schools began in 1986 with a collaboration between a community group in Fort Worth, Texas, and the Morningside Middle School. The Alliance Schools network grew to 32 schools in 1992 to 1993; currently, over 100 schools, many in disadvantaged communities in Texas, are network members. The goal of the Alliance Schools is to develop a constituency of parents, community leaders, and educators who will work together to improve student achievement in low-income communities.

Hatch (1998) described a range of community efforts to "reduce danger and stress, improve students' health, provide more and better facilities and resources for learning, and protect improvements" (p. 17). At Morningside Middle School, for example, members of the school and the surrounding community forced the closing of a store near the school. The store often sold alcohol to minors. At Ysleta Elementary School in El Paso, members of the school and the community got public commitment from city officials and monitored their follow-through to install crosswalks and traffic lights around the school. Other Alliance Schools communities have raised funds for building repair, construction of libraries and gyms, establishment of health and social service clinics, and numerous after-school programs and activities to give children a safe place to go at the end of the day.

Communities in Schools, Inc. Lewis and Morris (1998) reported that the Communities in Schools program has been in existence since 1977. It has brought parents, volunteers, and community resources and services into schools to create a safe, caring community inside the school, so that students' basic needs can be met and they can concentrate on learning. Currently, more than 300,000 children and youth in more than 1,000 public schools across the country are served annually by Communities in Schools programs. In 21 schools in the Charlotte-Mecklenburg, North Carolina, area, for example:

> More than 900 volunteers from 170 area corporations spend time each week with Charlotte-Mecklenburg students as tutors, mentors, lunch buddies, and pen pals. . . . Civic organizations such as the Junior League, the Kiwanis Clubs, and the Rotary Clubs provide career mentors, tutors, and financial support. . . . Health service providers, such as dentists and dental hygienists, volunteer each week to clean teeth and give basic exams to students. . . . Hands On Charlotte and the Junior League work with Communities in Schools to help students develop community-service projects in their neighborhoods. (p. 35)

Lewis and Morris also described efforts in El Paso, Texas, where more than 15,000 students in 53 schools throughout the city are served:

> The Cesar Chavez Academy provides a safe place to learn for 130 students who are former gang members. The students have been expelled from their home schools, have been court-ordered to attend, or are living in a halfway home after having attended a state school. . . . Youth Opportunities Unlimited motivates younger students by providing summer work experiences at a local university. . . . A family literacy program, Even Start, presents English as a Second Language for adults who speak only Spanish. (pp. 35-36)

The Relevance Counts Institute Bottge and Osterman (1998) observed that the Relevance Counts Institute was the result of a partnership among three central Minnesota school districts, the Chamber of Commerce, business representatives, and public service organizations. The institute prepares teachers to understand the skills employees need for success in various workplaces. Teachers, for example, "learn specific examples of how job skills are used, such as determining pressure, volume, and coverage of fire sprinklers and extinguishers at the fire department or clear, concise technical writing at a metal fabrication company that designs and manufactures computer-controlled machines" (p. 76). A more in-depth experience is available to teachers through Teachers in Business, which pairs a teacher with a business partner for 80 hours during the summer. Teachers receive college credit for completing the experience and a $500 stipend that can be applied to tuition or taken as cash. Businesses supply the $600 that covers these incentives for teachers.

Bottge and Osterman also described applications of teachers' experiences in the classroom. A fifth-grade teacher, for example, worked at a bank. In her classroom the next year, she emphasized accuracy in math class: "She explained how tellers are accountable for their computations and that seemingly insignificant errors are critical to the bank and its customers. For the entire school year, she required students to keep a math ledger with simulated banking transactions" (p. 77). The teacher's firsthand experiences with transfer of academic content to on-the-job skills provided her with a very different perspective on the application of academic content to real-world situations. The Teachers in Business program enables teachers to understand workplaces other than the classroom. Teachers' "work" experiences then enable the teachers to make more meaningful connections between school work and "real" work for students.

SUMMARY

Beginning teachers will have their hands full inside the classroom. They are expected to understand their students' developmental levels, diversity of needs and experiences, learning strategies and problems, and motivation. Beginning teachers are also expected to plan outcome-oriented instruction, use a variety of instructional strategies that develop thinking and problem solving, use a variety of instructional materials and resources, use a range of informal and formal assessments, and manage a learning environment effectively.

Beginning teachers, however, are also expected to understand and develop strong professional skills such as effective communication with parents or guardians; reflective practice and professional growth; cooperation and collaboration with other teachers, administrators, and school staff; and adherence to specific expectations and requirements of teaching in Texas. It is in this realm of professional skills that understanding the significance of the school-community relationship falls.

With all of the skills and perspectives that the beginning teacher will have to develop in the first years of teaching, why is an understanding of the school-community relationship important? Student learning and self-image are influenced by many factors *outside* the classroom. To not understand the school's community is to not understand the students.

SUGGESTED ACTIVITIES

Process

1. Gather printed materials that provide information on a community in which you have completed a field placement or internship. What do you learn about the challenges facing the community? What do you learn about the demographic characteristics of the community? What do you learn about potential community resources? What are resources for students' leisure time and entertainment after school and on weekends? What agencies, interest groups, and businesses exist in the community?

2. Gather printed materials that have been developed by the school and/or school district about the school. What do you learn about the school's mission? What do you learn about the school's efforts to reach out and connect with parents and community members? What services does the school make available to the community? How is the community represented in projects, programs, and decision-making structures in the school? Does the school have key community liaisons?

3. Gather communications from the school to parents and the community. What do you learn about the content and tone of these communications? Do the communications reflect a personal touch? What do the communications say about what is important to the school? Are there any aspects of the communications that would intimidate or alienate those reading the communications?

Application

1. Add a section to your lesson plans called "Community Connections." Make it a part of your overall curriculum planning.

2. Generate a list of possible community resources for the school in which you did a field placement or an internship. What resources might be used in your classroom? For what purpose? Are there ways in which you might connect academic content to those resources?

3. Review the community challenges that you identified in Process item 1. Is there a way to involve students in a problem-based unit that would connect academic content to the exploration and/or resolution of a real problem in the community?

4. Are there individuals in the community who have a long and/or unique history in the community? Develop an oral history project that would involve students in conversations with these individuals and in the development of a history of their community.

Reflection

1. Think about your own experiences in school. How were your school and your school experiences influenced by characteristics of your community? How similar or different was your community from the community in which you have taught?

2. Think about your communications with parents and community members. Evaluate the extent to which your communications reflected or did not reflect a personal touch.

3. Think about your involvement in the community in which you have taught. Were you out there?

Were you engaged in the day-to-day events or celebrations of the community?

PRACTICE DECISION SET

1. During the past five years at Easton Middle School, the number of students who are recent immigrants has increased. Ms. Jenkins wants to make her classroom curriculum more connected to her students and their experiences. Which of the following would be the best instructional strategy for Ms. Jenkins to try?

   a. Call on students individually in the classroom to present their cultural and ethnic experiences in relation to issues being studied in the class

   b. Develop a mini-unit designed to highlight the largest cultural group represented in the classroom

   c. Regularly implement classroom activities that involve small, mixed groups of students

   d. Ask students to describe their cultural backgrounds and have teams of students develop research units to study the cultures represented in the classroom

2. Ms. Jenkins has also given some thought to how she might communicate with her students' families and communities. She decides to write a biweekly newsletter to send home with her students. What information sources would be useful to Ms. Jenkins as she develops her newsletter?

   I. Demographic characteristics of her students and their families

   II. Local community newspapers

   III. A history of the city

IV. The community watch group
   a. I and II only
   b. II and III only
   c. I, III, and IV only
   d. II and IV only

3. During a class discussion, students raise the issue of sharing what they learn with their parents and neighborhoods. As the discussion continues, the class decides that they want to use an empty billboard about a block away from the school to tell their story. What is Ms. Jenkins's first step in addressing the students' idea?

   a. Assign the students to work committees

   b. Send a permission letter home to parents

   c. Talk to the principal about the idea

   d. Call the district's public relations office

Answer 1: An important focus in Competency 14 is getting students to understand their community, its characteristics, its culture and heritage, and its challenges. Although students' viewpoints and experiences are important in the classroom, calling on them individually to state their views on issues under study does little to foster a sense of cooperation and collaboration, both of which are important skills in diverse communities. A teacher-developed mini-unit focusing on one culture may be interpreted as partiality or bias by students. Regularly getting students to work together in groups on class tasks would be helpful over time in building student relationships, but there is no connection made to students' learning about their community. Response *d* is the correct response, providing opportunities for students to work cooperatively, to learn about all the cultures represented in their classroom, and to study those cultures in the context of their own community.

Answer 2: Response *a* is correct. It focuses on the students and their families. Community newspapers provide a source of information about the language differences in the community and the writing format that is easily understood within the community. While a city history is useful, because many of the families are newly immigrated, their backgrounds may or may not be represented. A community watch group could provide information

about the safety concerns within the neighborhood. The group may be useful at a later date if Ms. Jenkins and her students would like to explore community problems.

Answer 3: Response *c* is correct. The teacher's first step is talking to her principal about the idea. Although students' working in committees might help to develop the project and parent permission may be needed for some of the activities the committees select, Ms. Jenkins must first know whether the project is feasible within school and district guidelines. The principal is the best source of that information. The district's public relations office might prove to be a useful partner in the project if the project idea is approved.

WEB LINKS

Remember that website locations may change. If any of these sites have moved or cannot be located, use the Terms to Know in this chapter to search for further information.

www.unl.edu/websat/alpha.html
Alphabetized Internet Education Resources provides an alphabetical listing and linking of all resources listed by the Internet Education Clearinghouse. This site contains just about every educational topic imaginable from elementary to college level.

www.classroom.net/home.asp
Classroom Connect provides search tools linking to thousands of schools online, online resource materials for teachers, and online teacher contact groups.

www.ed.gov/EdRes/EdCurric.html
Curriculum Resources gives access to curriculum resources from the federal government.

www.brown.edu/Research/The_Education_Alliance
Education Alliance provides resources and research on the community-based projects and curricula developed by Education Alliance school sites.

www.education-world.com
Education World provides lesson plans, books in education, news in education, resources for administrators, and selected best sites. It includes a search engine for over 50,000 sites in the database.

www.nicsl.coled.umn.edu
National Service-Learning Clearinghouse gives a comprehensive listing of schools, projects, and programs focusing on service learning efforts across the nation.

http://teachers.work.co.nz
Teachers@work provides over 3,000 reviewed websites sorted into curriculum areas and a directory of the 1,000 best

Internet sites for educators. It includes a consultancy information resource as well.

www.txserve.org
The Texas Center for Service-Learning is a noteworthy site for what is going

on in service learning projects and programs across the state of Texas.

REFERENCES AND SUGGESTED READINGS

Abbott, J. (1995). Children need communities—communities need children. *Educational Leadership, 52*(8), 6–10.

Bottge, B. A., & Osterman, L. (1998). Bringing the workplace to the classroom. *Educational Leadership, 55*(8), 76–77.

The Carnegie Corporation of New York. (1996). *Years of promise: A comprehensive learning strategy for America's children. Executive summary.* New York: Carnegie Task Force on Learning.

Carroll, S. R., & Carroll, D. (1994). *How smart schools get and keep community support.* Bloomington, IN: National Educational Service.

Cummings, L., & Winston, M. (1998). Service-based solutions. *Science Teacher, 65*(1), 39–41.

Delisle, R. (1997). *How to use problem-based learning in the classroom.* Alexandria, VA: Association for Supervision and Curriculum Development.

Gabarino, J. (1997). Educating children in a socially toxic environment. *Educational Leadership, 54*(7), 12–16.

Gallagher, D. R., Bagin, D., & Kindred, L. W. (1997). *The school and community relations* (6th ed.). Boston: Allyn & Bacon.

Halford, J. M. (1998). For significant support, turn to seniors. *Educational Leadership, 55*(8), 49–51.

Harper, S. (1989). *School crisis prevention and response.* Malibu, CA: National School Safety Center. (ERIC Document Reproduction Services No. ED 311 600)

Hatch, T. (1998). How community action contributes to achievement. *Educational Leadership, 55*(8), 16–19.

"Honor thy children." (1995, February 27). *U.S. News and World Report,* 39–55.

Hope, W. C. (1997). Meeting the needs of middle level students through service learning. *NASSP Bulletin, 81*(587), 39–45.

Kinsley, C. W., & McPherson, K. (Eds.). (1995). *Enriching the curriculum through service learning.* Alexandria, VA: Association for Supervision and Curriculum Development.

Lewis, R., & Morris, J. (1998). Communities for children. *Educational Leadership, 55*(8), 34–36.

Lindle, J. (1989). What do parents want from principals and teachers? *Educational Leadership, 47*(2), 12–14.

McBride, M. E. (1995). The Italian restaurant project: Lessons of restructuring. *Educational Leadership, 52*(8), 64–66.

McFaden, D., & Nelson, B. (1995). A refuge for real-world learning. *Educational Leadership, 52*(8), 11–13.

Miller, P., Shambaugh, K., Robinson, C., & Wimberly, J. (1995). Applied learning for middle schoolers. *Educational Leadership, 52*(8), 22–25.

Miringoff, M. (1994). *Monitoring the social well-being of the nation: The index of social health.* Tarrytown, NY: Fordham Institute for Social Policy.

Morehouse, P. (1995). The building of an airplane (with a little help from friends). *Educational Leadership, 52*(8), 56–57.

Rose, L. C., & Gallup, A. M. (1998). The 30th annual Phi Delta Kappa/Gallup poll of the public's attitudes toward the public schools. *Phi Delta Kappan, 80*(1), 41–56.

Sandler, L., Vandegrift, J. A., & VerBrugghen, C. (1995). From desert to garden:

Reconnecting disconnected youth. *Educational Leadership, 52*(8), 14–16.

Scherer, M. (1996). Our changing family values: A conversation with David Elkind. *Educational Leadership, 53*(7), 4–9.

Thompson, S. (1995). The community as classroom. *Educational Leadership, 52*(8), 17–20.

Winger, M. (1995). Students and radio: Getting the good word out. *Educational Leadership, 52*(8), 36.

ABOUT THE AUTHOR

Judith Ponticell was a high school teacher and administrator in inner-city Chicago for 20 years. She received state of Illinois Outstanding Teacher and Outstanding Administrator awards and was a recipient of the Phi Delta Kappa Educator of the Year Award. She received her Ph.D. in Curriculum, Instruction, and Evaluation Leadership from the University of Illinois at Chicago in 1991 and is currently Associate Professor and Chair of the Division of Educational Leadership and Organizational Learning at the University of New Mexico. Her research focuses on personal, interpersonal, and organizational factors that influence individual and organizational learning and change. She is widely published in both education and business contexts and is a recipient of the Distinguished Research Award from the Association of Teacher Educators. She teaches courses in both teacher education and educational leadership, including courses in school and community relations, organizational communication theory, and public relations.

15

✳

Teaching in Texas

GARY R. CLAY
HOUSTON BAPTIST UNIVERSITY

This chapter will address Competency 15 of the Examination for Certification of Educators in Texas (ExCET). Competency 15 is a component of Domain III, Understanding the Teaching Environment, in the framework for professional development.

Competency 15: The teacher understands requirements, expectations, and constraints associated with teaching in Texas, and can apply this understanding in a variety of contexts.

The teacher is familiar with the various expectations (e.g., those of school boards, principals, colleagues, parents, students) and constraints (e.g., legal requirements, ethical responsibilities) placed on members of the teaching profession and is aware of the multiplicity of roles that teachers may be called upon to assume (e.g., instructor, resource person, problem solver, curriculum developer, school spokesperson). The teacher understands laws and guidelines relevant to education (e.g., those related to civil rights, special needs, confidentiality, child abuse) and ensures that his or her decisions and actions are in compliance with legal and ethical requirements and the legitimate interests of others. The teacher understands the structure of the Texas education system, recognizes types of authority and decision-making structures within the system (e.g., centralized systems, site-based management), and knows how to work within the system to address issues and make decisions appropriately.

TERMS TO KNOW

Code of ethics

Site-based decision making

Compensatory education programs

State Board of Education (SBOE)

State Board for Educator Certification (SBEC)

Commissioner of Education

Texas Education Agency (TEA)

Local school board

Texas Essential Knowledge and Skills (TEKS)

Texas Assessment of Academic Skills (TAAS)

Public Law 94-142

Section 504

Buckley Amendment (confidentiality)

Inclusion/mainstreaming

Admission, Review, and Dismissal (ARD) Committee

Individualized Education Program (IEP)

Least restrictive environment (LRE)

Professional Development Appraisal System (PDAS)

Bilingual education

English as a second language (ESL)

Gifted and talented (GT) education

Sexual harassment

Title IX

Child abuse reporting requirements

A person who accepts a position as a teacher in Texas schools must have awareness and understanding of the particular responsibilities and constraints of the position set out by state laws and regulations. The teacher is employed by the community, through its local board of education, for the primary task of delivering the approved curriculum and ensuring that students learn and achieve to their highest potential—quite a challenging task! Almost everyone knows, especially experienced teachers, that much more is expected of teachers in our schools today. In addition to the many individual responsibilities, the teacher must understand that he or she functions as part of an organization (typically a school and/or school district) that, like the individual teacher, is subject to governing authorities. These authorities provide directives, regulations, and policies for all levels of the educational environment. The regulations may include applicable federal and state laws, rulings from court decisions, and policy directives from governmental agencies including the U.S. Department of Education and other federal agencies, the Texas Education Agency, the State Board of Education, the Texas Commissioner of Education's office, the State Board for Educator Certification, and the local school board. The teacher is also subject to directives from authorities higher in the hierarchical structure in the district or school, including the school principal who is normally the direct supervisor of the classroom teacher and to whom the teacher is immediately accountable. With added regulations, accountability issues, and new responsibilities and roles, today's teacher in Texas must understand the context in which he or she serves in order to be a successful and effective teacher.

The statement that follows the competency at the beginning of this chapter describes in greater detail the types of knowledge and skills covered by Competency 15 and provides a comprehensive overview of the expectations and constraints placed upon Texas teachers in a variety of areas. This chapter is organized to follow the sequence of the main points listed in that narrative.

EXPECTATIONS OF TEACHERS IN TEXAS

Among the groups having expectations for teachers is the **local school board.** The responsibility for the oversight of the operations of the schools in a community in Texas belongs to an elected local school board whose members are called trustees. The local board of education may have from three to nine members, depending on the size of the school district, with most local boards of education in Texas having seven members who serve on the local board of education. The district may have members serving "at large," meaning they represent the entire district, regardless of where they live in the district; or the district may have a system of single-member districts that requires each member of the board to reside in and be elected by the voters in a specific geographical area of the district. A district may also have a combination of the two, wherein some members are elected to represent single districts and other members are elected at large, that is, from voters throughout the district. Each member of the board is elected to serve for a term of three or four years. To be eligible for election, the person must be a U.S. citizen, be registered to vote, and have resided in the district for at least six months. Elections are held in May or November each year.

The local school board has a variety of responsibilities, including adoption of policies that directly impact the teacher. The board establishes goals for the district, approves the annual budget, employs and evaluates the superintendent, and employs the professional personnel for the district, though that authority may be delegated to the superintendent. The board can only take action as a body when meeting in compliance with the Texas Open Meetings Law. No individual member has any authority to speak for or act on behalf of the board.

The Texas Open Meetings Law requires that all meetings be conducted as open meetings unless topics allowed by law for closed sessions or meetings are on the agenda. Examples of topics that may be discussed in closed session are personnel matters and legal issues. All votes by the board must occur in open session. The agenda for each meeting must be posted in a public place, normally the school administration building, for at least 72 hours prior to the meeting. Teachers frequently attend meetings of the board, particularly if there are items of particular interest to be discussed. Board meetings often include items to recognize or honor achievement by teachers, students, or schools. Teachers in Texas should strongly consider attending one or more meetings of their local board of education to see how the business of the district is conducted and to see the community members who have volunteered to serve in the most important position of trustee.

The Texas teacher is expected to follow the policies adopted by the local board of education. Copies of the policies are normally available on each campus and at the central administrative office. They may also be available on the website for the district. Often the district will reproduce the policies that directly impact the teacher and make them available to each teacher at the beginning of the school year.

The policies of the board are communicated to the district staff, students, and community by the district *superintendent*, who serves as the chief executive officer for the district. The superintendent is also responsible for implementing the policies and reporting regularly to the board about progress toward the goals of the district. The superintendent has a number of additional duties associated with the position of educational leader for the district. Dependent upon the size of the district, there are normally one or more administrators who have districtwide responsibilities over areas that impact the classroom teacher. Examples would include those with responsibilities for curriculum and instruction, finance, personnel, and general administration. Examples of job titles for these positions may include assistant superintendent, director, or coordinator. An organizational chart for the district, which identifies the areas of responsibility and the appropriate lines of authority, would be a useful source of information for classroom teachers as they become familiar with the organization of the district. This document, if developed for the district, will likely be available from the campus principal.

The primary person to whom the teacher is responsible is the campus *principal*. The principal is responsible for the daily operation of the school and its staff and students. Principals have been given increased responsibility and authority in recent years. In compliance with state and federal laws, state regulations, and district policies, the principal establishes procedures for the efficient operation of the school and has the primary responsibility for the employment, supervision, and professional development of the staff assigned to the campus. The principal is the instructional leader for the campus, and one responsibility is to ensure that the state-mandated **site-based decision-making** committee and procedures are instituted. Teachers in Texas have the opportunity and the obligation for input on the important decisions that impact the local campus through the site-based decision-making process. The purpose of this process is to allow shared decision making at the campus level for decisions that impact the campus. This committee is made up of a prescribed number of teachers, parents, and community members. Teacher representatives on the committee are elected by their colleagues on the campus, but all teachers have the opportunity and the professional responsibility to provide input or feedback for the committee's consideration. The committee's major tasks include: identification of goals for the school year, development of plans for accomplishing those goals including staff development, input on scheduling and student assignment, and evaluation of the results of any actions that may be taken. This committee most often meets outside the regular school day, as do other campus and district committees to which teachers may be assigned or elected.

Two other groups within the school community have expectations of the teacher. Parents have expectations that the teacher and school will provide a safe, secure environment where the students will be educated to their full potential. Parents expect the teacher to keep them informed of student progress and to enlist their aid when needed. Students have similar expectations and must have confidence that the teacher will be their advocate and treat them with respect while providing a challenging learning environment.

CONSTRAINTS ON TEACHERS IN TEXAS

Teachers should be aware that there are both legal requirements and ethical responsibilities that govern their employment and may serve as constraints on their actions. Teachers should be aware of the legal issues affecting education and their employment. Teachers are not expected to be fully knowledgeable of all education-related law, but they should be conversant with the constraints or requirements that may impact their daily experiences in the school. The *district* or *campus handbook* will most often outline these major issues that have a legal basis or ramifications. Specific areas of legal issues impacting the teacher will be discussed later in this chapter. An excellent resource for the Texas teacher is *The Legal Handbook for Texas Teachers* by Fernando C. Gomez and Kenneth R. Craycraft (1998). Ordering information for this handbook is available from the publisher.

As with other professions, a **code of ethics** has been developed that sets standards and expectations for the Texas teacher. This *Code of Ethics and Standard Practices* provides the framework for ethical conduct on the part of Texas teachers. A beginning Texas teacher should be familiar with the code and adhere to its tenets. The code and supporting information is reprinted in Figure 15.1.

MULTIPLE ROLES OF TEACHERS IN TEXAS

The teacher in Texas is called upon to fulfill many roles in addition to the primary role of instructional responsibility of the classroom. The teacher should have an understanding of those roles in order to be most effective and be prepared to fulfill the expectations associated with the roles. The descriptive statement with Competency 15 includes at least five specific roles for the teacher. Each will be discussed in this chapter, and teachers will likely identify other or related roles as they gain experience. The roles identified by the competency include: instructor, resource person, problem solver, curriculum developer, and school spokesperson.

The most important role of the classroom teacher is that of *instructor*. Teachers are expected to use their knowledge and skills to plan for and deliver an instructional program that results in student learning. The primary tool for the teacher's use is the curriculum approved for the particular content area, grade level, or course. Curriculum is the content or learning experiences provided to students in school. The curriculum to be taught may be provided in a document developed

Code of Ethics and Standard Practices for Texas Educators

In compliance with the Texas Education Code, the State Board for Educator Certification has adopted an educators' code of ethics and is solely responsible for enforcing the ethics code for purposes related to certification disciplinary proceedings. The Professional Responsibility statement and the five principles included in the code are reproduced below. A series of Standard Practices have been developed for each principle and may be found along with the code on the SBEC website, *www.sbec.state.tx.us.* The *Code of Ethics and Standard Practices* may also be found in the *ExCet Preparation Manual for Professional Development* produced by National Evaluation Systems, Inc.

Professional Responsibility. The Texas educator should strive to create an atmosphere that will nurture to fulfillment the potential of each student. The educator shall comply with standard practices and ethical conduct toward students, professional colleagues, school officials, parents, and members of the community. In conscientiously conducting his or her affairs, the educator shall exemplify the highest standards of professional commitment.

Principle I: Professional ethical conduct. The Texas educator shall maintain the dignity of the profession by respecting and obeying the law, demonstrating personal integrity, and exemplifying honesty.

Principle II: Professional practices and perfomance. The Texas educator after qualifying in a manner established by law or regulation, shall assume responsibilities for professional administrative or teaching practices and professional performance and shall demonstrate competence.

Principle III: Ethical conduct toward professional colleagues. The Texas educator, in exemplifying ethical relations with colleagues, shall accord just and equitable treatment to all members of the profession.

Principle IV: Ethical conduct toward students. The Texas educator, in accepting a position of public trust, should measure success by progress of each student toward realization of his or her potential as an effective citizen.

Principle V: Ethical conduct toward parents and community. The Texas educator, in fulfilling citizenship responsibilities in the community, should cooperate with parents and others to improve the public schools of the community.

FIGURE 15.1 This code of ethics sets standards and expectations for teachers in Texas.

by the district or school. The curriculum may be the teacher's manual for the student textbook to be used in the course or grade level provided to the teacher by the school or district. Educational publishing companies often produce a special edition of their textbooks and accompanying teacher's manual for use in Texas schools to ensure that the text includes the mandated Texas curriculum. A teacher may not receive a guide or a textbook and may lack sufficient resources for planning for instruction. Teachers may have to develop their own plans. Regardless, in Texas there exists a state-mandated curriculum, the **Texas Essential Knowledge and Skills (TEKS),** for each grade level and content area. In secondary schools, the TEKS is in place for each course. The TEKS represents a statewide content guide of essential information that all students should achieve. The TEKS can be found at the Texas Education Agency website and should be readily available in each school district. All teachers in Texas must be knowledgeable of the TEKS required for the course or grade level that they teach and be certain that the outcomes included in the TEKS are a part of their instructional plans. Students are tested on the outcomes included in the TEKS, and teachers are accountable for teaching them so that students may be successful in the assessments.

The statewide assessment program, the **Texas Assessment of Academic Skills,** or **TAAS,** is aligned with the TEKS and is used to ensure district and campus accountability based on student performance on the tests. The TAAS is a criterion-referenced evaluation instrument that assesses competencies in reading, writing, mathematics, science, and social studies. Reading and math are assessed in grades 3 through 8, with writing also assessed in grades 4 and 8. Teachers should understand that the grades and subjects tested are subject to change dependent upon legislative action. Social studies and science are currently assessed in grade 8. Students are required to perform satisfactorily on assessment instruments for English language arts and mathematics prior to being eligible to receive a high school diploma. Successful performance on the social studies and science assessments at the high school level will be an added requirement for graduation due to the passage of recent legislation. Student performance on the TAAS is the primary criteria used in rating schools and districts in the state's accountability system and adds additional importance and pressure on teachers to ensure that the students are well prepared to be successful on the TAAS. Additional state funds are granted to schools based on student performance on the TAAS and other accountability rating indicators. Districts and campuses are always working to improve or maintain their accountability rating. Texas teachers should remember that if students have mastered the appropriate TEKS and possess test-taking skills, they should be well prepared to pass the TAAS exam.

The teacher's skill and knowledge that contributes to student achievement is the primary component for the teacher appraisal system currently in place in Texas. The system used by most districts in Texas is the **Professional Development Appraisal System (PDAS),** which involves assessing teachers in a variety of areas, such as successful student participation in the learning process, evaluation of student progress, management of student discipline, and professional development. The local district may choose to develop its own appraisal system if it chooses to do so instead of adopting the state-approved system, though most use the PDAS. If a district chooses to develop its own system, it must contain a component that links teacher assessment to student achievement and be developed with active teacher participation and input. The PDAS and district-developed systems focus on the teacher's reflective practice, goal setting, and professional development. The local district is required to provide an orientation to the system for teachers new to the district.

A second role that teachers are called upon to assume is that of *resource person.* In this role, teachers may be asked to share their time, expertise, and experience in contributing to efforts that are designed to improve the profession. Teachers may be asked to serve on campus, district, or even state committees that develop or advise the development of curriculum resources. The campus often has a variety of committees on which teachers routinely serve or lead. Districts frequently have committees with representatives from each campus who give input or advice on a variety of topics from planning staff development activities to aiding in the selection of a new superintendent. An example of an area in which teachers are expected to participate is the review and evaluation of teaching resources. Teachers, along with others, are asked to review new textbooks that are available for adoption. New textbooks are adopted on a scheduled basis with the book for each subject area expected to be in use from six to eight years. The selection of the best textbook is critically important, as it has long-lasting implications. Teachers are also asked to review other resources, including technology-related items, supplementary teaching materials, and even specific programs the campus or district may be considering for implementation.

Teachers may also be asked to be mentor teachers to new teachers on the campus. In this capacity, teachers share their experience with the new teachers, which greatly assists the induction process for the new teachers. A teacher may also be asked to lead or facilitate a professional development session. If the teacher has recently attended a conference and gained new knowledge or skills, sharing that information with colleagues is logical and benefits all teachers. A teacher will likely be considered as a resource person on a variety of other topics, such as the selection of campus or district goals, identification of budget priorities, the employment of new teachers or administrators, and development of the campus or district annual improvement plan. The individual teacher's contributions will benefit the profession, the local district or campus, and the teacher's own ongoing professional development. Contributing to the improvement of the profession should be considered one of the obligations of being a teacher.

A teacher is also frequently called upon to be a *problem solver*. This role is closely related to that of resource person. The teacher may be asked to be a participant in the solution of a particular problem or to provide input and time on the solution of a long-term or controversial problem. Because schools involve people, there are no shortages of problems that arise.

Because teaching is by definition a helping profession, teachers are well equipped to give valuable input to the solution or resolution of problems. Teachers may be asked to be involved in the solution of problems that are seemingly simple to the most complex. From settling student-to-student issues in the classroom to working on committees to improve campus safety, teachers are relied upon to be problem solvers.

Another of the multiple roles of the teacher is one that directly and significantly contributes to improvement of teaching and learning opportunities. The Research and Education Association (1998) describes this role of teacher as *curriculum developer*. The development of new curriculum resources, the evaluation and revision of existing curriculum, and the successful implementation of new curriculum are ongoing tasks for educators, and the teacher is expected to be an active participant. In Texas, all curriculum development efforts include representative teachers who play a vital and important role in determining what Texas students should know and be able to do. A teacher may be asked to serve on a district or even statewide committee to rewrite or develop curriculum. This task often occurs in the summer, and teachers are paid for their participation, though usually not enough to match the expertise and time provided. The teacher may be asked to present the results of the curriculum development to their colleagues, parent and community groups, or in conference settings for other educators. Teachers should welcome the opportunity to have input on this issue that has such potential for impacting student achievement. Who is better positioned to contribute to curriculum development than the teacher who daily plans, delivers, and evaluates student learning based on the curriculum?

The final example of the roles Texas teachers are asked to assume (identified in the Competency 15 narrative) is that of *school spokesperson*. Each employee of the school or district is the primary source of information about the school or district to someone. The family, friends, and acquaintances of a teacher expect the teacher to "know about" everything that occurs in the school, the district, or even education in general. This expectation is both a challenge and an opportunity. The expectation may be unrealistic because the teacher is often most concerned with the education of the children in his or her classroom and may have little or no knowledge of the educational issues and events outside the school. The challenge is for the busy teacher to be a knowledgeable professional. Teachers should keep themselves aware of contemporary educational issues—whether they be what the proposed district bond will provide or the status of voucher programs in Texas. How is a busy professional who also has family responsibilities supposed to "keep up"? The teacher should read or at least skim metropolitan and local newspapers on a regular basis with an eye alerted to educational issues. News magazines, television news and specials, professional journals, newsletters, conferences, and conversation with colleagues are all good sources of information about contemporary educational issues. Teachers who "keep up" will be able to respond with facts or an informed opinion when asked by friends or family their views on education or when asked, "What's new at school?" The opportunity in being considered as a spokesperson is that teachers are best positioned to advance the cause of education and tell the "good news" about Texas schools, and a well-informed community will have greater confidence in and better support for their schools and teachers. The knowledge of contemporary educational issues also serves to advance the "professionalism" of teaching and allows the teacher to be seen as an informed decision maker, not simply as a monitor of learning activities designed or assigned by others.

Teachers in Texas must recognize that they are not official spokespersons for the campus or school. There are policies and procedures that direct the media to designated personnel in the district for the district's official response. Teachers who are asked their opinion by a media representative must, if a response is given, clearly state that the statement provided represents only their personal views and not the position of the district or school. Teachers should immediately consult with their principals if such a request is received.

The teacher has many additional roles besides those addressed in this section. During every school year, the teacher will likely be called upon to be a nurse, a counselor, a social service referral provider, a pseudoparent, a sponsor of student organizations, a chaperone, a conflict resolution expert, a technology expert, an accountant (grades, money, attendance, etc.), and many more things—and all while being an enthusiastic, well-planned, organized, and skilled teacher. Such a job description is overwhelming, yet it accurately represents the challenges and rewards associated with teaching.

LAWS AND GUIDELINES IMPACTING TEACHERS IN TEXAS

Teaching in Texas requires that practitioners be familiar with the laws and policy directives that influence their employment and always work in compliance with those laws and directives. The district and campus administration should provide staff development that orients teachers to their responsibilities in this area along with printed materials for assistance. The Competency 15 narrative provides examples of specific areas of legal concerns for which teachers should be aware. These include the areas of civil rights, special needs, confidentiality, and child abuse. Each of these areas and related legal areas will be discussed in detail to provide the Texas teacher with the basic knowledge to teach without fear of violating laws or policies. A word of advice and comfort is in order. Teachers should not feel the need to have expert knowledge of educational law in order to be a successful teacher. When a question arises, teachers should immediately consult their administrator for direction or advice. If the administrator needs legal advice to respond to a question, the school district will have access to attorneys.

In the area of *civil rights*, there exists a number of federal and state laws that guarantee students protection from discrimination and violations of their civil rights. Students are also afforded access to an "equal educational opportunity," which simply means that neither the teacher nor any school employee can refuse to permit a student to participate in any school program or activity due to the student's race, religion, gender, national origin, or disability. The teacher must show respect to his or her students at all times, and any negative reaction or evidence of prejudice to a student's gender, race, religion, or disability would never be appropriate. Such behavior may place the teacher in legal jeopardy and be an embarrassment to the school or community. The media is quick to report such allegations. The teacher must also make every effort to ensure that the classroom atmosphere is free of prejudice or bias. The teacher must act quickly and decisively if discriminatory comments are made by students and must never dismiss an action or statement that discriminates against a student or adult in the school as unimportant.

One phase of discrimination that has drawn attention recently, particularly in secondary schools, is violation of **Title IX** of the Education Amendments of 1972, which requires gender equity in all areas of the school's operations. A district or school that receives federal funds is subject to this law and may not segregate courses or activities by gender and generally may not treat males and females differently. Challenges that are most often lodged related to this issue deal with inequity in athletic programs between girls' and boys' teams. If coaching an athletic team is a part of a teacher's assignment, the teacher must be aware of equity and consult with school officials with questions or concerns. The classroom teacher is advised to be cautious in differentiating assignments, activities, or consequences based on gender. Reflective teachers must regularly review their expectations for all students and analyze their instructional practices to ensure equity for all groups within the class.

School districts are required to appoint a Title IX coordinator whose responsibility includes the receipt of allegations regarding potential violations of this law. Teachers should know the name and location of the Title IX coordinator for their district and remember that Title IX impacts all areas of school operations, not just athletic programs.

A related issue is **sexual harassment.** Sexual harassment is a form of sexual discrimination that is in violation of federal and state laws. Schools have a duty, which has been reinforced by court rulings, to protect students and employees from all forms of harassment, including sexual harassment. Districts are required to have policy that prohibits any form of sexual harassment by students or employees and to make that policy readily available to all employees and students. Procedures should be in place to ensure a prompt response to complaints, a complete investigation, and follow-up based on the results of the investigation. Teachers should be aware of the policy and procedures and never ignore a complaint of this nature. Districts, administrators, and teachers may be potentially liable if they do not take action on student or employee complaints of sexual harassment. Districts often schedule training sessions for employees on this topic as a part of staff development. A training session on sexual harassment serves as an excellent opportunity to gain the knowledge necessary to appropriately respond when this issue arises.

Teachers should be cautious to avoid any physical, inappropriate contact with students. Seemingly innocent intended actions may be perceived as inappropriate actions and jeopardize the reputation or career of an excellent teacher. The school or district may have in place specific guidelines for inappropriate touching of students. A related guideline is that teachers should not be alone with students in a closed room.

For general information and direction, the teacher should consult and follow his or her district policy for dealing with sexual harassment, and if a situation arises that may involve this issue, the teacher should immediately contact the administrator designated to deal with this matter.

Another area the competency narrative identifies relative to laws and guidelines for teacher awareness is the area of *special needs*. The laws and guidelines that impact the teaching and learning of students with special needs in Texas will be the focus of this section. Programs that will be briefly addressed include special education, Section 504, compensatory programs, bilingual and ESL programs, gifted and talented education, and alternative programs. Teachers are encouraged to review each of these programs in greater depth, particularly those that impact their classroom. Space allows for only a limited overview of how these programs impact Texas teachers. Teachers are encouraged to discuss with their supervisors and colleagues the areas addressed in this section if questions arise about proper procedures or compliance with legal guidelines or regulations.

SPECIAL EDUCATION

The time is opportune before beginning a discussion of special education to remind the reader that acronyms abound in education, particularly in the area of special education. Teachers will be well advised to ask questions when needing clarification and to make special efforts to help parents understand the "jargon," so that they may be full partners in the education process and not intimidated by lack of understanding.

McCune, Lowe, and Stephens (1995) provide a good overview of special education issues including the fact that federal and state law requires that a school district provide a "free appropriate public education," also known by the acronym FAPE, to all disabled students who are between the ages of 3 and 22 and who live within the district (services for the blind and deaf begin at birth). This federal requirement began with the implementation of **Public Law 94-142,** the Education for All Handicapped Children Act passed in 1975. The law has been revised several times, with the most current legislation being the Individuals with Disabilities Education Act (IDEA) Amendments of 1997.

The FAPE is not only for educational instruction to accommodate the academic needs of the students but also for related services that may be required for a student to be able to maximize the instructional opportunities provided. Related services may include such programs or services as physical therapy, special transportation, psychological services, counseling services, parent counseling and training, and many more. Disabilities of students that teachers may encounter include: learning disabilities, speech or language impairments, serious emotional disturbance, visual or hearing impairments, autism, orthopedic impairments, and other health impairments. The district must offer a full range of programs to meet the special educational needs of their students who have been identified as having disabilities.

Before a student who is suspected of having a disability may be placed in special education, an initial evaluation is made of the student following a referral. The referral may be initiated by a teacher or parent and includes all relevant information to the student's performance and difficulties encountered in school. The student's parent participates in the initial evaluation, and if a comprehensive evaluation is determined to be in order, consent is required of the parent. It is important to remember that the parent must give consent at every step in the process. Trained assessment personnel at the campus or within the district conduct the assessment. When the assessment results are available, the district or campus must hold an **Admission, Review, and Dismissal (ARD) Committee** meeting within 30 days to review the assessment data, determine the eligibility of the student, determine the appropriate placement and services to be provided, and develop an **Individualized Education Program (IEP)** for the student. The

IEP is a comprehensive plan for the special education student that includes the instructional objectives, the identification of services needed to achieve the objectives, any modifications required, and other legally required components.

The ARD committee includes representatives from the campus or district administration, assessment personnel, regular education teachers, special education teachers, the parent(s), the student, if age appropriate, and others who may be invited. Teachers should become knowledgeable of the legal guidelines and procedures related to ARD committees, as it is likely that they will serve on one or more ARD committees during the academic year. The ARD committee meets at least once per year to review the student's progress and update the IEP and also meets whenever a student is being considered for dismissal from special education.

If a student meets the eligibility criteria, options for services range from continued placement in the regular classroom with consultative services from special education personnel for the teacher to a range of more restrictive environments according to the needs of the student. The applicable law states that students eligible for special education services should be educated in the **least restrictive environment (LRE)** possible. The placement of students is determined by the ARD committee, and inclusion or mainstreaming is encouraged whenever deemed appropriate. **Inclusion,** also known as **mainstreaming,** is a philosophy and practice that allows special education students to be included, as much as possible, in the regular educational environment. The regular education teacher must be well informed and supported to make inclusion successful for all concerned.

The provision of special education services involves many procedures guided by law and administrative regulation. Teachers must be especially careful to carry out their responsibilities set out by the IEP and the ARD committee, including the provision of modified objectives, instruction, and assessment when required by the IEP. Teachers must also carefully document their modifications. Each campus normally has a person who is certified or has special training to oversee the special education program. When questions arise, teachers should not hesitate to contact the campus designee or the campus administrator.

A related but separate program to serve students with special needs is required of schools or districts as a result of **Section 504** of the Rehabilitation Act of 1973. This law is a civil rights law that prohibits discrimination on the basis of disability and requires public entities that receive federal funds to provide qualified individuals with disabilities special program services. The definition of disability in this law is broader than that in the IDEA (special education), and students who are not considered as disabled under IDEA may be defined as a person with disabilities under Section 504. Parents or teachers may request that students be assessed to determine if special services may be made available as a result of Section 504. The referral and assessment procedures are similar to those for special education. Examples of qualifying disabilities under Section 504 include dyslexia, attention deficit disorder (ADD), and hyperactivity. Each campus and district should have a Section 504 coordinator who will have the necessary information to answer teachers' questions.

Other programs for students who have special needs are collectively known as **compensatory education programs.** These programs provide supplementary services for academic assistance and are designed to meet the needs of at-risk students. At-risk students are those who are performing well below their grade level or meet any one of several criteria, usually associated with below-average academic performance, that places the student at risk of dropping out of school. Additional funding, normally from the federal level, is provided for these programs, and eligible students may be served in a wide variety of settings dependent upon the district's or school's program design. Some examples of compensatory programs would be reading or math laboratories, summer school programs, after or before school programs, and tutorials. Teachers should become aware of the compensatory programs that are in place on their campus and how the services provided benefit the students.

Bilingual education and **English as a second language (ESL)** programs are designed to meet the special needs of students whose home or native language is not English. Legal guidelines and procedures exist for determining student eligibility for these programs and how the programs are to be implemented. The process for identifying eligible students begins at the time of enrollment. The parent or student must complete a Home Language Survey that reports the language spoken most often in the home. For any student reporting a language other than English, an oral proficiency examination is administered. Students who are determined to be limited English proficient (LEP) are referred to a committee for placement and scheduling. The committee is the Language Proficiency Assessment Committee (LPAC), and it has similar responsibilities as the ARD Committee for special education students. Parent permission is required for placement in bilingual and ESL programs, and exiting procedures are also dependent upon the student meeting language proficiency guidelines. Teachers should become familiar with the nature of the programs and how they assist students who have difficulty speaking or comprehending the English language. With an increasing student population in Texas of students eligible for these programs, most schools have one or both programs in place. The goal of both programs is to provide the necessary academic instruction while the student transitions to being able to have all instruction in English.

Those students who meet criteria for being eligible for **gifted and talented (GT) education** represent another special needs population in Texas. Students may be referred for screening for this program by parents, teachers, other educators, or by the students themselves. The criteria for eligibility varies by school district, but the process includes both objective and subjective measures. Subjective measures may include checklists, rating forms, and interviews. Objective measures may include intelligence tests, achievement tests, and aptitude tests. Students placed in GT programs are reviewed annually for continuance or exiting from the program. In Texas, programs for students identified as gifted and talented are required by Texas law for all schools in grades kindergarten through 12. Special funding is made available to implement these programs, which may exist in any one of several models in a school or district. In elementary school, students may receive services in the regular classroom from a teacher who has received at least 30 workshop hours in gifted education topics, be pulled out for a portion of the day to be with a teacher of the gifted, or be self-contained all day in a class for the gifted. In secondary schools, certain courses are identified to serve the identified GT students. Teachers of these courses are also required to have special training. Teachers should find out which model is used at their schools and how their instructional programs may be related to those occurring for the students identified as gifted.

Another area that the Competency 15 narrative lists as important for teachers to understand the applicable laws and guidelines is **confidentiality.** McCune et al. (1995) discuss the Family Educational Rights and Privacy Act (FERPA) of 1972, also known as the **Buckley Amendment,** that gives students and their parents access to student records and restricts disclosure of record content. The district may release "directory information" unless the parents have notified the school that the information is not to be released. Directory information normally includes such items as the student's name, address, telephone number, and so on. As a practical matter, teachers must be very careful with whom they discuss personal information or the academic records of the students. Teachers must use good judgment, respect the privacy of student information, and follow carefully and with integrity the district or campus procedures for protecting the confidentiality of student records. For example, a teacher should not discuss student information with parents of other students or conduct conversations about students in a location where other students can easily hear the discussion.

A major concern for all teachers must be for the safety and welfare of students in their care. Teachers must be aware of the laws regarding the required reporting of suspected or potential **child abuse.** In Texas, teachers, nurses, and other "professional" educators are required to report child abuse or neglect to a child protective agency (Child Protective Service offices are located in each county) or law enforcement agency within 48 hours of first suspecting the child has been or may be abused or neglected. The identity of the professional who reports is kept confidential, and a teacher cannot be held liable for false reports unless the act of informing is determined to be a malicious act. Failure to report, however, may result in the teacher being found guilty of a misdemeanor. Teachers should be informed by the district of child abuse and neglect reporting requirements and learn to which agency reports should be made. When confronted with indications of abuse or neglect, the teacher should report as required by law. Incidents have occurred where teachers were reported for or charged with child abuse as a result of their disciplinary actions. Teachers must follow their district's policy on discipline and be particularly cautious about punishments involving physical contact or even restraining students.

STRUCTURE OF THE TEXAS
EDUCATION SYSTEM

Competency 15 has as its focus teaching in Texas. It is important for teachers in Texas to have a general understanding of how education in the state is organized so that they may recognize the types of authority and decision-making structures within the system. Under the United States Constitution, education is a state function. However, the federal government has a significant role in the governance of education if the state or local district accepts federal funds. If federal funds are accepted, the education entity must comply with the directives of legislation and abide by the regulations of the federal agencies, including the U.S. Department of Education that has the responsibility of administering federal education laws and regulations. In Texas, the state legislature has established school districts and a central education authority, the **Texas Education Agency (TEA),** to organize and administer the educational programs in the state. The constitution of the state empowers the legislature "to establish and make suitable provision for the support and maintenance of an efficient system of public free schools." The funding for schools in Texas comes from two primary sources, the budget of the state and local property taxes. The percentage from each source varies dependent upon the property wealth of the local district.

At the state level, the **State Board of Education (SBOE)** is a statewide policy board that has the responsibility of overseeing the TEA, among other duties. The board is a 15-member body elected for six-year terms, and each member represents one of fifteen geographic regions of the state. The chair of the board is appointed from the membership of the SBOE by the governor.

The management of the TEA rests with the **Commissioner of Education,** who is appointed by the governor and confirmed by the Texas Senate. He or she is seen as the educational leader of the state and works with the State Board of Education to achieve its goals for education in the state. The commissioner has a number of specific duties set by law including authority to develop regulations for the implementation of legislation. At the local community level, the authority for creation and oversight of educational programs rests with the local board of education, which was described earlier in this chapter.

A recent addition to the state agencies responsible for education is the **State Board for Educator Certification (SBEC).** This is a 15-member board responsible for the oversight of all aspects of public school educator certification, continuing education, and standards of conduct. The overall guiding principle of the board is set out in its vision statement found on the SBEC website, which states, "The board is guided by the philosophy that educators will create higher standards for preparation, practice, and conduct than others outside the profession, and that educators will rigorously uphold these standards." The board oversees the implementation of certification rules and is the agency to which a teacher applies for certification. The SBEC also governs all aspects of the ExCET and sets rules for teacher education programs in the state.

At the local district level, the superintendent of schools, central office personnel, building principals, and teachers represent the hierarchy of authority. The superintendent is accountable to the board of education, and the employees of the district are responsible to the superintendent in a manner reflected by the district's organization. The teachers are directly responsible to their campus administrator, most often the principal.

The Texas Education Agency (1998) has provided current demographics of students in Texas that will assist teachers in gaining an appreciation of the complexity and size of the education enterprise in Texas (*1997–98 Texas Public School Statistics*). In the 1997–98 school year, there were 1,042 school districts in the state, ranging in student population from over 200,000 to less than 25. There were 7,053 public schools in the state that enrolled approximately 3,900,000 students. The students in Texas schools are becoming increasingly diverse, and an increasing percentage are considered to be economically disadvantaged. Among Texas students, there is currently no majority ethnic group. African American students comprise 14 percent of the student population, white 45 percent, Hispanic 38 percent, and those students classified as other 3 percent. Hispanic students are the fastest growing segment of the population. For the same year, 48 percent of the students enrolled in Texas public schools qualified for free or reduced price meals based on family income, and thus were considered economically disadvantaged. The increasing diversity of students and the number of children living in poverty have implications for the teachers preparing to teach in Texas schools.

SUMMARY

This chapter has expanded on the Competency 15 statement that teachers in Texas must understand and respect the requirements, expectations, and constraints associated with teaching in Texas. Teachers should have a general understanding of how the educational system is organized and how the system practically works in Texas. Teachers must understand they are obligated to follow all laws, regulations, and policies that come from all levels of authority in education. One benefit of this knowledge put into practice is that the informed teacher is better equipped to be an effective teacher and to maximize learning opportunities for their students. With confidence based on knowledge and experience, teachers can focus their energies on their students who deserve the very best that educators in Texas can offer. The future of Texas as a state of educated and productive citizens requires no less.

SUGGESTED ACTIVITIES

To reinforce and expand on the information presented in this chapter, the teacher may consider the following activities.

1. Attend a meeting of a local board of education. (In larger districts, the meeting may be televised on local cable channels.)

2. Discuss with a campus administrator how site-based decision making works on his or her campus. Ask for copies of agendas or minutes to review topics discussed.

3. Explore the websites provided in this chapter.

4. Read newspapers, news magazines, journals, and other publications for current information related to topics discussed in the chapter.

5. Volunteer to serve on campus or district committees when given the opportunity.

6. Monitor new rules related to certification and required renewal of license every five years.

7. Meet with professors, program directors, or campus personnel who work with programs serving special populations.

8. For preservice teachers, request to observe an ARD meeting and/or a bilingual/ESL class.

9. Visit an inclusion school or classroom.

PRACTICE DECISION SET

Mr. Smith was hired during the summer to teach sixth-grade science at McGraw Elementary School and was looking forward to the new school year. He had enjoyed his three years of previous teaching and hoped to apply in the classroom what he had learned from that experience and from his summer enrollment in a graduate education course. The principal at McGraw assigned Mr. Smith a mentor to assist in the transition period. The mentor was Mr. Martinez, who had taught at the school for eight years. On the teacher preparation day before the students reported, Mr. Martinez took Mr. Smith on a tour of the school to meet members of the staff.

1. One of the first persons Mr. Smith met on his tour was Mrs. Redd, the counselor. Mrs. Redd said that she needed to meet with Mr. Smith soon to discuss a student who would be in his class for a part of each day in connection with the school's inclusion project. Mr. Smith was puzzled. What program was likely included in the inclusion project?

   a. Gifted and talented program
   b. Compensatory education program
   c. Special education program
   d. English as a second language program

2. As Mr. Smith's tour of the campus continued, Mr. Martinez pointed out a posted copy of the agenda of an upcoming meeting of the McGraw Collaborative Committee, which was the campus committee for site-based shared decision making. The topics on the agenda included:

   I. Hiring Mrs. Green as the new third-grade teacher
   II. Discussing the year's staff development plan
   III. Reviewing the campus budget proposals for the year
   IV. Determining bus stops for the year

   Which topics are appropriate items for campus SBDM committees to consider?

   a. I and II
   b. I and IV
   c. II and III
   d. III and IV

3. Mr. Martinez then introduced Mr. Smith to Mrs. Nguyen, the teacher of the gifted and talented class at the school. Mrs. Nguyen had just completed posting on the front hall bulletin board the names of the students who had qualified as GT students for the year based on the screening conducted last spring. The list also included the scores for the various tests taken, including IQ scores for each student. Mrs. Nguyen had likely violated which of the following laws by her actions?

   a. FERPA (Buckley Amendment)
   b. Title IX
   c. IDEA
   d. Section 504

4. Mr. Martinez then cautioned Mr. Smith to watch for any signs of child abuse among his students, since the school had seen several

cases in the past year. Mr. Martinez went on to say that if any potential abuse or neglect was noted, Mr. Smith should contact the principal, who would investigate the matter and determine if there was abuse. Mr. Smith was confused because this was not the procedure at his previous school. Whom should the teacher contact when child abuse or neglect is suspected?

a. The parents of the child
b. A child protection or law enforcement agency
c. The school nurse
d. The central administration office

5. As they concluded the tour, Mr. Martinez shared with Mr. Smith that he was a good friend of the president of the local school board, Mr. Benson. Mr. Benson was a great supporter of teachers and the district and always wanted to help teachers new to the district. Mr. Smith expressed thanks for the tour and, reflecting on Mr. Martinez's comments about the board president, thought about the student mentorship program that had worked so well in his prior school. What would be the best first step for Mr. Smith to begin the process of getting the mentorship program introduced to the school?

a. Call Mr. Benson and meet with him to discuss the program
b. Go to the next school board meeting and speak to the board about the program
c. Make an appointment with the principal to discuss the program
d. Begin to sign up adult mentors in the community to be ready for program implementation

Answer 1: The answer is *c*. *Inclusion* is a term most often associated with special education. Students receiving special

education services are "included" to the greatest extent possible in the regular education classroom or program. The ARD Committee determines the amount of time and in which classrooms the student will be scheduled. Inclusion may be described as both a philosophical position and a program. The major belief underlying inclusion is that all students, regardless of disabilities, can learn from and contribute to the learning of students in appropriate regular education settings. The other programs listed relate to the needs of special population students but are not associated with inclusion.

Answer 2: The correct answer is *c*. Determining which teacher applicant to recommend for employment (item I) is a decision reserved for the principal and the personnel department of the district. Teachers who will work directly with the new employee are often consulted in the decision-making process, but the decision is not appropriate for discussion by the site-based committee. Item IV on the agenda is an administrative decision most often determined by the district's transportation department, which has the best information upon which to base a decision. Items II and III are included as specific topics appropriate for discussion and decision in the Texas law that created these committees; thus, answer *c* is the correct answer.

Answer 3: The answer is *a*. The Buckley Amendment concerns the right of privacy of the records and information related to students and restricts who may have access to that information. Test scores of individuals are protected by this law and should never be posted in a public place or made available to anyone who does not have the legal right to access the records. Title IX deals with gender equity in educational programs. IDEA (Individuals with Disabilities Education Act, 1990) is the name of federal legislation that established rules and regulations related to educating students with special needs. Section 504 deals with rights of students with disabilities who are not eligible for services through special education.

Answer 4: The correct answer is *b*. Texas law places the responsibility to report suspected child abuse directly upon the teacher who observes or suspects the potential child abuse. The teacher should contact the local child protection agency or law enforcement agency. The teacher may inform the principal, nurse, or other colleagues of his or her suspicions, but this does not relieve the teacher of the responsibility to report as the law requires.

Answer 5: The answer is *c*. A teacher should always follow the chain of command or authority in relation to discussing school matters with superiors. The district policy will provide the correct sequence for the teacher. The campus principal is most often the direct supervisor of the teacher and should be the first contact regarding issues similar to the one related in this scenario. If a teacher has a complaint or grievance, he or she should follow the district policy that lists specific procedures as to how these concerns should be addressed. The teacher should keep the principal informed and advised at all times. Board members are not normally involved in the initial review of programs or curriculum issues.

WEB LINKS

Remember that website locations may change. If any of these sites have moved or cannot be located, use the Terms to Know in this chapter to search for further information.

www.tea.state.tx.us
This is the web address for the Texas Education Agency. The site includes current school-related laws and regulations, campus and district data, curriculum and assessment information, information on educational programs (including those for special needs students) and accountability and accreditation information. The site also has links to other education sites.

www.sbec.state.tx.us
This website for the State Board of Educator Certification includes information related to licensing, certification, testing, and applicable rules.

www.edinfo@inet.ed.gov
This U.S. Department of Education website contains links to related agencies.

www.tea.state.tx.us/esc/
This is the web address for the 20 regional Education Service Centers in Texas. The site contains links to each center.

www.sos.state.tx.us
This site for the Secretary of State's office includes the Texas Administrative Code, Texas Education Code, administrative rules, and links to related sites.

www.ed.gov/free/
This website address for the Department of Education in Washington includes a wide variety of useful topics for teachers and links to related sources.

REFERENCES AND SUGGESTED READINGS

Gomez, F. C., & Craycraft, K. R. (1998). *The legal handbook for Texas teachers.* Bulverde, TX: OMNI Publishers.

McCune, S. L., Lowe, M. E., & Stephens, D. E. (1995). *How to prepare for the ExCET.* Hauppauge, NY: Barron's Educational Series.

Research and Education Association. (1998). *The best test preparation for the ExCET.* Piscataway, NJ: Author.

Texas Education Agency. (1998). *1997–98 Texas public school statistics* (brochure). Austin, TX: Author.

ABOUT THE AUTHOR

Dr. Gary Clay is an Associate Professor of Education and Director of On Site Graduate Education Programs at Houston Baptist University. He worked in public schools for 28 years and held positions of teacher, principal, and superintendent. He currently teaches undergraduate and graduate courses in Curriculum and Instruction.

16

✷

Preparing For and Taking the ExCET Test

JANICE L. NATH
CYNTHIA G. HENRY

We hope that you have gained enough knowledge from these chapters to do well on your Professional Development ExCET. We also know that test-taking skills can have a great deal to do with whether or not you do well—even if you know the material very well. In this chapter, we offer a study plan and some helpful hints for test day.

Getting ready for your Professional Development ExCET test has four parts: (1) making sure that your registration is complete and sent in on time, (2) preparing for test day, (3) understanding the format of the test, and (4) planning a study routine well in advance of the test.

REGISTRATION

Register for only one test at a time. Research shows that taking two or more tests on the same day is risky. More information on this subject is provided later in this chapter.

Watch the deadlines for registration carefully. There is nothing that your certification preparer can do if you do not make your deadlines to NES (National Evaluation Systems, the testing entity). No exceptions to deadlines are made. If you are applying from another state, it is important that you contact the State Board for Educator Certification (SBEC) Information and Support Center. The address, telephone number, and e-mail address are provided at the end of this chapter.

Obtain your money order or check and send with your registration. If you do write a check, make *very sure* that your check will clear. Money orders are safer. One student's bank made a mistake and refused her check. Even though they sent NES a confirmation that it was *their* mistake, the student's scores had already been taken out of the computer.

Carefully complete all parts of the registration. If they are not completed correctly, your registration will be returned, and most likely, it will be too late to reregister for that particular date. Be careful to fill out your form with no mistakes.

Obtain your bar code from your university certification officer or preparation entity and affix it to your form. There may be an earlier deadline required by your preparer for this, so that your certification officer has time to process all documents. Be sure to watch for or ask about this.

Do not forget to put a stamp on your envelope. Students often forget this, especially if they are taking documents into a university or other entity to be mailed.

Sign your form. Many people do not sign their forms. Unsigned registration forms *will* be sent back!

When you receive any information from National Evaluation Systems (NES), check it for accuracy. The test site, time, and so on, that you requested may not have been available, and you may have been given another time or place. If any other information is wrong, your scores may be reported to someone else. Check everything!

Figure 16.1 provides a checklist for registration. *Things change often, so please double-check with the latest* ExCET Registration Bulletin *for current procedures. Read everything that applies to you carefully.*

Checklist for Registration

__ Registration form obtained

__ Deadline for registration noted

__ Money order (or check) ready to be sent with registration

__ All parts of registration form completed correctly

__ Deadline for obtaining university bar code checked

__ Bar code obtained and affixed to registration form

__ Stamp placed on envelope

__ Registration form signed

__ Test site, time, and so on confirmed by information from NES

FIGURE 16.1 A checklist to follow in registering for a test.

PREPARING FOR TEST DAY

You have heard enough teachers talk about test preparation to know many of the suggestions by heart. However, there are certain hints that are important enough to bear repeating.

Allowing plenty of time for arrival can make a difference between feeling rushed with some degree of anxiety or feeling calm and confidently ready to begin. One way to prepare is to start several days in advance. The test site may not be familiar to you, so having a map in your car, where you have already located your site, will help. If you live in a large city and are not familiar with the site, it may help to check its locale by driving there at some point prior to the test day. Some sites may be far enough from your home that you may want to consider driving there the night before and spending the night nearby. If so, arrange for that well in advance, as others may be thinking along the same lines, and hotels in the near proximity may be booked. The alternative might be an extremely early morning drive with a lot of anxiety about a timely arrival. In the past, test takers were required to arrive very early—by 7:30 for the morning test (1:30 for the afternoon). Check your required arrival time carefully. If you live far away, requesting an afternoon testing session may be the answer. Also, check the gas in your car. The last thing you want to have to worry about is finding a service station on the way to a site. There is a cutoff time where proctors do not allow late arrivals to enter, and no refunds are given for latecomers.

Have all your supplies ready and in the car the night before. You will need your admission/acceptance ticket(s), two pieces of identification (one must be a government issue with a picture), pencils, a jacket, an accurate watch, and some food and/or beverages. Rushing around the night before, or worse, the morning of the test may create a frantic feeling that is hard to overcome. A complete list of items needed (and a list of prohibited items) can be found in your ExCET Registration Bulletin (and later in this chapter). Be sure to look at the list from the current bulletin, as changes may be made from testing date to testing date.

Some people are nervous about waking up on time and do not sleep well the night before an event such as this one. A good night's sleep is essential, so set two alarm clocks, if needed, to make sure you are not waking up to check the clock. Partying or staying up late the night before for *any* reason can really make a difference in your concentration level. Also, arrange for this day to be a testing day *only*. Do not make plans to be at an event that would require you to rush to finish early or that would be exciting enough to break your concentration. At $72 a try and with the testing dates so far apart, it really makes sense to take the test seriously in every way. Even a point or two can make a difference in passing or failing. For a morning test, you should be in bed and asleep by at least 10:00 the night before your examination.

Breakfast and/or lunch (for an afternoon test) is another important part of test preparation. You may need the entire five hours to finish your test. Near the end of that time, your energy level may wane, causing a loss of concentration. Plan a moderate breakfast for a morning test and a moderate lunch for an afternoon test. Too heavy a meal may cause you to be drowsy. That lull in your concentration, as with being too tired if you do not get a proper night's sleep, may make a difference in obtaining just that point you need to pass. Foods high in protein and low in carbohydrates are recommended by nutritionists for optimal mental alertness (lean meats, fish, green and leafy vegetables, and peanuts; but avoid cereals, pastas, potatoes, and breads). Testing sites are often in high schools or other areas where their "quick fix" snack and beverage machines may or may not be available, but prepare for nonavailability by eating a proper (but not heavy) meal before your test. Backpacks have not been allowed in the past, so you may want to stick an energy bar and juice of some kind or bottled water in your pocket or purse for a midtest "pick-me-up." Eating, drinking, and smoking is not allowed inside the testing room or area, but you may want to take a quick break to have your snack outside. Also, you might persuade yourself that a large dose of caffeine before or during this test will help, but it can actually impair concentration with "the jitters" and, of course, can interrupt your test with multiple trips to the restroom. If you are taking two tests on one day (and we hope you are not; see information later in the chapter), it may be worth taking a lunch and leaving it in a cooler in your car. Testing sites may not be located close to fast-food restaurants, or everyone else may be trying to get a lunch quickly, too. You do not want to have to worry about finishing your first test quickly in order to get a lunch prior to the next test's starting time.

Another important part of test taking is the temperature variant. In the checklist in Figure 16.2, we urge you to wear layers of clothing and/or bring a jacket.

Checklist for Test Day

__ Admission/acceptance ticket(s). Each test will have its own ticket. If you are taking two tests, you must have both tickets. Read all information carefully for site locations and times, as NES does not have to give you the first site and time you requested

__ Map that shows the test site location (if needed)

__ Two pieces of identification, one with a picture (one government issued, bearing your signature and picture, such as a drivers' license or passport) and another (university ID, social security card, credit card, employee card, etc.)

__ Pencils (No. 2 are best)

__ Accurate watch that does *not* beep on the hour

__ Energy bar

__ Juice or bottled water

__ Layers of clothing/jacket

__ Lunch (if taking multiple tests)

FIGURE 16.2 A checklist to follow on test day.

This would be advised for all seasons. Sites often anticipate many, many people in a large room, so the temperature is turned down quite low when you arrive. In fact, it may seem to be "freezing"! As people arrive, however, the temperature may begin to climb and become quite warm throughout the testing time. Dress in layers that you can take off or add, so that you can concentrate on the test rather than on being uncomfortably cold or hot. Also, dress in loose-fitting, comfortable clothing.

Early arrival at the test site is important for many reasons. It will help reduce your anxiety level to arrive with plenty of time to spare. Parking is sometimes limited, and test takers may be forced to park quite some distance away. We have had a few reports of students believing that they had arrived early, but by having to park far away, they were rushed and running to get to the registration site on time. Again, allow enough driving *and* parking time. Even if you take a newspaper, novel, or review material and have to sit in your car for a bit, it is better than arriving late and in a frantic state.

Once you are checked in, take your seat. Be sure to sit in exactly your assigned seat (if applicable); do not be creative in seat selection, as it may make a difference on your reported scores. Listen carefully for instructions. If there are further written instructions, read them carefully. Even if you have taken a practice examination, there may be things that have changed. Be alert to that fact.

Figure 16.2 provides a checklist for test day. Note that the following items are prohibited during the professional development test:

backpacks	briefcases	cell phones	pagers
beeping watches	packages	sliderules	highlighters
cameras	tape recorders	notebooks	textbooks
scratch paper	dictionaries	spell checkers	calculators
audiotapes	written materials		

Things change often, so please double-check with the latest ExCET *Registration Bulletin for any changes. Read everything that applies to you carefully.*

THE TEST

Again, we hope that you have not signed up for multiple tests. Growing research shows that people who attempt multiple tests often do not pass one or both of their tests. If you have signed up for more than one and you find that you really do not have the energy to continue after a full morning, it may be to your benefit, psychologically, to forfeit your afternoon test. Though you will not receive a refund, it may better serve you to come back fresh on the next test date rather than experience failure due to fatigue. If you do have to take two tests, do not let the fact that you have an afternoon test affect your morning test by making you rush or putting you in a bad frame of mind, so that you do not put your best effort into your morning test. Again, the best advice is to take only one test per testing date.

When Texas first instituted a test for teachers, it consisted mostly of recall questions. For example:

Whose theory included a close examination of children's developmental levels?

(a)   Piaget
(b)   Bloom
(c)   Jamison
(d)   Jones

You either knew the answer or not, based on your level of knowledge. That is no longer the case. In many ways, taking the test now is easier; and in many ways, it is harder. There is no longer a list of names, dates, and so forth to memorize for the professional development test. However, for the professional development ExCET, Texas gives teacher candidates 15 competencies that encompass the skills, knowledge, attitudes, and philosophies that Texas wants in its teachers. Questions now are at the application and evaluation level. They do not ask you to repeat or restate any of the competencies. Instead, they ask you to know the competencies well and apply them to typical school scenarios according to what Texas wants in its teachers—as given to you exactly through the competencies. Do not answer in *any way* other than those aligned with the Texas philosophies—if you want to pass! You may have grown up in a school where students sat quietly in individual desks and cooperative groups were never used. You may (though we hope you do not) believe that that is the correct way to run your classroom all the time. The competencies tell us, however, that Texas wants us to use cooperative groups often—where children learn through interactions and talking to each other. If you want to pass, do not select your preference if it does not happen to match that of Texas. We hope that you will match your actions to the philosophies set forth by the competencies because they are all good for children. But again, if you do not have such a match, and you should persist in answering *your* way, be prepared to get the wrong answer.

Answering questions in accordance with the competencies may be particularly difficult if you went to school in another country or even to a strict private school where your experiences were in direct opposition to the competencies. Be very sure that if this is the case, you understand the importance of matching your answers on the ExCET to those of the Texas competencies rather than those of your experience—should your experience not be as these competencies state. Another population that may have difficulty in matching views with these competencies is those who are already teaching in certain types of schools where these Texas philosophies are not often seen. There are still many schools in Texas and in other areas where, sadly, these competencies are not a part of daily school life. We hope that you do not see schools that are gloomy places for students with negative actions by teachers *they* say are examples of "what needs to be done in the real world." If for some reason you have never known a school that is a wonderful and positive place for all kinds of students and teachers, and you *persist* in answering in ways that are negative and contrary to the competencies, you will not succeed on this test. A good question to ask yourself as you select an answer is, "What does Texas say it wants a teacher to do in this situation?"

Test Format

Teacher Decision Sets Let us continue to look at the test layout more carefully, now that you understand the importance of aligning your answers with the views of Texas. It is critical that you understand the amount of reading comprehension required for passing the test. The test is organized into large reading blocks, or "Teacher Decision Sets." Each Teacher Decision Set or school scenario is first introduced with several paragraphs—perhaps a half page of reading. This is followed by questions, usually several pages in length, all related to the opening situation. These questions may also have several paragraphs that introduce new information into the scenario. Competencies are mixed at random throughout the test. In other words, one Teacher Decision Set covers several competencies but will not contain test questions over just *one* competency.

Slower Readers If you are a slower reader or an ESL learner with difficulty reading rapidly in English, you will need to keep a close eye on your time. Prepare thoroughly by learning the terms listed in the competencies and boldfaced in this text. Practice your reading skills in order to get through the vast amount of reading on this five-hour test. If your university or certifying agency gives a practice ExCET, you should make sure that you take it. It will help you understand exactly the time element involved in reading and answering this type of lengthy test. If reading fast enough is difficult, review by rereading all your teacher education texts and answering questions from the chapters, after you have reread the chapters in this book. Carefully establish and maintain a long-term study program (see hints later in this chapter) with these skills in mind.

Tips for Answering Questions There are some tips for answering the actual questions on the examination that may be of help. First, make sure to read the opening scenario carefully. This will set the whole stage for the next few pages. One strategy that you may have used on *other* tests is to read the questions before you read the scenario. This *can* be inappropriate for the Professional Development ExCET *only*. This is because the opening scenario often continues along throughout a Teacher Decision Set in smaller scenarios, and information continues to be added as you read the other paragraphs. If you read *all* the questions up front belonging to the Teacher Decision Set, you may find that it is too time-consuming and too confusing, and that you miss important information added along the way. It *is* a good strategy, however, to read the questions prior to reading the *smaller* scenario questions after the stage has been set by the introduction of the Teacher Decision Set.

This examination is written in multiple-choice format. The answers are designed to make you think by recalling factual information, analyzing, then evaluating information, and finally applying it to the current scenario. As you read the scenario and questions, underline key information and circle key words or phrases that you have seen in the competencies. Also, carefully underline or circle words and phrases that may *negate* an answer (such as *not, never,* and so forth), as well as other words that would change an answer (*always, frequently,* etc.). Read all of the answer choices before making your selection. There will usually be four answers from which to choose, and you will mark your answer on a separate scantron.

The process of elimination will help you considerably. As you read each question, you may often find that one or two answers clearly stand out as incorrect. Put an "X" by those and do not waste further time on them. Two answers, however, often are straight from the competencies and clearly sound correct according to the views of Texas. Your task now is to go back to the question and determine *exactly* what the question is asking. Though both answers sound good, only one will be the true answer to the question. Thus, in this test, the distracters are often designed to look great and are often written in excellent educational terms, *but they do not match the question.* Be careful!! Quite often this is where many people make mistakes, especially if they are in a hurry. There are also some very tricky differences to discern between two of the best answers. For example, let us look at the following question:

Mr. Nguyen wanted his students to participate in helping the librarian select new books and games that were to be available from a large PTO gift. He proposed that students in his class read and review books from ordering lists, and that some games on the list also be made available to be played and reviewed. He wanted his class to survey teachers and students from each grade level about their favorite authors and the games they liked and present the survey to the librarian. First, he went to the principal, librarian, and the grade-level committees to ask if this was feasible. In doing this, he shows that he can:

a. Continue professional development by seeking direction from other professionals
b. Collaborate with others for his lesson objectives
c. Communicate with others to accomplish educational goals
d. Demonstrate to students how collaboration accomplishes objectives in the real world

Let us analyze this problem. Answer *a* is not correct at all because (1) he is not asking any direction, but rather asking only for time and permission to run his surveys, and (2) there is not anything to do with professional development in his actions, so we can put an "X" by that answer. Answer *d* is also not applicable because there is no mention of the students even knowing that he went to these other professionals. There are some distracters here, though. We know that Texas wants its teachers to continue professional development and to show how school relates to the real world. Answers *a* and *d* are written nicely to distract. We are then left with answers *b* and *c*—both of which sound very good. We know that Texas wants us to collaborate with others (straight from the competencies), so we might be drawn to answer *b*, but if we look closely, there really is no collaboration going on here. Mr. Nguyen is just communicating his proposition to the other parties. He already has his ideas, and rather than asking others to work together with him to design his lessons, he wants permission to implement them. His ideas also involve more than just one lesson's objectives (since this would no doubt be a series of lessons), so the proposition would be for a broader set of goals. These are such small details, but taking the answers apart in this way is what you will want to do in order to pass.

Another strategy is to try to discern exactly which *competency* the question is trying to test. If you can determine this, you can often select the answer easily. If you know the competencies very well, it will be easier for you to analyze the possible answers for this strategy. For example, if you can determine that a question is testing Competency 8, some of the key concepts of that competency are higher-level thinking, real-world application, and use of a variety of strategies. If you see those concepts in one of the answers, then you can be fairly sure that is the correct answer. Let us look at an example with another competency:

> Miss Huff was a new teacher who grew up in another area of the country. She was having difficulties with one of her seventh graders, Jorge. She went to ask her mentor, Ms. Faseler, what she should do because she was sure that Jorge was lying to her. "The last time I asked him if he was the one who made the noises, I told him to look me and tell me that he didn't do it. He kept saying that it wasn't him, but he must be lying because he wouldn't look me in the eye. What am I going to do with him?" Ms. Faseler told Miss Huff that often both Hispanic and Asian children will not look directly at an adult (especially a teacher or parent), and this is learned as a sign of respect for their elders—though in middle-class white culture it is taken to mean "guilty" if someone refuses to make eye contact. The next time that Miss Huff wanted to question Jorge about his behavior, she had him wait after school and sit down beside her rather than in front of her. She calmly asked him to tell her about what had happened through a series of questions. She was pleasantly surprised that they actually had a nice conversation, and she was enlightened in several areas of class behavior. She used this information the next day to make some changes that improved the entire classroom environment. This teacher now understands that:
>
> a. Collaboration with other professionals increases learning and a sense of a community of learners
>
> b. Students develop in different ways according to their culture
>
> c. Establishing management techniques through collaboration is mutually supportive
>
> d. Being sensitive to nonverbal cues is an important part of communication in a classroom of learners

All of these sound like they might work. First, let us eliminate! Answer *a* cannot be the correct answer because we are not really talking about *learning* here. The answer cannot be *b* because there are no developmental problems being discussed—even though we could be distracted about the cultural issue, especially since that is the only reference to culture in all the answers. Now, let us closely examine our remaining two best items by looking at the question to see if we can decide from which competency it has been taken. Certainly, there is a management issue and there was collaboration going on with a mentor teacher, but there were really no management techniques discussed in the conversation with Ms. Faseler—as answer *c* states. It was a communication issue, and the main thrust of the question involved Miss Huff's misreading a student's nonverbal cues. Letter *d* is correct because she used her new information to question Jorge with supportive interactions that helped to change the classroom environment. This is all about the part of Competency 7 that states, "The teacher models effective communication strategies (e.g., monitoring the effects of messages, being a reflective listener, simplifying and restating, being sensitive to nonverbal cues given and received). . . . " When we can analyze the main idea of the scenario, the questions, and the possible answers, it is easy to go to our knowledge of the language of the competencies and pick out the answer. We must certainly know those competencies well!

Marking Your Scantron Test takers often make some mistakes that are very easy to control—yet cost points. Not bearing down hard enough to ensure that a clear mark is made, not erasing clearly, not coloring in a full circle, or marking outside of the lines on your scantron answer sheet can cause the machine that marks your paper to read the answers incorrectly. If you do not want to worry about these mistakes during the test, allow for several minutes at the end to go back over your scantron and correct these types of marks. If you run completely out of time and believe that there could be a possibility that your scantron might have been misread through these types of errors, you may want to have your test rescored by hand. The cost is about $25, and the information on how to request a rescoring is in your registration booklet. It is unlikely that many items have been misread, so this would only be suggested if you had a question about the state of your scantron and if you were within a very few points of passing.

One mistake that is common is mismatching the number of the test question in your booklet with that on the scantron. Be sure to stop every so often to check that you are actually on the same numbers on both parts of your test. Two good places to check are at the end of each Teacher Decision Set and when you begin a new column on your scantron. Catching a mismatch after a good portion of the test or not at all can be devastating! This can also happen when you want to skip a question and come back to it later. A better suggestion is *not* to skip questions on the Professional Development ExCET. Answer every question as you come to it, but mark a light mark beside those that you wish to revisit—if time remains. If you still feel compelled to skip a question, do so only until the end of each Teacher Decision Set rather than at the end of the test. Why? The scenario format of the test involves quite a lot of reading time. Again, there is a long introduction with many questions following each Teacher Decision Set. If you have many questions that you skip, you will find yourself practically rereading all of the test. It will also be very confusing to try to reinsert yourself into each scenario without reading the whole situation. Your first inclination is often the best answer, and you are penalized for leaving a question blank, so go ahead and take your "best shot" the first time. Leave a light mark, and come back to check it later *if* there is time.

Timing Your Test Time may or may not be a concern for you. The ExCET test changes often—not only the items, but also the number of items. Your certification entity may have prepared you to take a test of 150 items, and there may be only 100 on the test you are given *this* day or 180 on another day! Before you begin, check the number of questions so that you will see how to divide your time. If there are 100 items, you know that you should be covering about 20 to 25 items per hour. If there are more, divide your time accordingly. Plan your breaks as well. Taking several short breaks on the hour or even more closely spaced is usually more profitable than plowing through the bulk of the test. Physical exercises developed for long flights (stretches in place and isometrics) can be helpful, or lay your head down for a minute or so—though be careful not to doze off. Do keep an eye on your watch, so you are not surprised. We advise you to bring a watch that you know is accurate because the clock in your room may not be accurate or visible from where you are seated. You want to make sure that there is time to mark every question. Again, you *are* penalized for wrong answers and blanks, but not for guesses if they turn out to be correct. If you should run out of time at the end, quickly mark all remaining blanks with *any* answer. Do leave enough time to recheck your scantron for stray marks or incomplete circles.

Test Anxiety Test anxiety can be a debilitating part of test taking. Here are some suggestions to help combat these feelings. If you have followed our suggestions about arriving in plenty of time with your supplies, you are one step ahead of test anxiety. If you allocate your time and breaks to the number of questions and maintain a schedule accordingly so that you will not run out of time, it should help reduce your anxiety. If you have arranged your day such that your focus is on the test *only* rather than on another big event such as leaving town for the semester or other exciting plans following the test, you should be calmer. If it makes you nervous that someone seated near you is noisy, you may want to ask a proctor whether there is another seat—or ask the proctor to request that that person be quieter. However, overall, the best strategy is to know your material very well and to practice with the terms and the format as often as possible. The following is a discussion of a long-term plan to make sure you feel confident in your knowledge.

LONG-TERM STUDY SKILLS

The amount of material in this book is extensive, and it may seem overwhelming. Breaking the information down into smaller, more manageable steps is really a key to preparation.

Time Management

It is easy to let time slip away and find yourself with only a few weeks or a few days before your test. This can certainly cause anxiety, so try to avoid it by setting up manageable goals for study time. The amount of time that you set aside will depend on the time you have prior to the test day. If, for example, you begin to study for the examination four months before the test date, plan to study about three days a week for 30 minutes or an hour. If you have only one or two months, however, you will need to study more often and for a longer period of time each session. Both can be fairly manageable, but to keep to your schedule, write your study times on your calendar as you would with an appointment. This will help to remind you each week and emphasize the importance of this time for you. It will help to establish a more consistent study routine if you develop and maintain about the same times each day or evening as study times.

How to Study

Everyone has a favorite environmental learning style. If you need to be cozy on your favorite couch with low light and no sound at all, or if you cannot seem to learn without sitting at your desk with the radio, find that spot! Our brains are strange in many ways. Remembering the first and last items that we read are much easier for us than information we read in the middle. What does this mean to our study habits? Take frequent breaks so that your brain has a chance to begin and end more often, thereby cutting out the "forgettable middles." A brief two- to five-minute break is often what is needed to make that happen. Stretch, do an exercise set or so, get up for a drink or a snack, listen to a song, give your animal a petting, or close your eyes for just a second to rest your mind just enough to help absorb the material you have read. You know your own body rhythms. Try to schedule your study time when you are more energetic rather than tired and ready for bed.

How Much Is Enough? This question is one we often ask when faced with a heavy workload. Setting a goal on how much to accomplish each time helps you to overcome your study blocks. Again, look at the time you have and divide your pages into the days you have set aside. A reasonable amount of work for long-term study should be about 5 to 10 pages each time with time for review of the pages you studied earlier. You may also want to include working through some practice questions each time.

Material Management We often waste time with disorganization because it takes time to locate study materials, books, and so forth each time we want to use them. If there is one place where you can keep your ExCET materials, you will find it easier to study because you are not wasting time in hunting what you need.

Organization of materials is also important. Using different-colored file folders, coded labels, and so forth makes it easy to locate just what you want for that day. You may want to organize your materials by competency or by another system such as "Know," "Need to Review," and "Still to Learn."

Study Environment Other suggestions cover your environment more closely. Temperature affects our mental alertness. Keeping the room at 68 degrees can help maintain concentration and memory. A study area free of visual distractions can be helpful—a blank wall can be more conducive than a wall of bright posters or pictures. Lighting factors also make a difference. Many people do not study well in softer light, as it often increases mental fatigue (though a very few are low-light learners).

Use Your Senses and Memory Techniques There is a huge amount of material to remember for the ExCET. Try to use as many sensory avenues as possible to help you remember the main concepts. One idea is to paraphrase each competency and to put that information on index/flash cards to help memorize the important concepts or do the same with words at the beginning of each chapter in this text listed as "Terms to Know." Use these in a typical flashcard way or in a matching game with the answers on another set of flashcards or on the back.

Another method called the memory model technique comes in handy, as well. For example, Competency 8 involves several key concepts. You might draw a picture of a globe (for "relating instruction to the real world"), and out of that globe might be a huge flower with six petals (for Bloom's taxonomy) with the top three petals drawn in an exaggerated way and labeled "analysis," "synthesis," and "evaluation" for the importance of higher-level thinking. Then to the side, you might have a teacher juggling several hats, each labeled for the various roles that teachers perform, such as facilitator, audience, coach, and guide. You may want to add other areas that are important for you to remember in this competency. Memory techniques are very personal, so try to make up your own visuals that make sense to you for each competency. This is a good technique because you "wrestle" with the material in creating your memory "picture," but then it also easily flashes into your head if you study with it, because it is easy to visualize a ridiculous association.

Mnemonics are helpful as well. KCAASE for the six levels of Bloom's taxonomy may become, "No Candy Apples for Ana," says Eva (*No* for knowledge level, *Candy* for comprehension, *Apples* for application, *Ana* for analysis, *says* for synthesis, and *Eva* for evaluation). Again, this must make sense for you, so either design your own or take someone else's that works for *you*.

Talk concepts over to yourself alone in the car, so that you "hear" them often. Nobody will know that you are not singing along with the radio.

Another method that can be helpful in internalizing concepts is to make up your own questions. Creating these will help you think like the test developers, and you may be surprised at how closely your questions match those of the real test!

Make the Most of Your Time Focusing on the materials will be to your advantage, so give all of your attention to them when you study. Changing topics can help keep your mind fresh and maintain alertness when your attention is waning. Taking notes or underlining as you read also helps you to focus on what seems really important. As you come to a term or concept, try to visualize a classroom example of it. Note that example beside the term or concept. Basically, these techniques will stop you from arriving at the end of your reading wondering what you have just read. Do a bit of psychology on yourself by trying to begin and end on a positive note. In other words, visualize yourself confident and ready for the test because you have completed your study goals regularly, and see yourself with your certification in your hand. Do not go past your time allotments too often, especially when you are feeling tired and irritated with your learning abilities. "Making a deal" to give yourself a reward at the end of your study period can be quite effective, too. Plan something fun or enjoyable after your sessions. It does require hard work and commitment to "stay with it." This is one way to make it happen.

Study Groups   You may be with a group of teachers from your school or district who all need to pass this test to continue teaching, or you may be in a preservice program where your fellow students are facing the examination. Study groups can be a great source of support and learning for you. Try to organize or become a part of such a group. Often more minds than one offer new insight into the materials and ways to approach certain questions. Just discussing the concepts of the test engages you in the material in an active way, while we all know that teaching others, which you will do in a group, is also one of the best ways to learn. Working in a group often seems like it is "not working" when it comes to studying, so your energy often stays at a higher level. Put up notices in your school, university, or district to see if you can organize or gain access to an ExCET study group. Going over concepts, generating practice questions and answers, and talking over test-taking skills with others is a most effective way of preparing for this important examination.

ExCET Review Sessions   Attending an ExCET session that is commercially sponsored may be a sound investment if you have not been recently prepared by a college of education or have not done well by the second time you have taken the test. These sessions may offer additional insights into the material or an opportunity to work with a practice examination that will closely match the real ExCET. Regional service centers, school districts, universities, and others may offer these sessions. Find out about them early, however, because some are limited in size, and universities *may* limit their sessions to their students only. If you are unable to find a group in your area, you may want to establish an online review with someone who is further away but with whom you can still maintain a computer study time.

CONTACT NUMBERS

If you have questions about completing the forms, payment, test dates and registration deadlines, admission tickets, score reports, study guides, or ordering registration bulletins, you may want to call or write:

ExCET Program
National Evaluation Systems, Inc.
P.O. Box 140467
Austin, TX 78714-0467
Telephone: (512) 927-5151
Telecommunications for the Deaf: (512) 926-1248

If you have certification questions or questions about which tests you need, you may want to call or write:

State Board for Educator Certification Information and Support Center
(SBEC ISC)
1314 Hines Avenue
San Antonio, TX 78208-1899
Telephone: (888) 863-5880 (toll-free)
E-mail address: SBEC@esc20.net

Telephone numbers and e-mail addresses sometimes change, so you may need to call telephone information or do another computer search if that is the case.

This is not the first test you have taken and will probably not be the last. It is, perhaps, one of the most important because it will be your ticket to your chosen career in teaching. Prepare well. By following an organized study schedule and by reducing anxiety on your test day, you should do well. Above all, you should have the knowledge and skills to enter the classroom as a competent and confident educator.

Name Index

Subject Index